MW00953795

I'd Rather Be Sorry

The Third Note in the Life of a
Northland Musician

Dottie Lou Bolme

authorHOUSE®

AuthorHouse™
1663 Liberty Drive
Bloomington, IN 47403
www.authorhouse.com
Phone: 1-800-839-8640

First published by AuthorHouse 6/28/2010

ISBN: 978-1-4520-0378-8 (e)
ISBN: 978-1-4520-0379-5 (sc)

Library of Congress Control Number: 2010908373

Printed in the United States of America
Bloomington, Indiana

This book is printed on acid-free paper.

PREFACE

My most gratuitous thanks to all those assisting in gathered information through interviews and informal chitchats. Mother amusingly thanks Dale, Charmaine and Roger for their input on all the revealed past mischievous teen-age escapades that occurred in Mother's unaware absences.

Much appreciation to Larry vonGillern for all his information on auto mechanics, racing snow machines, etc, enabling me to pen the data in a knowledgeable vein.

Many thanks for humorous, enlightening tidbits revealed by Arlene Sorlie, Barb jurek, Ione DeBauche, Vickie Norell and many others.

Some research was gathered from old newspaper items, Country Music Roundup, Minneapolis CountrYSide Magazines etc.. If your name should get missed it's not intentional, just the factual state of an old memory or lack of.

I cannot apologize for my life and my memories. If one should disagree with my story versions, one must consider we all remember the same incidents differently.

Observations, opinions and assumptions herein are those of the author, alone. I'm hoping not to offend, however, I retrospectively embrace Scott Spenser's insight when he penned, a quote, "A writer who will not risk hurting someone's feelings is no more effective than a firefighter who will not smash a window." unquote.

Some names have been changed to protect the innocent and the guilty. Conversation dialogue is partially improvised and enhanced around nonfiction facts to create more interest, intrigue, and humor.

I dedicate this book to the memory of all those living in the pages of my memories that are no longer with us.

Following; My philosophy of life from which I determined the books Title.

If you hurt me, you won't be the first or the last
On life's journey of many mistakes.
But I won't waste pristine moments regretting
the past,
Or for chances that I didn't take.
'Cuz **I'd Rather Be Sorry** for something I've done,
Than for something that I didn't do!

When you touch me it's easy to be filled with belief
That tomorrow won't take you away,
But I'll wager whatever my choices may bring
In the love that I'm living today.
'Cuz **I'd Rather Be Sorry** for something I've done,
Than for something that I didn't do.

CHAPTER ONE

It was late June and the household was filled with activity as usual. Larry's stock car circuit people were in the garage and in and out of the house. The kids were scattered over the neighborhood. Rogie somewhere on his bike with Bryan, Charmaine hanging out with Roberta and Dale in the garage with Larry.

I concocted a huge stack of sandwiches for the kids and whoever else might be hungry and placed them on a large platter in the center of the kitchen table. I retired to my toilette basics and bath in preparedness for my gig at the Gopher.

While in my robe, after a leisure bath, Larry tore into the kitchen, apparently in search of some urgent, essential item, needed or required in his mechanics. Detecting the sandwiches on the table, with black greasy soiled hands, he ravenously seized one and greedily began munching as he earnestly and diligently searched the junk drawer for some item seemingly of importance.

He scrounged through the interior of the drawer with one hand, clutching the half-eaten sandwich with the other, and in-between bites, with a full mouth, he garbled, in a mushy food laden drawl, "Sorlie's and Jurek's are going camping this weekend, around Minong. Totogatic Campgrounds. They want us to join them, I thought maybe with the kids. Big "M" is going too, with her kids."

"Really. How could I ever manipulate that?" I inquired. "With the music gigs, I mean. And what about your racing schedule for the weekend?"

"I thought I'd let someone else, maybe Redenbaugh, drive my car and I'd take the kids camping. They need some family oriented time and support right now to help them cope with the aftershocks and grief of their Dad's death. Swimming, hot dogs, mini bikes can do just

1

wonders for kids! Get their minds on other things. I think it's essentially of foremost importance right now." he stated, imperiously.

It was just ten days since my three children had lost their 36 year old father in a truck accident. He had been killed instantly as he was thrown from the truck when the passenger door accidentally swung open. He landed, head first, against a concrete guard rail in Pattison Park. The driver had lost control while groping to catch their Dad, Roger Sr., from the fall. The gesture resulted in a roll-over and Mr. Gross was briefly hospitalized, but without serious injury.

The children were still in limbo from the aftershocks of the trauma. All three were dealing with their grief from three different personality aspects. Charmaine, having prior cried incessantly, would still instantaneously burst into unanticipated tears. Dale was displaying a relentless, a stern tough attitude; Fronting a control that masked a disguised denial. Rogie was somehow transfixed in a metaphor, picturing them as a likeness to a deck of cards. "We been dealt a really bad hand here. A really bad hand!"

Larry, my new husband of merely ten months was striving generously to permeate his role of Surrogate Dad, overcompensating to usher the children through the anguish of the grief that had asphyxiated their adolescent minds.

"Camping!! That would be wonderful, Larry." I assessed. "How very thoughtful and caring of you! I never thought I'd see the day you'd renege a week-end of racing fun for anything!"

"So if I can, how about you? How about them sharing their mother's company too?" he retorted, in a credible, convincing contention.

"Well. Hon, this is what I've decided. I'll drive to the campsite Saturday night after the gig." I proposed, "And that way we can have all of Sunday, together to spend with the kids."

"That, I'm sure will be very important to them." he remarked. He grabbed another sandwich, attacked it hungrily and rushed back to his garage activities.

As I dressed for my job the sandwiches, little by little disappeared from the kitchen table as did the pitcher of Kool-aid I had mixed up for the kids. Before my departure I stopped for a brief visit with Larry in the garage. He was stretched, full length on a creeper beneath his #61 Ford. I stooped down to peer at him under the frame of his stock car, carefully keeping my clothes from coming in contact with spilled oil and grease and clutter adorning the concrete floor, the usual decor of a macho garage!

"Hey, I need directions, Larry," I shrieked, above the roar of welders and sanders and engines. "How else am I going to find you guys at the campground?"

He rolled out from under the car, rose and briefed me on directions to Totogatic.

"When will you be going?" I asked.

"We'll leave this evening as soon as I finish the final details on my car for Bill. So I won't see you 'til you arrive at the campground tomorrow night. Be sure and bring some warm clothes. It still gets cold at night sometimes. And clothes for the daytime too—shorts or slacks." he conscientiously suggested.

"And my swim suit." I added. "Where will we sleep?" I asked.

"In a tent," he laughed and winked, toying with me. "Where else? Jurek's have reserved a cabin, but most of us sleep in tents." he explained amiably.

"How about blankets?" I inquired.

"I'll have everything there." he assured me "Haven't you been camping before?"

"No. Never!"

"Oh, you'll love it. It's so incredibly invigorating to sleep in a tent! Waking up to fresh air. No pollution of anykind!"

"Yah, and mosquitoes and ants and all kinds of creepy things." I grimaced, crinkling up my nose and pursing my lips in a repulsed expression.

"Not in a tent!" he chuckled, shaking his head. "They can't get inside a tent. For a farm gal You're sure awfully dumb!" he chided me.

"Well, we didn't have tents on the farm!" I muttered. "Farm life is all work, not play!!" Embarrassed, I changed the subject, "Where will the kids sleep?" I asked, with parental concern.

"Don't worry. I'll have tents and sleeping bags for them too. You just get yourself there. Have **you** ever made love in a tent?" he asked mischievously, changing the subject.

"I haven't ever even been in a tent!" I admitted, flustered.

"I'll initiate you there." was his equivocal summation. "It's incredible! You'll see! You haven't made love 'til you've done it in a tent!"

"I'll bet." was my ambivalent reply as a frivolous chuckle accidentally escaped.

"I'm an expert teacher! It'll be your unforgettable debut!" was his roguish promise.

"And I'll be the coquettish debutante!" I laughed and bantering, probed, "Is that a guarantee or just playful teasing?"

"You just show up and find our for yourself!" he interjected confidently as he leaned against the hood of his car smiling, displaying that devious, half-closed, foxy eye demeanor, supposedly intending to fill me with heated anticipation of coming attractions!!

"You're crazy!" I chuckled, "Absolutely NUTS!"

"That too!" he laughed in agreement.

"I'll see you Saturday night then, Hon." I conceded, a bit intrigued.

A quick peck on the cheek Goodbye and he as back on the creeper and under his car before I got into my Chevy.

"Gosh, he is really incredible!" I mused. "So good for the kids." His numerous altruistic attempts to console them hadn't gone unnoticed by me. His struggle to keep the boys busy with errands and projects to saturate their leisure time, though devious, left them with little time for negative, sad meditation. I had overheard him consoling Charmaine the previous afternoon in the living room. I shamelessly had been eavesdropping. "I'm here for you, Charmaine. Just like I'm here for your brothers. Don't worry. You have me as a Dad now. I know it's not the same, but I'll do as much as I can to help you get through this. We'll see it together. Okay?" Then he had hugged her with fatherly care and compassion.

This was the therapy they really needed in these traumatic times. "It just couldn't get any better than that!" I thought silently.

I threw the Chevy into reverse and spun away out of the driveway. It was Friday night and the Gopher would be jam packed, three deep at the bar, crowded to the hilt as usual. My heart was happy, my mind at ease. All was well in my positive world. The children would soon overcome. Time heals.

I arrived at Totogetic around 2:00 A.M. and the campground was still, occupied in silent slumber.

Larry scurried toward my deliberately slow-moving Chevy, waving his arms, emphatically, in the dimly-lit roadway to direct me to his location. He was fully aware of my atrocious sense of direction and had forcefully remained awake in anticipation of my arrival, so I would be able to find the gangs campsites.

I parked my auto on the side of the roadway, grabbed my little overnight camping tote and prepensely followed him to his tent.

It was my first adventure of rugged, brusque life in a tent. I apprehended there would be many such firsts with Larry who was always eager for experiencing anything new. Always enthusiastic for new beginnings and challenges.

I crawled into the tent intimacy where he had laid an open sleeping bag on the plastic tent bottom in lieu of a mattress and another on top as a cover. In the diminutive quarters I wriggled, uncomfortably, out of my stage clothes and slipped into a long, large, flannel night shirt. A cool breeze was filtering, whispering through a miniature screen window to the head of the sleeping arrangement.

"This is no nice." I thought. "Fascinating", ♪ 'The Games People Play'♪ Korn's song dancing in my mind. "Brusque excitement but with intriguing charm as well." I mused.

I rolled my meretricious stage attire into a tight bundle and squeezed it against the side wall of the tent, out of the way.

"This is really 'NIFTY'!" I said, paraphrasing a Toby expression, as I snuggled my cool frame next to Larry's warm, conditioned physique. He was disrobed down to a pair of briefs.

"Are you ready for an enchanting, out-of-this-world initiation?" he asked mischievously, as he wriggled his shorts down and off his legs, flippantly tossing them against the outer tent wall.

"Of course." I giggled, as I pulled my flannel shirt over my head. "I've been tossing your invitation around in my mind, all the way up here from the Gopher, looking forward to your beguiling promises, so this better be good!" I teased, deviously.

* * * * * * *

"What's so thrilling about a bed this hard and lumpy?" I soliloquized. A stick or pebbles were poking me in several places in my back as he rhythmically pressed me into the bottom sleeping bag with his exuberant thrusts! "Sure he's got the best spot! I'm his mattress and I'm soft and fluffy—well maybe just fat. ha!" I thought, silently. My mind traveled to a magnet posted on my refrigerator at home, a little white painted sheep, 'Ewes not fat! Ewes just Fluffy!' "Try the bottom, Cowboy!" I imagined telling him. "Then see how comfortable and exciting it is down here on the bottom!" No I was not mesmerized or impressed with the initiation of **'Love in a Tent!"**

He was way too swift for me. The strained awkward, uncomfortable boudoir did nothing to kindle an exotic, amorous mood for me, slowing my libido to an indolent crawl. As Larry sighed his release, I was almost relieved it was over. He fell asleep almost immediately. I assumed he was exhausted, having waited up for my arrival. He was seldom able to embrace the late hour night life. Except, of course if it involved racing. I had mastered, over the years the endurance of the night life people, having been thrown into the graveyard shifts of music.

I wasn't yet thoroughly unwound. As Larry rolled over I laid quietly staring into the darkness, lighted faintly by the campground security lights filtering through the tiny window screen, thinking with low spirited disillusionment, "Well maybe tomorrow will be more fun. I'll hang out with my kids, Probably go swimming." The water was one of my nondescript, infectious passions.

I must have dozed, as I was abruptly awakened by a piercing, loud stringent bang, followed consecutively by a flood of rumbles. I flinched and bolted upright into a sitting position. They were numerous, diverse blasts of thunder.

Larry just snored lightly, oblivious to the streaks of lightning cascading across the opaque sky, I could perceive through the little window screen. Deafening and crashing louder, closer, the claps of thunder and electrical streaks of lightning dashed across the sky, creating a 4th of July fireworks display.

Larry just continued bombarding the tent with a copious sequence of rumbling zzzz's, unaware and unconcerned. Sawing logs with the stamina and exuberance of a Paul Bunyan lumberjack!

I sat up, wide awake and apprehensive. "What happens if it starts to rain?" I mused. I probed Larry gently. "Hon, I think it's going to rain pretty soon°" I blurted, perplexed.

"Hummmmmmph----------" he mumbled, sleepily incoherent. "Okay—we'll go." he stammered, disconnected.

"But what will happen in the tent when it rains?" I questioned, with uncertainty.

Sleepily, drifting into reality, he assured me in an ambiguous monotone, "Water just rolls off a tent. It's waterproof." Then more zzz's droned on.

I lowered my head to my pillow. My eyes were wide, in a quandary state of mind, fully awake and then I heard the soft peck-peck-peck of raindrops cascading the roof of the tent. Like the drone of a softly puttering engine the pitter, patter of the rain lullabied me off to dreamland and the soothing music of Mr. Sandman.

* * * * * * *

"WHAT THE HELL!" I gasped, **"I'm all wet! Hey Larry! What's Happening?"**

"What? What? Did you piss the bed?" He bolted upright to the retrospect of reality!

There was one to one½ inches of water rushing around us and the whipping angry wind was violently shaking the tent. It was about to take flight except for the two anchors. The weight of our two bodies.

"Let's get the hell out of here!" Larry shrieked.

We grabbed our soaking clothes and drenched sleeping bags and wrapped them around us like beach towels. I luckily and mercilessly snatched the top one which was not very wet. In fact it was almost dry. Larry was untimely left with the soaked bottom sleeping bag, as we made a mad, accelerated dash to Jurek's cabin.

"A helluva storm!" Larry shrieked, as he intensely pounded the cabin door in frustration.

"What about the kids?" I asked, fearfully apprehensive.

"Oh they're high and dry in Sorlie's camper!" he reasured me. He fumbled, inspecting the door knob to discover it was not locked so we burst, unannounced into the cabin looking and feeling like a couple drowned rodents, wakening all the cabin occupants in our noisy frenzy.

"OH, so the water just rolls off of a tent!!" I rebuked, in a verbal assault, reminding Larry of his previous obstinate statement of knowledgeable enlightenment. "It's waterproof!" I stated impetuously. Smiled wryly.

"Well it usually does roll off." he explained apologetically. "I borrowed it from Bill. It must be real old." was his penitent expertise.

Barb located some dry garments for us and brewed a pot of coffee to warm our shivering bodies. Our short night had come to an abrupt halt!

The sky was beginning to lighten in the east as dawn was surreptitiously approaching, with a Mother Nature derisive smile! As we visited and sipped caffein with Barb and Bud, outside a gentle mustering began as the campsites began coming alive.

I peeked through the cabin window, viewing kids, mine too, scurrying around, chasing each other playfully. I could see Sylvia and Kenny folding up a wet tent in preparation to calling their camping excursion **QUITS!!**

Bit "M" was perched glumly on a saturated lawn chair, beside an extinguished campfire, as she kept confidently tossing paper and tid-bits at a tiny diminutive flame. She was determined to foster a new blaze under a huge campfire coffeepot. Parker's were packing up their gear in the distance, as were Bunny and Bill.

"UH-Oh! Looks like everyone is packing up. It's only 7:00 A.M.!" I attested glumly.

"The storm is chasing everyone home!" Larry babbled.

"But it's over now!" I grumbled. "The sky is clear. It will probably be a great day at this lake!"

"I guess they're all pretty disgusted." Bud piped in. "All their gear soaked. I really can't blame them. We may as well head back too."

"I s'pose." Barb muttered. "We've been camping and fishing and boozin' for two days already. I'm kinda tired, too."

"Well, I may as well get home, get my trusty #61 and race Proctor. No use us hangin' around by ourselves if everyone is going home." Larry sputtered with forced, feigned laughter.

"So much for my first camping experience!" I babbled, trying hard not to divulge my aggravation with the outcome. "You'll really love camping and sleeping in a tent," Unquote, "I've had such a fantastic, incredible, delightful, exciting, enough adjectives time! I think I'll do it again! In say, maybe 15 years or so!!"

"Don't give up that easily." Barb chuckled, timidly. "It's usually a lot of fun, Dottie."

"Well you guys have been here since Friday to do stuff. It really was stupid of me to come for such a short time anyway! Never again. And I'm so so tired! I'm gonna go home and get some shut-eye this whole afternoon!"

My first camping experience was, as Larry said, definitely Something to be Remembered. but not something I planned to entertain in my lifetime, **AGAIN!**

I precisely was not a nature enthusiast! "Yes" I mused, "I'll trade my sweat shirt and jeans for my sparkle of sequins and satin and chiffon and my hi-heeled Pumps any day!!"

♫♫♫

CHAPTER TWO

I was surprised and delighted to discover Support Payments arriving in the mail from Roger Sr. It was the very first time in six years he was actually assisting with the support of his three children. Checks were consistently arriving to purchase school clothes and supplies! Food for the table! Money for Doctors and dentists and other miscellaneous maintenance, even for recreation! I was flabbergasted!

Roger was conscientiously, consistently supplying $58 a month for each child. **In DEATH**, he had become the provider for some of their sustenance! A responsibility he had never accepted, had never acknowledged, accountably to contribute to their support when he was number **among the LIVING!** Trusty Social Security Survivor Benefit checks of $174 for three minor children arrived, constant, each month.

I had never badgered him for funds. If I could pursue him at precisely the specific time he'd pick up his meager check and cash it, he would offer it, in it's complete entirety to me. However, he gratuitously responded to his friends, drinking buddies, and his mother with identically the same perspective. To establish exact time and place to snare him was unfeasible, next to impossible. So whoever got there first emptied his jeans and incorrigibly there would be nothing left for his children, by the time I was able to locate his whereabouts. I'd have to research and analyze a definite, accurate time he'd get a check and the location to nab him with it, before it disappeared! I remember only one time having successfully accomplished this.

He still had $80 on his person when I found him in a local pub. I asked him for some cash for grub for the kids. He gave me the entire $80. I asked him boldly, what asinine plan would he come up with to survive, broke, until his next pay-day arrived. He just indifferently shrugged his shoulders, offering not a word of explanation nor a hint of rebuttal.

I couldn't bring myself to completely annihilate his funds, and leave him credulously broke. Although, I assumed it would all be flushed away on booze. My conscience just wouldn't extricate me into taking his last buck so I pragmatically returned the entire $80, musing imperviously, "Do I really need his money? It's just for the principal of the thing. To make him aware of his responsibility and he doesn't seem to grasp that anyway!"

It was the one and only time I had momentarily held any of his cash in my possession. It just wasn't worth the effort and the lost time in research to locate and harass him into giving us any support. Therefore I had just complaisantly relinquished asking for any assistance in the last five or six years.

Now after all this time, with Social Security Survivor Dependency Benefits for his kids, they were finally being provided for by **Roger Sr., through** his DEATH! I had **very mixed emotions** over the credulity and trepidation of the windfall! I know God works in mysterious ways!! But is He this **Unmerciful?!!** I tried not to dwell on the **"WHY"** the ambivalence of it all.

They were not immense checks, by any means, but they did effectively assist in financing some of the children's needs.

The benefit was based on Roger's earnings at Jeno Paulucci's Chun Kink Sales, Inc. where he had remained employed for the longest duration of time and his most recent job, as well. He had a brief employment at the Steel Plant in Morgan Park, where he had remained a mere two pay periods. And a very short time he had been employed by the Fraser Shipyards of the Great Lakes, on the boats.

* * * * * * *

"Hey, Your folks are here, Dottie." Larry announced, sauntering in from the living room.

"I didn't know they were coming to visit us!" I declared.

"Surprise! Surprise!" he smirked, as through the window we watched them exit their auto and shuffle toward the house.

"How come, today?" I queried. "Why?"

"At Roger's funeral I mentioned to your Dad that I had a few unfinished tidbits and tasks on the garage, I still needed to do, like window trim, a few more plug-ins etc. etc. He offered to take a week-end and come and help me. You know how little I know about carpentry! I thought, I may as well take advantage of **THAT** offer!"

"I guess that's fine, but I wish I had known, I'd have put a large beef roast or a turkey in the oven to feed everyone. Nothin' but bologna sandwiches around here now!" I joshed.

"I knew you had to work tonight so I just thought I'd take them out for supper." Larry purred, proudly.

"Great! That's better yet!" I laughed, shamelessly.

They stayed overnight and visited with Larry and the kids in my absence.

The next day I tossed together a couple chickens, with rutabaga and carrots, into a roaster, cooked up a kettle of potatoes and prepared a roast chicken dinner for everyone. I called Barb and invited her to join us for dinner, as she was alone with her kids, Scott and Debbie. Gerry was stationed, in the Guards, for a couple of weeks somewhere on the east coast. Their family lived only a mile from us on Maple Grove Road. Often when the kids were in school, I would jog to Barb's, have coffee with her and jog back. It was a two mile exercise work-out for me with bonding fellowship thrown in for desert!

Char sprightly set the table and I heaped on the grub for the fortuitous celebration of a family Sunday afternoon get-together.

"Did you take the axe to the chicken shed, chop off their heads, scald and pull their feathers on these chickens this morning?" Dad japed with witticism, "So we'll have **FRESH** meat?"

"Oh yes, Just like on the farm. Like old times." I bantered, giggling, but was soon reluctantly forced to admit, "They're Piggly Wiggly Specials from Piedmont Heights!"

"Didn't we get those chickens from Shopper's City?" Larry asked, casually indifferent.

"Could be." I grinned.

"No matter!" Dale piped in. "They sure are good." as he heaped another serving of chicken and mashed potatoes onto his plate, smothering the pile in white chicken gravy.

"How are you doin', Rogie?" Dad complaisantly coaxed some conversation from him at the other end of the table. "Do you have guitar lessons or some place you have to be next week?" he asked inquisitively.

"Nope, no school now. Nothing to do, only play with my friends" he replied. "Well maybe a guitar lesson." He looked in my direction for answers, or guidance.

"Maybe to clean your room!" I intercepted, simpering slyly. "And a guitar lesson." I added.

"How would you like to come back with Grandma and me for a week in Bruno?" Dad asked.

Rogie's eyes lit up, glistening with infectious vitality. He drew a deep breath and blurted, "Could I bring my bike?"

"Sure can. We can put it in the trunk and tie it down." Dad suggested. "You can stay with us some of the time and some of the time with Monette's, your cousins and aunts and uncles."

"WOW! That would be fun! Could I go swimming in Sand Creek?"

"Sure, with your cousins." Mom answered. "Maybe we could go fishing there too, huh? Catch some fish for supper. Like Dale and I did when he was your age."

"Yipee!"

"That's great." I added, "Hey pass me the buns, please and the butter too. Rogie can get out of his guitar lesson. One time won't matter. I'll call Uncle Harry to let him know Rogie is bummin' around."

"We'll pack up a little bag of clothes and his stuff, toilettries, whatever." Larry suggested. "I just took them all camping a couple weeks ago." he assessed with exorbitance. "It was a helluva lot of fun 'til we got rained out!"

"Larry has been just super with the kids, keeping them busy and their minds off of painful thoughts."

"This is a great meal, Dort." Barb piped in. "Too bad Gerry isn't here to enjoy it with us."

"Yeah, he's stuck out East with Army Slop!" Larry snickered, mischievously. "Too bad!"

"There's something I wanna talk to you about, Dort." Barb initiated another subject. "I'm flying out to meet Gerry in Philadelphia in a week."

"That sounds like a great get-away! Uh-huh! Yeah, A Secluded Amore!!" I teased in Italian melody, ♪'Amoretto ♪ Amore'!y—Will Gerry have completed his Guard Stint by then?" I asked.

"Oh Yes, Then we're going to visit Aunt Helen in New Jersey and take in Washington D.C. A whole two week vacation!"

"Fabulous! Wonderful, Barb. I've never been to the East Coast, ever. You lucky stiff! And Washington D.C. What an opportunity!"

"We've been to the West Coast, though." Larry promptly interrupted. "That was really great! Wasn't it Dottie?"

"That we have, Larry and yes it was great." I humored his interruption with a simpered smile, denoting a little twinge of envy in Larry's demeanor.

"But the thing is," Barb continued, "I'll need a baby-sitter to stay with Scott whenever Gerry and I go out, on the town, in the evenings." She raised her arm, motioning to Mom, "Please pass me another piece of chicken—oh well—the potatoes too."

"What do you have in mind?" I probed apprehensively.

"How about loaning me your daughter?" She impishly winked at Char. "I thought maybe, I could take Charmaine with me to help with that. That's if she'd like to go on a two week vacation with us!"

"Wow, would I ever!" she exclaimed, excitedly.

"I'd just pay for her flight ticket, food and fun! No wages."

"Yes! Yes! Yes! I'll go. I'll go."

"She'd have to take care of Debbie too!" I pondered dubiously. "She's barely a year old, Barb. I don't know. That's a big job for a twelve year old, away from home."

"No." Barb explained. "I'm going to finagle Lorraine into taking Debbie for two weeks. You know how she loves babies!"

We all laughed, well aware of Lorraine's obsession with little babies. She would have had a dozen of her own by now if it hadn't been for miscarriages.

"I've never been on a plane!" Charmaine giggled. "Boy will that be fun! Boy, will that be scary!"

"Gerry will come and pick us up at the airport and then we'll just travel, visit, sight see and vacation all the way up the East Coast and back home again by automobile." Barb promised. "Is that okay with you, Dort. Well you too, Larry?"

"Sounds fine to me. No hassle for two weeks with these BRATS, Monsters!" Larry chided. "Dale can spend it with me at the races. I'll lie again that he's 16 so he can be in the pits with my Pit Crew. Okay Dale?"

"Sure." Dale replied elusively, showing no emotion. Dale was my one offspring who always displayed a passive, complacent savoir-faire in almost every situation.

So it was settled. The kids had a couple weeks ahead to extinguish timely, boring routines. Just to hang out, enjoy the moments, smell the roses! Not Larry or I, however. We should be so lucky!

Dale, go get the ice cream from the freezer in the basement I said. "It's time for apple pie!"

So Rogie left for Bruno with Mom and Dad, and one week later, Charmaine, Barb and Scotty boarded a plane in Duluth for Pennsylvania.

* * * * * * *

There was a persistent, urgent pounding at the kitchen door. I quickly drew my immersed hands from the dirty dishwater and hastily wiped them on the hand towel hanging at the sink, finishing off the dampness on my hips as I rushed to answer the relentless pounding at the entrance.

Who could be so impatient and commanding? I was home alone. Char and Rogie, both were absent on their mini vacations and Dale was, somewhere loafing with his neighborhood friends. Larry was at work.

As I swung open the kitchen door, I discovered the irritated party was knocking on the outside door. I conceived it had to be a stranger. Anyone who knew us or frequented our residence always stepped inside to the second, interior door.

"Probably a Damn Salesman!" I thought, "Wasting my time, tensely annoying me, forcing me to rush around unnecessarily."

As I opened the door, there depicted a neatly pressed, immaculate uniform, stood a Police Officer! I glanced beyond his derisive eyes to the official lettering of his vehicle parked in the driveway, reading in bold, macho, bright black letters, **"Sheriff's Department"**. A little unnerved with unsettling thoughts. I stumbled over my words as I inquired in a forced, fictitiously polite, benevolent voice.

"What can I do for you, Officer?" I asked, trying to hide the tremble in my poise.

"I'm looking for a Larry vonGillern? This is the address I have in my file." The officer stated, addressing me in a cold, stringent voice.

"Why?" I stammered.

"Are you his wife?" he asked, smiling wryly, ignoring my question.

"Yes, for a year." I replied.

"Oh." A long pause as he casually reviewed the papers he was holding in his hand. "I have papers here, to serve on Mr. vonGillern." he briefed me somewhat indifferently.

"Papers? For what?!" I scowled, seething inside with indignation.

"This states," he was examining his official looking document, "That he owes a lot of money to an Ernest Brottom from Zim, Minnesota." He slowly scrutinized, as he turned pages. "Hmmm-Uh-huh—It appears Mr. Brottom is apparently pressing charges against Mr. vonGillern for money owed him. Nonpayment for an X number of years for labor and parts on rebuilding of several engines for him. Do you know this Mr. Brottom?" he asked.

"No, not really. Though I've heard his name often from my husband and his associates in the hobby racing circuit."

He scanned the pages, back and forth, slowly, half reading, half memory, softly, in a monotone, as though reviewing the information to himself.

"Is he here?" he finally inquired.

"No, he's at work. He works until 5:00 P.M. If you want to return 5:30 or 6:00 P.M. or unless I can sign for the papers," I suggested, "and give them to him when he returns home."

"I'd love to see his face," I mused, silently, "when he tries to explain this situation to gullible me!"

"No." the Officer retorted, "I can't do that. I have to serve him the papers directly, in person. Where does he work?"

"He works at Muntz T.V., uptown. He's the manager of the store there."

"That's a fairly new business, isn't it?" squinting his eyes, furrowing his brow in attempted recall.

"It's new here, in Duluth, but it's a branch of an old business, I guess, that's been around since 1949."

"I'll catch him there," the Officer stated flatly. "Thanks for your time." and he was gone.

I poured a cup of coffee and slithered into a chair at the kitchen table, amply necessitating a caffein break after that befuddled embarrassment. I pondered, weighing the situation in a confusing muddle of disbelief.

Larry idolized the ground this man walked on. Praised him endlessly, fervently. Boasted to all his companions and neighbors of Ernie Brottom's uncomparible skill and talent in the mechanics of engines. Larry had profoundly promoted his name in the racing vocabulary as prominently popular, as A.T&T was to the telephone. He incessantly bragged of their benevolent friendship. He placed Ernie's devotion on a pedestal, equivalent to that of the Blessed Virgin Mary! There was never a hint of the fragility of a precarious relationship, ever present. Ernie was his confidant, his Special Friend!

Why would Larry do such a thing to a dear friend? Apparently Ernie in his easy-going, complaisant nature had let the debt slide for a number of years. It must have taken the proverbial **"Last straw on**

the Camels Back" to incite the degree of anger in Ernie, to instigate serving papers.

In my own analysis, I assumed Larry would do just about anything, say almost anything, promise almost anything, to persuade and con almost anyone, if it enabled achieving the accessability to build a competitive Race Car!!

He never weighed the slight possibility that, on his meager wages to financially afford the six or seven thousand it took to build and maintain his Hobby Stock would ever be unfeasible! This much I had observed in the short year and one-half I had known Larry.

He would certainly, without guilt, likely Botch a close friendship if the need was requisite. The subject of money or friendship or loyalty was never an issue or a priority when the goal was a **FAST ENGINE! A WINNER on the track!!**

As I hugged my mug, sipping and relishing my caffein break in the quiet, peaceful still of my kitchen, I reminisced, retrospectively recalling Larry's sister Kay's warning words, scribbled in her letter to me a few weeks prior.

Quote, "You say, poor misunderstood, Good-hearted, Compassionate, Good-'ole-Larry!! You have a lot of awakening to do in your future. Good Luck! You're going to need it!!" Unquote.

Larry burst into the house around 6:30, sputtering. "I need a quick fix! I'm starved! A quick sandwich or soup or somethin' to tide me over. I've gotta hit that garage and tackle that Ford, probably 'most of the night! Has Bill called? Or Kenny?"

"No, I haven't heard from either." I stated flatly.

"They're suppose to come and help me change that engine tonight." he scowled, perplexed.

"Oh yes, I remember. You blew your engine in Proctor, Sunday night. I'll make you a quick sandwich."

"Make it two." he concisely muttered.

"Well, how was your day?" I asked, waiting to hear Larry's version of the Sheriff's department versus Brottom incident.

"Oh, it was okay, I guess," he glibly replied, as he intently watched my construction of two thick ham sandwiches. "Only sold two T.V's and some small stuff, though."

"Nothing unordinary?" I pried obtrusively.

"No, but they're gonna fold up if they don't get off their fanny's and do some serious heavy promotion. Too much competition to just sit around waiting for someone to walk in. Will see you later and you know where I'll be all night if you need anything." He chuckled as he swiftly grasped the plate supporting his two ham sandwiches and sprinted for the door. Stopping short, he exclaimed, "Oh, I almost forgot. Grab me the half-gallon of milk from the 'frig. Can't eat sandwiches without milk!"

"Need a glass?"

"No. I've got my mug in the garage."

He was quickly out the door with never a mention of Ernie or the sherrif's visit.

I never did bring up the subject in the days that followed and he never relayed one diminutive bit of information of any kind on the subject. I never was informed of any aftermath or end result of the situation. It was as if it had, unphenomenally, never happened!

♪♪♪

CHAPTER THREE

"Do you realize next Sunday is our first anniversary?" I asked, while sharing the evening meal with Larry and the boys.

"Boy, I guess it is! That sure came fast!" he replied. "Where did that year go?"

"It just flew by!" I agreed. "There's so much going on all the time. Grand Central Station around here every day!"

"What would you like to do and where would you like to go?" he asked, "ON Sunday for our Anniversary?"

"I'm playing in Rutledge at the Flamingo Sunday night and you're racing at the Proctor Races, so how can we do anything together on Sunday? We sure do see a lot of each other, don't we?"

"No wonder we never fight!" he impishly snickered,

"Well, I s'pose we could go out to dinner on Monday night instead of Sunday." I suggested. We both love to eat. That's the one thing we do have in common! The only thing!" I giggled.

"Yeah. Maybe we could go someplace real fancy, where they might even have dinner music to dance to."

"Sure, like the Highland Supper Club has a piano bar. A lot of supper clubs have piano bars." I responded.

"Okay." he agreed, dispassionately. "It's a date, Dottie. You pick the place and we'll dress up in our "Fancy Rags" as Toby would say and just pretend it's a wile roarin' Saturday Night!"

FIRST ANNIVERSARY ? LONDON HOUSE

And gussied in fancy attire we certainly were. Larry impetuously surprised me with a lustrous, impeccable corsage of yellow Sweetheart Roses, tenderly embracing a plush, elegant Orchid.

"Now I am confused!" I giggled and began nonsensically crooning, "I over-♪looked an Orchid, while searching for a Rose.♪ The Orchid that I over-looked was You.♪ The Rose that I was searching for has proved to be--♪--" I sang to him, flippant and saucy.

"But, am I the Sweetheart Rose or am I the Elegant Orchid?" I teased.

"It's not about you!" he tittered, bursting my bubble. "It's about me! I'm a Gemini, you know. The Twins! Split Personality! So of course I couldn't make up my mind, which was the nicer so I had to take both."

"Well I better be the Both!" I chortled, a warned reproval on my tongue. "Gemini's are known to be fickle! They have a reputation for collecting women like women collect jewelry!" I said, bantering lightly, with a simpered grin splashed across my face.

We shared a superb dinner at the London House on Duluth's east end, relished a couple Old Fashioned's, slowly swayed to a couple Fox Trots and we were home by 11:00 P.M.. Both of us untimely exhausted from our extravagant week-end commitments and cherishing more the snuggle and comfort of our bedroom and our pillows to the constant rumble of a melodious concert of peaceful sonorous zzzz's.

* * * * * * *

Char burst through the kitchen door, dragging behind her with one hand a large garbage bag filled with the paraphernalia of her two week vacation on the East Coast. Her other arm was clinging to her jacket and a pair of sandals I didn't recognize as her belongings.

"Where's Barb and Gerry?" I asked.

"They just let me off." she replied, "and then they went home."

"Are you tired?"

"No, not too much. We stayed at Grandma's and Grandpa's last night in Bruno and I went to bed early."

"How was your trip?" I pumped her enthusiastically, for details.

"Okay, I guess."

"Just okay? I thought you'd be speechless with excitement over such an adventure. A whole two weeks of a holiday!"

"Yes it was fun, only I got sick for a couple days in the beginning."

"That was probably from the change of water or maybe too much excitement or stress over your first ride on a plane." I explained. "How did you like the plane ride?"

"It was real scary when you looked down. Like a really, really big ferris wheel. The cars were so small they looked like little bugs!" she giggled.

"Yes, and I know how much you like **BUGS!**" I joshed. "What all did you do?" I queried, obtrusively, beside myself with curiosity, trying to encourage and accelerate her narration.

"Barb and Gerry visited----well, we all did visit Aunt Helen in New Jersey and I baby-sat with Scott. When we stayed in the hotels, Barb and Gerry would go out and Scott and I would stay in the room and watch television." and then abruptly diverting her inert emotion, she excitedly exclaimed. "but Gerry taught me a new song and I know it by heart already!!"

"What about New York? And the Skyscrappers?"

Ignoring my questions, she continued. "I left my shoes in the motel so when we got to New York I had to go barefoot. I'm so used to going barefoot in the summer, you know, I forgot to put my shoes on."

"I saw you carrying a pair of sandals when you came in." I divulged, tittering.

"Yes, Barb bought me a pair at the store. But, I gotta tell you about this new song Gerry taught me. Is it ever funny. I know it my h----"

"What did you think of the skyscrappers?" I interposed. "Really tall, huh?"

"They're okay."

"What about Washington D.C.?"

"Oh it was okay, but you should hear that song that Gerry taught me. I can sing it all the way through."

"Did you see the president? or the oval room?" I queried, tersely, disregarding her indifference.

"I don't know. It was all kinda boring. But we sang that song all the way home. Scotty and Gerry and I, in the car. Barb sang sometimes too! Was that ever fun!!" she exclaimed, her eyes dancing impishly, with sparkling, electrifing delight.

Okay! okay! Okay!" I surrendered, impatiently. "What song?"

Char began warbling excitedly, with animation, "♪ Oh, mairzy doats and dozey doats and liddle lamzy divey,♪ a kiddledee divey too, wouldn't you? ♪ Oh, mairzy doats and dozey doatsa nd liddle lamzy divey. A kiddledee divey too wouldn't you?"♪

"That's cute." I snickered, reminiscing my childhood, having sung the same ditty also as a little girl, and also fascinated with the lyrics.

"But Mom, do you know what it really, really means?" she mischievously queried.

I anticipated she was advancing my interest to the approaching element of surprise, so I replied, pretending ignorance.

"No, I don't know what it means!" I did not want to burst the proverbial bubble she was embracing with zest. "What does it mean?"

♪ She immediately began serenading my counterfeit curiosity, "If the words sound queer and funny to your ear," she melodiously crooned. "A little bit jumbled and ♪ jivey." then articulously added," Mares eat oats and does eat oats and little lambs eat ivy!" Then squealing with delight, she went on, bouncing about the room, rhythmically as she crooned, " ♪ Mairzy doats and dozey doats and liddle lamzy divey--♪--" chanting the lyrics that fascinated her.

"Oh my gosh!" I pretended surprise. "That's really cute and clever. I'll have to learn that one. Will you teach it to me?"

"Sure I will. It's real easy, Mom. To learn, I mean."

Charmaine, in her 12 year old innocence had experienced for the very first time, a flight on a plane; seen Broadway and the streets of New York; Skyscrappers; Washington D.C.; the terrain of countryside across one-half of the United States and the very highlight of her two-week trip was a little ditty called "Marzy Doats and Dozey Doats" plus the sharing of that little ditty with family!

I discovered in that moment, how true the concept, that all we need to learn, experience, and remember, "We Learned in Kindergarten". Children have an insight, a unique secret perception of what is really important and necessary in our existence. The capacity to relish what is real priority in life!

No, I've never been to Broadway, viewed skyscrappers or the streets of New York or the patriotism and politics of Washington D.C., but I had the thrill of witnessing my daughter's exuberant excitement over the sharing of a song she had learned on a two-week trip with her Aunt and Uncle to the East Coast!

There is no adventure that could ever surpass that Memory!

* * * * * * *

Sunday was the upcoming Spectacular of the Dave Dudley "Double D" Country Music Festival. It was an annual August outdoor concert presented at Dave Dudle's resort on Staples Lake, in Danbury Wisconsin.

Korn had, prior, played Bass for Dave, on the road in his concerts, during Dave's huge success with "Six Days on the Road", so we were naturally the choice to front all the artists performances as the front band. Dave hired all the talent as singles.

Sunday was arriving so quickly and I was agglutinated to my electric sewing machine in the concoction of a new gold, metallic sparkle dress for the show.

The guys planned wearing the purple, black trimmed suit jackets Marilyn MacDonald had tailored for them. Marilyn was everybody's special friend, had a heart of gold and we all lovingly called her "Big M". I remember, retrospectively, she did remark on occasion, that she abhorred the tag. Little did she realize it was in fact a term of endearment to us. Of love and warm friendship! We never meant anything, but that, by the use of the nick name. There have been a lot of Marilyn's in my life's memories, but only One "Big M."

As I hammered away at the machine, I was mentally jolted by a subconscious reflection of a pending dentist appointment. I threw the switch on my sewing machine and exited my bedroom.

"When is that dentist appointment, Char?" I queried blatantly to reach her ears in the living room, as I intently reviewed my kitchen calendar scribblings. "WOW!" I gasped. "Looks like it's today!"

"Yes it's today." Char yelled from the living room. "I'm already dressed. Ready to go." she added.

Whenever I was engrossed in a seamstress project, it wasn't unusual for me to completely lose track of time.

I sauntered to the living room, Larry casually following behind. Char was standing, her eyes drifting back and forth to a TV program in progress.

She was attired in a white turtle-neck sweater, with a black vinyl mini-skirt and black sandals, completing the ensemble. As my eyes grazed her appearance I discerned, apprenhensively, that my little girl was maturing so fast, before my eyes. She appeared so much older than her twelve years, I mused reflectively I had purchased her first bra at age nine. Soon she'd be fully fledged and spreading her innocent wings to fly. What a reluctant thought.

"Let's see. It's 1:00 P.M. now." I scrutinized. "The appointment is for 2:15. If it takes an hour I can still be back at my machine by at least 4:00 P.M. That'll give me a couple more hours on my dress before I have to think supper and Gopher Lounge."

"Why don't I take her to the dentist?" Larry piped in.

"You'd do that?!" I sputtered in surprise. "Don't you need to get back to work at Muntz?"

"I'm pretty much free to come and go as I please" he explained. "The advantage of being the manager, I guess." he smiled nobly. "I'll take her, that way you can work on your costume a couple extra hours."

"That's really great, Larry. Thanks , Hon. You're a Sweetheart".

It was incredible how well Larry had adjusted to the responsibility of a ready made family. The role of a Surrogate Dad, incomparable! I hoped the kids were aware of his selfless contributions to our needs.

* * * * * * *

Dave Dudley outdid himself again, as usual, with a Country Spectacular Show, staging an incredible variety of talent! National and local as well. With continuous music throbbing through-out the day. Talented, versatile performances were enjoyed from such National Stars as Bobby Bare, Tom T. Hall, and George Kent. More locally from the Twin Cities and the Twin Ports areas, talent such as Johnny Lidel of "Primrose Lane" popularity; Dorothy, "Everybody's Mother" from Minneapolis, and of course, ahem, Dottie Lou and the Tumbleweeds also appeared; Betty Jo from the Twin Cities performed a superb rendition of Patsy Cline favorites.

Dave Dudley, who had an incredible rapport with an audience, wound up the finale of the evening with an hour production of his own renditions of his signature songs, plus a few interpretations of other artists strains, as well, while the devoted fans consistantly tipped their beers and cocktails and exuberantly, danced barefoot in the grass!

Two days after the concert at the Double D Lodge, Larry and I embarked on a five day mini vacation to visit Larry's relatives in Iowa and Nebraska. He wanted to introduce me and my kids to his sibblings.

We diligently packed up the five of us in Gerry's and Barb's tent camper they sogenerously loaned to us.

We spent an afternoon at the Wisconsin Dells, sight-seeing and taking tour boat rides through the gully's and caverns of the Dells, enroute to Iowa.

We spent a day in Waterloo, Iowa with Larry's Mom and her new husband, Arnold. Lu was such a Sweetheart. Everyone loved her. She tossed together a family picnic for us, entertaining everyone in her gracious demeanor. Lu and Arnold had visited us the previous year, in Duluth just a month before Larry and I had wed so we were not strangers.

Kissing and hugging a tearful goodbye, the following morning, we expeditiously launched our trusty, little caravan in the westerly direction of Lincoln, Nebraska to meet and visit with some of Larry's sibblings.

I was able to meet Larry's sister, Kay for the first time in person. Our contacts had previously been encountered by telephone and by mail, only, when she had tartly enlightened my mind on the irresponsible side of Larry. Yes, the Larry with the split personality of the Gemini Twins!

We gathered at Larry's brother Paul's home, where we stayed for the night.

Rogie and Char had crashed in an extra upstairs bedroom that Paul's wife had improvised for them. Char claimed the small ¾ size bed and Sue had added a mattress to the floor for Rogie while Dale had retired outside to the top bunk of the tent camper.

With the kids crashed and quiet, the adults visited and played cards late into the night. Then after a few consecutive lethargic yawns from Kay around midnight, she excused herself with a decision to scuddle across town to her own residence and **"call it a night"**.

After Kay had made her exit, Sue announced she was ravenously hungry. "Wouldn't a pizza hit the spot?" she suggested.

"She's always hungry!" Paul apologetically teased. "She must be eating for three or four, not two!" he chuckled.

I noticed Paul had Larry's smile and the same sense of humor. A very close resemblance, except Paul was dark with olive skin and ebony black hair.

"I don't know," I gibed. "**I'm not expecting** and pizza sure sounds good to me!"

"Yeah." Larry agreed. "It's a long time since dinner and almost time for breakfast. Sounds like yummy for the tummy." he laughed. "You got milk in the 'frig, I hope. Don't you?" Larry would not have anything to eat unless it was washed down with gobs of milk.

"He's just a growing boy, you know." I joshed.

Sue volunteered to pick up the phone-ordered pizza and Larry insisted on accompanying her. I refused tagging along and leaving the kids behind in an unfamiliar place lest they should awaken and wonder where they were. Paul conscientiously agreed to stay behind and keep me company.

It was all new territory, getting so suddenly acquainted with all the new siblings I had not previously met. As is my way, I immediately struck up amiable conversation with Paul in what I hoped were male interests to fill gaps of awkward silence.

"I s'pose, like most guys, you're into cars and auto racing like brother Larry? HUh?" I asked.

"Hey, we have very little time now before my very pregnant wife and your very ugly husband returns," Paul sniggered. "Would be a cryin' shame to waste it on conversation! Don't you think?"

"What do you have in mind?" I asked bewildered and in disbelief.

And within a very few moments he physically answered my question and in a very few moments I answered his as well, physically and verbally, in indignant, brusque squelch, thus creating an uncomfortable silence between us. The minutes waiting for the arrival of pizza developed into an awkward, long drawn-out stretch of time. Paul was dead set on getting to know me better in the absence of our spouses, a whole lot better than I was willing to explore.

Then the giggling at the door vented a sigh of utter relief from the depths of my diaphragm as pizza and a gallon of milk was deposited on the kitchen table.

"What a family!" I mused. What an initiation into the male species of those Proud, arrogant Germans. Descendants of the Morton Salt Empire, so Larry had often pretentiously claimed and boasted. How much of those claims were credible, remain to be explored.

"The Womanizing vonGillern Species." I ruminated, smiling to myself. I hadn't met the male gene's of the species, as Larry had ignored any possibility of looking up his dad, in Waterloo, when we had visited his Mom. He seemingly wanted to discourage any family contact with his father at all.

* * * * * *

Upon our return to Duluth we glumly received the news that Gerry had accepted a transfer from the Duluth Public School System to a new teaching position in Aitkin, Minnesota, sadly severing the close bonding between our two families, we had so embraced. Time spent together would now become tenuous and sparse.

The very next weekend they loaded their belongings into a u-haul truck and trailer and were on their way to a new residence and a new teaching niche.

♪♪♪

CHAPTER FOUR

Larry popped in at the Gopher just shortly before our closing set. It was much later than he usually appeared from the Friday night stock car races.

I stepped off the stage from the final set and with cocktail in hand, joined him at the congested bar.

"How did you do?" I asked in a disinterested voice.

"I came in second, tonight." he casually replied. "Boy, what a night! Cops called me. Didn't they call you here, too?"

"No. For what?"

"Dale was caught stealing a bottle of wine from the Red Carpet, that's what!"

"No!" I gasped.

"Yeah. I had to go to the Police Station, uptown, where they were holding him and they gave him a choice to go home with me or to stay in jail!"

"Why didn't they call me?" I assertively questioned.

"I thought they had called you."

"Course, maybe they did. It's pretty hard to get a message through to anyone here in all this noise and commotion."

"Well anyway, he made the choice to go with me. I took him right home to save his ass!"

"Where is he now?"

"He better be at home where he belongs!" Larry scoffed, indignantly. "I hope he learned a lesson about the consequences of stealing!"

"Boy oh boy! Teenagers!!" I scowled. **BIG TROUBLE!!**

"Then, just as I got home, with him," he continued, "Charmaine and a couple of her rowdy friends wandered in, strolling in from a party somewhere. Lunds, I think. I could tell they'd been drinkin'. They started mouthin' off to me too, and Dale and I got into it. **Big fight!"**

"Fist Fight?"

"Yeah, A big one!" he divulged. "We rolled around on the ground for quite awhile."

"But he didn't have to stay in jail at all then." I retorted incisively.

"No. He's lucky I got him out of that. The charges were dropped and they let him go, warning him not to ever show his face there ever again or he'd be in **DEEP TROUBLE!"**

"But, then he's home now?" I asked, searching for reassurance.

"As far as I know. That's where He'd better be!!" Larry thundered.

"Wow, the dilemma with kids!" I mused, staring into space in silence. "It's a miracle Larry doesn't just up and leave." Wrapped up in my own guilt thoughts, "I'm never there to discipline or address their actions, supervise their activities, or oversee any direction at all." I assessed with cutting self-reproach.

Back to reality, "Well then, I 'spose I'd better get my fanny home too." I declared, "See you at home, Larry."

"Okay, I'll be along as soon as I finish this drink."

When I arrived at my Walnut Avenue residence around 2:00 A.M., the house and garage were lighted up like Christmas. Upon entering the kitchen I found the kids all still up and mustering around.

Dale was seated in a chair next to the basement stairway in front of the duct vent that threw a fluent flow of heat from the furnace below. He was apparently trying to warm and comfort his shivering body, which was in a shocking, deplorable, wretched state.

I gasped in horror as I discerned his unsightly bruised condition. Bloody, bulging bumps were protruding from his forehead and the side of his skull. One eye was swollen shut and the other was cut and caked with dried blood. Bruise on top of bruise, Black and blue and bloody.

He was hardly recognizable as my young teen-age son. Blood oozing from broken skin, some dried and caked. One leg and foot, twice it's normal size, was futilely useless. They were not, however, broken, but mercilessly bruised and severely injured.

Utterly speechless, I began to cry. I didn't know what to do or say to banish this unforgivable scene from having taken place.

Char shrieked, sobbing, a quiver in her voice and gurgling her words. "I thought Larry was going to kill Dale. He kept pounding his head against the cement floor in the garage, over and over again! I screamed for help. Didn't know what to do! How to stop him! I called someone on the phone. I don't even know who I called, but Jeff Lund and Jeff Halverson must have pulled Larry off of Dale. I don't remember how, but someway they must have stopped him!"

"And then---?"

"And then Larry just got in his car and left."

"He came to the Gopher." I replied. "He said, Dale had gotten caught stealing a bottle of wine from the Red Carpet and that he had bailed Dale out of jail and that he and Dale had a fight over that!!"

"Oh—uh--," Char muttered, a strange expression etched on her face as she glanced in Dale's direction. Dubiously and apprehensively, and Dale returned a puzzled look on his battered face, with neither child volunteering any insight or scrutiny or analysis of the incident.

"I don't care what Dale did!!" I screamed with animosity. "This is no ordinary man to man squabble. This was no regular, orthodox fight. This was mutilation!!! Attempted Murder! Just look at him!" I cried, trembling redundantly. "How barbaric. Look how crippled he is! Larry had no marks on him at all when he came into the Gopher!!" I ranted.

I tried gently, to touch Dale's swollen, scratched arms, his bruised face. I was trying to soothe and comfort my maimed child, but he only whimpered and cringed in pain.

"Don't, Mom. Oh no. Don't! No, it hurts too much."

"Can you walk at all?" I asked, hopeful.

"I don't know." dejected, he replied, dispiritedly.

"Let me help you stand up, Dale. Char, come over here. Help me to get him up on his feet."

We bolstered him to his feet, but he was able to put his weight only on the one side.

"It's best if we can get you to your bed so you can rest these wounds." I insisted. "In the morning we'll see how you feel and how you look. If you've not improved I'll have to take you to see our doctor. Just to make sure you don't have a concussion."

Char and I assisted Dale in his struggle to his bedroom. He hopped and limped the distance on one leg as we steadied him from each side. He wasn't able to step on the other leg without excruciating pain.

I fetched a pan of lukewarm water to his night stand and attempted to sponge, very gently, his broken skin and smudged blood stains and bruises, alternating soft, warm, wet cotton batting.

"How could Larry possibly justify doing such a thing to Dale?" I soliloquized, forlornly meditative. "What can I do?" I thought, contemplating some kind of intervention. "They got along so well." I mused. "Heads together under #61 hood. A male mechanic common bond."

"Larry as an adult," I surmised, "should know discipline is not **Fists.** It's reasoning and communication. Removing privileges is normal punishment for misbehavior, not physical attack! That's what **TOUGH LOVE** is all about. What have I gotten us into? What have I subjected my kids to? Dale was brought up knowing I never condone Theft!

Taking what didn't belong to him certainly did deserve reprimanding and serious punishment. **But This?!!"**

Inadvertently, I silently wished the police had just incarcerated him. Had thrown him in jail instead. It would never have been so ravaging. The only thing hurting would have been his pride and his dignity!

It necessitated a week of nursing and rehab to nurture Dale back to normal. School would soon be back in session. Hopefully I assessed, perhaps things would mellow and improve when the kids were back in classes and we were again on a firm, fixed, impervious schedule, allotting them no idle time to get into mischief!

* * * * * * *

"Hey Kids, you know registration for school is next week." I casually reminded Dale and Charmaine at breakfast after Larry had left for Muntz TV. "Monday, I think. I'll look it up. I know Rogie's registration is this week. I'll have to take him to Lowell tomorrow."

"Yes,, I know." Dale replied. "It's next week on Tuesday."

The three would each be in separate, different schools this term. Rogie would be in Lowell, Char in Washington, and Dale at Central.

"Mom, there's something I wanna talk to you about." Charmaine muttered in a soft dubious voice. With Dale and Rogie looking on, scrutinizing and listening, she threw a derisive facial gesture in their direction, scowled and added, "In Private!"

While the boys sat at the table crunching and munching their cheerios, Char and I withdrew to the living room. As we plopped ourselves on the couch I casually inquired, with an earthy grin.

"What's the Scoop, Char? You got a boyfriend, I bet." I teased. "Ah Ha, You've been smitten!"

In oblivion, she wasn't picking up on my dry humor, and with a perplexed expression, blurted out, "I wanna go and live with Barb and

Gerry in Aitkin and go to school there. Would that be okay?" she asked uneasily, lowering her gaze.

"Really!! Well, I don't think Barb and Gerry would want another kid hangin' around to be responsible for!" I winced. "Why in the world would you want to do such a thing?" A painful twinge of impending loss stabbed at my heart.

"I already asked them." she replied, "and they sa----"

"When were all these plans and decisions being made?" I grimly interrupted, obviously disturbed.

"They said it's okay with them." Char continued, "If it's okay with you."

"Really!" I was stunned. I reflected in silence. "Where was I when all this was conspiring? It's pretty obvious I don't spend enough time with my children." I reasoned with the usual unsettling guilt. "And now they don't even want to live here!"

"But, why would you ever want to live there?" I pleaded. "For God's Sake, don't you like your own home? I love you. I dearly love all my kids."

I was fighting to hold back tears that were pressing at the base of my lids. I felt my heart would shatter with the unexpected heaviness in my bosom.

"I know, Mom. I love you too, but I have to get away from Larry!" she blurted, abruptly, with tears. It was reminiscent of **my pleading with my Mom** to help me get away from **my Dad!**

"But, why in the world---- he's so good to you kids. Takes you guys everywhere, well most of the time anyway, 'cept maybe for that awful fight with Dale, when Dale stole wine from The Red Carpet."

"No Mom. He's not **So Good To Us!** You don't know. You're never here."

I felt condescendingly ashamed at her words, perhaps because they were true. I was always gone, either working or socializing, partying.

"What does he do that's so bad? So bad that you have to run away and live somewhere else?" I asked, diffidently.

"He hits on me!"

"Hits on you? What do you mean?" I was jolted by the thirteen year old use of a popular adult slang. Surely she didn't mean what the term actually meant. "You mean with his fists." I stated matter-of-factly, ignoring the obvious analogy.

"No, Mom, not with his fists! You know what I mean!"

"And how do you know that? For sure?" I dug for details.

"Well, whenever I watch TV, when he's home, he comes into the living room, sits down alongside of me. Then he rubs his hands up and down my legs and if I'm standing up he hugs me real hard and says he is now my Dad and will be there for me whenever I need him."

"Maybe you're putting much more into it than what' actually meant. Maybe it's just fatherly affection and compassion for you." I explained.

"No, I'm not!" she stated indignantly and she began to cry, softly, continuing, "He took me into the basement to play pool." she stammered through muffled sobs. "And then he said he would show me how a man kisses a woman. He put his **"yuk"** sloppy tongue in my mouth!"

"How long has this been going on?" I asked, anger mounting. Without waiting for a reply, I blurted, "When did this all start?"

"Right after Daddy died. He told me he was going to protect me, take care of me now that I had no real live Dad to take care of me anymore. Whenever I would feel sad, that I should come and talk to him!" Then emphatically she added. "I don't want to be around him!!"

"What a sick excuse for a man!" I angrily uttered, then ruminated in silent disgust. "What kind of a creep would try to take advantage of the vulnerability of a young girl who is mourning for her father.?"

I was poignantly trying to digest the situation. The trauma of death, in itself, is an overwhelming dilemma for a young girl, making her unconsciously vulnerable for comfort, solace and understanding. And a grown man preying on this vulnerability is sickening. I was appalled and very disturbed.

"Remember when he took me to the dentist?" Char asked.

"Sure. That was just last month."

"Well, I was really, really scared. I didn't want him to take me 'cuz I could see how he was looking at me. That awful way. He was looking at my shiny leather mini skirt and I had a turtleneck sweater on and he was staring at my boobs." It came as no surprise to me as endowed she filled a sweater. I had purchased her first bra at age nine.

Then I remembered how I had glimpsed Larrys hand brushing, on one occasion, across her precociously developed bosom and I remembered, in denial, thinking, "I must be mistaken. Just an innocent accident."

Char went on, "After I was done at the dentist he drove me down a little gravel road into the woods and stopped the car. It was someplace close around here. He knew the place but I didn't. I think he'd been there before."

Agitated, I stammered, "Did anything happen?" Probing and searching for pertinent facts.

She hesitated momentarily, as though intending to tell me more, but then capriciously added, "No nothing happened. I threatened to tell you so he took me home."

Foreboding thoughts clouded my mind, ostensibly adding fuel to my confusion. "What to do?!" I mused.

Repugnant memories swept through my mind of a dad with lustful, manipulative controlling behavior. And Larry was the choice I had made as a considerate, compassionate, responsible surrogate dad for my children!" I had married a **clone** of my father! How dirigibly stupid is that? How blind to credulously believe in him! I had been duped.

Char was crying and I hugged her gently, gibbering little terms of consoling support. "It's okay, Char. Don't cry. Everything will be okay. I'll call Barb this afternoon. Don't worry, Sweetheart. You can stay in Aitkin for awhile. We'll try it out for one school term and see how it goes."

As her sobs subsided, she exclaimed overtly, "Everything bad around here that happens is my fault! When I'm gone everything will be lots better!"

"It's definitely not **YOUR** fault!" I doggedly persisted. "Not one single bit of this is your fault!"

Holding her gently in a lengthy cuddle, I casually combed my fingers through her long, straight, blond tresses, rambling on, "Don't ever, even once, think it's your fault." Then under my breath, I muttered, "The dirty Bastard. It's his fault and don't you ever forget that. He's the adult here." I sputtered with indignation, attempting to dissuade her unwarranted thoughts of guilt and shame.

"But, it's even my fault Dale got beat up!" she religiously insisted.

"How can that be? Absurd! No way! Absolutely not! How ever in the world could you begin to think it was your fault?" I asked, rekindling my pented up anger toward Larry over his shocking perverted conduct.

"That night of the fight, when we came home from Lund's, Larry was by the garage unloading his stock car. He asked where we'd been and then he started calling me names, like a dirty tramp, a slut. He said, 'I was whorin' around the Heights with all the boys!' Dale stepped in to stick up for me and started arguing with Larry. 'You can't call my sister names!' he said. That's how the fight started. When he started calling me names, I knew what he was up to. And he was real mad 'cuz he knew I had told Dale and my friends what he tried to do!"

"What about the stealing of wine from the Red Carpet?" I asked.

"That happened a different time." Char emitted. "Dale got caught stealing a week before that, by the owner. He was tryin' to steal some beer, but that was a different time."

"The police hauled him off to jail, then?" I asked.

"No. There wasn't any policemen there at all. The owner just told Dale to get out and never come back!"

"There was no fight over Larry at all about stealing wine?"

"No."

"Larry didn't have to go to the Police Department, the jail uptown to get Dale released?" I dumbfoundedly probed.

"No. Larry musta' made that up." she asserted. Pondering the brutal struggle, with docile eyes, she lowered her head and sadly continued, "Larry almost killed Dale. He could have killed him if Halvorson and Jeff hadn't stopped him! Maybe me calling on the phone helped stop him too. I can't remember for sure, but anyway it was my fault. If I wasn't there it wouldn't hav-----,"

"No, no no!!" In firm audacious interruption, I exclaimed, "I don't wanna hear anymore of that! I'll call Barb and Gerry to discuss this and set up some plans. I'll make arrangements for you to attend school in Aitkin this term. And to live with them, of course. Maybe we could trade some baby-sitting too.

So in September Charmaine was enrolled in the Aitkin School District. It tugged at my heart painfully to be forced to separate my daughter from my home and my arms. My close, intimate bonded relationship with my daughter would now be divided, out of my control. My daughter's welfare had to be my first concern. The outcome of this division of my family was the result of the bungling, incompetent choices I had made.

Larry had convinced me, under the guise of a warm, compassionate and caring surrogate Dad that he would be magnificent support and assistance in the raising of my kids. I had been credulously gullible in my assessment, as I had viewed it all through those **rose-colored** glasses I wear.

It was no mystery to me that I had married Larry primarily to obtain a father-figure for my boys. To give them some male direction, authority and discipline that I, as a female parent would never be able to achieve.

And likewise, I was convinced Larry had alternative motives for this union as well. Firstly, I was fairly positive he thought I had **Big Buck$** as a recording artist and that I would be a financial avenue for funds to support his Racing Hobby and secondly, just to show his friends, fans and acquaintances **that he could !!**

When I cornered Larry with all the charges, he of course, obstinately denied all the accusations, professing only devotion and compassion for the welfare of my kids, shrugging it off as the usual teen-age rebuttal to authority and discipline.

"Remember, Hon," he asserted, "The very last words Reverend Michael Zacker said as we left Holy Cross Church?"

"Hmmm---."

"He said, let's make this one last! Let's make it work this time. **Pray Together and Stay Together!**"

"I remember. But sometimes things get beyond repair and even prayer can't fix the problem."

"Kids are not always as truthful as a Mother wants to believe! We knew it wouldn't be easy. Not with teen-age kids to raise." he smiled, furtively smug.

At 27 he was barely a kid himself, and I assesed, perhaps not mature enough to fill the role of a father.

♪♪♪

CHAPTER FIVE

Larry took his pit crew to the Canadian Invitationals and upon their return he threw an appreciation Keg Party at the private Hunting Shack get-away on Fox Farm Road for the Pit Crew, their wives, and friends. Dale was just a month shy of turning 16 and some of his friends were even younger. What a mature, decisive surveillance for a surrogate dad to perpetrate. Fill the kids full of beer in a secluded hide-a-way and really show them the ropes. Lessons in honesty and responsibility, not to mention encouraging illicit sexual encounters!

In October I hosted my first **DOUBLE** party at our home, consisting of Larry's racing crowd and my music coterie. The party was set up as an after-hour fest to begin at the conclusion of the Proctor Racing Banquet and our usual Gopher Gig.

I counted 106 people almost breast to breast in our house, sufficiently inadequate to accommodate a crowd that size.

The living room was alive with guitars and voices in unrehearsed song, equivalent to any planned Jam Session. Laughter exploded as an occasional humorous joke was shared. Ice cubes tinkled in cocktail glasses and foam fuzzed, now and then, as a beer can was popped.

As I squeezed through the racers, mechanics, pit men and racing fans congested in my small kitchen, in an effort to concoct a cocktail at the sink, my ears were drumming with amplified, exuberant conversation, extremely diversified from the chit-chat of the living room:

"I think, maybe I can raise some compression to that 63½ Ford if I---------"

"What kind of gas and oil are--------?"

"I think maybe my crank shaft is----------"

"But, the suspension is all-----------"

"I gotta get a hold of Ernie again about that ratio so---------"

Arlene Sorlie, my neighbor friend, wedged in beside me to mix a drink at the temporary make-shift bar I had improvised upon the sink drainboard area.

"Boy oh boy!" she ejaculated, "It sure is like night and day. The difference, I mean, in the sounds erupting from one room to another!" commenting as we poured liquor.

"Well. I guess!" I agreed. "Sure is different than my usual party's of 30 or 40 people." I declared, as we squirmed, unnoticed through the chit-chat of roll-bars, crank shafts, pistons and rebuilt engines. "I counted 106 people stuffed in these three rooms." I giggled. "I maybe even missed a few. And what a difference in the two worlds! Huh?"

"I would guess you and Larry don't see too much of each other." Arlene commented as we loitered in the hallway between the two party scenes where conversation was less difficult. "You two must really get along well that way." she quiped.

"That's for sure." I laughed. "No fights. He goes his way and I go mine!"

"But I bet you two meet in-between those two worlds quite often." Arlene bantered, giggling mischievously. "One day a little eight pound auto racer will pop into this crazy world, really upsetting your apple cart! Huh?"

"Are you kidding!?" I laughed. "I think you have to have sex to get pregnant!"

"I bet you two manage that musical symphony in perfect harmony." she punned facetiously.

"No way! He spends all his time under the car, in the garage or else he's gone racing. To get any lovin' from Larry would take some kind of a miracle." I quipped, returning her banter.

Jokingly, she replied, "Knowing your creative nature, Dottie I'm sure you could think of something to entice him to meet you between the sheets."

"HUH!" I grunted. "He never even gives me a second look, anymore. Honeymoon's over I guess."

"Nah, It's too soon for that!" she twitted.

"Well, yes, Arlene, I do have a plan and yes, it's creative and yes it's funny and it just might do the trick to get Larry to show s--------"

"Hey Dottie, get your fanny in here and sing." Korn scolded as he brusquely pushed his way toward the make-shift bar, brushing boldly against us in his pursuit of Old Thompson.

"Okay! Okay!" I sputtered. "In just a New York minute!" and addressing Arlene with a giggle, "I guess I don't have an option, as the crowd is unknowingly pushing me in that general direction anyway!"

"What kind of a plan are you instigating?" Arlene queried, returning to our previous conversation.

"Well, I've been thinkin', my attire is all wrong! That is, It's not suitable to interest a mechanic or an auto enthusiast. Competition is what drives an auto racer to electrified enthusiasm and surrounded by garage and automobile attmosphere!"

"Whatta' you mean? You're always dressed so elegant and elaborate." Arlene emitted.

"Sure, maybe on stage, but not around home. That's an entirely different situation!"

"I s'pose that's possible."

Very fictitiously serious, I continued. "I thought I could hang two headlights from my boobs, attach a piston ring in front, at my V patch, dangle a muffler from my rearend, with a red tail light attached, an air cleaner on my head and roll around the garage on a creeper and maybe, just maybe I could get a spark from Larry. A goad to fire up his libido!"

"It would sure be fun to see that!" she chuckled.

"You know me! Don't be surprised if you see me crash our next party done up in car parts. If I can get a hold of the necessary parts!" I promised incisively.

How I embellished pulling pranks on people. How I loved to laugh! How I passionately doted on coercing others to laugh with me. And sometimes I made them laugh at me, as well. I'd instigate almost anything just to tickle someone's fancy. I had to reluctantly admit this segment of my personality stemmed from my father's genes.

Vickie, Korn's wife and I spent many leisure, socializing hours together during the years she and Korn were married. Vickie was very adept at creating humorous antics and situations, as well, and often we were in amiable competition with each other. We were almost afraid of **WHO** would come up with **WHAT**, next!!

One such afternoon we casually sipped cocktails at our favorite get-away, the Amber Flow. A close friend of Vickie's, Delores, had joined us this particular afternoon. As Delores excused herself to the restroom, Vickie winked, mischievously in my direction, suggesting, in Delores's absence, "Why don't you pull that Pooper Machine prank on Delores. I don't think she has ever seen that one."

"Sure." I giggled as I pulled the improvised contraption from the depths of the gigantic purse I toted.

In the early devious origin of this gadget I had improvised this concoction as such: Unwinding a heavy metal clothes hanger, I had cut an 18 inch section of the wire and bent it to devise a letter U shape. Leaving approximately six inches across the open end of the U. I bent the ends of the letter to form a hook on each end. I looped two large sturdy rubber bands through a jagged edged washer and each rubber band was stretched taut and attached to each hook to form a straight tight line across the open length of the U wire. Then I would wind the attached rubber bands with the centered washer very rigid and taut and place the wound gadget snugly under one side of my buttocks. As I perched upon the impish device, I'd gently raise my fanny just a smidgen as if releasing air. The washer would roll gently across the preferably vinyl covered seat of a chair or in this case a booth, creating the authentic sound of a little harmless fart!

If I was very careful to not let it roll too rapidly, the wound gadget would last for approximately three farts before it was totally unwound. There was definitely an accomplished, artistic talent in controlling the reeling of this toy to achieve it's greatest potential! Ahem!! It did not require a diploma or a degree, I'm sure, but acquired ability and genius was precise, never-the-less! Ha!

I wound up the thingamajig up tight and positioned it under my butt, ready for action, in anticipation of Delores's return from the restroom. As we casually conversed in friendly chit-chat I raised my butt, ever so slightly, allowing a little gush to escape. Delores flinched a bit, scanned my facial expression, questioningly. However, I just continued talking and sipping my cocktail, completely ignoring her skepticism. When the third little burst of fictitious fart emerged, Delores, obviously annoyed, with an unsettling look on her face, rose from the booth to leave and sputtered tersely,

"I just can't sit here any longer. The disgusting smell is just getting to me!"

Vickie and I cracked-up in infectious laughter.

"Oh no, Please stay," she urged between bouts of giggling. "It's only a joke, Delores!"

I had to clarify by demonstrating to Delores the feat of my little toy and that it was indeed a joke to convince her to return to our jovial, unpredictable company.

The **Power of Suggestion** is certainly more over-powering than we had imagined!

Vickie is quite the card herself, often out-doing anything I could muster. Here she is demonstrating, with a friend, How sex looks if you could see it from the other end!

Vickie, at one of our luncheons, tagged each of us with invented nick names. She had, earlier, during the recording of 'One More Memory' in Nashville, in '67 tagged me with the alias of **Thelma Thudpucker**, explaining jovially, that Englebert Humperdink became a smash overnight HIT with 'Please Release Me' not because of the power of the song, but because he had changed his name to something different and bizarre! Therefore if I wanted 'One More Memory' to make a similar fracas I'd have to change my name to her suggestion of Thelma Thudpucker! So at this afternoon luncheon, our little clique was blessed with Vickie's fabricated nick names.

Delores became **Asmirilla Lipshit**, Irene was **Dirty Girdie Giddleschnidt**, Patty was tagged **Patsy Clapsaddle**, and "Big M", Marilyn was christened **Ruby Rottencrotch**. Vickie said she had named Korn **happy Harry Hollowpeter**, but of course he wasn't allowed to attend our female coterie. I couldn't tolerate not being in competition, adding my two cents of creativity, so Larry became **Jerry Jolly Jockey Jingleballs!** Oh yes, Jane was Pollyanna Hootinpile.

One Sunday night when the Tumbleweeds weren't scheduled for a gig, Vickie and I visited one of our favorite bands at the Venture Club. We met as usual at the Amber Flow and stopped off at my house, briefly, on the way to visit my bathroom. While there, I compiled a couple brandy mixed drinks for Vickie and I to enjoy and then a couple more to relish enroute to the Venture Club. I had failed to use a measuring shot glass in the preparation and I assume the cocktails ended up rather potent!

As we came to a halt at our destination and I parked my Chevy, I strode around to the passenger side, wondering what was keeping Vickie.

"Come on, Vickie, let's crash this joint!" I retorted.

I opened the door to assist. Alas, Vickie fell right out of the seat and on to the parking lot pavement. She just layed there, looking up at me, giggling incessantly. I took her hand to assist her to her feet. I seized her contagious laughter and we both convulsively giggled our way into the Club, where we pleasured the establishment with our simpered adorable, intoxicated demeanor! I guess you had to be there!

We had hardly located a table and ordered beverages when the band, without my beforehand approval announced emphatically, "Dottie Lou is in the Club and I'm sure if you'll give her an enthusiastic round of applause, she'd surely delight us with her rendition of her smash hit of 'One More Memory'!

Vickie resolved to sing along with me and rendered her famous, well remembered **DEBUT!** Live on stage with a live band! A vocal fiasco!

After her embarrassment had dwindled and her courage returned, she admitted to me, defending her honor with a passive explanation, "I can't drink brandy, Dottie! It quickly puts me out of commission!"

Vickie ordinarily, fashionably coasted on screw-drivers, while I, on the otherhand, could never tolerate Vodka. What a pair!

The passing of time eventually found us, retrospectively enjoying the humor of the memory. We loved to laugh and laugh we always certainly did!

My music circle of friends, of which Vickie's associates were a part of, enjoyed our nonpernicious gossip, jokes and frivolous chit-chat gatherings in the atmosphere of warm indoor comfort.

On the other hand, my Duluth Heights clique of lady friends had little similarity. They were in an opposite realm of taste. Most of the gals were snowmobilers, campers, or racing addicts and loved the outdoors in all elements of weather. Our only idiosyncrasy, in common, was our bantering chit-chat, flavored with the recent gossip. We were marvelously diverse.

At our luncheons we were clad in snowmobile suits and rode sleds, so it was no surprise when at an afternoon luncheon clutch we unanimously voted to organize a ladies snowmobile club! After all, the guys sporting their own 'Hardway Team' couldn't have one over on us! "If the guys can do it, so can we!"

We resolved, over much cocktail deliberation, that we would call our team "The Devils Darlings".

We had professional patches fashioned and sewed them on our snowmobile attire. We met twice a month at a selected residence and from there we'd ride our machines around the outskirts of Duluth. We'd pause at a previously selected Honky Tonk location for lunch and ride around the area between bologna and beer interventions, making it a point to conclude our festive afternoon around 5:00 P.M. in time to prepare dinner for our families. This part of the plan was to avoid antagonizing irate husbands into putting the kibosh on our afternoon capers.

The club consisted of approximately 15 gals. My memory recollects some of our companions. Among them, Barb Jurek, Arlene Sorlie, Betty Mattila, Vi Nelson, Eileen Parker, Darlene Wallner, Gineen Razkowski, Nora Nystrom, Marlene Nelson, Barb Huttle, Judy Razitallo, and of course Dottie Lou.

We relished, with zest, our afternoon mischief in the absence of men. We coddled our prides over our expertise sufficiency. We nurtured our susceptible egos, speculating a growing independence over the unnecessary need of men to run and service our machines. We proudly stocked our own individual, little criteria's of "Mechanic Maintenance Kits", supporting a supply of spark plugs, starting fluid, a few basic wrenches: pliers, sockets, cresent wrenches, tow ropes, etc., semblance of a security blanket.

We were soon to encounter our first "Number One Episode of Irate Husband!!"

We were torpedoing our caravan of ladies along the trail parallel to Calvary Road and had to cross Rice Lake Road to zoom over to a steak house where we intended to savor our luncheon washed down with a mug or two of Budweiser.

We were there, confronted with a gigantic, apprehensive snow bank, so enormous, so high, we were unable to see the sleds on the other side after they had crossed over. Betty Mattila was selected to stand on the summit of the snow bank and wave each sled over when she could see the coast was clear on the blinded side, when a sled had cleared the snow bank and parked out of the path of the next gal. One by one we zinged over the bank and lined up along the row to wait for the next one.

My turn: I gunned my little ski-doo, Cleared the summit, but unfortunately, when the machine nosed downward, it came to a sudden halt, imobilized at the bottom of the bank. I quickly jumped from my sled to manually wriggle it loose, to no avail. Barb Jurek, following me, however did not wait for the safety hand signal from Betty and **KA—BOOOOM!** there she was "hell bent for election", nosed right into the rear-end of my sled!

"Oh! Oh!" she exclaimed, "Just look at my hood, loose and Wow, a big crack! Boy, is Bud ever going to be Hot, Hot over that!"

"Well no one's hurt," Arlene volunteered. "He should be happy over that."

"But you know men," Barb retorted. "They're machines are more important than people and Bud's no exception."

"Well how can we fix it so he won't know?" we all chuckled, sheepishly.

"I know." Barb blurted a suggestion. ♪"I have a package of chewing gum, Wriggly's Doublemint." Double your flavor, double your fun," Barb sing-songed cheerfully, "Also for patching. ♫ ♪ that doublemint gum." We'll smudge the crack shut so Bud won't notice it right away. Then when he goes for a ride, he does ride most every evening after work, I'll pretend he must have done it!"

She handed out sticks of gum to each of us as we giggled infectiously over our clever scheme. She instructed us to chew until they were softened. A devious expertise plan to camouflage the casualty that took some authentic feminine ingenuity on Barb's part. However Barb related at a later time how Bud hit the ceiling when he attempted to remove the gum. The more he ground it the hotter and more sticky it became and the more smeared all over the hood! He hadn't bought her innocent story, either!

It was the first episode of our ability to Antagonize Husbands on our Club efforts that had never actually been endorsed or welcomed or encouraged by any of them! They had chauvinistically insisted that women cannot function or maintain or service a snowmobile club without the assistance of men!

Then befell Number Two Episode of **Irate Men!**

With the kids off to school and Larry at work, I hopped my little Ski-Doo and scooted through the woods to Morgan Street and Arlene Sorlie's house. As I approached the residence I observed several sleds were already parked in readiness for our prepensive gal gallivanting.

"What a gorgeous day for a ride!" I exclaimed as I removed my boots and unzipped my snowmobile jacket. "It must be 20 degree or better out there."

"And snowing ever so lightly." Arlene added. "It really is pretty awesome."

"We're still waiting for four more to join us." Darlene Wallner announced as she sipped coffee from a mug.

"I'll have some of that hot stuff too." I affirmed while removing my yellow Ski-Doo jacket.

And what a gorgeous, pleasurable, superb ride it was! We zipped here and there with gratifying pizzazz, nonchalantly stopping occasionally to share a bottle of wine or schnapps, passing it around mouth to mouth for **Ahem!** winter warmth!

A unanimous decision was conspired to eat and chat at the Fall Inn on Martin Road around 1:00 P.M.

We were so engrossed in our inimitable visit that we became oblivious to the escape of time. We were startled to discover two hours had slipped away unnoticed, during our diversion at the Fall Inn over sandwiches, beer and brandy.

As we exited the Inn and mounted our machines we were stunned over the drastic, dramatic change in the elements. It was now snowing furiously and a bitter cold harsh, wind had developed during our lunch, whipping across our cheeks, taking our breath away and viciously slapping our faces.

"What in the world is this **SHIT?**" Betty gasped. "We're in the middle of a **DAMN, DAMN, BLIZZARD!!** What happened to our warm beautiful day?"

Pulling our jacket zippers tightly up to our chins and securely tying our winter scarves around our throats, we began, one by one, attempting to start our snowmobiles for what had developed into an unpleasant, cold, uncomfortable dilemma.

Vi retorted in dismay, "My machine won't start!"

"What the HELL!", Eileen Parker scoffed, "Neither will mine!"

I tried to turn the ignition key on my electric start and the key refused to move. It was frozen, immovable!

"Oh MY God!" I scowled in distress. "My ignition key won't even turn!"

One by one, most of the ladies, very unsettling, discovered their machines were immobilized!

Around four or five machines finally took off and whimpered a mile distance, only to find they would soon join the disabled parade. Machines were now scattered everywhere.

The assistance of ether from a can sprayed into paralyzed engine carburetors, from Arlene's "First Aid Mechanic Kit" resulted in successfully coaxing her machine and Betty Mattila's to start. Their's were the only two sleds to continue percolating! Machines were scattered around the parking lot, some across the road, some a quarter mile away. A drastic sudden change of temperature in the frenzy of an angry approaching blizzard had resulted in gas line freeze-up in almost every sled. Some would run, briefly, only to die out in a mile or two, scattering snowmobiles all over the white terrain of the outskirts of Duluth. And to add to the tormenting adversity, a belligerent wind whistled and whipped, slashing knife-like snow against our freezing cheeks, to the violent rhapsodic tune of an antagonistic Northerly.

Arlene and Betty suggested they go to summon help. as they were the only two sleds left operating.

Needless to say, our outing resulted in a mammoth display of intimidation and imminent anger from a large group of divisive, irate husbands, when the S.O.S. of our debilitating predicament reached their ears. While shaking their heads, bursts of, under their breath, profanity and some with profanity not quite so subdued emerged as they collected our stranded machines. They indicated we were walking, no riding, on **THIN ICE!** (oops, that's another story).

We were bluntly informed, quote, **"We had better consider terminating the stupidity of riding without men, or else the Devils Darlings had better initiate hiring a male mechanic to ride in their company on their absurd, ASININE, ESCAPADES, or else call their STUPID, SILLY CAPERS QUITS!!"** unquote.

Many of our luncheons were playfully without complications or disaster and just filled with bonded fun and laughter.

However, we were frequently warned by our spouses that the Devil's Darling's escapades had better remain uneventful or our Bizarre, Bird-Brained schemes would not be tolerated by the men!

Then in March when the weather was breaking and had become quite comfortably warm, on the verge of thawing at times, we initiated a ride of utmost ludicrous, inane sporting, to again foolhardily infuriate the men!! Our recourse, at the time, always being, **"The Devil Made Me Do It!"** But it was never met with any merciful leniency from the men. They didn't share our humor.

And so "Irate Husbands #3 Episode" transpired:

"Gosh, isn't it great to be riding when the harsh weather has finally broken like this? We don't even need a scarf or an extra sweater anymore." Marlene Nelson commented as we exited my house to mount and gather our caravan of machines on this warm, gentle breezy morning in the middle of March.

The sun was shining and a hint of melting slush splashed against our boots now and then. I emitted a heavy audible sigh and inhaled deeply a burst of warm spring air into the depths of my diaphragm and mused,

"Yes, what a gorgeous lazy day for a snowmobile ride." Twelve gals had gathered at my home this day for a scheduled excursion.

"The season of the winter storm is about over." Marlene remarked as she revved the engine in impatient anticipation of our departure.

"I don't know!" Judy opined dubiously, "I've seen some pretty vicious, ferocious, savage storms paralyze us in late March in past years!"

"It's possible." I added in agreement, "But I'm sure our guys are not too worried about us today. We definitely won't be yelling an S.O.S. for their assistance on a beautiful spring day like this!" I chuckled, reminiscing the February snow storm.

"You got that right!" Eileen emitted confidently.

And off we were, gallivanting, blasting down the trails in childlike fervor, playfully intrigued. We roamed the white terrain, melting somewhat under the slides of our sleds, north of Duluth in the Martin Road and Rice Lake Road areas. We ensued a couple impromptu pit stops in the area and reversed our direction back toward the origin of our departure, planning to arrive at the designated "Red Carpet" across Miller Trunk Highway 53 for lunch.

The only way to cross the highway by snowmobile in the 70's, where a gigantic 21st century Mall now stands, was to drive under the highway through a concrete tunnel and down Miller Creek. The only businesses at that era in time was "Cozy Corner'" general store on the north side and Target and the Red Carpet across on the south side.

Miller Creek was a diminutive, unperilous little stream of minuscule depth, harmlessly unforeboding in risk to cross in any way.

We all lapsed on the north side of Highway 53 for an interval, a few minutes of small talk before tackling the tunnel and the stream and the mini embankment into the Red Carpet parking lot for a 2:00 P.M. luncheon.

We'd all be arriving home a wee bit early this trip as our last stop was in the vicinity of the back doors of all our homes, with only a five or ten minute ride to our domestic duties.

"I'm starved!" Nora quipped. "Let's get our fanny's in gear. What we waitin' for? We can talk anywhere! 'Nuf Chit-Chat. Quit the Cshit! I mean Chat!" We all giggled convulsively.

"Okay! Okay! Let's go."

The caravan, as usual, ambiguously lined up in a row and bolted off with Barb Jurek in the lead, scooting confidently through the tunnel and down Miller Creek. However, we soon, skeptically became aware that we were traveling over spans of open water, here and there. No problem! Miller Creek was comparatively shallow. Those of us bringing up the rear all yelled in unison, "Give 'er gas!! Gun 'er! Don't slow down, whatever you do!!"

Arlene followed Barb up the slight incline into the Red Carpet parking lot, with Barb Matilla right on her tail and Vi directly behind her.

Vi was in her very first season on a snow machine and quite inexperienced. When she viewed the open water beneath her sled, she froze in fear!

"Don't Stop!" Eileen, following her, screamed, audaciously. Of course all audio was lost to the roar of snowmobile engines and Vi stopped dead, and watched her sled slowly sink into a foot of slush and water. It was merely a short, brief span of open water and everyone could have easily, with a little common sense and effort scaled their sleds to the parking lot.

With Vi in the drink, directly in front of the rest of us and no way around her, we were forced to stop as well, creating a chain reaction of several sleds being submerged and stranded in a foot of spring mush and water.

We dismounted and abandoned our machines and slushed to the top of the incline with boots full of water, drenched sox and saturated snow suit leggings.

"Oh Boy!" someone moaned. "Another S.O.S."

In one direction I could hear, under their breath, "Oh—Oh—ohing, Now what?" Some were swearing. Some were laughing, it resting solely on their individual premonition of varied husband rebuttal awaiting them at home.

I was laughing hysterically, along with a couple other gals, as we sat on the bank, removed and emptied our boots and wrung the water from our saturated sox, returning them to our wet wrinkled footsies.

Larry never took anything very seriously concerning our escapades, good or bad, so it never resulted in anger from him. He'd just, good humoredly, pick up the pieces and tote the disaster home, shaking his head with, "Will you gals ever learn and admit how much you need us?" Not all the gals had husbands with passive attitudes as Larry.

After squeezing some of the water from our clothes, we lumbered up the incline, slushing in our boots as we entered the Red Carpet for cocktail time and numerous phone calls to **IRATE HUSBANDS**, again admitting failure, wounding, again, our already battered prides!

Needless to mention, this caper incited the proverbial "Last straw on the camels back" to 80% of the **Irate Husbands** of the Devils Darlings as they retrieved our submerged sleds from the the DRINK!! So, not totally unexpected to us, they firmly put the KIBOSH on our afternoon snowmobile luncheons and our Impetuous Devil's Darling's Club, short-lived, had survived only one season!!

♫♫

CHAPTER SIX

Christmas rolled around and I missed having my daughter with us during the holidays. Of course she was a part of the Christmas Day celebration at Pauline and Don's having arrived with Gerry and Barb and their family. I promised we'd spend a couple days after the holidays with her and Barb and Gerry's family in Aitkin.

One evening, shortly before Christmas, Larry presented me with a gorgeous, black, hand knitted, wool sweater, with D.V.G. knitted near the shoulder in large yellow letters.

"It's a matching set, Hon." he sputtered. "See mine says L.V.G. They'll be so nice and warm for snowmobiling."

"Wow! Where did you get these?" I scrutinized, with raised brows. "They're hand knit!" he responded.

"Yes I can see that. Who made them?" I inquired.

"A dear friend of mine from the racing gang. Betty Garnet."

"I don't know her. I'm sure she doesn't know me." I said. "Why me?"

"Well, cuz you're my wife I suppose." he chuckled. "She has a **Thing** for me!" he vaunted, assertively.

"Isn't she married?" I asked.

"Oh sure, but we had a thing going a while back. Way before your time!" he quickly added.

"How did her husband take to that?" I rebuked.

"He never knew. I'd give her a ride home from the Stock Car Races and we'd fool around. The first time I walked her to her door, we stepped in between the two doors, like a porch or vestibule and we kissed goodnight there. She was quite passionately receptive and I knew she wanted me!"

"Where was her husband all this time?" I asked with flamboyant curiosity.

"She said he was in bed, sleeping, so we screwed, standing up, between the doors. **Who said it can't be done!!**" he sniggered, self-assuredly pleased with himself and his conquering, memory abilities. "That was before your time, of course!" he blurted, shamelessly.

Larry always vaunted, neurotically of his sexual conquests. He was endlessly, emphatically proud of his skills at swindling someone out of something, be it a wife or a material possession or a favor in labor, or a debt he had escaped paying.

"The **Power Obsession** of a little man, and not merely in stature." I mused, silently amused.

"Oh Gosh, Larry!!" I ironically gushed to my mendacious husband. "I'll cherish this sweater with my whole heart, forever!"

I never wore it.

* * * * * * *

Just before Christmas Larry indulged the kids with a large, new color TV from Muntz TV. The boys were mesmerized. The screen was gigantic in comparison to our little obsolete black and white.

A twinge of heartfelt, forgiving compassion tugged at my heart as I realized Larry was bending over backward, making a colossal attempt at reconciliation with my children. A staunch effort to get back into their graces and their hearts.

I had a hunch he probably hadn't paid for the set, but I deemed it was not my responsibility or concern and I didn't even want to know the details.

Christmas Eve he supriseingly indulged me, as well, with an admirable gift of a new Bass Fiddle. It was an electric Ampeg Bass and a new concept in electronics. The pick-up unit was built inside equivalent to the electronic structure of an electric guitar. I would be able, now, to chuck my old Doghouse of fifteen years, equiped with an improvised outside pick-up unit under the strings beside the bridge, which always dispensed an uneven volume.

"It's one thing to have physical stage presence," Larry said, "and you do, but it's also important to impress the public, your fans, by parading and flaunting a prestigious instrument of excellence! It reeks of success and prestige." he explained. "How well this will look on stage compared to that **Shabby piece of Crap** you have been playing since I've known you!"

"I'm impressed!" I managed to squeeze out after catching my breath from the shock.

Larry's Ladies were mere trophy's to him. The more trophy's he could line up and display, the more recognition he perceived he'd acclaim. The more evidence of his dauntless power and success! We, his ladies must be displayed with elegance and eminent quality status.

By comparison, analogically, I was still in the middle of an undertaking Larry had arranged, of having bridges placed in my mouth where my back molars were missing on all four sides.

Larry had sold a snowmobile to a dentist the previous year at a super rock bottom steal of a price and he had bartered with the dentist an arrangement to devise dental bridge work on his wife for ½ price in lieu of the favor. Larry had complained, that the holes in my mouth masked my otherwise beautiful smile when I sang or laughed.

"It is not becoming to someone with your status!" he asserted. "someone involved with performing before an audience!"

I, of course, received no assistance with the financial burden of the dental work, but the price was very feasible with my income. I did appreciate his suggestion and efforts creating the necessary nudge to spring me into action to improve my appearance. Subsequently, I realized the appearance of his Trophy wife's Bass Fiddle was as important to him as was her smile.

I was ecstatic with the beauty of the new instrument!

"It is so gorgeous, Larry!" I squealed. "Thank you! Thank you! What a wonderful gift. It must have cost you a Bundle!!"

He ignored my frugal curiosity over the finances and continued, "They made these Electric Ampegs for only two years. 1969 and this year is their last. They're closing them out. This Bass will eventually, in years to come be a Collectors item!"

"You're kidding! WOW! That's fantastic!" I beamed, as I glided my palms over the glossy finish of the body.

"They make an Ampeg Bass Amp that's made 'specially for it, but I couldn't go that much money. You'll have to buy that yourself." he added.

"I'll just use the amp I already have." I compromised. "That should work just as well. IT's made for a Bass. An amp is an amp is an amp is an amp, I think. This Bass Fiddle is really an incredible gift, Larry. Thanks, Hon." I repeated as we hugged.

"Merry Christmas." he said. "You'll have many years of music, memory and service out of that instrument." he added proudly.

"Yes, memories of you too, Hon." I giggled, elvishly.

To play a Country Bass Fiddle one straddles the body sideways to keep it from twisting or slipping as you run the notes up and down the fingerboard with the left hand fingers and simultaneously pull the strings at the base of the neck, directly above the bridge with your right hand index finger. Occasionally, a technique for effect, is created by slapping the strings with the palm of the hand, creating a double accentuated staccato beat. In country music the bass is not usually played with a bow.

"Whatta ya mean? Memory of me?" he cut a wisecrack in jest. "You planning on ditching me and movin' on?"

"No, no. But you're never, ever around when I'm doing my thing." I replied, explaining, "So whenever I'll straddle the body of that bass between my legs, I'll think of you and pretend it's you between my legs." I giggled deviously. "And however brusquely or however softly, tenderly I **Slap The Strings**, will indicate, at the time, what I'm feeling for you! Tender Passion or Raging Anger, depending entirely on your Behavior!!"

"In that case you'll probably be breaking strings all the time from **TOO MUCH GUSTO!!**" he laughed heartily.

"More than likely." I giggled as we squeezed and exchanged Holiday Hugs. Little did he realize how close to the truth was that little innocent statement in witticism.

* * * * * * *

Shortly after the Holidays, Larry surrendered his position at Muntz TV and initiated new employment as a salesman for Arrow Chevrolet. He insisted the reason for the transition was because Arrow Chevrolet would tolerate his racing schedules, where as Muntz TV was not very understanding concerning his Hobby absences.

After the holidays, Sharon finally allowed Collette, Larry's little daughter to visit with us at length. Larry and I married 1½ years now and Sharon finally felt secure enough to allow Collette to share our life. She confessed her change of heart was because she now trusted me, not her ex!

"Hey Dottie, do you have to work tonight?" Larry asked. It was Sunday and yes, I had a rare reprieve from music.

"No, we don't have a booking for tonight." I glibly replied.

"A bunch of us are going to play around at the Work Farm tonight. I've never taken you there. It's an excellent place to snowmobile. You wanna go?"

"Sure. Sounds like fun." I emitted affirmatively.

The hills and meadows of the white terrain were packed like pavement from the incessant pounding of snow machines at play over previous days, previous riders. It was exciting and exhilarating to dash, repeatedly, up and down the crystal white hills.

The rolling meadows were bordered on all sides with deciduous and an evergreen tree mixture.

Larry, in his usual, unconventional hambone stunting, didn't follow the posted rules of the accepted area in which to play. Ordinary buffoonery didn't quite suffice his perpetually, hungry for attention, ego. Not heroic enough to just **Race** passing machines on the hillsides, or swinging, sharply in front of sleds, clowning zanily to cut off their maneuvers in jest.

Proudly displaying his skill and expertise, he took off hell-bent, into the surrounding, **No Trespassing** posted, forest which bordered the rolling hills. I deduced he was anticipating an assumed eagerness for us to follow his lead into the untraveled unexplored terrain. However, the remaindeer of the group dispassionately ignored Larry's frolicking and just continued playing in the designated, approved area.

Suddenly a shrill scream screeched from the hidden midst of the forest area and we all darted our machines to the edge of the woods to investigate. We dismounted our sleds and entered the woods on foot.

There we found Larry, sprawled eagle, face down in the soft fluffy snow! The guys lifted him and carried him to the traveled area.

He had cascaded across a deep, but narrow ditch and dropped his sled into the hole with a sudden jolt, torpedoing him into the air, like from a cannon in a frolicking carnival. He bashed against the sled's handlebar in the flight and dislocated his shoulder.

"Are you okay?" Kenny inquired, as they slowly supported him to his feet. He wavered unsteadily, appearing wobbly and a trifle disoriented.

"Yeah! Yeah! Yeah!" he scoffed, audaciously. "Only my shoulder is OUT-----Again!"

With his right hand he began pushing intensely against his left arm, which was loosely dangling in a futile position. A loud crack penetrated the silence as we stood watching, aghast. With confident physical persuasion he relocated his shoulder joint back into it's normal socket position!

I was flabbergasted! I had never witnessed such an inimitable, mind wrenching undertaking before. However, I came to learn this incident was a frequently repeated occurrence with Larry! He assured me this happened often and he was indubitably okay with it!

"How does it feel?" Bud asked.

"It hurts like hell!" Larry admitted, sheepishly. "It always does at first!"

The guys lifted his sled from the miniscule ravine and drove it out of the forest, into the meadow.

"We can let Sylvia get the sled home for you." Kenny suggested, as she had been riding double and was available.

"Why?" Larry retorted. Without waiting for a reply, he blurted. "Hell No! Let's ride! That's what we came for! RIGHT?"

"Are you sure?" Bud asked. "You okay to ride your machine?"

"HELL YEAH! No problem!" he quipped and off he sprinted, spurting and throwing snow in several directions as he burned the white stuff, leaving diminutive gully's in the hard packed snow behind him! He flew up the hill as if nothing out of the ordinary had occurred.

At home, later, as we yawned and disrobed for bed, I teasingly remarked, "I guess I' m really out of luck for any thoughts or plans of lovin' feelins' tonight. Your lunatic behavior took care of that, I guess!"

"WHY?"

"Well, you must be in quite a lot of pain after tonights nose dive off of your sled!" I needled, with tantalizing speculation.

"Hey, I dislocated my shoulder, not my family jewels!" he laughed, adding, "I did hurt my back some. It's pretty sore, no doubt of that.

But that only means we'll have to reverse positions!" he chuckled, mischievously. "Is that okay with you?"

"OKAY? Not just okay!" I jovially smirked. "It's fabulous, Incredible! Wonderful! Out of all bad comes some good!!"

A curious, baffled expression flashed across his face at my remarks. However the following amorous encounter did give Larry an abundance of insight into what was really pleasing to frugal, usually lukewarm Dottie.

Larry, even the scoundrel that he was in the guise of altruism, had the narcissistic drive to powerfully be the best at everything, be it salesmanship, mechanics, racing, or boudoir skill! He determined I needed release and fullfillment twice a month, scheduling us to meet every other week for a culmination; scheduling me faithfully. In between his other lady prospects and encounters I suspected?

* * * * * *

Early winter was saturated with Snowmobiling racing events and frolickign snowmobile excursions.

Larry had just purchased a 292 Blizzard and was fanatically antsy about getting it on the tracks to bolster his inflated ego, in his adept expertise in snowmobiles and racing. This was the first of the Bombadier Blizzard Line and Larry was itching to Outshine—Outlast—Outrace any other competitor on the tracks.

Dale and his buddies accompanied Larry to many of the Snowmobile Races. At the time Dale was hanging with Leslie Knutson and was captivated with her allure. He was definitely, explosively in love, or maybe in Lust! At 16 it is difficult to distinguish between the two.

He and Leslie were all wrapped up in each other, smooching and petting in Larry's parked truck at the Proctor Speedway Snowmobile races. They weren't much interested in participation with the fans that had gathered to view the racing events. They were more strongly interested in the participation of swapin' spit in the warmth and privacy of Larry's truck!

A loud tap on the window untangled their elusive detachment from the festivities and they bolted to attention, as they broke 'kissy-face', realizing it was Larry at the window.

"Hey, Dale," Larry excitedly buzzed, "I entered you in the Junior Class to race my Blizzard. You're already signed in. You gotta come and race! You're up next. Come on! Now!"

"Oh, I don't know." Dale protested with languid, lethargic indifference.

"OH WOW! Boy oh Boy! Awesome!" Leslie exclaimed excitedly.

Dale glanced down at his petite, young love and suddenly digested the devotional light in her eyes, the proud excitement in her mesmerized demeanor and it was evident a "No" answer would not be wise!

"This just might make some **Browny Points** for me with Leslie!" he mused, smiling presumptuously to himself. So he mumbled a "Yah, I guess I'm in."

As Dale followed Larry into the pits, he was still half-heartedly protesting, with a lack of confidence, about his dubious skill to race.

"I don't even know what I'm doing here, Larry. I've never ever raced before!"

"I know, but you'll do okay!" Larry cajoled enthusiastically. "It'll be a piece of cake on my new Blizzard!" he sniggered convulsively.

Dale mounted the sled and scooted around the pits several times, trying to get the feel of the machine.

"Boy, this thing is really fast!" he affirmed as he slid the machine beside Larry and braked. "Wow! This Blizzard is sure a lot faster than Mom's 16 Horse electric start! Yah!"

"Lots more **THUNDER** under that hood? Huh?" Larry glibly boasted.

Dale coasted the sled onto the track to the starting line, as Larry lumbered beside him, assertively instructing him with a few appropriate racing tips.

"Make sure you lift the butt end of the machine and bounce it to clear any snow or ice that might be stuck and then jump, hard, several times on the back end before you start to make sure you're getting traction. That's so it will dig in good at the start."

"Okay." Dale nodded acknowledging, and began bouncing the rear of the sled in prep.

"When you get in the corners, make sure you lean, cuz, well, the G force, you know. Otherwise you might tip over."

"You Bet! Okay! I can do that!!" he replied, fostering some necessary courage and confidence.

In Dale's Own Words:

"I get on the starting line and they drop the green flag and I do all Larry says and **Boom!** all of a sudden, I'm out in front. WOW! This thing is fast! Yah! As soon as I hit the corner I forget to lean, so I flipped it right away, coming out on the back straight-away. I get back on again, but by then everybody's passed me, so I was in last place, but not way far back. I ended up catching them on the 4th corner and I passed them all again by then. I sure remembered, then, to lean and when I got around the 4th corner I punched 'er and **BOOM**. Here I am a whole straight-away length in front of everybody else! It was only a five or six lap race and I finished ½ lap ahead of everyone—**Taking First Place!** Then they gave me a checkered flag and I had to drive around one lap carrying that flag. It was a thrill, but what I remember most was when Ronnie DeGrio, Mike's younger brother, jumped out of the stands and sprinted into the pits to shake my hand!!"

"Oh boy, You did a great job, Dale!" he exclaimed, overwelmed and awestruck over his buddy winning the race.

And of course Larry was proud and beaming, "That's my step-son! You're going to see a lot more of him around the tracks!" he warned the fans, boastfully.

So that winter Larry started signing Dale into numerous Junior Snowmobile races; Poplar, Birchwood, Duluth Heights Community Club, Winter Frolics, etc. but Proctor had been Dale's only thrilling, **First Place Win!! FIRST RACE! FIRST PLACE!!**

* * * * * * *

There never seemed to be a lull in the snowmobile activities that winter. It was the winter of the birth of **The Devil's Darlings,** as well and I spent many, many hours of leisure time straddling and bouncing on my old 16 horse Ski Doo!

"Hey Dottie, me and the Hardway Team and a whole bunch of our friends are going on a snowmobile week-end ride to Grand Marais!" Larry exclaimed, excitedly. "Do you want to go?"

"On a week-end?" I inquired, wistfully.

"Yes. We'll leave Saturday, early A.M., ride to Grand Marais with a few pit stops here and there, stay overnight and ride back Sunday morning. We start from Two Harbors, leave our vehicles there."

"But I'd have to get a replacement for Saturday Night at the Gopher." I whined with disappointment. "I can't afford to take time off from work! It would be impossible to find a fill-in this late, anyway."

"The gang has been talking about this. They all want you to come with us this time. They do this week-end every year. Well you know that. I went last year. Anyway, we put our heads together and we've come up with an idea. A way you can join us."

"How's that?" I asked, apprehensively.

"Howard Hanson said he'd drive your machine to Grand Marais and after you get through with your gig at the Gopher, you could drive your car to Grand Marais. Then Sunday, you could ride your own sled back with all of us and Howie would drive your Chevy back to Two Harbors."

"Gee, you know that sounds like a Blast! That should be a barrel of fun!" I spiritedly agreed.

Sports never pushed my buttons, especially competitive sports. But I loved snowmobiling, when I could engineer my own sled, when I was in complete, shrewd control of speed, the piloting of curves and hills. It was, then, sheer delight and adventure!! Not the dismal, competitive sport of Stock Car Races.

I had never become intrigued, even as a spectator, in the Stock Car Racing circuit. I actually abhorred it; detested the breathing and eating of dirty dust and gravel. The horrid thundering of myriad engines throbbing against my ear drums, did absolutely nothing for my artistic appetite!

But snowmobiling with an affable group of friends was an entirely different ballgame. The feel of control, with the sled beneath my buttocks, as I snugly straddled the seat and body of the sled with my thighs was overwhelming. Flowing with the sway of the machine, around curves and up and down the hills, vibrations elated me to the sensuous momentum and abandonment of an awesome, gratifying sex experience. **WOW! ooooh ooooh awwwwhhh!** Yes, I loved snowmobiling! Wow! **Did I love snowmobiling!!**

"Yes I think I could do that. No, in fact, I **know** I could do that!" I responded, eagerly. . 'I wouldn't get much sleep, but what's one day without sleep? How hard can that be?" I went on reasoning with self assertive logic.

"Sure, you can do it!!" Larry diplomatically reassured me, wheedling an affirmative decision from me.

"But how would I ever find you guys at three in the morning?" I asked. "Everyone will be sleeping. The town will be pitch black. Kinda dark and spooky and overwhelming."

"I would give you the name of the motel and the number of my room as soon as I found out where we'd be crashing. I'd call you at the Gopher during your gig to give you directions."

"Sounds like a plan!" I squealed with accelerated emotions. "Sure I'll go. I'll have my warm snowmobile rags all packed ahead of time and in my Chevy, so when I storm Grand Marais, I'll be all set!"

"Okay! That's the plan then." he grinned and I felt he really did want my company. We seldom did anything together. It was a rare treat to spend any quality time together in each others company.

As the evening came to a close at the Gopher Lounge, I diffidently consulted my chunky, dear friend, Delores as she collected soiled glasses, wiping tables, behind departing customers to a soon almost vacated lounge.

"Dee, I need a very, very, special favor from you?"

She stopped cleaning, wiping, a filled tray in her grasp and inquired, "And what might that be, Dottie?"

We moseyed, casually to the service station where she chucked her loaded tray.

"Delores, how about giving me two or three of your special diet pills? I have to ride a snow machine 75 miles tomorrow on three or four hours sleep! I'll really need some solid, reliable help! I know that for sure!"

Delores always carried on her person a sufficient supply of diet pills. She had a very liberal, compromising M.D. who very agreeably offered her whatever she requested in medication.

"Sure, no problem. she replied with congeniality as she searched the contents of her purse.

"You're an angel, a sweetheart!" I exclaimed, squeezing her corpulent form with a gigantic bear hug! "See you next week." and off, down Highway 61 to Grand Marais I flew, hugging the highway shooting ahead of me; an arrow of clear, clean asphalt. Luckily no perilous ice coats were apparent to hinder my pursuit.

Grand Marais is a small, winter sport community, nestled in the far north of Minnesota with a diminutive population of eleven hundred, so it wasn't difficult to locate Larry's whereabouts in probably the only motel in the vicinity. Hurriedly tearing off my clothes, I plopped my head on the pillow in anticipation of some real fast ZZZZ's. It was four A.M.

I had just closed my sand filled eyes when, what seemed like mere seconds later, I was harshly awakened to a loud, boisterous pounding on the motel door and a husky, raucous voice thundering, "It's six A.M. and breakfast is being served at the Town Hall for all you snowmobilers! Pancakes, eggs, sausages and ham, **THE WORKS!!!** Time to rise and shine!" Finalizing the announcement was another burst of repeated audacious hammering on the door!

"Yeah! Okay, Okay." Larry finally replied, sleepily. "Come on Dottie. Time to get movin'. Breakfast and then down the trail we'll blast off!!" he eagerly added, in seconds, ambiguously fluctuating from a sleepy, languid **LOW GEAR** to a Pompous **FAST LANE!** But that was Larry.

"My guess is you guys all hit the sack at 10:00 P.M." I blurted, a mite annoyed.

"Oh No!" he quiped, derisively. "Not 'til 11:00."

"Yeah, yeah. I've had a measly two hours of shut eye!" I grudgingly exclaimed. "Why do we have to ride so early?"

"Come on now, Dottie. No whining, Dottie." he chuckled, enjoying my annoyance. "It's a beautiful day for a ride on a sled!" He began vigorously pulling on his garments for riding, from shorts to heavy pants to sweat shirt, concluding with a snowmobile suit zipped halfway up to the waist, with the remaining jacket and arms dangling in back, empty. All snowmobilers dressed this way when entering a building to stay cool.

"Well, It's breakfast time for us!" he announced. "I'm starved! hungry as a bear. Could sure go for some pancakes!"

I slowly, stoically dressed, yawning and rubbing my sand-filled, listless eyes that did not want to focus on anything but the alluring boudoir and some inviting slumber. I attempted, tenaciously to convince my tired body that, **This Was Fun!!**

Before departing our motel room, I popped two of Delores' little crutches down with half a glass of water and joined the others for breakfast.

What a Ride! What control! What Energy!! I found myself whizzing past experienced, skilled riders. I impetuously left the trail to play, around and around in a deeply drifted meadow. If I'd have stopped before re-entering the groomed trail, I would have buried **ME AND MY SLED!** Probably buried and embedded in the drifts for hours. My stamina just wouldn't quit! Everyone marveled at my maneuvers, my energy, strength and control. Giggling, I'd whiz and zing past people. I'd then stop and wait for them, being absorbed in convulsive laughter as they'd catch up! I had intently and impressively taken over Larry's role of exhibitionist!

DOTTIE LOU ON HER SKI DOO

"Delores, Delores, You're an angel in disguise!!" I mused, smiling to myself. "You can fill an order for me for 200 plus of these little **"NIFTY DUGANS",** anytime! Boy could these become habit!"

It was a fabulous 75 mile ride! I loved every impassioned mile of it. However, the following morning, I couldn't fathom why my body was as stiff as Pinnockio's nose. I couldn't comprehend why every muscle of my lower body; calves, thighs, buttocks surged with excruciating pain, with every movement. My shoulders ached, as well, as did the palms of my hands, reflecting they were the strained muscles from the continuous hearty grasp of the handlebars, controlling speed and braking. I found I couldn't handle the stairs to my basement. I discovered I was subject to agonizing pain merely in the lowering of my buttocks to the toilet seat! I could do so only with the support from my aching arms, by holding the sides of the commode and slowly, gently lowering my fanny to the seat.

By the time Wednesday rolled around, I was able to convince my healing body to abandon the torrential pain enough to manage the steps of the Gopher Lounge stairways.

But I had to admit, the incredible 75 mile Sunday Snowmobiling Experience was well worth the pain!

♪♪♪

CHAPTER SEVEN

The end of January found the Tumbleweeds saying farewell to their leisure Tuesday Nights. Connie Lukovsky, owner of the Venture Supper Club on Highway 53, in the Pike Lake outskirts of Duluth, insisted we fill those evenings entertaining his clientele, in the downstairs lounge of his establishment. We were in constant demand in the Twin Ports area to pick and grin" and it was exhilarating! It felt wonderful!

The economy of the country was prospering. Perhaps the Vietnam War, in full swing, was somewhat responsible for the boom in economy.

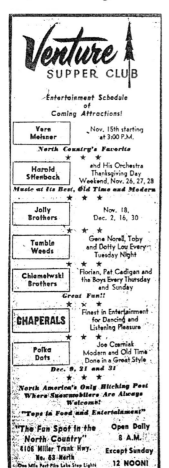

South Vietnam and U.S. troops had just invaded Laos, in an attempt to sever the Ho Chi Mnhs Trail. The war had been met with severe opposition; protest from many angry Anericans!

In March of the previous year (1970), four students had met their demise. Our National Guard had been responsible for their deaths at the Kent State University of Ohio, where the students had been involved in protest activities. It sparked hundreds of similar such activities across college campuses all over the U.S. Some were encountered with violence as in Ohio and New Mexico. In May of that year 100 colleges closed because of angry student riots, protesting the invasion of Cambodia and our involvement in what was considered and analyzed by most, as a pointless war with pointless loss of our young boys!

It was not a Patriotic, supportive, acceptable war to the masses, but we Tumbleweeds, enthusiastically zealous, and happily involved in our own little world of music and laughter and party, didn't really concern ourselves with the chatter or actions of the Vietnam War!

Connie Lukovsky always invited and welcomed the band to stay and visit with him, after closing, with pro bona cocktails to savor.

"You Tumbleweeds really are a HOT ITEM right now!" Connie shot the exagerated compliment our way. "You fill the Lounge on an off Tuesday Night like it was Saturday!"

We gracefully smiled, accepting his amiable comments with sincere, cogenial gratitude, tickled that he was pleased.

"You know, I been thinking," he continued. "What do you think would really give this place some sophisticated Pizazz!? Plus, the frosting on the cake would include some incredible advertising for my Supper Club, as well?" Without waiting for our reply, he went on. "I've been rollin' this idea around in my brain for days. The possibility of a TV show, originating right here, from the Venture Lounge, taped here on a feasible afternoon, but to be viewed on Prime time, like maybe Saturday or Sunday!"

It was difficult to suppress my profound enthusiasm of the possibility of TV, but I remained silent and composed and continued listening intently, as Connie and Korn thrashed their various ideas around.

"My brother, Wayne, works on WDSM, Channel six." Korn remarked. "He's employed by WDSM as their primary photographer and camera man. I could get some info on this idea through him, maybe. He did stuff for us on Dottie's first album. All the art work. Right, Dottie? And we did it all right there at the Channel six studio."

"Sure, Wayne did an incredible job!" I added.

"It was all photofinished at Channel six. We used all their equipement, their props." Korn responded.

"Does Wayne have any inside pull or authority?" Connie quiped, with a touch of sarcasm.

"Well, no. But I could get some insight and it wouldn't be awkward, getting some introductions through him to the Big Shots, the people who are in charge, that he knows and works for." Korn depicted.

"Well Gene, why don't we look into it? Give it a shot!" Connie suggested. "See what kinda money we're talkin' about. I'd sponsor the entire project. I'd want complete, controlled saturation of the advertising package. I don't want a bunch of other little peon sponsors abducting some of the prime time. It would be totally, carried by the Venture Supper Club."

"Do you want me to check it out, Connie? Or would you rather go it on your own? I'm not exactly green when it comes to selling entertainment!" Korn emitted, diminutively irritated with Connie's obvious lack of confidence in his ability. "I've worked for Jimmy Key's Talent Agency in Nashville, booking the Big Names, not to mention the Country Western Arena Shows right here in town!!"

"I know! I know!" Connie blurted, retreating, penitently. "Well then let's do it. We'll present our ideas to them this week. Together. How about Monday afternoon?"

"Sure." Korn agreed.

"I've got the money, If they've got the time!" Connie spurted a line from an old Hank Williams retrospective repertoire, followed by a stream of arrogant, confident chuckles.

So 18 weeks of "Arrowhead Country", a half-hour Country Western Music Show, a Hee-Haw of the North, was born.

The WDSM management wouldn't assess the expense or drudgery of the production being devised at the Venture. However they accepted the format of a Night Club atmosphere. They provided their own props, tables, decor, etc. eloquently displaying the appearance and impression that we were indeed, performing at the Venture Supper Club.

Many of our local, loyal fans attended the Wednesday afternoon tapings. They were ecstatic and flying on cloud nine, to be included, sitting at pretend night club tables, sipping fictitious cocktails. It enabled them to view themselves, live and prestigious on the Saturday Night TV line up.

It was parallel to the public dancing viewed on the KDAL, Channel three Chmielewski Fun Time shows, where people swarmed to attend merely to obtain a glimpse of themselves dancing on TV.

As producer and Director, Korn was able to capture the essence of Country Music equal (Ahem! We thought) to any National TV syndicate. He barricaded his time and talent into the success of the show, and also doubled as emcee of the weekly production.

Wayne, Korn's brother, donated his expertise on the camera.

Korn selected many name talents to grace our stage as guests, A different unique artist each week, creating a format of highly exquisite eminence to please even the most critical of audiences. We were very proud! Headliners included names like Dave Dudley of "Six Days On The Road" fame; Marvin Rainwater, "Gonna Find Me a Bluebird"; Bobby Bare, etc, etc. Many weeks also, guests of local talent caliber were invited to perform with the Tumbleweeds on Arrowhead Country, as well.

And of course, Dottie Lou sung various selections from her record releases each week. This of course, resulted in prodigious promotion, abundantly increasing record sales and air play. The program introduced us to television audiences that normaly had never seen or heard us before. Local talents included such names as; yodeling Freddie Osberg,

Ronnie Light, BeeBee and Rick Allen, Dick Porter, Lorrie Clemmens, Big Bad John Volt, Frankie Dell, Jimmy Luhm, etc. etc.

The TV time slot ran for 18 weeks.

* * * * * * *

Midst the work, gigs and TV, I surprisingly, miraculously coerced a consecutive Sunday and Monday, liberty free! I tearfully suggested we take a trip to Aitkin, to Barb's and Gerry's. "Larry, I miss my daughter!" I fretfully emitted.

"Okay! Okay!" he agreed. "I'll loan a motor home from Elliot and we'll take our snowmobiles and really make it a two-day Holiday!"

"We don't really need to go through all that fuss!" I assessed.

"Why not? I love to ride! You love to ride! The kids love to ride! So why not?"

"Gerry and Barb aren't into snowmobiling." I explained.

"But it's Charmaine we're going for! Right! She likes to ride." he argued.

"Well, okay then. I guess we can fit visiting and riding in together. You just think you'll be bored, just **visiting** with my relatives! Huh?"

He grinned at me, ignoring the remark. "I'll give Bill Elliot a call right away!"

So Rogie cheerfully played Hookey from his school activities on Monday. Dale stayed behind, as he was working after school, a couple hours each afternoon at Bridgeman's Store in the Heights. He'd debark the school bus on Bridgeman's corner and walk home after his Bus Boy chores were completed.

We arrived in Aitkin Sunday forenoon in Bill Elliot's 69 Pathfinder Motor home, toting two Ski Doo's on a trailor behind it.

DAUGHTER, CHARMAINE ON SKI DOO

Larry located trails and roadsides to scuttle over, on Sunday afternoon with our sleds. We talked, we gorged our appetites, we sipped cocktails and lo and behold, evening found us singing songs together at the piano, as Barb tinkeled the ivory, to everyone's delight, We crominized! (A Toby Term) Then to my amazement and shock, Larry scrambled to the piano bench and Butt against butt, he shoved Barb aside and proceeded playing the piano!! It wasn't, after all, one of his pathological lies, as I had assumed from his previous boisterous vaunting! He could, indeed, actually play the piano, as he had boasted!!

ROGIE & cousin
scott knapp

* * * * * * *

Larry, Big M, Dale and Knutson and Dave Willis left early on a Saturday morning to race snowmobiles in Hibbing. I sent my movie camera along with them and fleetingly suggested that someone, anyone, shoot some video pictures, especially of Dale, if he should race.

In the midst of my second set at the Gopher Lounge, Larry and some of his friends clambered down the stairway. I was anxious to hear the reports on the outcome of their Hibbing escapade. On intermission I joined them at the bar to chat and catch the results of their racing achievements.

"Did you get some good action pictures?" I queried with ebullience.

"I don't know. I put Marilyn in charge of the camera." Larry replied ruefully. "Only time will tell! After we get them developed."

"I'm not guaranteeing anything!!" Marilyn chortled. "I never ran that kind of camera, ever before. I think it was a disaster!"

"Did Dale race?"

"Oh sure." Big "M" quiped. "Lot's 'a racin', lot's 'a breakin' lot's 'a losin'. Not much to brag about!"

"Well, we had a good time, anyway, didn't we?" Larry sniggered, jovially.

"We always do!" Marilyn ejaculated with gusto.

I had barely returned to the stage and the music when Larry came barreling down the stairs, two steps at a time, in an apparent uproar! Engrossed in music, I hadn't observed when he had departed.

As he shuffled his way, brusquely, through the crowded dancing conglomeration to the bar, he hardly even glanced in the direction of the bandstand and seemed to be preoccupied and in a tense angry state of mind. He was still socializing in the lounge as I concluded the music set. I scurried to his booth, where he was perched, communicating with his friends, flailing fervent gestures and expounding in a raised voice.

"What's up Larry?" I queried, with indulgent curiosity. "You seem kinda **Perturbed!**"

"**Perturbed?!** You call it **Perturbed?!** No, it's more like, **I'm really, really PISSED!!** Some Son-of-a-Bitch stole my two snowmobiles, tied up on my trailer, from right behind the Gopher. Right beside the back door!!"

"No Way!"

"Oh yeah. They must 'ov just quick hooked up to my trailer and took off! A very professional heist! A Mafia type of theft!"

"Was'nt it hooked to your truck?"

"I unhooked it and pushed the trailer way back against the Gopher wall by the back door. Kinda cornered in the dark area, out of sight, cuz we wanted to bar hop with my truck."

"Have you searched for it?" I asked.

"We drove all over town. All over West Duluth. No sign of the sleds anywhere!"

"Did you call the cops?"

"Sure. What good will that do?!" he scoffed, infuriated, as he chewed nervously on a cocktail straw. "May as well kiss those machines **GOODBYE!**"

After we left the bar for the evening, Larry drove around all of West Duluth and West End, searching for hours, investigating every dark alley, nook and garage access in the hope of finding his snow machines stashed somewhere. However, it was all in vain, with no results of success. Larry never did locate his sleds or the party responsible for the theft. It did certainly appear to be a very professional burglary.

＊ ＊ ＊ ＊ ＊ ＊ ＊

It was apparent Charmaine missed us just as much as we missed her. She made the decision to return home to us in time for Easter. To celebrate her official return, Larry treated us all to Easter Dinner at Mr. Steak in the Heights, including Dales girlfriend, Leslie.

Being all "♪Together Again" Our ♫ tears did stop fallin'. I was intensely ecstatic to have my daughter home. Collette also spent the week of Easter with us, but spent Easter Sunday with her Grandma, June Peterson in Poplar, Wisconsin.

Things seemed quite back to normal again—School-Work-Party-time! Yes, all a part of Marriage, Melody and Mischief!

♪♪♪

CHAPTER EIGHT

"I,m sorry Sir. We don't have Cutty Sark downstairs." I heard Dick Grantly, the bartender politely attempting to explain. "Only in the restaurant, upstairs. How about Black and White or Johnny Walker?"

"I always drink Cutty Sark. Cutty Sark and Soda. Nothin' else!" I heard the well dressed stranger mutter as he chewed on the end of a cigar.

"I see him around here, occasionally." I mused, "A loner, I think. Always by himself. Definitely not one of the locals. Always in a suit and tie. The finesse of his choice of attire, however, doesn't fit the disposition or insolence of the guy. He certainly is a cocky S.O.B." I thought as I overheard the conversation.

He was leaning, impassively, on the waitress station, unaware that I stood directly behind him, waiting to order a cocktail.

"Delores?" Dick motioned to the waitress. "Do you s'pose you could go upstairs and bring me a bottle of Cutty Sark from the stock up there?"

"Sure, it's not very busy down here, yet." she replied in her usual good-natured demeanor. "For you, Dick? Anything!!" she purred, flirtatiously.

I didn't remember **When** I'd first noticed his presence in the Club, but I did know **Why** I remembered him. It was because he'd plop himself, audaciously in the first booth, to my right, adjacent to the stage and incessantly puff cigars. Sometimes a pipe. The smoke would rise and drift to the stage transversely across my nostrils and my throat and I'd be tenaciously annoyed inside, but unable to react and object verbally.

"What a conceited Ass" I thought. "Good looking? Yes, but very, very spoiled! It was evident he was used to getting his way!"

"You're the singer!?" he said to me, just aware at the moment of my presence behind him. I couldn't assess if he was asking a question or merely making a flat statement. "You have a fine voice. Really nice." he added.

And I thought, "Well not a very new line." as I gazed into penetrating brown eyes. A simpered smile escaped my lips. "Same old corny garbage." I soliloquized.

"What's your first name?" I asked, not being able to think of anything brilliant to add to the conversation and to conceal my embarrassment over the compliment. I always found it uncomfortable and difficult to gracefully accept praise.

Following the unanswered question, I went on, "I never bother with last names anyway, I rarely remember the first ones."

"I've been watching you sing for weeks." he babbled, ignoring my question. "I love country music and you sure can warble a country ballad."

"Oh no, not another gushing old line blather." I mused.

"Really! Oh thank you so much." I heard my voice muttering appreciative nonsense, noting, inwardly, "I have to divert the subject and soon! All this artificial admiration will soon make my stomach churn!"

"You know, you have very nice eyes." I crooned, changing the subject from me to him. "They're quite coy and impish and a very nice chocolate brown." I gushed soft coquettish sighs as I slowly ran my quivering tongue across my lips, moistening them, back and forth. "Yes! Yes!" I sighed. "Very, very Brown," then with austere, "and very, very **Full of Shit!!**"

He laughed heartily. "You're somethin' else!" he said. "Do you mind if I sit in the booth next to you?"

"Yes I mind!" I scowled. I noted a surprised look spread across his face. Obviously rattled, he continued to aggressively pounce on the end of his cigar. His turn to be embarrassed and lost for words. I gloated.

"The smoke from that first booth just kills me." I tried to tactfully explain. "The fan from the entrance to the upstairs bar," I motioned to it's position at the foot of the stairway, "pulls or sucks the smoke directly into my mouth from that first booth's direction. And especially the fumes of a cigar or a pipe is the worst. Have you ever tried to sing with smoke pouring into your lungs? It's quite a handicap, you know. I don't smoke and I guess that makes it even harder to handle."

"Well, I'm really sorry about that." he sputtered, almost timidly. "I didn't know it was so crucial. You certainly know how to burst a guy's bubble!" Abased, he retreated to a table across the room from the bandstand.

His jet black hair, with a definite, orderly part, not a strand misplaced, was waved neatly to the right. His eyes, brown as chocolate fudge, seemed to suggest intrigue and savoir-fare, masquerading as timid reticence. A few tiny crow lines beginning to creep from the corners of his eyes made it difficult to estimate his age. Scrutinizing his smart, precise attire and polished demeanor, suggested he portrayed a striking, debonair difference to this dismal, dark and drab Basement Lounge. And he seemed well aware of his attributes, even as out of place as he appeared. Likely pursued by any number of women. Yes, a Ladies Man, I assumed. Plausibly, more than likely, a well practiced, experienced **Womanizer!**

Definitely not my type, even if I were single. I chuckled inwardly. Dark complexion, like Greek or Italian, very dark hair and eyes. Not the kind of features that exploded any remarkable chemistry in my Heart, or my Groins, for that matter!!

"Tumbleweeds" came over the mike and my inner trance came to a halt as Korn's summons indicated it was that time again. Time to begin our usual evening gig of Melody and Chatter and Laughter. Just another "Night Life" at the Gopher Lounge in selected career choices.

Being a limited, small scale musician in a local night club wasn't all the glory fans believed to be. The smoke filled, congested room only added to the discomfort and unrevealed outrage over the many cigarette burns in my stage clothing. Chain smoking fans loved to chatter with me while flinging a clutched lighted cigarette, to profoundly express themselves. Sometimes encircleing an arm around my shoulders, toting alit cigarette dropping coals in their pursuit to praise and declare their admiration. It would be in bad taste to object. It was just the occupational hazard of being in the limelight. Being in the dense smoke, four consecutive nights often resulted in emitting bloody phlem from the depths of my vocal chords from the incessant nicotine irritations. The hot, unconditioned air seemed to suffocate at times, as the large fan at the foot of the stairway entrance, merely pushed the smoke and dead air from one end of the room to the other.

The basement Lounge harbored low ceilings with no windows, no air cleaners to absorb the smoke, three stairways being the only release to the freedom of outdoors and the restaurant and Bar above.

Yes indeed, the establishment didn't triumph in a "Touch o' Class". It had been uniquely and veritably named The Gopher. The construction and decor certainly did justice to it's name. A dark, dingy, stifling Gopher Hole!

First set, first hour was always on the slow side, so the brown eyed stranger managed to send up a couple requests to me, scribbled on a Lounge cocktail napkin. "Funny Face" and Barbara Fairchild's "Teddy Bear" seemed to tickle his fancy. When I tried to acknowledge him, I realized he actually hadn't ever relinquished his name.

"We'll be right back, so don't go away." I heard Korn glibly announce over amplification and I realized the first hour had rather swiftly, as usual become 'One More Memory'.

As I approached the waitress station, a heavy rumble on the stairway overhead indicated another group was about to join the bash downstairs. However, I was totally surprised, discovering it was Larry and a wolloping portion of his Pit Crew from the Superior Friday Night Stock Car races. He motioned for me to join him and his friends and associates. They were loitering and chattering in the bar area off from the dancing lounge.

"What in the world are you doing here?!" I ejaculated, "It's only 10 o'clock!"

"What? Not glad to see me?" he teased.

"Of course, I'm **Not** glad to see you!" I cajoled, laughing.

"Have you been outside lately?" he buzzed. "It's raining buckets and buckets! Pouring Cats and Dogs and Nigger Babies! So, of course, we got rained out!"

"My Gosh! Well, you really filled up the place with your crew!" Some of them I knew casually. Some I just recognized faces, but some were strangers to me. The racing circuit were not music fans, generally, so they, except for a small handfull, weren't consistent, faithful patrons.

"Yeah!" Larry grinned. "Don't I always!! That's the vonGillern way!" Beaming, chest heaved out like the Mother Hen gloating over her brood of chicks. But that was Larry! "I did some talking!" Larry continued, "To get them all to come over here. Promised I'd buy the first round."

"Oh, You bribed them! Well, whatever works."

"Come over here. I want you to meet some of **MY Friends!**" He led me to the far side of the barroom. "Hey Guys, this is my wife Dottie Lou." He introduced me, prestigiously puffed, then continued. "She's the singer in the band." then turning to me said, "and Dottie, this is Pete and his wife April. Pete is a guy I've known way back when—well—since I was in the guards at the base. He's the one, at the air base, who fills my cans with that AV 100 octane, pure liguid gold for the **Thunder** of # 61 on the race track!"

Everyone giggled.

"And you know Kenny and Sylvia of course. and the Parkers, Eileen and Ray. And of course you know the Powder Puff Queen, Delores Johnson and her teacher, hubby Johnny who is my stiff competition! And this is Pat and Earl Winnin. They are involved in horses----."

"I know Pat and Earl." I interrupted. "We met some time ago. We **Tumbleweeds** played for a Horse Show Competition in Lake Nebagamon where they were riding in competition. Even their wee bitty son, a rider only Yay high!" I gestured, arm out and palm down in a three foot approximate measure, "Dashed around a bunch of barrels too, just as proficient as mommy and dad."

"We got kinda wet." Pat added. "Didn't we?"

"We sure did. We were drenched." I replied. "It rained a fine drizzle all day long. We had plastic, kinda thin plastic, hung over us on a truck bed and huge bubbles of collected rain water, about to burst, hung in between every little beam."

"Did they burst?" Earl Asked.

"No. We kept hand pushing them up to empty them." I said.

Larry continued, focusing on his usual sales ability in expressive description, "And this is---" he introduced Folks from his pit crew, people involved in synthetic oil, mechanics that assist him and staff from the Skiroule Shop—etc.

He rattled on a number of names I forgot almost as soon as they had left his lips, adding history of each in connection and regards to their part in the support of his racing agenda.

"Nice to meet you all." I emitted. Korn was at the mike, so I politely excused myself from the presence of Larry's little clutch and ambled toward the stage for our second set of the night.

"Wait!" Larry sputtered, as he shuffled along beside me. "We'll probably l eave before your next break, so if we're gone—well, anyway, you know—I'll see you at home."

"Okay, see you at home." I flipped, nonchalantly.

A cocktail awaited me at the bandstand when I stepped up, to my microphone. One for Korn and Toby, as well. .

"Where did this come from?" I asked, then added as an afterthought. "A round from Larry, I reckon."

"No" Korn whispered furtively, "It's from that guy across the room, there, at the table. The one in the suit and tie, puffin' a cigar."

"Oh. Must be because of his request I did for "Funny Face" and "Teddy Bear." Do you know his name, Korn?"

"Nope. Not a clue."

"Thank you, Sir." I said, with raised glass, I motioned toward him, acknowledging his gift.

"How about "Help Me Make It Through The Night?" he buzzed in a raised voice from across the room, above the hum drum noise of the festivities. "I need all the help I can get!" he chuckled, amused with his own buffoonery.

We concluded the finale song of the gig, "I'm Ragged, But I'm Right" in mine and Korn's Ray Price cloned voice. Holding in harmony the last note. It was our nightly challenge to see who could hold it the longest. The trick was to remember before hand to completely fill our diaphragms with air.

I snatched my purse and wrap and scrambled up the back stairs through the restaurant to collect my wages. The policy was to get reimbursed nightly. I assumed the owner thought it was good business sense to make sure we had money to spend each evening, as we were plausibly, some of his best customer!

I shuffled past Ralph, Dandrea's cleaning boy. He was a teenager who tidied up the restaurant after closing most nights, vacuuming, wiping furniture down, cleaning rest rooms etc. This night as I greeted Ralph with my usual "Hi", I observed a gal perched, with knees bent, her arms clenched around her knees in a fetal position, sitting sideways in a booth.

"Uh—oh!" I grinned at Ralph as I questionably, repeatedly pointed, a couple head nods, without looking, in the general direction of his guest.

"Hanky Panky, Ralph? Huh! Shame, Shame, Shame." I laughed.

"Oh no. Just my girlfriend waiting for me to finish my work here."

"Oh." I smiled raising my eyebrows in mischief and took a second scrutiny of the girlfriend. To my shocking discovery on second glance I realized it was Leslie Knutson, Dales heartthrob! Wow! "Oh the ♪Games People Play♪ now. Every Night and ♪ Every Day, Now" I hummed, softly. As I headed toward Dandrea's office I muttered to myself, "Should I tell Dale, or shouldn't I? Oh, the heart break! Maybe I should let him discover on his own, the truth. About Life?! About People?! About reality!!

As I approached the office door, I could see the light stream from beneath the door, telling me John was still busy in his office, head engrossed in management particulars, as usual.

"Come in." addressing the usual invitation.

"Just me, Dottie. Pickin' up my pay." I jovially replied.

John smiled politely, droned, "Dottie, your wages for tonight are gone. In fact, a portion of tomorrows as well."

"Gone? Whatta you mean, gone?"

"Larry ran a tab, downstairs on your wages."

"You're kidding, I hope!"

"No. He bought for all the people he brought with him from the races. He bought all their drinks the whole time they were here, I guess."

"Well, you guessed wrong!!" I **replied despondently**, "Apparently, **I BOUGHT** all their drinks while they were here!" I mumbled, disconcertedly. "Well then," I shrugged my shoulders in dismay, "See you tomorrow night, John." I could feel the hair tingling as it rose on the back of my neck and the heat rush to my face in pented up anger. Better leave before I say things I may be sorry for.

Instead of an exit, I scrambled back down the stairway, retreating to the lounge. Employees were still chattering and a handful of customers remained as well.

"Who ever gave permission to run a tab on my wages?!" I screamed, out of control with fury, attacking Dick and Cal, the two bartenders left behind the bar, sipping after hour drinks.

"Well Delores said---" Cal began.

"I don't care what anyone said," I barked. "No one puts their drinks on my tab! I **don't** even put **MY DRINKS** on a tab! **I don't ever run a tab!** If I don't have money, I don't drink!!"

"Well, He's your husband and I thought---" Dick began timidly defending Larry. I resolutely interrupted his feeble defense, assaulting any possible rebutal.

"There's absolutely no excuse for this!" I thundered. "It better never happen again!" I dejectedly scuttled to the stairway in retreat to my vehicle parked at the back entrance. Feeling resentful and used, I floored the Chevy and peeled out of the parking lot, babbling, irately to myself.

"What nerve! Two Night Wages! ZILTCH! Down the tube! He'd never gone quite this far before! But of course that was Larry!! How well

I knew that. Playing **BIG SHOT** as always! On my money, now! HA! I could have at least been given credit for my generosity. No status or esteem for Good "Ole Larry," however, if he'd told them it was on me. There was no halting that bombastic, pompous, power drive. He had to be on top, no matter the cost, no matter who got smothered in his dust! He was evidently obsessed with making an overblown impression on **his friends.**

He must impress people, always! Larry, the last of the Big Spenders, must be recognized and admired with awe!"

I glanced down at my speedometer and realized, in my frenzy, I was doing 55 in a 30 mile speed zone. Frustrated, with pedal to the metal, I vowed, the proverbial cliche was about to become reality! **The Shit Will, indeed, Hit The Fan** on Walnut Street tonight!!

* * * * * * *

Saturday night Larry, rather abased, returned from Ashland, Glum, Dejected, and disappointed. I was glad! I was Gloating! He had blown his engine at the races, running, testing the performance of Synthetic Motor Oil in his Stock 63½ Ford engine.

"Yes! Yes!" I chuckled inwardly. "He gets what he deserves." I reasoned, without guilt. "There is justice after all!" I thought. "He steals—his sleds are stolen. He uses people—they use him." I wasn't glorifying in the failure and disappointment **of synthetic oil testing,** but felt there was justice for Larry's Grey dishonest dealings and I had to Gloat some.

He'd be tenaciously dedicated to rebuilding his engine for tomorrows Sunday night Proctor Races. Yes it would ruffle his finances, Not Mine!

Indubitably, he'd be zealously, mechanically engaged in his garage all night and all the following day until race time. It was imminent he would religiously present a completely rebuilt engine by Sunday Night Racing Schedule. Larry's drive and resolute endurance was surpassed by no one!

He did, however, with all his efforts, and justifiably, earn the honor and the prestige of being the first one and the first automobile to dramatically and successfully ply a synthetic lubricant, in it's performance. Although the first trial, a disappointment, had been a fiasco, later innovative experiments eventually were met with undaunted success.

♪♪♪

CHAPTER NINE

I quickly tossed my paring knife and half-peeled potatoe on to the sink drainboard, abruptly drying my hands on the hanging hand towel and picked up the wall phone that was incessantly interrupting my preparations for supper. The kids would soon be bursting through the kitchen doorway in the usual hustle, bustle; bags and books tossing everywhere, in their arrival off the School Bus. Hungry, they'd be opening cupboards and slamming refrigerator doors in search of snacks.

"Hello."

"Dottie?"

"Yes, and who is this?"

"A concerned neighbor and friend."

"A neighbor. A friend. Who? Why?"

"Dottie, I know you're so very busy, You're probably not aware of what's going on with the neighborhood kids. Your kids, My kids and their friends." The female voice explained audaciously.

"Hmmmm-" I mused. "Is the person truly concerned or just nosey or intrusive?"

"You mean they're having party's?" I sputtered, trying to remain cool.

"Well, maybe that too. I don't know." she replied with tenacity. "But I'm really calling about Dale's girlfriend, Leslie Knutson. You probably don't even know she's the little slut of the Heights, pardon my terminology. She's trashing around with a number of the neighborhood boys!"

"I am aware she is far from a "Goody Two Shoes". I replied. "I saw her just last week, after hours with John Dandrea's cleaning boy at the Gopher, two or three A.M. He called her his girl friend. I thought she was suppose to be Dale's girlfriend. I s'pose Ralph thinks he's the only one too!" I tittered, suppressing an overpowering urge to giggle.

"She's been shootin' her mouth off on the school bus, sayin' She's tryin' to get PG. Then she's going to name Dale as the Father, cuz I guess she likes him the best!"

"Really!? Maybe it's just idle kids talk!" I said. "Maybe she's just tryin' to get attention."

"Could be, Dottie, but we all think a lot of you and we thought, anyway, you should know what she's been saying. You sure wouldn't want to be strapped with a Paternity Suit!"

"Who is this?" I asked again.

"A bunch of concerned neighbors suggested I call you. Just so you know what's goin' on. I don't want to mention names."

"I'm glad you think enough of me to let me know, anyway. Thanks. I appreciate your concern."

"Maybe it's none of our business, but I know if it was my son that was going with her, I'd sure wanna know what she's saying, planning or threatening. We think too much of you, Dottie to just let it go by."

"Thanks for calling me." I conceded, propitiously.

"Sure. Bye now."

I returned the phone to it's cradle and stood silently staring into space, pondering over the ambivalent phone call. I hadn't yet disclosed to Dale the betrayal of Leslie with Ralph at the Gopher. I had mixed emotions over revealing the incident. I usually let my children pick friends of their own choosing. Most of the time I remained unbiased in the creation of their own little bonding clique's. I didn't delight in making unnecessary waves over minor things. Dale was soon approaching seventeen and a precocious individual. He attended school diligently and worked part time after school at Bridgemans. Larry had also finagled a week-end stint for Dale as a Lot Boy at Arrow Chevrolet. He was a hard-working, responsible achiever, so I didn't admonish interfering in his social life. I didn't want to rain on his dutiful, trusty Parade. I guess I wasn't very proficient in the "Tough Love" department.

When Dale returned from Bridgemans it was nearly time for me to depart for the Gopher Gig.

"Did you just come from work or from Leslie's?" I tried to casually, bring up the subject to probe a little information, unsuspectingly, I hoped.

"From Bridgeman's."

"How are you and Leslie doing? Madly in love, I s'pose!" I laughed, benevolently.

"We're fine."

Dale was my quiet, reserved son. It was like pulling teeth to manipulate him into small-talk chatter. He almost always, never volunteered any information on his activities or his personal feelings.

DALE WITH LESLIE KNUTSON

"How did you meet Leslie? In school?" I asked, probing lightly in a docile tone.

"No. Not at school. She baby sits for Sandy McConnikey right close to Bridgeman's."

"Oh, does she come over to Bridgeman's then?"

"Sometimes, but mostly I met her when I'd walk past Sandy's house. It's on the way home. She yelled at me from the porch, so I stopped and talked to her."

"That's how you met?"

"I guess." he submissively mumbled.

"Where does she live?"

"She lives with Sandy."

"How old is this Sandy?"

"I don't know. Maybe 24 or 25."

"Do you go over there when Leslie baby sits?"

"Sometimes. Why all the questions, Mom?"

"Oh, just curious, I guess. Well, I'm off to work. There's left-overs, Dale, from supper on the stove and some in the 'frig, if you're still hungry. I suppose you filled up on ice cream at Bridgeman's." I decided against revealing anything about Ralph or the anonymous phone call until I could muster sufficient quality time to disguss it, Heart to Heart.

"Who's turn for dishes? There's a sink full. I want to see a clean sink when I get home." I switched the subject, turning the chatter to domestic parental discipline.

"It's Rogie's turn." Char volunteered.

"Well, get on it, Rogie." I buzzed. "Bye, Bye, Kids." and out the door I hurriedly departed.

The Heights in the 70's was not as we see Duluth Heights today. Tons and tons of concrete and blacktop has disguised and concealed what was once beautiful. House, now, touching house. So inhabited that yards are diminutive, surrendering cherished privacy. One must be afraid to spit in the wind, lest it whisk the unsuspecting cheek of your neighbor. Solid commercial enterprise prevails where once hills rolled and rocks mounding against the sky. Rocks and hills, which provided winter slides for energetic, fanciful frolic of happy children. It's called **'PROGRESS'!!**

Retrospectively, in the 70's, the area was embraced with wild life in forest and paths into the semi-wilderness, intriguing to the young. Peaceful and Private for the old. Kids would slide for hours down the hills and rock formations on large sections of cardboard and the more financially blessed kids slid on commercial, capacious plastic saucers, they shared with friends. Summer found children with their many pets, allowed in a country environment. Dale had chickens, some with rabbits, cats and dogs, etc. because the surroundings complimented animals. The roads were all gravel, bordered everywhere with majestic trees.

And many were the little paths that originated, interlacing in the woods from street to street and home to home. It established a minuscule pioneer highway of travel for the young to visit and hang out with their playmates and friends. Life was simplified. Recreation as well.

With school cessation for the term and kids with excess idle time on their hands it urged their creative, yet nevertheless, mischievous minds to collaborate and invent numerous adventures. Some of the projects were constructive and educational. Some were impish and naughty.

Girls giggled and prattled of clothes and make up and BOYS! Boys confiscated and drank beer. They rambled verbally of party experiences, cars and construction. Oh yes, of GIRLS! They're impatient incentives reeked with enthusiasm to build secluded, obscure, hidden party sights without adult interference. These improvised little structures cropped up in the forests with paths leading to their whereabouts, behind many of our homes. And I, suspect much innocence was surrendered in those party Shacks!!

Some parents were fully aware of our boys expertise skill in carpentry, real estate renovation and suburban architecture! Some were aware of the teenage party Bashes going on. But many parents, of which I was one, didn't have a clue! Of course, naive, gullible me was not aware of much.

Dale, as a teenager, had spoken, casually, in small talk with me about an A frame the boys were building behind DeGrio's for the kids to hang out, play cards, swap stories etc. Just boys with something to do. Slumber Party's he called them. And I was quite pleased that they were spending their summer doing something constructive. It never occurred to me to investigate the authenticity of the project.

So I was, of course, rather stunned and dumbfounded, when Dale, at 40+ revealed to me some of the antics of teenagers at play, while I, in oblivion worked. I interviewed Dale to gather material, insight and research for my books. But of course now, what would have then resulted in chaos and punishment, only brought smiles and laughter, unabashed. It certainly became an enlightening and entertaining interview!

Going back in time, as Dale testifys to these activities he affirms, earlier the boys had a shack behind Dave Willis's house, built by Dave's older brothers. They called their shack "Erma". The older boys brought girls there and the younger kids, of course, were adding constructive (ahem) material to their education. Dale quotes, "The shack ceiling was so low you had to stoop inside, even as a kid." He and Dave giggled together, discreetly, renaming it the "Dog House". As they watched with young enthusiasm they concluded, unanimously, the two of them, that they undoubtedly, could build a much better shack. So they emerged on their own in the creative construction of *their* shack at the top of DeGrio Hill!

Dale, facetiously confessed his teenage, borderline, grey involvements in the development of these architectural projects. Minnesota Power and Light were absorbed in construction of some new power lines in the vicinity, so Dale and Dave snitched a roll of their cable, stored beside the road.

They connected the cable to the electric power in DeGrio's garage and ran it all the way up the hill to their shack, thus electric lights to party by. Also giving them a party atmosphere, with donated lighted beer signs and miscellaneous decor from the kids homes.

However, after just beginning to enjoy the completion of their efforts, someone anonymously tipped the B.P.M.'s, a notorious motorcycle gang, of the location of the party shack. They blatantly thundered up the hill with beer and older guys and gals to mold an obtrusive adult party, raiding and intimidating the kids with bullying control. Being bombarded with motorcycles and harassment infuriated the kids. The next day they turned off the power, unplugged their M.P.&L. cable, collected their beer signs, other decor and belongings, rolled up the cable, abandoned their new Party Shack and moved on.

Going ahead with Dale's interview, he continued: "So we contemplated a new location for a party shack, closer to Walnut Street. Between our house and Lindbergs there was already in existence, a path from our house to DeGrios.

My buddy's and I used to admire the "A" frame construction of the Mini Golf Course on Maple Grove Road. Then one day it was moved about three blocks further down the road with a FOR SALE sign posted on it. Of course we had no money to buy it, so we went there and studied how it was put together, took some notes and put our teenage brains together to come up with a less than perfect or professional blue print of our plans.

All the neighborhood kids were excited at the prospect of building a new party shack, so they all pooled their finances together to help. We purchased lumber from a lumber company that offered cheaper lumber. **They sold** seconds. Ritchie Razidilo came up with a hunk of cash. Everyone donated whatever they could, as it became a neighborhood project and the kids all wanted to be a part of it." Some lumber came from Mattila's torn down barn."

Dale chuckled, displaying a simpered grin, "You know, Mom, you're the one responsible for all this building hanky-panky anyway."

"No way!" I smirked. "How do you figure that?"

"Well it all started when you made me build that dog house, you know. You said if I wanted to have a dog, I'd have to build a dog house. No dog house! No dog!"

"I did?"

"Yes. I was only eleven and you showed me how to do it and I've been in the building craze ever since."

We both guffawed heartily.

"I guess I did fester some "Tough Love" at times, after all." I added.

Dale continued. "What we couldn't afford to buy we stole. If you take only a few boards from many lumber piles, they won't notice the shortage as if you took a bunch from one place!"

"One night, Dave Willis and I *took*, well, we *borrowed* Larry's Stock Car truck hauler & hot wired it, to go stealing lumber. As we were parked beside a business lumber pile, the cops came. Someone must have called t hem. We scuttled, lickety-split into the cover of the woods. Our scheme for stealing and hauling lumber for our shack backfired! The police confiscated the truck, as we peeked between the trees, about to shit our pants! Larry was called. It was a race night. He had to retrieve his truck, where it was impounded in order to haul his stock car to the races."

Talk about naive. All this information I acquired at the ripe old age of 71. I guess we never really change! Still naive and gullible! Old dogs don't learn new tricks. I assumed my kids were absolutely honest. Not angels, partying some, but nothing more serious than a little beer drinking, I surmised.

I was always intimidated by old **Grumpy, Nosey, Antagonistic, Malicious, Mean-Spirited, HORRID** Harry Benson, Our next door neighbor.

"Remember when Benson Called The Welfare on me, or the cops, telling them I left my children alone and without food? He sure caused us a lot of grief." I mumbled. "Didn't he?" I was trying to keep the interview flowing, in Dale's recollection of their teen-age Hanky Panky.

"Oh yes. He sure did." Dale emitted, "There was this one time. Oh it was before the building of shacks and shack parties. We had parties at our house and sometimes at Lunds. As soon as you left for work at the Gopher on Friday Nights, the party would start. Everyone knew when you left and when the coast would be clear. Kids would pour in from all over the neighborhood. Hoban's, Hanson's, Mesadahl's, Mattila's, Willis, Thompson's, Pheister's, Swizlak, Razidilo's, Halverson's, Bennets, Lund's, and of yes, of course, last but not least, the Loukes's!

Sandy, Leslie's employer, was our beer supplier. Trading for baby-sitting. She was 24 or 25 so she could get served.

Harry Benson, the grumpy old coot, this one night called the cops. The kids were bewildered when the police arrived and raided the place.

Lights were flashing, kids were flying in every direction to hide. Into the surrounding woods, in ditches, in the bedrooms, in the basement. Two kids battled for occupancy of the empty freezer in the basement. Annie Bennett and many others sprinted up the stairs to the unfinished attic, jumping across unfinished floors, pivoting unsteadily on exposed studs in between poured insulation. It was chaos on Walnut Street!!"

"I scurried to my bedroom to hide." Dale said. "Several other neighbor kids followed me. I'll be dammed! I screeched as I looked up and saw a pair of legs dangling from the ceiling between studs. they had broken through the ceiling tiles of my room."

"Do you recognize the legs?" Richie laughed, then spurted. "Hey, pull them legs up. The cops are coming!!"

"I think it's Annie's!" I said. Then Bruce Hanson dived for cover under my bed.

"They'll hold me responsible!" Bruce shrieked. "And probably throw me in the slammer if they find me, 'cuz I'm the only one here of legal age!"

"My mattress was old and thin and dilapidated, without much shape or form so when Bruce, being a big kid, squeezed beneath the small space, his big belly pushed the center up, making a big hilly bulge, obviously noticeable in the center of the thin mattress. So Dave ruffled the covers up to camouflage the hump."

Then Dale continued to explain how Holly and Jeff had scuttled down the stairs to the basement and clambered into my huge empty abandoned freezer, leaving just a little crack of the lid to watch the commotion. Boy, how dangerous was that! Those two pair of eyeballs kept diligent watch, back and forth, taking in all the chaos and clamor as police officers investigated the basement and its teen-age occupant activity. Kids were playing pool, Dale explained, in the recreation area of the basement which had diverted the cops awareness of the miniscule crack of the freezer lid.

As the cops left, Bruce crawled out from his snug residence under the bed, sighed relief and casually reached for another beer and thundered, "Hot Damn, I'm thirsty'!"

Holly and Jeff lumbered up the basement stairs, giggling and gloating in the spin-off of their sly, devious, secret hiding place that had duped and outsmarted the maneuvers of the cops!

Dale went on, "With the departure of the cops and the return of all the party kids, I went to work and Dave helped me repair the damage in my room ceiling. We patched it with masking tape and covered the tape with paint to hide the evidence."

"Hey, this must have escalated your interest in carpentry as we know of it today!" I laughed. "It turned out to be your calling."

"Didn't you ever notice any evidence that we were having parties, Mom?"

"No. I never really suspected anything like that."

"Char and I and our friends had organized a clean up crew." Dale percolated a little memory chuckle. "We had a boys detail to confiscate beer cans and dispose of garbage. And a girls crew to clean the house, mop the floor and wipe any messes we might have made. We must have done an excellent job of leaving no evidence."

"Sneaky, sneaky Kids! Not my kids!" I glibly snickered. adding, "And Mom just returned after her gigs to disciplined kids, well behaved, studious, hard working, a clean house and a secure feeling that all was well and in order on Walnut Street! Huh!?"

It was strange that the police had never notified me of this disturbance. My assumption was, they must have tired of Grumpy Old Benson's constant, persistent intervention in our lives with his crank calls.

* * * * * * *

Dale decided to chuck his Lot Boy position at Arrow Chevrolet and began working, part time in West Duluth for Dave Bjorklund at Dave's Auto Transmission Shop. The change was proposed by Larry in persuasion from his contacts in the racing circuit, mainly Dave Bjorklund. This created a disadvantage, as Dale had no transportation to West Duluth. He had, had competent transit to Arrow Chevrolet each day with Larry.

Dale's only alternative was to loan Rogie's five speed bike and peddle the six miles to his job. This didn't settle very well with Rogie. It was his summer vacation fun! Biking and hanging out with Bryan and other neighborhood kids. The bike had been a recent gratuitous token, unexpectedly from Larry. Roger treasured his Roloflex with pride and very grudgingly was forced to loan it to his big brother. I didn't interfere with the decision, suggested by Larry, as I was convinced Dales employment would help purchase school clothes and also put a damper on teenage mischief. Not much time left on their hands for misconduct! Right? **Wrong!!** Kids always **MAKE TIME** for MISCHIEF!

* * * * * * *

I came bounding into the house from my gig to surprisingly find Larry already at home, puttering in his garage. Upon noticing the arrival of my trusty 'old Chevy, he quickly dropped his, whatever, and barged into the kitchen to greet me.

"Hi Hon. You home already!?"

"Sure. You workin' alone tonight?" I asked.

"Yeah. Just a few loose ends to get ready for the races in Ashland tomorrow night. Do you happen to know where **YOUR DALE** is tonight? He didn't pit for me tonight in Superior."

"Oh sure. He's at a teenage boys get together. I think he called it an overnight "Hangin' Out" or maybe an overnight "Slumber" thing. Just a bunch of boys goofin' off. Maybe a little sneaky beer drinkin', but very harmless."

"I don't **Think** so!" Larry quipped sarcastically. "I think it's time you become aware of the Hanky Panky your kids are up to, most of the time while you're gone working!"

"Whatta you mean?" I asked, testily.

"They built a shack in the woods, down a path toward DeGrio's." he subtly briefed me, on what he assumed I was unaware of.

"Oh, I know about that!" I defensively attacked the implication of misbehavior. "Dale told me the guys built an A frame, just for something to do, just for fun. I think that's great! They're doing something constructive with their leisure time, instead of drinkin' beer, chasin' chicks and getting into all sorts of Trouble!"

"You're so, so gullible, Dottie! This shack stuff is **TROUBLE!** Do you know where it is? Do you even know about all the paths in these woods between neighbor's houses?"

"No. You're right! I haven't a CLUE!"

"I think it's time you woke up, Dottie! I'll take you there and show you how constructive and innocent and harmless their shenanigans **really are!** They sure know how to pull the wool over your eyes!"

Larry located a big, foot-long flashlight from the garage paraphernalia while I swapped my high heel pumps for a pair of tennys. I clumsily, in the pitch black of night, followed him through the woods down an obviously well traveled path.

We came upon a fairly big, fairly well constructed building in an A frame design. Laughter and conversation buzzed from within. The exterior of the structure was merely one inch boards of various widths, with no siding or covering of any kind. Therefore between the boards, crack spaces were obvious, where light streamed out from inside.

Larry and I slowly crept to the building, noiseless as a cat stalking it's prey. We stood silently, peeking through the cracks to visually investigate the party in progress.

Swizlak sat at a small table drinking beer with Dave Willis, Dale and Leslie. Two other couples were lethargically settled on an old dilapidated sofa across the room.

The room was approximately twelve or fourteen foot square and was to my amazement installed with electric lights. A heater was positioned next to an outer wall with stove pipes emerging through the roof.

Jeff Halvorson sat on the couch with arms cozily squeezed around Annie Bennett as they intimately petted and cuddled. Jeanie Thompson and Jeff Lund were busily engrossed smooching and swapping spit at the other end of the couch. Some kids were clutching beer bottles or some form of beverage. A case of bottle beer was stacked upon the floor beside the table, arms length from where Dale perched.

Inaudibly I sighed, and gratefully made a sign of the cross, relieved to discover there was no indication of any kind of dope present at the teenage Bash!

Larry pressed his mouth against my ear in a whisper, "See what **really** goes on when you're busy at work?"

"Well I never ---" my quivering, aphonic voice trailed off, not finishing my thoughts.

"Yeah, a regular teen-age Orgy, Shack-up!" Larry quipped in a quiet murmur. "What do you think we should do?" he queried furtively.

"I think we should, Number One, definitely break this up." I replied softly, lips against his ear drum. I moved to the right for a better view, through a larger, wider crack.

"Hey, Dale," Swizlak burbled. "I need another beer!"

"Yeah, me too." Dave piped in.

Dale passed beers from the case on the floor, to the boys.

"Hand me the church key." Dave muttered. "Dale, you have another beer too."

"No. I think I'll pass." Dale mumbled, as he pressed his palm to his mouth, enacting a bogus half yawn. "I think Leslie and I will hit the sack."

"Good idea. It must be three A.M. by now. I'm really tired." Leslie added.

Dave snickered, implying secret understanding as they rose and ascended a ladder construed against a square opening to what appeared to be a second floor attic entrance!

"Quite skilled, expertise talent for a bunch of teen-age boys!" I mused with a simpered smile on my lips.

"I think it's time we Crash this party." I grumbled, indignantly, under my breath.

"I'm for that."

We shuffled to the front of the structure, to the one door entrance. Larry pounded, forcefully on the door for admittance.

"Someone's at the door." we heard someone comment.

"Ask for the password."

"What's the password?" Swizlak bellowed.

We remained silent.

"What's the password?" Swizlak thundered in repetition.

No answer.

"Ah, it must be Ritchie." Dave commented, matter-of-factly. "Come on in."

The expressions on their faces as we emerged through the door could have warranted an Academy Award Oscar in a movie, next door to Gone With The Wind!!

"Quite a Slumber Party goin' on here!" I barked angrily. A **BOYS** hangout? Huh?"

Larry just stood by gloating, a triumphant ensued expression on his face, eminently enjoying the kids dishonesty being discovered by mother.

"Where's Dale?" I asked, already having witnessed through the cracks where he and Knutson had disappeared to. However I wanted to entrap the kids to see what kind of story they'd invent.

"He went to bed." Dave emitted passively.

"Give me that flashlight, Larry." I muttered.

With the flashlight gripped in my hand, I sashayed up the ladder to the second floor. In a sleeping bag, snug as a bug, stretched out on a bare hard floor, I found Dale. Only a part of his bare chest was visible as he leaned, nonchalantly on one elbow while pulling the sleeping blanket snuggly to him with his free hand. tiny, petite Knutson was completely out of sight, scuttled inside, way down to the foot of the sleeping bag. Apparently hiding!

"What are you doing here, Mom?" Dale asked with bogus innocence, suavely spewing like the awe of Niagra Falls!

"Don't pretend innocence with me, Dale!" I shrieked angrily. "Some boy hang out!! Where's Leslie?"

"Baby sitting, I guess."

"Yeah, Baby Sitting! Get your ass out of that sleeping bag, Leslie. No point in hiding. Larry and I have been watching the goings-on here for over an hour, through the cracks in the walls!"

They began squirming, abashed, out of their little love nest, disconcertedly scrambling for their clothes as I descended the ladder.

"The rest of you kids can get your sneaky, lyin' butts home and out of here." I assaulted in a stringent voice. "Unless, of course, you'd rather I call the cops to break up this little love nest?!"

Larry and I plodded down the unlit, shadowy path back to our house. I immediately seized the phone book and began calling every parent of every teenager that had been present at the shack. It was three A.M. and most parents, upon beig abruptly awakened, were lethargically trying to grasp the situation.

I asked each unaware parent where their teen-ager was spending the night. A varied list of fabricated alibis and invented activity excuses emerged; a girl friends house slumber party, movies, school dance, pizza and overnight stay, etc. etc. the list went on. However, when I attempted to call a parent for Leslie, there was NO ONE to call! The only person in charge of her life, as a guardian, was Sandy McConnikey whom she lived with and baby-sat for. Sandy certainly was not a reputable guardian, fostering discipline and direction. She was, in fact, their **supplier for beer and alcohol!!**

A lump rose and adhered to my dry throat. It was a sad, unsettling result. She had no one! With no other option available I called the police matron and explained the situation to her. I don't recall exactly what developed, what happened to Leslie, but I believe she was removed from Sandy's home and placed in Foster Care elsewhere.

An irate parent burned the shack to the ground.

♪♪♪

CHAPTER TEN

After the A frame incident, things became rather tense and icy cold between Dale and I. Leslie was out of the picture. I could see Dale was painfully crushed over the termination of his puppy-love affair.

I attempted to have a tété-a-tété talk with him to cushion the weight of his heartache. With prevalent, oscillating mood-swings, I found him in his room apathetically staring out his bedroom window.

"Dale, I know how much this must hurt!" I murmured, with tears pressing for release in my sand-grained eye lids. I gently pressed my arm around his shoulder, trying to comfort him. I felt his body go rigid, which was Dales way, always of dealing with the embarrassment of a display of emotion.

"Dale, Leslie had many many other boyfriends too. One, at the Gopher, even I knew about. I know you don't wanna hear this right now, but this break-up is really for your own good. Someday you'll look back and understand. I know it's painful right now and hurts like hell, but----"

"I Hate You! I Hate You!" he interrupted, adamantly, brusquely shrugging my arm from his shoulder.

Tears welled in my eyes so I left the room, not wanting him to see my emotion. It takes an abundance of **TOUGH LOVE** and **HEARTACHE** to raise children. It's definitely much more difficult to administer **"NO'S"** than to surrender to easy-way-out, passive **"YES"S**!

Month's later, after Dale had begun a new relationship with Barbara Tomanio, the news arrived that Leslie had given birth to a set of twins! I believe, Dale then realized it could have been him!! It could have been a rude awakening to the surrender of teen-age freedom in exchange for a sudden thrust into the mature responsibility and problems of an adult!

* * * * * * *

Swinging the door wide, Larry sprinted through the kitchen and snatched some auto keys dangling from the key bracket organizer beside the kitchen door.

"Where are you going?" I asked. "I'm just about ready to put supper on the table. In no more than five minutes."

"Oh—oh, that's okay. I gotta scoot out to the airport. Get some **AV gas** 110 octane for my stock car, and I need to touch **base on some synthetic oil too.**"

"Right now?"

"Yeah. I gotta get ready for the races."

"What about supper?"

"Just fix me a plate, put it in the oven on warm. I'll scarf it up later, when I get back."

"I won't keep it warm for you. You never eat left overs 'til they're stale and dry. It'll be in the 'frig."

"That's okay."

And out the door be bolted.

Larry had rebuilt his late model and had spent a lot of time and effort trial testing the synthetic oil with a lot of problems researching the new concept of a synthetic lubricant.

* * * * * * *

Life went on pretty much as normal at our house, as was feasible, considering the career differences between an Auto Racer and a Country Western Musician! We passed in the halls, so to speak, neither of us inconsiderately over stepping the turf of the other.

Larry invited an abundance of his friends, pit crew, racing and Arrow Chevrolet associates to help him celebrate his birthday by throwing a keg party in the new garage. Many of these folks had previously assisted in gratuitously building the structure. I invited my music coterie crowd to join in the festivities as well.

"I'll show you **HOW** to really put on a Party Bash!" Larry boasted. It was usually my 'cup of tea' to entertain flamboyantly, but I stepped aside, and refrained from any interference, letting him conquer the "Spotlight".

"You two get along pretty well." Arlene fleetingly sputtered in small talk at the bash. "And John sure admires Larry."

"Not as much as Larry admires John." I piped in. "He really looks up to John and his skills. Often I hear him brag to others of John's expertise ability in so many trades. He calls John his **"Second Dad"**. Not very complimentary" I tittered. "He should call John his other Brother, whom he admires and looks up to as a doting mentor or a wise teacher."

"John wouldn't care. Age doesn't concern him like it does us gals!"

"Larry and I do get along super well, cuz we don't see much of each other." I giggled. "We're hardly ever shoulder to shoulder in anything. He's gone racing and I'm absorbed in my career."

"But not **Every** night." she shyly implied coupling, with raised eyebrows. "Always time for you know What!"

"Not much." I replied. "The nights he and I are both home, like I told you before, he spends the entire time in the garage with his mechanic helpers, working on engines, trannys, rear ends, welding roll bars, so forth and so on. Oh a couple times a month he makes an appointment! Ahem! To make me happy, he says. He insists that keeps me from getting moody." I giggled and winked. "He knows very little, I guess, about **PMS.**"

"Keeps the worry of getting PG, anyway, out of likelyhood. Not much of a chance of that happening?" Arlene jovially taunted.

"You got that right."

"Did you ever try that costume you talked about before?" she asked. "You know, the one with head lights hanging from your boobs and a tail light hanging from your fanny and rolling under his car, in the garage on a creeper to get his attention?"

"Nah!" I wriggled my nose. "But I still have that plan on the back burner for future reference, if the appropriate time should arrise."

Arlene and I tittered together, sharing frivolous chit chat and laughter over hi-balls.

It was an elongated drawn-out Birthday Bash. Larry ultimately pooped out and decided he'd had **Enough Birthday!** He deviously slipped away, heading for our bedroom. Flopping across the bed, he collapsed, believing he had cleverly outfoxed us all and secretly escaped the Party Animals.

However, Alas, I shot home 8mm movie pictures, as Barb Jurek smeared lipstick all over his face. As he continued snoring she inserted a candle in his belly-button. Big "M" added her clever touch by delicately lighting the candle, as we all stood bye, camera rolling and laughing convulsively!

All this hanky-panky witticism was imperceptive to oblivious Larry, gushing a stream of zzzz's. He had always implied to me privately, that my friends and I were all alcoholics and drunks. In his assessment, low life were the drunks and the more sophisticated drinkers were the alcoholics. His racing friends and associates, in his opinion, were just very conservative, social tippers.

Here, incoherently at his own Bash, he was the first to topple and become ludicrously harassed by his own, **Oh so Conservative,** folk. His Friends! Ahem!

The laugh was indubitably on Larry! And I had pictures to prove it wasn't fabricated. I couldn't help but gloat a little.

* * * * * * *

It was Wednesday forenoon, kids had left for school, Larry had departed for Arrow Chevrolet or whatever was his plan for the day. I wasn't in the habit of questioning his whereabouts.

With the bonus of a quiet peaceful house, finally materializing, after all the chaos of school preps, I soaked blissfully in a tub of bubble bath for a half hour almost falling asleep. Then I dressed in sparkle and sequin in preparation for another taping of our weekly TV, "Arrowhead Country" show. Taking extra care and patience in the art work on my face, I dabbed a second coat of mascara and eye shadow, and fluffed extra pink blush on my cheeks. A flashy outrageous pair of dangling earrings completed the stage ensemble.

DULUTH HERALD, FRIDAY, FEBRUARY 20, 1971

COUNTRY MUSIC
THE
TUMBLEWEEDS
Featuring
Gene Norell—Toby—Dottie Lou
"Stars of the Weekly TV Show"
Arrowhead Country
Appearing in Person Every
Wed., Thurs., Fri., Sat.,
9 P.M. to 1 A.M.
gopher
RESTAURANT and LOUNGE
402 Central Avenue, West Duluth
Serving the Finest Italian and American Food

When I arrived at W.D.S.M., Channel six, the camera crew and stage hands were vigorously pushing tables around; placing cocktail glasses, candles, and a lone flower at each table to create the atmosphere of a night club in action. Our sponsor, Connie Lukovsky, insisted the set give the impression we were, indeed, performing, LIVE, from his Club, "The Venture".

A number of our fans were present to sit at small cocktail tables to simulate the authenticity. They would sit, during tapings, and sip on half-filled glasses of soda or water and applaud dynamically on cue.

I didn't relish the production coming to closure, but the final episode was approaching rapidly. It had been exhilarating emotionally and we fancied the rewards of saturated exposure to TV audiences we would otherwise, never have reached. My record sales had doubled and music performances, at live gigs had increased immeasurably. The birth of "Arrowhead Country" had filled my Wednesday afternoons with incredible rapport diversion.

Korn concocted a format of various local artists each week to add variety and interest among local viewers. He was, himself, an impressive addition to the production with his numerous talents. He was the producer, the emcee, the front man, lead vocalist and musician, having acquired his many skills in earlier years as a D.J. on local country stations and performing live, in many clubs with his own band. Most recently he had been employed as manager and booking agent of the Key's Talent Agency, based out of Nashville. He also produced and booked the Duluth Arena Country Shows with popular Headliners.

His format for this particular segment was yodeling Freddie Osberg of the Chaperals as headliner, plus a brief guest shot from Frankie Dell, a local country vocalist.

I casually greeted our usual stream of fans mustering about, loitering, hanging with friends. They were basically the same faces week after week. Now and then a few new faces would emerge out of curiosity and join the cluster of enthusiast's, taking an active part in our fabricated Night Club setting.

Upon closer scrutiny I spotted Gladie, our own "Tumbleweed Sweetheart" whom we all adored. She was a regular Saturday Afternoon guest at our Jam Sessions at Freddie's Town Pump.

"Hi Gladie! Wow! What a surprise!" I exclaimed, astonished. "So nice to have you join our team." I beamed as we shared a warm, amiable bear Hug.

"I had to show up just once to see what mischief you guys are all up to." she grinned as she gracefully accepted a hug from Korn.

"Lookin' good, Kiddo." he declared politely.

Gladie was the oldest guest on our weekly Jam Sessions. I estimated her age to be around sixty. She majestically flaunted a staunch, matronly figure and a coiffure of steel grey hair. She nurtured a spirited sense of humor and bantering was a consistent attribute that never took a vacation. This was her personality resume. She was a cocktail waitress from across the street at "Norman's Bar" and her shift ceased just about the time our Jam Sessions began, so she faithfully spent her afternoons with us.

In her younger years Gladie had pursued the entertainment circuit as well. It was obvious in her outgoing desire to entertain. She had been one-half of a musical duo and she had shared the spotlight with her late husband, Earl. The "Derosiers" had played many of the night spots in the Twin Ports area and were known for their comedy routines as well.

Most of the unabashed tunes Gladie belted were parodies of her own creativity. Her improvised words to "Alley Cat" brought tickled smiles of amusement to many listeners:

♪"He goes on the prowl each night,
   like an alley cat.
   He's looking for some new delight,
   Just like an Alley Cat!
   She can't trust him out of sight,
   There's no doubt of that!
   Don't you feel really sorry for
   Her and her Alley Cat?
      He woo's 'em---Mee-ow,
      He loves 'em---Mee-ow,
      He leaves 'em,
      Like that cat's a NO GOOD CAT!! etc. etc.

or sometimes she would make us all blush with her rendition of—

♪"I wanna play piano in a whorehouse.
That's always been my one desire.
Some folks own ranches, elegant homes in Butte.
But I wanna tinkle the ivory in a house of ill repute.
Don't laugh at my humble avocation,
'Cuz copulation's here to stay.
I don't need fame or riches.
I just wanna play for them 'ole Bitches.
♪I wanna play piano in a whorehouse!"

Her parodies were never ending. She had a repertoire of hundreds of such powerful ditty's.

I was so absorbed in visiting with Gladie on the sidelines, I became somewhat oblivious to the progress of the taping. I glanced up to the sudden reality that yodeling Freddie was leaving the microphone, having finished his rendition of "Chime Bells."

Korn scooted hurriedly to the mike and buzzed with the usual stream of praise.

"A nice hand for Freddie, from the Chaparel Band. Thank you Fred, for some very fine entertaining yoleling. And the singing too wasn't all that bad! Just kidding." Everyone chuckled.

A large card was raised, displaying the word "APPLAUSE" in gigantic letters to cue the audience to make a thunderous explosion of fervent hand clapping.

As the applause diminished to a halt Korn piped in, "For our next guest, well it goes without saying, you all know Frankie Dell. Let's get those hands outta your pockets, Folks and make him feel real welcome here at the Venture Club." More cued applause.

Frank scrambled to the microphone, guitar strapped across his back, guitar pick in hand, between thumb and forefinger in "pickin' grinnin'" readiness.

"And what are you going to treat us to tonight, Frank?" Korn asked as the applause subsided.

"A Conway Twitty tune." he replied, "Called "Fifteen Years Ago.""

Korn sauntered to the immediate sidelines, joining Gladie and I, relinquishing the mike to Frankie.

Frank slowly, dramatically strummed a chord, dragging his pick melodically across the strings. We assumed he was etching the key pitch of "Fifteen Years Ago" in his mind. However he stopped cold and abrupt. Addressing the camera, he brusquely, melodramatically blurted,

"You know, folks, I'm a sinner! You're a sinner as well. In fact no one is innocent! We all fall short of God's approval. But there's still time yet, for us all to become worthy enough to enter the Pearly Gates of Heaven. We need only to **REPENT!**" He raised his voice, theatrically for effect in the boisterous clout and essence of a Southern Baptist

Preacher. **"REPENT! I say! REPENT!"** He slowly fanned his arm in a politician wave, gesturing for dramatic impact. **"REPENT!** And the time, Folks is **NOW!! TODAY!** Don't wait another minute! Let Jesus set you free!!"

I heard a snicker or two emerge from behind me, and Gladie, in a quiet, stifled voice gasped. "Omigod!!"

I chuckled. "See, Gladie, you're already getting his message." I teased. "I heard that little acknowledgement there of God."

The room became silently stunned for a brief moment and then I heard "Cut" as Korn sprinted to Frankie's side at the mike. Bouncing back to reality of production, he began barking miscellaneous orders. "Back up that tape right past Frank's introduction of the song title he will be singing." Korn dictated, addressing the engineer at the controls.

"Frank, you're entitled to your religious beliefs. But nobody **HERE** gives a Rats Ass about your beliefs! This is neither the time nor the place to address them. This is a Country Western Music Variety Show and listeners tune in to see and hear good 'ole Country Music. So sing your song! Damn it!!"

Cameras were earnestly moving about, trying to capture the best possible angles. "Take two" came over the speakers, "on track six" and sheepishly Frank began. "Fifteen years ago ♫ ♪ and I still feel the same. Why did he have to mention---"

"Boy oh boy, For asinine." Korn spurted, shrugging his shoulders imperviously, as he returned to the sidelines. "You know, it takes all kinds! And you know, I feel more like I do now than I did a little while ago." he added in nonsense.

We all laughed in an effort to stifle the tension of the ridiculous.

♫ "It takes a mighty long time, to get a real love off your mind. I know cuz it's been fif--"♪

"You know, the Fart does sing a pretty good song, however." Korn added as Frank warbled his stuff.

As we concluded the Wednesday afternoon TV segment, Gladie stood beside me and with Goodbye's in order, we hugged.

"Hey Dottie, I almost forgot." she blurted. I have something for you."

"Something for me? Why? Hey, it's way past my birthday and it's a helluva long time 'till Christmas!"

"Okay, it's cuz it's Wednesday, then." she smirked, "It's something I've wanted to give you for quite some time." She rummaged with frenzy through a cluttered purse, searching, and finally came up with a tiny white box. "Oh, here it is." she exclaimed. "I've thought of bringing it to Freddie's but you're always so busy there."

She opened the box displaying a pair of dangling guitar earrings in turquoise with rhinestone trim and little silver leaves dangling from the bottom.

"They're so exquisite." I said, "but why me?"

"Cuz you're a musician, so you'd appreciate the fine intricate design of the hand made guitars."

"Wow, Gladie. I'm flattered. In fact, I'm stunned!"

"I've had these since my hubby and I played the clubs here in the Twin Ports. **HMMM—a hundred years ago!**" she tittered. "Of course I don't play anymore and it would just fill me with so much joy if you'd wear them sometimes on stage in your "gigs". They always were my favorite piece of jewelry and Earl had them hand made for me on some Special Occasion."

"Are you sure you wanna part with these Gladie?" I asked. "They are a very sentimental token of some very special times for you. Those kind of token memories can never be replaced. How about if I just loan them and wear them for you at Freddies?"

"No I want you to have them. Little guitars are really not the fashion for little grey haired old ladies!" she smirked wryly. "Of course when you are an active musician, for you they're always in style. No sense to just let them lay unused in a dresser drawer."

"They're really elegant, gorgeous." I purred.

"Yes, but they are meant for the stage. So what better place to plant them for display then on your ears, Dottie. Earl would be delighted. He'd like that too." She glanced upward briefly in retrospect as if to acknowledge his approval. "And I can't think of anyone I'd rather have wear them than Miss Dottie Lou!" Tears shyly slipped from the corners of her eyes and her tears contagiously exploded mine. WE hugged and I mused, thoughtfully,

"I hope I can, someday, at her age still entertain people as vibrantly as she. She's a Special Angel!"

"Sure Gladie," I mumbled, my lips quivering. "I'll be so proud to wear them. Thank you for even considering me with such a sentimental memory and for sharing it with me. They're very precious, Gladie and so are you."

Gladie is long gone to the band in the sky, but I still carry those little guitars close to my heart, in her memory, and I still wear them on occasion.

I taped a few of her parodies and always regretted having not recorded a lot more of them. It was her unbridled, daffy humor that inspired me in later years to write and sing many parodies of my own.

* * * * * * *

Home at 4:30 I prepared a prepense, prompt macaroni goulash supper for the soon arrival of the kids from school. Larry was a no-show, busy I assumed with some Arrow Chevrolet project or Stock Car politics.

After scarfing down a plate of goulash with the kids, I dressed for my regular commitment at the Gopher Lounge. We were engaged in our fourth consecutive year, four nights a week for John Dandrea.

Occasionally, we Tumbleweeds would schedule a two hour early arrival, around six or seven to learn and rehearse new releases that were topping the charts and requested by our fans. The downstairs Lounge was not opened to the public until 9:00 P.M. so we were able to go over arrangements, words, chords, etc. in complete privacy.

My life was completely occupied with career and children, mostly career, leaving little time for leisure relaxation or recreation. So as weeks, months slipped away I was unable to share much quality time with Larry or take part in camping jaunts, racing hi-lights, whatever functions resulted in weekend pleasure. With four nights at the Gopher, an afternoon Jam Session at Freddie's and Tuesdays at the Venture Club, I was overly self-indulged in my own career and **LOVING** every impassioned moment of it!

♪♪♪

CHAPTER ELEVEN

When I arrived at the Gopher Toby and Korn had just arrived and were casually mulling about, each absorbed in their own tasks. Korn was earnestly engrossed in downing his first cocktail of the evening, which consisted of a couple sizzling alka-seltzer in a half glass of lukewarm water. He regularly began his evening with this medicinal cocktail. He complained of a persistant upset acid stomach. I gently badgered and scolded, suggesting that he see a doctor about it. However men are noted to ignore any advice or seek the assistance of doctors.

A few stragglers were already inadvertently flitting about the deserted lounge.

As I began arranging my music paraphernalia, plugging in mike and speaker cords into receptacles, I raised my eyes and noted the dark brown-eyed stranger, of earlier weeks was already perched at a table across the dance floor. "So **he's** in town again." I mused. "He sticks out like a sore thumb, attired in an expensive suit and tie in **this** saloon atmosphere. How could I have not noticed him?" Most patrons in the Gopher dressed in jeans, casual sportswear or work clothes. I pondered why I hadn't observed his visits sooner, in lieu of his conspicuous sophisticated get-up. "But then, I'm really never very observant," I chuckled to myself. "Too self-absorbed, I guess."

Changing my train of thought, I sashayed through the silver, sparkly drapes adorning the back of the stage, which also camoflaged an entrance, beyond the stage to a small adequate dressing room. There I toted my purse, make-up, an extra change of wardrobe and miscellaneous personal belongings. A couch stretched against one wall on which to relax if the need be. On a small stand I stashed a liquor decanter, into which I disposed of liquor sent up to me by fans of the band. I drank very conservatively when I performed, so whenever customers graciously wanted to treat me to a cocktail, rather than offend them in refusal of their hospitality, I'd order straight shots of Petri Brandy and on break I'd pour them into my decanter to use at my many, many parties on Walnut Street. I frequently entertained friends, neighbors and music fans. People in the 70's were a generous lot and were constantly sending drinks to the bandstand. Parties were inevitable whenever we fronted the Country Shows at the Arena, as they were when someone was celebrating a birthday or an anniversay. And sometimes because it was Saturday, or because the rain had subsided or the boss got lucky!! Well, obviously we were all a bunch of **Party Animals!** Parties regularily took place at Korn's, or Sundown Mary's or my house.

With twenty minutes remaining before the nine o'clock onset of music, I clambered upstairs to the dining room and poured myself a cup of coffee from behind the counter. This was **my** habitual first cocktail of the evening. Returning with a refill in hand, I shuffled downstairs and sashayed to the table of the dark-haired, tastefully clad infrequently present, visitor.

"May I join you?" I asked.

"I'd be proud." he replied.

"You know, the last time you were here, two or three weeks ago, I asked you your name and you ignored my question. You never did tell me!" I grinned as I nonchalantly plopped myself on the chair across the table from him.

"Eugene O'Demarra." he smirked, smiling glibly. "I hadn't ignored the question. I guess I just didn't realize I hadn't introduced myself."

"Hmmmm—Eugene O'Demarra."

"But everybody calls me Gene."

"Oh.—Gene. If I may ask, where do you disappear to for weeks at a time?" I tittered jovially.

"I'm a sales rep, on the road for Mack Manufacturing Company Incorporated and owned by Jack Grappler." he beamed with gusto. "The company was initially based here in Duluth, but just recently moved to Prichard, Alabama. They only support a miniscule office on this end now. I was based here, for quite some time, and I frequented the Gopher often, but you just never noticed."

"Oh-oh, I'm sorry."

"I was here long enough to accumulate some ties and bonding in Duluth."

"But now, you're just a Salesman." I quiped. "Oh no, I didn't mean that, like it sounded." I conceded, apologetically.

"I prefer to call myself a Sales Rep." he sputtered.

"You live in Alabama, then?"

"No. I live in Holiday Inns!" he chuckled. "I'm on the road, almost all of the time. I call on potential buyers across the whole East Coast, west through Louisiana and then north through Tennessee and Alabama, Mississippi, so forth and so on."

"But you **live** in Prichard, Alabama."

"No. I have a desk in Prichard, Alabama!" he laughed. "A desk in my office there. I work there sometimes, but no, I don't live there." was his unequivocal, tittered answer. "I can't call it home."

"Is this some kind of a riddle, a trick question?" I joked.

"Oh yes, there's more than one answer." he smirked.

"I've never heard of Prichard, Alabama." I rolled my eyes.

"It's s suburb of Mobile. You've heard of Mobile, haven't you?" he ribbed me, obviously taxing my sense of humor.

"No, I've never even heard of Alabama! Smart Aleck!" Grinning, I shot another question in his direction. "What do they manufacture?" I went on, making indolent conversation.

"Large, massive, machinery. It's a **Gigantic Trucking Business**. You've heard of Big Mack trucks?"

"I guess." I shrugged indifferently.

"It's all affiliated. Many channels of production in machinery, but that would only bore you to death. Let's talk about you."

"What's there to tell? Not much I'm afraid." I squirmed, feeling ambushed and a bit uncomfortable.

"Well where do **YOU** disappear to, when the lights go out here?"

"Well, I live in Duluth Heights. I work here, Freddie's Town Pump and the Venture Supper Club; have a TV show, soon to be finalized—and—emm, uh," Feeling a bit abashed at blowing my own horn, I arose to change the subject, and went on, "and, hmmm—It's time for me to go to work." Ambling toward the stage, I stopped abruptly, looked back and buzzed, "Oh yes, Nice to officially meet you Gene. The leader we call Korn is a Gene also."

Life at the Gopher Lounge was never dull. And I was showered with so much fond admiration and attention, my self esteem always soared as did my heart for love of my fans.

There was, as an example, sad, brown **puppy-eyed** Sonny, who was as dependable a nightly sight as were the musicians. He had never missed an evening at the Gopher in as long as we'd been there.

In the middle of my set he lollygagged to the band stand and between numbers we chatted. He leaned on the band stand railing and purred, cajoling me as was his usual dramatics. "When is it going to be my turn, Dottie?"

"Turn for what?"

"To marry you, of course. I've been in love with you," he droned with prurient optimism, "since way before Larry."

"You wouldn't wanna marry a musician, Sonny. They're never home! They're self centered! I'd be primping instead of cooking. Musicians are mere Ego Trips."

"I could handle that." he tittered.

"Don't be too sure. Besides, I'm married."

"I know that. But you could at least give me a little hope for the next time you're single!" he joshed.

"Oh, you're a Sweetheart, Sonny, but—"

"But—I know the line, 'we can still be friends'," he sighed a fabricated disappointment. "Well, as long as you won't marry me," his soft puppy eyes twinkled in mirth, "and as long as I can't get you between the sheets, I guess I'll have to settle for second choice."

"And what might that be, Sonny?"

"Just sing "Satin Sheets" for me."

"Okay, Sweetie. Sounds like a 'more better' choice anyway." I giggled. "You won't have to be sorry later!" I laughed.

It was intermission. I descended the stage steps and hurried to the restroom, succumbing to a screaming bladder. I scurried through the restroom lounge and stooped to peer under the toilet partitions, only to discover pairs of feet occupying every stool. Turning to the adjacent lounge I became aware of Arlene, Toby's wife, sitting patiently waiting a turn at the commodes as well.

"Hi." I responded, as I leaned against the wall, crossing my thighs, trying to, obviously subdue my need to relieve myself.

Arlene nodded a casual hello.

We could hear someone sobbing in one of the toilet booths and on another stool an apparent confidant, trying to console her friend.

"Don't take it to heart, Deb." she said. "He'll come around. Just give it time. I'm sure he loves you, too."

"Then why did he and Gene come over to my apartment and rip my phone off the wall? Just cuz I threatened to call Toby's wife and tell her about us?"

"Toby was just mad. Real mad! It'll all blow over!"

"I don't know. I just don't know. I don't know what I'll do if I lose him!" She sobbed hysterically. "I love Toby. I love him so much! I don't care about his god damm wife. She can drop dead for all I care!"

I glanced over at Arlene, quietly perched on the couch, a somber, enigmatic expression on her face. No tears. No anger. She gaped at me, rolled her eyes, shrugged her shoulders and never uttered a sound.

I pondered, "How do spouses ever cope with the perpetual philandering, the womanizing. Yes it was not a Magnificent Holiday to be married to a musician." Being one-third of a band I observed way too much. Being intimately close to most of my fans I was given, 'Too Much Information', as well. I had promised myself to never, ever date or become emotionally involved with an entertainer. "And even more crazy and stupid was to get involved with a married man." I ruminated. It's only a haven for heartache, loss of self esteem and the ultimate pay-back time of discovering having been used. **Not me! Never!** I had never in my single years, ever involved myself with married men. I had strutted, vaunted, boasted in my mind a **self-righteous** superiority of self controlled choices most women do not achieve or embrace. I had never been a wee bit proficient at SHARING!

The gals came out, washed their hands, exited the restroom without a glance in Arlene's direction and I wondered if they ever realized Toby's wife was there.

"How stressful it must be to have a girlfriend and a wife in attendance at the club simultaneously." I mused, with a placid smirk. "How nerve racking! How distressing and ahem! How well deserving!"

No, life was never dull at the Gopher!

I moved from table to table, stopping briefly to chat with various patrons I knew and some I didn't. Booth to booth trying to acknowledge and share a fond "Hello" to all our fans, trying not to miss anyone.

I looked up and there approached the **"Potatoe Chip Kids"**.

They were a small group of four fans who were obsessively devoted to Toby. Every time they visited the Lounge, they would bring a gigantic bag of potato chips, boldly march up to the stage and present the gift to Toby, hence we nicknamed them **"The Potato Chip Kids"**! Korn and I were invisible to them and we were never included in their production. It was an uninterpeted bonding to Toby. We often pondered why, the ceremonious ritual was lavished on Toby.

Marlene, Rita, David and Don made up the foursome. They were somehow related to each other. Their explanations were confusing. They claimed to be cousins or aunt and uncles or whatever. Some were "Downs" Special People and some were minutely retarded or slow, more accurately described as Special people with Special Needs. They were tender-hearted and trying hard to please in their own way.

We never did discover the reason for the spectacular upstaged ritual or their undaunted devotion to Toby. Our theory was that sometime along the way Toby must have indulged them with very "Special" attention and apparently, casually, in idle conversation told them **"He loved potato chips!!"**

Thus they became tagged with the handle of "The Potato Chip Kids". Korn and I showered much time and dedicated special songs to them, but no matter how much we doted time and attention we were invisibly cast aside. It brought simpered smiles to our faces as they vented worship on Toby. However, we, all three of us, received annual Christmas cards from them, passed to us in person. The minds of these Special People cascade in very different channels than ours. Thirty years later, I still receive Christmas cards from them, Rita's, quite illegibly hand printed in large letters, but her heart is there in adequate penmanship. It must be legible for the Postal Service to find it's way to my home in Wisconsin, from Melrose, Minnesota.

Another music set dissolved into memory and as I stepped down from the stage, Shirley, nonchalantly leaned on the rail and began chattering incessantly, intensely bending Korn's indifferent ear.

Shirley was dark, olive-skinned, a smidgen corpulent, stocky with very distinct Italian features. She was in her late thirty's as we all were. Her ebony black hair bobbed in soft curls around a round face as she tossed them about in expressive demeanor. She was average in beauty, perhaps a number five, and a **fuzzy** mustache nestled above her upper lip. It was very black and very conspicuous even in the concealing dim neon lights of the lounge. I wondered why she didn't shave it off. I was 'ahem' also blessed with my dad's hairy genes above my upper lip, so I was aware of the aggravated nuisance. I regularly shaved my fuzz away. "Shaving makes it grow faster and thicker!" was the usual rumor of advice. **NOT TRUE,** It's only in the genes. Shirley could have been a lot prettier, I thought with a little friendly visit from Pink Lady Bic!

Korn pushed past me, leaving Shirley behind in the middle of a sentence, so she turned to me with an amiable "Hi". "He's ignoring me tonight." she gibbered.

"Who?"

"Korn. Who else?"

"He's probably not ignoring you on purpose." I defended his behavior. "I'm sure he must have something on his mind demanding his immediate attention. Perhaps a little room with a sign on the door that reads MEN." I tittered. "In fact, I'm heading there too. A whole hour of music, prancing and bouncing and I have to--------"

"You're heading for the men's room?" was her equivocal reply, literally deciphering my words.

Catching her pun I joshed in reply. "Well, I'd like to investigate and find out if it's really true. That there really are MEN in there. Easy way to catch one if it's true, huh?"

We giggled. Shirley followed me to the ladies lounge.

As we waited our turns for the busy stalls, we exchanged frivolous, idle chit-chat.

"It's funny how they ignore you the night after." she diplomatically divulged, unabashed.

"You mean Korn?"

"Yeah, Korn. Last night I called him, here, from home on his break. God, was I horney!! So horney I would have honked if someone touched me."

We both snickered.

"I told him how I needed him **SO BAD,** that I could hardly sit on **IT!!"**

"Nah, Shirley. You're puttin' the shuck on me!" I tittered.

"Hell No! Christ, I was really hurtin', that squeezin' throbbin' feelin'. You know what I mean?"

A couple gals were evidently evesdropping, as they washed their hands in lengthy detail, at the sink. As they faced each other, tearing paper towels from the dispenser, they toweled and toweled, then toweled some more, obviously extending the time to absorb all this juicy gossip. With simpered smiles etched on their faces, they raised eyebrows at each other in nebulous disbelief.

"I confess, I don't know much about that." I remarked. Sex is not one of my best attributes. I can take it or leave it. Mostly I leave it." I added, forcing an uncomfortable giggle, as I glanced at the audience still toweling and loitering. We both remained silent and piercingly gawked at them. They finally grasped the hint and exited the restroom. The lounge was empty.

"Well anyway," Shirley continued. "Korn told me to come and park behind the Gopher and wait for him 'til after he was done playin' for the night. He told me not to wear a lot of clothes. Dress scanty, he said, so we don't have to waste a lotta time. He promised he'd make love to me and take away all my frustrated anxiety." she chuckled, with accelerated emotion, remembering.

"And you did?"

"Oh yes! Did I ever and did he ever!" she winked roquishly. "Just like that duet you and Korn sing. '"Did you ever—not so much that you could notice' ♫ and Yes, Oh! **Did We Ever!!**♪ I had only my nightgown on and an open cardigan sweater. Nothin' else. No bra! No undies! Oh well I guess I did have slippers on my feet!"

"Oh—oh—"

"Wow! What a lover! What a Sweetheart!" She moistened her lips, slowly, back and forth, with her tongue, her eyes half-closed in retrospect. Women seemed to have a passion for conquest of musicians on stage, perhaps seeking to feel a part of the awe of the limelight or the magnetic charisma embracing their worlds.

A toilet flushed loudly in the restroom we had assumed vacant. My face was hot as ripples cascaded from my throat and at the base of my neck, upwards. I swallowed hard, feeling somewhat embarrassed. "Too much information, Shirley!" I burbled as I nabbed entrance to the vacated stall. "Way too much information!"

As Shirley and I washed and dried our hands, she continued her intriguing tale. "I really like Korn. It's just **DAMN GOOD SEX!** No strings attached. ♪ 'It's Not Love, But It's Not Bad' ♫ she amiably crooned the popular Merle Haggaard tune in an, out of tune, untrained, husky wavering voice.

"Can't say you lack guts, Shirley. And you're certainly not a bit shy. You know what you want and when you want it. Well, I'd say Go For It!!" I giggled.

"At least I'm not as off the wall and bold as Candy is in her pursuits. no where's near as blunt in snagging a stud."

"I can't picture Candy and Korn." I said a wee bit arrears in comprehension.

"No. Not Korn. She's got the HOTS for Toby."

"You gals are all nuts! There's no future with married men!" I replied negatively. "It's just an invitation to a helluva a lot of pain and heartache! They never leave their wives."

"For some maybe, but not for me. What the hell do I want with a complicated future? I'm already married, so who cares?"

"And Toby would surly be the last choice on my list. He's hard-hearted, self centered and insensitive to women. On the other hand," I winked deviously, "Korn is a warm hearted hunk. I can visualize an attraction there."

"Yeah, I guess Candy is pretty blind at that."

"And Toby's boinkin' her, huh?"

"I don' tknow. She said, tonight, she offered him a blow-job, on his break, if he'd meet her out in the parking lot."

"No, not really! You gotta be kidding!" I exclaimed, "I don't believe it!!"

"That's what she said."

"Did he go for it:?"

"I don't thi—nk----so." she trailed off, thoughtfully weighing the possibility or probability, "But the night is young. We'll just have to keep an eye on Toby." she winked mischievously. "And see if he disappears on any of the breaks." a short pondering pause. "And see if he returns flushed in the face!" She burst into infectious laughter.

"Too much information, Shirley." I tittered. "Way-way, too-too much information!!"

We exited the Ladies Lounge and Shirley headed for the bar area where Korn was tipping a cocktail.

Men have no insighted conception of how copiously women share their innermost secrets with other women friends.

No, there was never a dull moment at the Gopher!

"Hey, Dottie." Delores retorted in a raised voice, as I neared the waitress service station. "There's a drink for you waiting at that front table. That guy in a suit and tie. He bought it but insists you drink it there with him. In his company. I think he's got the **HOTS** for you." she teased.

"Pretty innocuous." I mused. "Not likely, Delores." I giggled facetiously. "He's just another loner, looking for companionship to pass the time in a lonely town."

"A lonely town? I think not."

"Well for him anyway, I'd guess."

I joined him at his table. A brandy water in a tall glass beckoned an invitation.

"You don't need that **straight stuff!** he assertively announced, "So I ordered your brandy with water, mixed. I drink Cutty Sark Scotch and water. Water is always a good mix. No hangovers from a water mix. Right?"

"Yes that's fine. Of course, hangovers always develop from the mix, not the booze." I flashed an enigmatic smile. "You don't approve of my two-fisted straight shots?"

"It's not very appropriate for someone with class, like you."

"Oh I see," I smiled to myself. "I noticed you like to dance."

"Sure do and that waitress, Delores or Dee, She usually will dance with me if she's not too busy. She's very light on her feet, considering her being quite heavy. She loves to talk too. She'll talk your arm off, if you let her."

"Maybe Jan, the other waitress, would dance too if you ask her."

"No, she seems kinda aloof, not very friendly."

"She goes with a disc jockey from KDAL. She wouldn't be much fun anyway. She's so in love with her breasts, that's all she talks about. How big they are!"

He briefly glanced in her direction. "They don't appear to be a Dolly Parton!" he laughed.

"Well, she thinks so! Oh, Oh, Shame on me!" I scolded myself as a lightly planted a bogus slap across my mouth, as a reprimanded time out. "Pull those claws in, Dottie" I mumbled. "Not very nice." and I quickly went on. "Yes. Delores is a much better choice. She has a nice sense of humor, too. Her and I are real good friends."

"I can see that."

"She goes on the road with me a lot."

"Whatta you mean? On the road?"

"Quite often, on my days off, I travel around, promoting my music, pushing records, gathering publicity and exposure. Many of my gal friends travel with me then. Like Delores."

"Where do you travel to?"

"Mostly to radio stations across the two states, for spur of the moment, over the waves, interviews. I convince them to spin my record at the same time. Sometimes we visit jukebox operators too."

"But **where** do you do this?"

"In a two state area. It's different directions everytime. A jukebox operator from Moose Lake, Gordy Rundberg, really was responsible for moving my first release 'One More Memory' around the Midwest. And did I have a time, at first, to convince him to try my record on his locations. It was like pulling teeth. He wanted absolutely nothing to do with local talent. When I finally convinced him to take a box of 25 free 45's, they played so profusely he purchased enough for all 200 of his jukeboxes. I'd go with him sometimes on his route, put up autographed pictures and get acquainted with the club owners and their patrons. Other operators would hear about my record being a smash, making a lot of green stuff for Gordy, they'd, in turn call Gordy or me to obtain records for their jukeboxes, as well."

"Boy, that sounds like a lot of work!"

"A lotta work, but a lotta fun too. We'd spend the whole day in serious business promotion, but I'd reward my gals with an evening out somewhere, where live Country dance music prevailed." I chuckled. "Cocktails and a nice dinner somewhere too."

"Tumbleweeds." came warbling over the P.A. and over the hum drum laughing and chattering of the crowded lounge.

"That's my cue, Gene. Thank you for the drink. Gotta go crominize a bit."

On the third break I sauntered into the bar area, curious to see who all was carousing there. Vivian was already downstairs, perched in a booth by herself.

"You're finished upstairs, already?" I asked as I plunked myself into the booth she was using to privately count her tips.

"Yes it sure was slow tonight. The restaurant closed early. I can tell by my tips it was a slow one. Only $38.80 tonight." she retorted, as she gathered up her green backs, folded them she stuffed them into an apron pocket, along **with** her change.

"Sure not slow down here." I remarked.

"They're a lot more into drinkin' than eatin' tonight." she replied as she sipped vodka, on the rocks, in a low ball glass.

Vivian was my favorite upstairs waitress, as Delores was my favorite server downstairs. Vivian and Delores were like night and day, however, each beautiful in their own way. Vivian was a matronly figured, impetuous, impish, golden blond coiffured lady. Impish was the only adjective they had in similarity. Vivian was perfection. A hair, never out of place, poised demeanor, elegant gestures of class, a demure manner. The frosting on the cake was, aside all sophistication, she was a down-to-earth confidant and a true friend.

Vivian was presently, hopelessly infatuated with a **"terrific"** cop. (terrific, her adjective) He usually arrived around closing, after completing his shift on the force. Policemen, like nuns, usually travel in twos and Randy, Vivian's Cop was always accompanied by his partner, Hank. They usually tipped cocktails with us after hours. Vivian and Randy, on several occasions tried diligently, to persuade me to make it a foursome, but I always reneged on their petitions. Hank was married, as was Randy, as was Dottie. But more logical was the fact there was no chemistry on my part, at all.

"Is Randy on the agenda for tonight?" I cognizably asked. Vivian and I frequently shared many empathetic tete-a-tete's.

"Oh sure. He'll show up before long, usually toward the end of your last set of music." her eyes twinkled in profound mystic anticipation. I pondered the chassis and make up of Randy and wondered how someone so elegant as Vivian could find him attractive, Perhaps it was the Police Uniform, Cap and Badge, because when he removed the cap he displayed a spherical dome glistening in the neon lights. 'Different Strokes for Different Folks' I guess.

"How are things going with you and Randy?" I asked.

"Pretty, pretty torrid. I mean real fiery, sizzling sex!"

"Well, don't complain!" I smirked.

"Who's complaining?" she giggled like a teenager. "I can't get enough of him! He can't get enough of me!"

"I guess I've never known that kind of frenzied delirium. Hmm— Let me think. Roger? Too long ago. Bob? He'd rather play his accordion than make love. Larry? Pretty indifferent, and apathetic. Well, maybe someday, Vivian, I'll have that glow too. The glow you sparkle with. But as of now, it's only in the movies. I can always fantasize. Clark Gable or Clint Eastwood."

"It's difficult for me to imagine you haven't." Vivian replied "With all the attention and invitations you get from men."

"I love the attention, but that's it. Attention."

"Dottie, can I ask you something very personal?" Vivian awkwardly inquired.

"Of course. Not that I'll have the answers."

She arose half-way out of her seat, leaned across the booth, hand cupped over her mouth against my ear and in a soft whisper timidly queried. "What do you so with the stuff?"

"What stuff?"

She rolled her eyes. "You know." She diffidently whispered, as she sat back down in her seat. "If it results in more than just foreplay?"

"Well," I stammered, somewhat taken back by the unprecedented question. "Spit it out, I guess. What else?"

"But what if there's no place to spit? Randy is kinda obsessed with the Sweet Potato Queen's 'Promise'."

"And benevolent Vivian aims to please!" I giggled.

"No seriously, what would you do?"

"It's all protein, Vivian," I cracked up, spuriously laughing.

"Whatta' you mean?"

"It's a seed. The seed of life." I didn't want to display my naive ignorance. "All seeds are protein. I guess, swallow it."

"You're not being serious, Dottie."

"It's nutrition, I guess. Extra nourishment." I was uncomfortable. Again, **Way Too Much Information!!**

"What do you do?"

"Larry never suggests me "tweeking his mushroom". I think maybe he's never experienced the "Promise". All his ex-wives were religious Baptists. I really don't know." I adversely replied.

"Haven't you ever----you know what?"

"Oh yes, but it's such a long time ago. I don't really remember." I lied, trying to diplomatically weasel out of the embarrassing topic. "It was way before Larry's time. I aimed to please too. I guess, maybe I was smashed." I replied, abashed and feeling a need to defend my actions.

The Sweet Potatoe Queens called it the "Promise" and testified, in their book (which was a later book than my story of Vivian) that a gal could get just about anything out of a man with just a "Promise", never having to actually follow through. However, I don't believe the Sweet Potato Queens strategy actually works. Men will not just let you abandon your commitment to the "Promise", and their memory of your "Promise" is the strength of an elephants! I think the Sweet Potato Queens just didn't actually tell **The Rest Of The Story.!!** In my days, Oral Sex was usually never admittedly expressed, but if apprised at all, it was only in odious, guilt-ridden whispers!

No, there was never a dull moment in the GOPHER!!

Korn's deep resonant voice boomed across the PA waves, ♫ "That's more than any loafer at the Gopher can afford"♪ then articulating a few brief messages to our fans about our gratitude and a line up of our current engagements, ending with his usual cliche, his own creation, "If you like us half as much as we like you, we're in Good Shape!"

Then returning to the closing song:

♫A big electric fan keeps me cool while I sleep,
A little baby boy playin' round Dottie's feet.♪

And I chant "No! No! No Way!"

He continues:

&♪ I'm a Rounder and a Rambler, I stay out every night.♪

I tell you folks, I'm ragged but I'm Ri------------------ht.♪ and another night at the Gopher came to conclusion

I gathered my purse and sweater from the dressing room and scooted to the bar room adjacent to the dance lounge to explore a smidgen of visitation before ambling home. Vivian was still plopped in her booth and the stranger to our crowd, Gene O'Demarra had joined her. As I approached them I became aware of what a remarkably striking couple they were. His sleek, slicked back, neatly combed ebony black hair, in contrast to her sophisticated, not a hair out of place, golden coiffure. "Now there's an elegant couple!" I mused. "No comparison to a bald-headed, married, carousing cop!"

"Come join us, Dottie." Gene persuaded. "For a night cap. Hey, Delores," he called, "One for Dottie over here and I'll have another. Vivian, how about you? Nothing but ice rattling in that glass."

"No, Gene. But thank you. Some people I know just came in. I guess I should talk to them." She winked at me and arose to leave. I spotted **Randy at the far end** of the bar. I took her seat in the booth to visit with Gene.

He was an interesting, affable conversationalist, with a personality that definitely shouted Charisma. It was evident he was a Charmer, not my first impression as I remembered. It was a characteristic that obviously was an asset to a salesmanship vocation. His eyes twinkled mischieviously and his cheeks dimpled, slightly when he laughed.

"Are you married?" he asked as our ice cubes tinkled.

"Isn't everyone?" I giggled.

"No". he replied. "Not me."

"Well, you're one of, perhaps, the lucky few." I bantered.

"Where's your husband?"

"He's around somewhere."

"Here? I'd like to meet him."

"No. Not here, but somewhere."

"He doesn't come to watch you sing?"

"Sometimes he does. But he's a stock car racing enthusist. He builds his own car from street stock, so he's more likely in the garage working on engines. That's whenever he's not racing. Always fixing whatever went Kapoot at the last previous race."

"Where does he race?"

"He races three nights a week around this area. They have races around the Twin Ports Friday, Saturday and Sunday. Friday races are in Superior, Saturdays in Ashland and Sunday's in Proctor."

"That's where he races?"

"That's some of the places he races, but he goes out of town to other events too. The Dakota's and sometimes even into Canada. I'm not sure exactly where he goes. Oh, on the Range sometimes, too." I added.

"He must be pretty famous."

"Famous?" I burst into ludicrous laughter. "Yes, he's famous alright. Just like I'm famous. A couple of ambitious peons, just doin' our thing!"

"Not peons. Never belittle what you do." he dismissively remarked. "Do you go to the races?" he asked.

My intuition perceived Gene's rather accomplished ability at knowing how to make 'brownie Points' with people. It was a part of his charismatic charm, always darting questions, forcing his companions to ultimately talk about themselves. A very fine, noble, if honest, attribute. He displayed an altruistic, sensitive interest in their activities, their history's. My insight was unable, however, to discern if it was bogus or just a genuine interest in people.

"Yes. I have attended the races a couple times, to please Larry, my husband, but it's so dirty and so, so loud, noisy, well, it's just not my cup 'o tea."

"I bet I'd like them." he beamed.

"Most men do. I can just picture you sitting there on those hard, wooden benches in the stands with sand and dirt all over your elegant suit and tie." I sniggered. "Wind blowing your neatly groomed hair all apart, in every which way. You'd sure have to dress a lot differently than you're accustomed to!" I teased.

"I could do that." he replied, good naturedly.

I arose to depart, gathered my purse and sweater and jovially remarked. "thank you for the night cap, Gene. It's been fun chatting with you."

"Yes, me too."

"And don't forget about us Tumbleweeds next time you're in town."

"I sure won't. I love Country Music!"

Shirley rambled past the booth and said, "'Nite Dottie. You know that Bugger is still surely avoiding me."

"That's too bad. Hey, you know we forgot to watch Toby, to see if he left the lounge on any of his breaks!"

We both laughed heartily.

"Yeah, we sure did, didn't we? Oh well, Candy will fill me in." she giggled.

"See you next time I see you, Shirley."

Yes, the Gopher was definitely never dull, never boring. Mostly it relinquished **"Too Much Information."**

♫♫♫

CHAPTER TWELVE

Mother called on Monday to inform me Dad had suffered a heart attack at Scott Graff's and was in St. Mary's Hospital in Duluth. I met Mom there to see Dad. He was out of the I.C.U. and resting in a private room. Dr. Henry had diagnosed Heart Failure and advised Dad would no longer be able to work at Scott Graff in his former physical capacity. He was only 59. His life of continuous overindulgence of liquor and cigarettes had taken their toll.

Sharon, Larry's ex and his daughter, Collette were visiting Sharon's Mom, June peterson at June's farm in Poplar, Wisconsin. It was just a few miles from the Twin Ports. Sharon had remarried. The new husband was a Baptist Minister and they were now residing in Michigan, which was a distance unfeasible and impossible for the frequent over-night visits of the past with Collette.

In an arranged meeting, Sharon very reasonably compromised and agreed to let Collette spend three consecutive weeks with us if we'd accept the responsibility of returning her to Michigan at the conclusion of her stay. We were tickled with the arrangement. This was a pleasant surprise, as Sharon had previously disclosed an obsessive, overly protective concern over Collette spending even a day with us.

I made arrangements to take a weeks vacation time from the Gopher to spend with our children. Larry and I rented a cabin for one week at Stewart's Lodge on Deep Lake near Iron River, Wisconsin. Bill Griffith, a bass player and a mutual friend of the Tumbleweeds, very graciously agreed to fill in for me with Korn and Toby, in my absence.

I designed and sewed matching swim suits for Collette and I, for our aquatic frolicking during her visit with us. The kid in me was enjoying a pompous kick out of playing house with this little petite four year old live doll! I'd fix her hair in curls, comb, brush and play with it, creating numerous different hair styles. I'd dress her in fancy duds I purchased. And pretend tea parties arose at her insistence.

Char and Rogie were likewise mesmerized with their little playmate addition to our family. Rogie would carry her around, over and over again and again, giving her piggy back rides. She soon learned how to indulge our attention. The kids embraced the water frolic of tire inner tubes, rock collecting, making sand picture mounds or just loafing on the beach. It was a rare commodity, having mother around.

Charmaine and Rogie and I taught her how to sing "Twinkle, ♪ twinkle little star." and my own country ditty of "Here comes Bossy♪ Cow, strollin' down the lane. ♪ Good 'ole Bossy Cow. What does Bossy bring? ♪ Sweet milk for us all! Tinkle, tinkle ting." ♪ And Charmaine taught her all about a spider that came up a water spout. I giggled, tickled over all the gestures that accompanied that little children's ditty. Collette would stand on my little kitchen step stool, and using a pop bottle for a micraphone in her hand she'd sing and pretend she was like me. Who wouldn't love the dickens out of her?

Dale had part time summer employment at Dave's Transmission Shop and also at Bridgeman's so he was unable to join us at the lake and Larry scooted off to work each day so he spent only evenings with his daughter and then not consistently. So Collette's visit with her Dad developed more into a visit with Char, Rogie and I.

I took the kids to the races Friday Night in Superior, so Collette could watch her Daddy race. I had never learned to relish the sport of auto racing, but this evening I discovered I did enjoy some aspects of the sport more than I had anticipated. Included in the nights events, following the serious competition, was a Powder Puff race and "Big M" was going to drive Larry's #61 for the event! I couldn't believe my own excitement and enthusiasm.

I just knew Marilyn would win! No doubt in my mind. She was a real avid, spirited racing enthusiast. A dedicated fan, never ever missing a race! She had tremendous determination and testified to an undaunted abundance of indomitable courage!! Yes, I agreed. Marilyn had Clout. Marilyn had guts! "There's not a fearful bone in her body." I ruminated.

Delores Johnson had pull position, but Marilyn was in second best spot. Position was determined by time trials, in advance, as each driver would be stop-watch timed as they circled around the track for one lap. Of course they'd be punching their best speed and endurance, as position was foremost in importance. It could be the decisive factor in **win** or **lose.**

We were perched half way up in the center of the bleachers and directly below us was Marilyn's brood of youngsters. The green "GO" flag flipped about furiously and Marilyn took off like a bullet in Larry's Ford, immediately pulling two or three car lengths ahead of all the other gals.

"Go, Ma, Go! Punch 'er, Ma! Punch 'er! Giver, Giver!" Marilyn's kids were standing up screaming and shouting, waving arms and fist punching the air for emphasis. Their excitement was contagious and intoxicating and I found myself getting caught up in the moment, along with my kids, yelling and screaming as well. Yes, we could all see and we all knew without a doubt, "Big M" had what it would take to show up all these Powder Puff Pansies! How a winner really does it!

Then Marilyn approached the first corner and abruptly slowed to a crawling putsy—putsy—putsy drive of an old woman! We all broke into convulsive laughter! All the cars passed her and then on the straight-away she punched it with guts again, flying like a bat-outa-hell, almost catching the others, but too little too late, then losing it all again, choking in the next corner!

One car was always significantly trying to push ahead of Delores Johnson who was in the lead, sometimes almost roughly, with a nasty punch in the rearend. The car spun around Delores to shoot ahead for first place. However, the car was later disqualified when we all learned it was Andy Rearden, dressed as a woman, adding a little spiced up humor and comedy to the show!

Delores Johnson took the checkered flag and carried it around the winners lap. She was way out in First with little competition from the rest.

"Well she wins them all!" Big M good-naturedly grumbled. "Why wouldn't she win? She has Johnny Johnson for a teacher! She's bound to win!"

"But you had Larry'd **Red Not Number 61!!**" I teased.

"I can't drive unless I'm drunk!" she laughed, shrugging her shoulders in indifference.

We tried every possible way we could invent to entertain our little guest to the fullest. Larry treated her and Rogie to the Ringling Barnum Baily Bros. circus at the Arena one evening. I took her with me for my weekly set and style appointment with Judy, my hairdresser, at the Beauty Shop. I requested Judy to set and style Collette's hair just like Dottie Lou's. Collette looked so cute and elegant in her adult hair style, I had Professional photos taken. It was the prepense plan of the day. Then suddenly I surfaced an impulse to take a speedy, innocuous jaunt to Arrow Chevrolet to show Larry Collette's new coiffure.

COLETTE

"Let's go show Daddy your new hair do." I sputtered. "He will be so surprised and so pleased when he sees his beautiful sophisticated little lady!"

"Uh—hmmm." she tipped her head slowly, sideways as though she was deeply thinking, apparently trying to digest what I had said.

"Do you know what sophisticated means?" I asked.

"Umm, Soft Cake." she replied.

"Well, not quite." I tittered, "but we'll go and surprise Daddy anyway. Okay?"

"We'll surprise Daddy!" she giggled, as she jumped up and down and skipped along the sidewalk. And **"Surprise him"** we, ahem, certainly did.

"Surprise! Surprise!" I announced as we scuttled through the large glass show room double doors.

Larry was perched beside a large desk in the company of a well tailored, comely young gal sitting with him, with their hands clasped. Their executive swivel chairs were facing each other, knees touching and their faces so close, in an almost butterfly kissing position and gazing into each others eyes in a way that didn't suggest serious, secretarial duties!

"Oh. Hi!" he sputtered as he sprang sheepishly from his chair, a guilty, embarrassed expression on his face.

"I just dropped by to show you Collette's new hair do." I said, as the lady at the desk quietly, discreetly disappeared. "We're scheduled to be on the "MR TOOTS" show at 4:00 P.M. Doesn't Collette look incredible, all decked out for the TV show?" I added. "I bet she'll be the prettiest one of all."

"Well, well. Daddy's girl sure looks nice." Larry said as he scooped her up into his arms. "You got a kiss for Daddy?" he urged. She giggled and planted a wet, drooly, slobbery, mooshy kiss, smack on his lips. I burst out laughing as he sleeve wiped the mushy Collette smooch from his mouth.

"Doesn't she look elegant?"

"She sure does." he agreed, with a chuckle, "but her kisses are something else, to be desired!"

"I wanted her to look classy for the Mr Toot show. A little replica of Dottie Lou, not the grubby, messy auto mechanic scene, like a Stock Car Racing Queen. Hah!" I teased, enjoying the pun.

"I've seen some pretty spectacular Speedway Queens in my time. Like Laurie Johnson in 1968, for instance. They're always single, between 17 and 21, firm butts, slicked up and smelling nice and definitely **not full of greese!**"

"OH, bye the way, Who was that woman you were almost eating up when I came in!?" I queried in an ironic coolness.

"Oh she's just a secretary from National Bank of Commerce, just down the street from us." he glibly replied. "They finance all our loans for customers purchasing our automobiles. She does the book work there for Arrow Chevrolet."

"They why isn't she **THERE** instead of **HERE?**" I meditated, concealing my irritation.

"Oh I sold a new one today." he announced, immediately changing the subject. "Nice commission there."

But my mind was not presently occupied with auto sales or commissions. I was still trying to digest the credibility of the presence of a secretary from the bank, To analyze her subtle speedy exit. She was somewhat attractive, except for an obvious, unusual imperfection. She seemed to tote a cranium disproportionately sized to her body, like the defects of water babies. (Hydrocephalus) She donned, in poor taste, a bouffant hair style which magnified the size difference, as well.

"OH WELL, Who cares?" I soliloquized. "Big Head is probably another one of Larry's Trophies." Trophies he imagined I was too naive or too stupid to be aware of. I could have mustered some rage and animosity if I had cared more!!

"Well, we have to skidaddle." I announced. "It'll be quite a challenge to keep this hyper four year old neat and clean for another hour. Try to save the hair do 'til we're finished with "Mr. Toot."

"What time is that?" He obviously hadn't been listening. His mind was elsewhere.

"It's on at 4:00 PM." I said in repetition. "Now be sure and watch the show. Don't forget. It took some real high pressure sales-pitch to get a ticket reservation, 'cuz there's so many on a waiting list. I gave a sad, sob story about Collette living way in Michigan and not being here very often, making it next to impossible to schedule a visit in advance."

"Daddy will be watching you, Sweetie." he addressed Collette and picked her up again. "Be a good girl for Dottie."

"Okay." she responded in a light carefree tone.

"I'm going to take home movie pictures if the studio will let me." I added. "Well bye now. Say bye to Daddy." I prompted as I clasped her teensy little hand in mine and slowly started toward the exit.

"Bye, bye Daddy, bye bye." she waved.

I hesitated, then added.

"Larry, be sure and turn the company TV on and watch. This will happen only once in her lifetime. It means a lot to a little girl."

"TV's always on here anyway."

"Don't forget. 4:00 P.M."

"What channel?"

"It's on WDSM, Channel six."

"I'll set it on six right away. Okay, Collette. I'll be watching for my little Angel. Daddy loves you."

"Bye, bye, Daddy."

* * * * * * *

Collette and I arrived at the studio a half-hour early. I spoke with the management for permission to take home movies. My camera required a light bar and I wasn't sure it wouldn't interfere with their cameras or their production. They very courteously granted me permission to set up whatever I needed. I was excited, while Collette just skipped around and played with other children present. She seemed unconcerned that they were strangers. She was not the least bit timid or fearful.

Mr Toot (Ray Paulson) was to our Arrowhead Country fans, what Mr. Roberts is to National TV fame. It was a children's half-hour production well received in the Twin Ports viewing area.

Mr. Toot spent a few minutes rehearsing with the kids beforehand, teaching them their parts, their cues of what to do and when. They were tutored on singing a couple lines of a skit, then instructed to turn around, face their chairs, and bend over like a bow. Mr Toot would then paddle their little behinds with a big soft paddle. When he had gently paddled each of them, they were told to turn around, face the audience and sit back down in their assigned chairs. I believe it was a birthday skit for everyone who had a birthday that week.

Only eight children, out of an audience of 25 or 30 were selected to be on stage. Collette was by far the youngest chosen. The tiniest of them all. A diminutive frame with a big personality. She wasn't the least bit shy or afraid, following all instructions to a tee, and smiling all the while as she answered his questions.

The eight children selected all received books, crayons and "Mr. Toot" certificates, as they perched in their special chairs. At the conclusion of the live taping of the program, the entire childrens audience in the studio received special treats of candy, cookies and juice. Mr Toot had interviewed all eight children, individually, on stage, asking them the usual questions. What's your name, where do you live, how old are you? What's your very favorite thing to do? I chuckled to myself, when Collette attested, She loved to sing, like Dottie.

I was so proud of Collette, but inwardly and reluctantly, I had to admit she definitely displayed the diverse, gregarious, ham, off the wall gene's of her dad. Silently I pondered, "I hope she also inherited, somewhere, a sense of honesty and value to put these attributes to admirable use."

"That was so fun!" she exclaimed as she skipped, bobbing up and down the sidewalk to the car, as we left the studio.

"Yes, and you were not afraid!" I added.

"Yes, and I was not afraid!" she chanted in repetition.

At home, I immediately called Arrow Chevrolet to touch base with Larry.

"Wasn't Collette just somethin' else? Such a little Princess." I clamored. "She's a gem. How did you like the show?" I asked, but without waiting for an answer, I gushed, complacently. "Didn't she do you proud?!! Only four, the youngest, the tiniest one there and remembering all her lines and instructions. How did **that grab you?** Daddy popped some buttons there, I bet!"

Silence on the line! "Hey, are you still there, Larry?"

"Yes, I'm here. Uh—oh—uh, Sorry, I forgot to watch."

* * * * * * *

"I can't baby-sit with Collette tonight." Charmaine announced at the supper table. "I promised to baby-sit for Sandy. I promised to watch her little girl."

"Wow! Larry is gone to Zimm. Something, some business with Ernie Brottom." I rambled on slowly, in thoughtful assessment. "Rogie, can I trust you to baby-sit for me? Could you watch over Collette while I work?"

Bryan, Rogies nine year old buddy was hangin' out with Rogie. "You can help too, Bryan." I added. "But you have to go home by nine, cuz the bigger kids will be gone." Bryan was two years younger than Rogie and I was skeptical about them being together, alone, without supervision. After all, two heads are better than one in inventing mischief.

"Are you sure you can handle this responsibility, Rogie? Without getting into trouble?"

"Sure, I can. How much money do I get?"

Rogie was always adamant and concerned with money and allowances. He was a little devious, juvenile King Midas."

I recalled one recent incident in particular, when I had been confronted with Larry, spontaneously inviting the **Winnen's** to come to our home for after-hour cocktails, without having first consulted me on the feasibility of such a plan.

The Winen's had never previously been to our residence. I was disturbed over the possible chaos condition of my house with unsupervised kids about, tossing toys and clothes, eating food and snacks and pop in every room. It could prove to be a disaster!

I quickly phoned home from the Gopher on my break. Roger answered and was home alone. Char was baby-sitting and Dale was galavanting somewhere. I issued instructions to Rogie. Told him to make sure the house was tidy and picked up. No dirty dishes strewed around in the sink or anywhere. The floor must be swept. I promised him $2 to clean and straighten it up, above and beyond his regular allowance. I explained, we were bringing first time guests, rather well-to-do guests home and didn't want to make a bad impression.

As we sashayed through the kitchen door with **Earl** and **Pat**, I marveled at how neat and clean it all appeared. Rogie had done an excellent job and was still up, leaning against the kitchen sink. Before I even removed my wrap, he rudely, disrespectfully thundered, "Where's my **TWO BUCKS?!**"

I was completely stunned and humiliated in front of our sophisticated guests, Embarrassed and annoyed by my eleven year old's insolence. "What are you doing still up?" I barked angrily, ignoring his comment. "You get straight to bed this minute. Right now! I'll deal with you in the morning."

* * * * * * *

"How much money do I get?" Rogie repeated.

"Two bucks." I said, "to watch Collette. It's only a short time before bed and then she'll just be sleeping, anyway. How hard can that be? **Everyone** to bed at nine. Remember at nine and that means you too, Rogie. No exceptions. Do you think you can handle that?"

"Sure I can." Rogie emphatically agreed.

I returned home immediately after my gig to make sure everything was okay and not in disarray. It would take merely a mild slip-up to prompt Sharon to discontinue our visitations with Collette as she was very obsessively over protective.

I sauntered to Dale's room to check on Collette, where we had set up an extra cot for her to sleep on. She was awake and softly whimpering, like a baby puppy.

"Rogie threw beer all over me. I'm all wet."

I examined her nightie. It seemed a bit damp. I marched upstairs to Rogie's bedroom to confront him & investigate the credibility of Collette's story.

Rogie was sprawled, face down, across his bed, fully clothed, A strong, stringent stench of stale beer or booze reeked and wrenched at my nostrils. On closer scrutiny I discovered Rogie was totally drunk and had barfed all over his bedsheet! He hadn't only tossed liquor on Collette, he had tossed it into his gullet as well!!

I was infuriated, losing my cool altogether! One of the first serious responsibilities I had placed on Rogie and he had bungled it. I yanked at his arms and mercilessly pulled him from his bed to the floor. I rolled up the soiled sheet and literally dragged the inebriated eleven year old down the stairs and into the bathroom, with him stumbling and tripping all the way down.

His eyes were incoherent and rolling as was his stomach, I assumed. He lowered his eyes, avoiding my intense angry glare.

"You're Smashed! What kind of baby-sitting do you call this?" I screamed. "I can see you've really been watching Collette HUH!" I turned the bath water on and let it run warm until the tub was half full.

"At eleven you think you're a Big Man, Rogie? Old enough to drink booze, huh! You're not even old enough to be trusted with a little job! If you think you're so Big. Big enough to get smashed, you're big enough to clean up after yourself. So, clean up your Puked Up Mess!!" I shrieked.

"Do I still get my two dollars?" he garbled, in muddled enunciation.

"Are you crazy? Absolutely Not! Two dollars for What?" I barked. "You can wash that sheet in the tub 'til it's spotlessly clean. **That's what YOU can do!!"**

He was on his knees, leaning on the tub. I chucked the vomit sheet into the tub water, tossed in some oxydol and disgruntled, left the room.

Rogie, in his drunken stupor, spent a half-hour tugging the big sheet back and forth, washing it in the sudsy water. I finally excused him from the bathroom, with the sheet still floating around and sent him back to bed. I was left to finish the mess.

Beer was not usually in stock at our house, so I investigated the liquor cabinet, and discovered, with a little studying, a half empty quart bottle of Petri Brandy, which had been a full unsealed bottle. Yes, Rogie had indeed raided my liquor cabinet.

After my severe, spontaneous reprimanding, and Rogie's up-chuck stomach experience, I hoped he'd not initiate that little fiasco a second time. And a lock was immediately installed on a once unguarded liquor cabinet!

* * * * * * *

"How are we going to get Collette home?" I asked Larry in conversation at the kitchen table. Her visit with us was about to end. It had disappeared so quickly.

"It's a long way to Lansing. We can't very well put her on a bus. She's too young for that. By automobile? Do you 'spose? You'd have to go it alone, cuz I 'd have to work. That's a long way, unless we traveled on my days off. Then, maybe I could go too."

"It's 690 miles to Lansing, one way." he muttered. "I'm goona have to think awhile on that one."

The following day Larry disclosed to my anxious surprise, "I've decided we'll take Collette back home by private plane. It's so much faster."

"Private Plane!? Holy Cow! How can we do that?"

"I have a friend, Doug Duncan, who owns his own plane. He's had a Pilot License for years, and he owes me." Larry chuckled cunningly. But I didn't ask why.

"That's a helluva long way by private plane!" I exclaimed.

"It's because it's a helluva long way, that private plane is the best, besides, I've already asked Doug. It's all arranged." Larry piped. "We'll leave from Superior early Sunday morning. Stop in Pellston, that's a half-way spot, refuel and have lunch, and then on to Lansing. We should be there by 15 hundred hours."

"That's scary!" I replied, in skeptical overtones.

"It's just as safe as commercial!" Larry quipped. "Doug is a very proficient, experienced pilot."

Sunday morning we boarded the one engine, four passenger plane. Larry up front with Doug. Collette and I slithered into the back seats. There were dual controls in the front, a set for each seat.

Before take-off, Doug began explaining the various uses for each gadget. Larry was in his glory, mesmerized, entranced by anything involving engines, be it assembly, composition, operating, whatever.

"How fast will this plane go?" Larry asked.

"You can't burn rubber in the sky, Larry!" I joshed, giggling as I volunteered my input, adding a little humor, I thought.

But they simply ignored my remark and continued. "We'll mostly stay in a cruising speed of 140 to 150 miles per hour." Doug retorted.

"That's top speed?"

"Oh no. This 'ole crate of mine can do up to 200 miles an hour, but for fuel economy it's best to keep 'er at about 140. Then the fuel will last for about 500 miles. Of course, take off power is the fastest. Faster than normal or cruising speeds."

"Sounds pretty simple. A piece of cake." Larry chortled.

"Not always. Speed depends a lot on the speed and direction of the wind, also. It can even change your course. Then adjustments have to be made, accordingly."

"Boy, I'd sure like to get my paws in control, flyin' one of these Baby's." Larry wistfully remarked, bursting with enthusiasm.

Collette was tenaciously engrossed with the new doll we had purchased for her. Our motive was to keep her occupied so she wouldn't be afraid of the flight. As I strapped myself and Collette into our seats for take-off, It was already obvious this trip would involve hours of boring, mechanical conversation. I already wished I had thought to bring something to read.

"What do these flight instruments achieve? What's their functions?" Larry asked, as we zoomed across the vibrant blue, embracing a scattered, fluffy nimbus cloud here and there.

"They inform me how my engine is operating and functioning. Some of the devices also instruct me in navigating correctly, directions etc. There are 12 gauges and meters for me to watch. Indicators for rate of climb, air speed, air pressure, fuel, etc. This one" he pointed, "the omnidirection finder is radio controlled and shows me what course to steer to reach destination." Doug chuckled, "You wouldn't want me to lose my way, now, would you?"

The plane handled rough and choppy in comparison to the flight we had made to California on a commercial aircraft.

"Seems kinda bumpy back here." I sputtered. "Is that normal?"

"Oh, we just hit little pockets now and then." Doug indifferently replied. "Not to worry. After all, this isn't the comfort of a commercial jet liner." he tittered, dismissing my skepticism.

"Oh Boy," I sighed. "I sure wish I had thought ahead and visited the restroom at the airport before we took off. This is going to be a long, uncomfortable ride, I'm afraid!" I confessed.

"No sweat!" Doug smirked. "We're just nearing the little Solon Springs airstrip. I'll land there for a brief Potty Call. Okay?"

In no time at all he landed and taxied to a stop.

"Wow!" I beamed. "This is really Nifty, after all! Makes me feel like a Rich Bitch! Not too shabby!!"

I hardly had my slacks zipped up and we were off again wingin' it, soaring the majestic skies.

"I know we're above water. We must have flown over Pellston, cuz I'm sure it's one of the small lakes, Burt or Douglas. Gas is getting low. We have to refuel pretty soon. I know that airstrip's here close." I heard Doug muttering and I realized I must have dozed off, for some time. We were half-way to Lansing!

Collette was still absorbed in dressing and undressing her new doll, and combing the tresses with a brush, which we had included in the ensemble.

Gawking out the window, I noticed the blue sunny sky had disappeared. Vanished while I slept, in lieu of fog, black clouds and threatening thunder,

"Well, where in the hell is that damn airstrip?" I heard Doug say. "I'll swing around again."

"It's gotta be right here. We're real close, according to the gauges. Aren't we?" Larry asked. He pointed. "What does this indicator tell us?"

Doug burst out laughing. "It tells us we're lost!!"

That remark immediately alerted my laid-back languid state of mind, bolting me into an uneasy perspective start. I suddenly sprung to a ninety degree upright position.

"We're lost!?" I gasped. "You're kidding!---------Aren't you?"

"Not to worry." Doug drawled, trying to assure me all was well.

"We'll soon find that airstrip, Dottie. Don't get your panties in a bundle!" Larry chided, in his usual flippant, complacent manner.

I maintained they were spoofing me or maybe the disappearance of clear blue sky created havoc with indicator direction info. Or perhaps the lack of visibility had become chaotic. I had heard Doug, earlier, explain that much of the course is determined by the pilot and his ability to locate visual air markers displayed on roads or roofs; names of towns, arrows, miles to this and that. Much information is annihilated when visibility becomes poor or nonexistant.

The innovative elements had completely reversed to tumultuous fury. The sky seemed to be predicting a turbulent storm approaching. With astronomical gusts of wind, the aircraft rocked and swayed and seemed wobbly and diminutive in the vast expanse of galaxy, struggling for leveling direction.

A sign of the cross was followed by several "Our Father's" and "Hail Mary's" erupting from the rear seat.

Oh to be four again! There was Collette, unaware of the turbulence and entertaining her dolly with zest, singing 'Itsy Bitsy Spider' and Twinkle Twinkle Little Star.

"Oh, there it is. The airstrip! I see it now." Doug exclaimed, chuckling. "I knew it was there all the time."

"You didn't have any doubt, did you?" Larry teased.

"Hell No!"

"Yeah, I believe you, Doug." Larry quirked. "Anyway, look, Your approach is perfect."

I circle rolled my arms, stretched my legs, wriggled my toes in pure inundated relief when my feet had touched the earth of Pellston, Michigan.

"We'll fuel up and find a little diner for some yummy for the tummy and then be on our way. Right Doug?" Larry dictated, imperviously, scrounging support from Doug in his decision.

"Sure, as soon as we can. This is the half-way mark to Lansing, Michigan." Doug added.

"No way are you getting Collette and I back on that plane today! Unless it clears up in a hurry! No Way!!" I screeched with adamant closure.

"You're kidding." Larry asserted, disgruntled. "This is only a very brief stop here, to fill up our plane and to fill up our tummy's. We're going to make Lansing today, and celebrate our anniversary. Remember? Our plans? A big fat steak at a fancy restaurant?"

"Our anniversary isn't 'til tomorrow. Anyway, whatever. I'm not getting on that plane in a storm!"

We had both appropriately dressed, moderately elaborate, at home, without a subsequent change of attire due to lack of luggage space on a small plane. Accommodations on a plane this size offered luggage space equivalent to our overnight bath and cosmetic cases plus Collette's clothes and toys.

"You'd have to use a tranquillizer gun and plug me with a dart to get me back on that plane in this advancing storm that's on our tail!" I tenaciously sputtered. "Just look at that sky! Are you crazy? You would jeopardize our lives?! Especially, your daughter's life?!"

"What's a little shower?" Larry quipped, "To get all hot and bothered about?"

The sky was a formidable black, shutting out the sun, precariously, making day appear to be late dusk. Ominous, ebony clouds were rolling angrily across the sky. Streaks of lightning were cascading, perpetually, dancing furiously, downward and across the horizon. The possibility of a premature speedy break in the weather seemed remote.

"I'll mosey over to the control tower and get a current report on the elements and flying conditions." Doug pensively proposed, with dampened enthusiasm. "These clouds and the storm track may just be hugging the surface and not very thick. Above this dilemma could be clear blue sky."

"Sure, we can probably fly way above this crap." Larry, unwavering, boomed resolutely. "A piece of cake. Where's your spirit of adventure, Dottie? Scared of a little shower! Hummmph!"

"You may be crazy, Larry, but I'm not. Don't undermine my prudent sense of danger. No way am I getting on that plane 'til it clears up!"

"This little whistle stop has a population of four or five hundred. Probably doesn't even have a motel." Larry argued. "A helluva place to be marooned."

"If it isn't too small to have an airstrip, it isn't too small to have a motel." I fired back at him defensively. Nothing, or no one would convince me to board that plane until the elements had reversed to clear blue sky.

Pellston is a little town of 429 people, nestled between Burt and Douglas Lakes, approximately twenty miles straight south of the Mackinac Straits.

We ambled around and luckily found a wee Ma's and Pa's cozy diner where the four of us shared delectable cusines of choice. I raised my coffee cup and proclaimed a toast, to planted feet on solid ground, the added a toast to our second Anniversary just hours away.

On private plane taking colette
home to Michigan (Pilot) Doug Duncan

Simpered smiles finally crossed their glum, sullen facial expressions when I gushed and giggled. "And they said it wouldn't last!"

We found a Hotel nearby, where we spent the night, as the winds raged and the rain pattered the window panes,

After an early breakfast we reboarded Dougs aircraft in smiles, but feeling a bit raunchy without a change in apparel.

"Happy Anniversary, Hon!" I giggled as we took to the sky.

"Yeah. yeah. yeah." Larry mumbled, indifferently.

♪♪♪

CHAPTER THIRTEEN

Shortly after we returned from Lansing, Mom called to let me know all my siblings were getting together Saturday morning to butcher chickens.

Each year Mom would purchase approximately 110 chicks from the catalog. I think it was from Montgomery Ward. The mailman delivered the chicks directly to the farm. They'd arrive in early May. Mom would care for the chicks and raise them to maturity to butcher and supply fresh poultry for five families. My siblings and I would divide, amongst the four of us, the cost of the chicks and the grain to adequately nourish them to adult size. Mom and Dad would receive one-fifth of the poultry for their efforts. These were not leghorn, laying hens, but the heavy breeds, Plymouth Rocks and Rhode Island Reds, with good meat-producing qualities, for the sole purpose of filling our freezers with fresh poultry for the winter.

"Gosh, Mom, Larry and I can't come Saturday, this Saturday or any Saturday for that matter, cuz of my work and his racing." I explained.

"Yes, I figured that," she replied, "but the other siblings have only week-ends off from their jobs so they have to butcher then."

"That's okay, Mom. Just keep our chickens squawking 'til Monday. That's my only night off and Larry can always get away from his job anytime. His position is fairly liberal. He can come and go pretty much as he pleases."

"Monday?"

"If that's okay?"

"Sure. I have no place to go and neither does Dad."

"How's Dad recuperating?"

"He gets tired easy, but he's getting better. He's glad to be home. Does a few easy chores around the house. He can rest so much better here, he says. In the hospital they woke him up to give him a sleeping pill!"

We both laughed.

"We'll see you Monday then, Mom."

"Okay."

Our share from the chicken coop was 22 chickens.

Larry didn't have so much as a remote inkling of the procedure of butchering chickens, so Dad pitched in at the old chopping block. He and I, retrospectively, took on the role we had shared when I was a teen-ager.

I'd hold the chicken by it's legs as Dad grasped the birds beak with his left hand, stretching the nick across the chopping block. With the axe clutched in his right hand, he'd swing it down across the extended neck and **CA-BOOM,** goodbye chicken head, in one clean sweep. I'd immediately toss the blood-squirting bird across the grass, where voluntary muscles kept it hopping and jumping for a couple minutes.

"Boy, that's **GROSS!** Char blurted, with a screwed-up repulsed expression on her face.

Our scalding, plucking process was, probably another unconventional, obsolete procedure, as well. Mom maintained consistant boiling water on the kitchen stove. We'd fill milk pails approximately half-full of the boiling water and holding the chickens by the legs, we'd immerse the bird into the water, up and down several times, pause, then pull it out and test the feather resistance by attempting to detach a feather. If they were still adhering firmly to the stem, we'd reinsert the bird to the water, over and over, consecutively, until the feathers would easily release from the stems.

Char, Rogie and Larry assumed responsibility for scalding and plucking feathers.

Char crinkled her nose and again complained, "Yuk, this is really **GROSS** too!"

I chuckled, unsympathetically, unmoved. "Hey, everyone eats! So everyone works!"

I was unanimously elected, without a caucus, to gut the chickens. I had to remove the anus, the intestines and all unedible insides, separating the giblets and thoroughly washing the carcus. The country in me didn't find this process to be the least bit Gross, as my city-slicker family attested.

Larry assisted in the wrapping and packaging for the freezer.

Twenty-two chickens, dressed, furnished us with 95 pounds, thirteen ounces of fresh, farm-fed poultry. This was without injected hormones, like force fed growth at commercial farms. Absolute HEALTHY meat for winter sustenance.

The total cost for the chicks plus the grain, divided four ways was $28.84, bringing the price of our wholesome, healthy, lip-smackin', saliva drippin' meat to the colossal, enormous price of 30¢ a pound! The average size of the fowl was 4.4 pounds per bird of dressed meat.

These statistics are 100% accurate, as I attained them from Mothers Farm Journal of 1971.

Larry had in our brief two years of bumpy marriage, introduced me, persuaded me, acquainted me, launched me and often shocked me with innumerable unexpected **FIRSTS** in my life! I finally gloated, with pleasure, over this one profound (ahem) experience I had over on him! Butchering Chichens was a Very Definite **FIRST** for Larry!!

* * * * * * *

Larry was struggling with time to get his #61 in excellent tip top condition for the Labor Day Weekend. He was diligently attempting to iron out the bugs before the Canadian Invitationals were solely posted on the prime time of his agenda. Even after all the trial and error research, he was still having difficulties **trial testing** synthetic oil. He was hoping to annihilate some of these problems before Canada. Labor Day was the finale of the Stock Car Racing Season for the Tri-State Racing Association. I didn't see much of Larry during those crucial Stock Car preparation times for the two gigantic week-ends ahead.

Labor Day races were featuring Powder Puff and Demolition Derby's to awe the spectators. So I gave Larry my old, beat-up Buick that had seen a trip to Nashville to record "One More Memory" with Bob Logergren. She had also succumbed and then recovered from a crushed passenger side, procured from a speeding motorist torpedoing through a stop sign enroute to Minneapolis with Bob and his Dad, Louie to see a Twins game.

My poor Buick had been through a lot and I thought it was time to put her out to pasture. However, she didn't do much grazing before she met her demise, was crushed and ground up in the second lap, crumpled and rendered to scrap iron, pet food for the steel industry. Poor Thing.

* * * * * * *

The door burst open and in rushed Larry, just as I was finishing supper dishes.

"What's all the hurry?" I asked.

"I've just been offered a partnership in a snowmobile business with Kenny Anderson!" he exclaimed, out of breath. "And for only $300!"

"Gotta be a catch to that, somehow." I said. "Three hundred bucks! That's peanuts."

"I know, but these guys are broke and are pressed to come up with money for their expenses to Canada. They offered it to me for some quick cash."

"Who's that nuts?" I asked, slowly drying my hands on a kitchen towel, finishing the dampness on my slacks.

"Wilhelm and Eliason! Boy I scraped up 200 bucks in a hurry, before they changed their minds. Can you borrow me the other hundred?" he asked.

"I s'pose," I replied, going for my purse.

Larry purchased the franchise partnership for $300 from Dick Wilhelm and George Eliason. He and Kenny searched and discovered a suitable vacant shop on Grand Avenue available to rent. It was between West End and West Duluth and with adequate parking. They remodeled, decorated and quickly set up a presentable efficacious show room to display, in a grandeur manner their products plus an area to sell parts and service machines.

The snowmobile franchise was from the Coleman Company, offering, a first time, new line of snowmobiles called Skiroule. The machines were green and white and similar, I thought, in appearance, to the John Deere line of machinery. The Coleman Company also offered a sufficient line of snowmobile accessories and parts.

They supplied a full line of **pragmatic** snowmobile wear and also a **glamourous** line of attire and accessories to interest the flair of the ladies, designed in green and white color combinations, in elegant taste to smartly match their machines.

Larry, now worked the Skiroule Shop in the evenings and Arrow Chevrolet during the days, He'd be in and out of both places and it was almost impossible to locate his whereabouts most of the time. However, he always managed, somehow, to squeeze in and maneuver a number of hours in his garage to **Repair and Prepare his #61** for the Canadian Races.

Larry took most of his pit crew and his Hardway Team to accompany him to Canada. They were all engaged in packing for the gigantic week-end ahead, tents, grub, mini bikes, sleeping bags, the usual camping paraphernalia. He never once asked me to join him, as he had dogmatically persuaded, the one time before we were married, when he was persistantly hustling me.

Dale was always eager to take up with Larry because Larry's pit crew consisted of a lot of his buddies. Dave Willis and Tom Swizlak; learning welding in "Shop" at school, were using Larry's hobby as a learning process to achieve more skill. Dale, John Hoban and Dean Nevcaw were Larry's student mechanics and go-fers, changing tires, filling depleting gas tanks, wiping windshields, etc. etc.

What more could a group of teen-agers ask for than a free mini vacation with a teacher as liberal as Larry, supervising in the grey area kids love. Teaching them mechanics, welding, but also how to get what you want, even if it means cheating, lying or stealing, whatever it takes to come out on top. I had the assumption Larry was teaching the boys the art of womanizing as well and how to be discreet. If he only knew his discretions weren't at all as discreet and cryptic as he assumed. I just didn't bother pursuing or investigating the evidence. It didn't seem worth the trouble, just a waste of time. Once in a while he'd feign an impassioned need to ravish me. I was told, on several occasions, heresy, from some of his friends that, quote, "She's only good for once or twice a month." unquote. Maybe he was right. It would explain my blasé indifference.

Before I knew it, the middle of September had rolled around and he and the boys were gone, off to Rollerside Racetrack in Canada.

In Larry's and my boys absence I pampered myself and embraced my sudden freedom, basking in my complacent leisure time, mostly at the Gopher. I had no one to be accountable to. The only one at home was Charmaine and she would be asleep not needing my attention.

The upstairs restaurant and bar crew were organizing a Baby Shower party for Dick Grantley, our affable, loveable Bartender. They were arranging the private party to take place the next day, Sunday afternoon, downstairs, as the Gopher was closed on Sunday's.

None of us knew Dick's wife, so in the bizarre ingenuity of the Gopher coterie, it was planned, not as a serious, typical Baby Shower, but as a daffy, zaney get-together, honoring Dick as the new "Father in Waiting."

Saturday night after the bar closed and music was silenced, we all participated setting up party tables and decorating the downstairs for the approaching bash.

Gene O'Demarra had eminently popped in to visit the Tumbleweeds Friday and Saturday nights, consecutively. He always seemed, to me, so pensively alone and wistfully searching for conversation and companionship. Feeling empathetic, I casually invited him to stick around for a couple of after hour high balls if he so chose to and could tolerate the wacky, outrageous bunch!

"I'd love to." he purred, openly delighted.

We all pulled together to decorate a scroungy little tree at the far side of the bar room. It was grey and barren, having lost all it's summer green leaves. For ornaments we hung safety pins, 4oz. baby bottles, baby bibs, rattles, topping it off with condoms. The garland was a mixture, entwined together of pink and blue ribbon. We topped the tree with a little stuffed Teddy Bear.

"You people really are crazy!" Gene chuckled, as he investigated our improvised bizarre creations. Several folk added their own genius in the form of beer cans, cigarette packs and numerous other brain storms, adding to the ludicrous hysteria.

"Oh yes, I guess we do know how to have fun!" I chortled.

"And it's all such innocent fun!" Vivian winked.

"This is Dick's Private Bash. His wife isn't even invited tomorrow."
I giggled.

"Does she know about the party?" Gene asked.

"I don't know. It never occurred to me to ask. It's just a little get-together with Dick's working associates. Just a little nonsense, but of course we'll all bring baby gifts, tomorrow for Dick, just like a typical Baby Shower."

"What does Dick think about it?"

"Dick is kinda soft spoken and shy. We don't know how he'll respond. WE just told him it's a baby shower for him—**SHOW UP— and we hope he has a good sense of humor! He'll probably be** pretty embarrassed. Dick's rather modest."

"Everyone here at the Gopher loves to party." Delores snickered. "I don't think Dick will object a bit."

"Still waters run deep!" Cal grinned, with a sly wink.

As the crew, of an approximate dozen, finished the decorating set up, we all graduated to the bar and booths with beers and cocktails in hand, relaxing and admiring our trumped-up creativity. I plopped into a booth beside Vivian to visit. Gene and Delores joined us in the seat across from Vivian and I.

After a bit of nonsensical chit-chat Delores asked, "Where's Gene? He asked me to pick up something in a gift for Dick for tomorrow. I gotta go talk to him."

"I'm right here beside you!" Gene joshed, chuckling.

"No. No. I mean the other Gene." she laughed as she excused herself and slithered from the booth.

"He's over at the end of the bar." Vivian remarked, as she visually squinted, scanning the bar area. "He's talking to someone, ah—er—uh, I guess he's talking to Randy. When did he sneak into our midst?" she smiled coquetishly.

I winked, knowingly, at Vivian and rose to let her out of the booth.

"You know, I'm going to call you Geno." I babbled. "Korn is Gene to almost everyone. Just a few of us real close friends and old acquaintances call him Korn."

"That's fine." he replied. "I kinda like that."

"It would be less confusing." I added, "So when we gossip and talk behind your back, we'll be precise in who we're Puttin' the Shuck On!"

"Puttin' the Shuck On! Wherever do you come up with all that lingo?" he continued the banter.

"It's probably a Toby term." I laughed. "He has a vocabulary all of his own."

"It's better to be talked about, anyway, than never mentioned. Where's your hubby?"

"Who cares?" I sputtered, grinning in friendly banter. He smiled faintly and I couldn't distinguish if he knew I was jesting and trying to keep the conversation light and nonsensical.

"Is he here?" he asked again.

"He's in Canada, racing at the Canadian Invitationals." I seriously replied. "Just for the weekend. He attends every year. It's a big thing, I guess, with him and the Racing Association."

"He's really not around much, is he?"

"He comes in sometimes, after the local races. It gets to be old hat, watching your wife work, after awhile and he's not very hep on music or dancing anyway."

"How can anyone not like music?"

"It's not that he doesn't like music." I passively defended him. "It's just not one of his priorities. When racers and pit crews and their fans get together, all you hear is pistons and crank shafts and roll bars and rear ends and ratio's and top ends and well, they gibber for hours and hours about junk like that."

"It's not junk to them, I'd guess!" he assessed.

"No, I guess not. We had an after hours party at our house last fall, after the racing banquet in Proctor, the finale of the racing season. My husband invited his racing friends and fans and I invited my music bunch from the Gopher. We had 102 folk squeezed into my little, inadequate bungalow, wall to wall people. The living room was filled with music, guitars aplinkin', Korn and Toby pickin' and a grinnin', people crominizing. The kitchen was wall to wall dugans, wrestling opinions on building street stock, gas octane and synthetic oil versus whatever, so forth and so on."

"You don't sound a whole lot enthused." he chuckled.

"I guess not."

"Do you have children?" he asked, abruptly changing the subject.

"Doesn't everyone?" I tittered, trying to disperse the serious vein of conversation.

"How many kids do you have?" he asked.

"I have three. Two boys and a girl. The girl in the middle."

"Do they have names?" he teased.

"I have a Dale, a Roger, who are both with their father in Canada and a gal, my husband and I named Charmaine, after a favorite song we loved to dance to."

"I thought, or you said he didn't like to dance."

"They're not Larrys. My first husband was killed in an auto accident. The kids were all his."

"Your current husband is Larry? What's the last name, which would be your name."

"Oh ho ho, a sly way to weasel out my name." I blathered. "My last name is vonGillern."

"that definitely sounds German."

"It is. Boy are you full of questions tonight. I feel like I must be on Jeopardy! Let's talk about you. Enough about me! Do you have kids?"

"Sure do. Two boys, two girls. Rich and Leonard, Arlene and the baby is Jeanette."

"Where are you hiding them?"

"they are with their mother in Burtrum, Minnesota, that's near Alexandria."

"And you're divorced?"

"Well no, not exactly." he replied. I'm separated."

"But that's the same as being married!" I replied.

"No Way!" he asserted, intrusively. "Absolutely not! It's a four year legal separation. Awarded in Family Court. Papers were drawn up by a competent lawyer and executed by a residing Judge. Details of custody of children were listed in black and white and notarized like any divorce decree."

"Why go through all that rig-a-ma-row? Why not just get a divorce and be done with it?" I asked.

"Well, I'm Catholic." he revealed. "It seemed the only thing to do, at the time, when you don't get along with someone. The right thing to do."

"I'm catholic too," I responded, "But I sure wouldn't go that route. It gave you freedom, but you're not **FREE!** What a bummer!"

"I guess I'm more serious about my **religion**. The Catholic Church does not condone divorce, but will accept forgiveness for Separation."

"Forgive me, Geno, but I don't think the church is **God!**"

"Maybe not. I thought I had the calling to be a priest when I was a young lad. I was active as an alter boy for quite some time. Those teachings in adolescence just seem to adher and linger with a person. Even long after a wife and four kids, it influences you thinking."

We were so perceptively absorbed in our effusive, ambivalent exchange of ideas, I hadn't even noticed the Gopher gang had thinned out, with only four or five still exchanging conversation and hospitality, at the bar.

"I still regret at times, that I missed my real calling. I should have studied the priesthood, at least givin' it a try." he continued. "When I was an alter boy it seemed the appropriate direction for me, but then puberty arrived and my calling took flight. Raging Hormones bombarded my teenage groins and consumed my thoughts and WOW! I discovered **GIRLS!"**

"You're too attractive to be a priest anyway." I joshed, kidding him, trying to lighten the subject.

"If you have the calling, appearance has no bearing on the direction your life will take." He was dead serious.

"I s'pose not, but what a waste!" I giggled, raising my eyebrows and wetting my lips in a suggestive, sensuous flirt.

"It's never a **WASTE TO LOVE GOD!"** he voiced, intensely in earnest.

"Wow! Sorry!" I rolled my eyes and smacked my forehead with the heel of my palm in a **forgive me** gesture. I made a diffident sign of the cross. He didn't laugh. He didn't smile. I couldn't perceive his emotions. Perhaps he was thinking I was belittling his faith. Maybe ironically making light of his Spirituality. "Well, if somber seriousness is what he wants, Serious I can get too." I soliloquized and volunteered my indepth opinions on Catholicism!!

"The Catholic Church has a lot of rules I can't follow." I remarked. "I have my own convictions and so in many instances I just can't agree with their doctrine. However I could never be anything but Catholic."

"Yes, I believe I'm Catholic for life too." he replied.

"I just can't believe I'll go to Hell for missing Mass on Sunday, or eating meat on Friday, from an all merciful, forgiving God! And I just can't swallow the dogma of telling my sins to a priest. That his absolution makes it any more forgivable than my confessing directly to Jesus. He hears all, see's all, know's all. Isn't that correct? Isn't that in the Bible, somewhere?"

He divulged a faint diminutive smile and mini dimples creased the ruddy glow of his cheeks. "We're all entitled to our opinions I suppose." he timidly muttered, withdrawing a point of view.

"Furthermore, I don't believe in their celibacy thing, either. How can a priest be a competent counselor, instructing catholics on marriage, difficulties of raising children or struggling with finances and job security, when he's never experienced any of those problems himself. It's like learning to drive a car from a book, without road practice. I have trouble accepting that law as if it's the doctrine of the Lord! I think a priest should marry just like the Protestant Ministers do."

"That may be, but------"

"In my estimation," I interrupted, "Priests, bishops, cardinals are merely teachers. Teachers of religion and theology. My brother is a public school teacher, an educator in woodwork and Shop. Does that make him better? A teacher is not a God nor a Saint. A teacher is a teacher is a teacher."

"Well, well, you certainly are opinionated." he delicately responded, as he disconcertedly glanced around at the few remaining folks, as if checking to see if anyone might be evesdropping in our diverse discussion.

"Never discuss religion or politics is the rule." he remarked with a simpered smile. "No use to get hyper and stressed over the small stuff!"

"I agree. You better believe it. I guess I'd better call it a night and get my Dupa home! Dupa, that's polish for Fanny." I added.

"Oh, you're Polish? Hmmmm—no wonder. That explains the beautiful, profound, deep brown eyes. Of course, brown implying "She's Full of Shit", as I remember." he winked. "Your cliche, not mine. And I believe, I've heard told, the Polish are very stubborn and opinionated as well, I might add."

"And what nationality are you?"

"A smidgen of German, but mostly Irish."

"That explains why you're such a stinker, a leprechaun and opinionated seems to be a trait of the Irish as well." I bantered as I rose to depart, singing, ♪ "When Irish eyes are ♪ lyin', Sure 'tis hard to ♪ tell what's true. Cuz the guiling dimples in their cheeks,--and—and—it's time to say adieu. ♪ I couldn't think of another smart-aleck line to rhyme." I admitted, grinning. "So that will have to do."

"Hey! That rhymes too." he tittered. "Are you parked out back?"

"Yes, I always park right next to the back exit."

"I'll walk you to your car." he announced.

When we approached my Chevy, he opened the door and I slithered in behind the steering wheel. Rolling down my window, I babbled, "If you're still in town tomorrow, Geno, why don't you join our party downstairs tomorrow afternoon?"

"Gosh! It's private. Isn't it?"

"Yes, but I'm inviting you. We're allowed guests. When do you go back to Alabama?"

"I'm catching a flight Monday morning for Mobile."

"It's an afternoon Bash. The rest of the place is closed on Sundays and you know most of the gang. There'll be plenty of time left for you to catch some shut-eye before flight time." I paused, Then nonchalantly added, "Well, it's up to you."

"Maybe—hmm—I might just do that."

"okay, maybe we'll see you tomorrow." I buzzed as I threw my tranny into reverse. "See you. If not tomorrow, then whenever."

♪♪♪

CHAPTER FOURTEEN

"What are you wrapping, Mom?" Char asked.

We had just returned from Sunday Mass at St. Joseph's, followed by brunch at Bridgeman's. It resulted in a quiet Mother-Daughter time together with no male interference to disrupt our very connecting morning. It had been a one to one, incredible harmonious tété-a-tété, of which we had too few.

"Oh, it's just a gift for a Baby Shower." I replied.

"A Baby Shower gift! Ooooh—oooh—oooh! Let me see! Let me see!"

Char was mesmerized by babies. She loved baby-sitting for infants. She was always thrilled and elated wherever, whenever baby entities were present.

Upon her excited persuasion I allowed her to peek into the box, remove and examine the already folded baby garment, before final wrapping.

"Oh for cute!" she gushed, holding the garment up to view. She fondled it thoroughly and at length, then finally refolded and replaced it into the gift box. . It was a green and white Trundle Bundle, a sleepwear, with a diminutive applique of a tiny teddy bear in the upper right hand corner.

"Who is it for? Who's having a baby?"

"It's for a bartender at the Gopher" I replied. "He's been here several times at some of my parties, but I don't think you ever saw him. It's always late, after work. His name is Dick Grantly."

"A guy?!" she blurted and cracked up, laughing.

"Well he did have a little part in it, you know. A tiny part. It's mostly woman's work, having babies!" I giggled as I began rewrapping the gift, putting final touches on the package. Charmaine watched intensely, as I consstrued a large bow, with a rattle for a final touch on the gift box.

"I s'pose I'll soon be wrapping another gift box in a couple weeks. huh?" I remarked.

Charmaine's face lit up and she broke into a wide grin, knowingly grasping my implication. "Yes, in just two weeks you'll be fourteen! How about that?" I sighed thoughtfully, "Gosh, you kids are getting big." I murmured, under my breath, almost inaudible. "Three, six and nine. How long have I been telling people that—so they can't mathematically compute my age?"

"Three, six and nine?" Char disclosed an enigmatic smile and raised her eyebrows in question. "Three, six and nine. What does that mean—any—"

"It's a long story." I interrupted. "Some day I'll explain, but it wouldn't be interesting to you anyway." was my nebulous reply. "The shower is this afternoon, so I'll have to leave early. I hate to leave you all alone, Char, with nobody else home. That's kinda sad, huh?"

"No it's not. It's a relief with no Bossy Brothers around. Yipee! Roberta or Gary will probably come over, anyway."

"You don't mind?"

"No. It's okay, Mom. Where's the Shower?"

"It's downstairs of the Gopher, The Gopher is closed on Sundays so we have the place to ourselves to party. None of us know Dick's wife, so that's why we decided to have the Baby Shower On Dick instead."

"You guys are sure silly. Is it a surprise party?"

"No. He knows. We just sorta ordered him to show up at 3:00 P.M., to celebrate his soon becoming a daddy. His wife is due in three weeks. I'll be leaving at 2:30 so you will have to fend for yourself when you get hungry. Okay? There's pizza."

"Sure." she replied. "That's easy. Maybe Gary and Roberta can share a pizza with me."

"Yes, that's good."

"And there's umm—yum, ice cream in the freezer too!" she beamed a whimsical smile.

* * * * * * *

I slipped down the back stairway to the Gopher Bash at 3:00 P.M. through the one door left unlocked, and joined a sizeable group with party already in progress. Hearty voices and infectious laughter assaulted my ear drums as I blended into the intoxicating festivity of tipping cocktails and **swapping lies,** (A Toby idiom).

I deliberately scanned the lounge to locate Dick and realized he hadn't yet arrived. "Good." I told myself. I didn't want to miss his entry or the expression on his face when he observed our bizarre, decorative ingenuity!

I ordered a drink and joined Vivian, Delores, Judy and Val engrossed in idle chit chat, across the room. They were flocked in the typical waitress clutch. They all laughed, heartily as I approached.

"What's so funny?" I quipped.

"Oh that crazy joke! Delores, tell it to Dottie." Judy urged.

"Oh, okay." Delores eagerly began, "Oh this guy and his wife went to the husband's Boss's Appreciation Party for the employees and the husband got totally wiped out. The next morning he awoke, groaning, holding his head with a bursting headache and a hangover—Big Time! he said to his wife, "Boy, I sure got smashed last night. How did I do? Did I behave okay?"

"You made a complete ASS of yourself!" she replied. "You told the Boss, a chimpanzee could do a better job of running the business than him. That he was a Big PRICK and then you dropped your drawers and mooned him, right there, in front of everyone!!"

"NO! What did he do?" he asked.

"Whatta you think he did? **He FIRED YOU!"**

"Well, he's an ass, anyway. Who cares!? **Fuck Him!!"**

"**I Did.** You go back to work on Monday." she replied.

Everyone chuckled a second time.

"I'd sure love to do that to Dandrea!" Val tittered. She had been intrigued and beguiled with the boss for sometime, with no apparent success.

Suddenly someone yelled. "Hey, Shushh! Everyone! Dick is now arriving at the top of the stairs!"

The buzz of the bar diminished and all eyes were turned to the opening at the foot of the enclosed stairway.

Coming around the corner from the stairway landing stood, quiet, timid, passive, modest, "ahem" Dick Grantley in all his glory. He was clad in ladies attire, donning make-up, eye shadow, mascara; a descript ensemble, topped off with bright, crimson lipstick. His crest was bedecked with a whispy, bouncy brown wig. A colossal, bulging belly protruded out front, gigantic and comparable to any expectant mother about to deliver. Breasts, as well, were prominent and rounded, appearing about to lactate.

A mischievous grin stretched across Dick's face as we all roared with contagious laughter. We were obviously, deviously fooled.

"Damn, I'm good!!" he snickered.

We had all been, unassumingly initiated into observing another side of quiet, reserved Dick. We realized he had been truly "IN Waiting", in on the gag all along, playing his role to the fullest, with droll genius.

A long restaurant table was brimming over with scrumptious pot luck. A small cocktail table was piled sky-high with wrapped gifts for

Dick. John Dandrea had set the jukebox for free music and the pool table for free pool.

"What a Boss!! What a Boss!" someone exclaimed.

The three employed Gopher Bartenders, Cal, Dick and Steve donated their time, taking turns, serving our cocktail orders from behind the bar. Dick, however, was soon forced to dismiss his chic, lady hi heels in exchange for his trusty old loafters. He was unable to function fixing cocktails in heels, nor fancy toe tappin' frolic on the dance floor.

Delores scrounged up a 30 cup percolator from upstairs and began brewing coffee for a select few who preferred coffee to beer or liquor.

The Pregnant Dick asked me to dance.

"I can't get close to you, Dick." I teased. "What a bummer!! My one chance to legitimately hug and squeeze the livin' daylights out of you and I can't even get near!"

"Yeah!" faking disappointment, "I've been waiting for a chance like this too, for—well for a long time and now my one and only chance has bombed!!" returning the innocent banter.

We both snickered. Then a tap on my shoulder and on Dick's, as well, found others cutting into our toe tappin' extravaganza. Judy grabbed Dick and swiftly twirled him around to the beat of the music. As I turned to leave the floor, looking over my shoulder, I came face to face with Geno, his slightly dimpled cheeks embracing a small, sly smile.

"Well, Hi there. Glad you could join us." I breathlessly sputtered, winded from the fast two-steps Dick and I had just shared.

I began to sashay toward the bar room.

"Hey! Not so fast." Geno purred. "This dance is mine!" He caught my arm and prepensely led me into a fast gitter-bug that soon left us both spent, gasping for air. We plopped ourselves in a near-by booth, surrendering the dance to catch our breath.

"Whew! I—I—I think I need to enroll myself into some kind of physical fitness program." he muttered, out of wind.

"Hey, that was only one dance for you!" I teased. "I just finished bouncing around a two-step with Dick, besides, --Oh no, not one, we actually whirled a couple two-steps. Anyway I guess I could actually use a little weight-lifting calisthenics, as well. I'm not supporting the greatest of energy levels either. I admitted.

Jan joined us and quickly coaxed Geno to dance with her. "That's if you're careful and don't hold me too close, 'cuz my big boobs might get in the way and throw off your balance and lose the beat." she laughed sanctimoniously.

With a simpered smile Geno rose to dance, looked my way and winked. "Oh—yes." he droned. "I see the bosom handicap. I promise I'll try to be ever so careful." with a hint of ironic laughter emerging.

"Hey, Dottie P. Lou, let's get out there and step on each others toes." Korn joshed and I could see Delores still tugging persuasively on Toby's arm trying to convince him to get out on the floor with her, to no avail. Toby never ever danced.

As we tipped cocktails with party gusto, someone suggested we jam a bit. That we dig out the guitar and do some **crominizing.** Toby sashayed over to our conglomeration of instruments all covered, on the stage and confiscated Korn's flat top from under the storage sheet covers. And the singing began in earnest with everyone joining in in sync with Korn's accompaniment. Everyone crooned the usual **Tumbleweed** favorites as beautiful controlled refrains and some not so beautiful bounced off the Gopher walls!

Toby warbled his usual two songs, **My Bucket's Got a Hole In It** and **You Always Hurt The One You Love,** then handed the rhythm guitar back to Korn.

"Dottie, sing a song or crominize one with me." Korn suggested.

"Sure. How about a parody of **The Party's Over?**"

"Where'd that come from?"

"I wrote it of course. Me and my Naughty Dottie mind. I began singing as he accompanied me on the guitar. "Turn out ♪ the lights, the party's startin'. That's when all good things begin.♪ Turn out the lights, the party's swingin' ♪ When the lights come on we'll all be more than friends." Everyone giggled.

"Hey, there's more!" I interrupted the laughter.

♪"What a crazy, crazy party." I belted. "Never seen such ♪ horney people. Kissin', neckin', boinkin', look at them, they're havin' fun. But look at me, ♪ I'm almost cryin', got my period ♪ just this mornin' and for me, you see, tonight **The Party's Over!"** ♪

I had front stage and was royally rewarded with laughter and applause, a fanning for my pampered ego.

"I can sure beat that! Piece of cake!" Delores, our favorite lounge waitress boasted, unabashed. She sang Norman's Bar, Gladdie's song. "I wanna play piano in a whorehouse.♪ That's always been my one desire.♪ Some folks own ranches or big homes down in Butte. But, I wanna tinkle the ivory in a house of ill repute. Don't laugh at my humble avocation,♪ 'cuz copulation's here to stay. To hell with fame and riches. I wanna play for them 'ole bitches. I wanna play piano in a whorehouse!" Delores dramatically stretched out her arms wide and sprang into a climactic curtsy as laughter emerged everywhere.

In competition I piped in, interrupting the laughter in a Connie Smith tune, belting loudly, "Once a day, every day ♪ all day long!" the ending tag of her hit. Then slowly, with drama, "I'm so tired." I fictionalized a tired yawn, hand to my mouth. "I'm losing sleep.♪ Can't we please cut down to once a week?" A parody contest seemed to be in progress.

Myrna had been eyeing us up in what I assumed was quiet embarrassment. She was a recent addition to the Gopher employees, upstairs, on kitchen detail, seemingly quiet and shy. Someone had thoughtfully invited her attempting, whole heartedly to include her in our Gopher functions above and beyond the hum drum of mere labor.

She had remained all afternoon, passively hugging the sidelines, not adding or joining in in anything. She was just placidly observing the **Party Animal** antics, I assumed. Perhaps too stunned to join in by our crazy, bold, risque mischief to get involved.

Then we noticed she waved, a half timid wave for attention. She muttered a soft, reluctant, almost inaudible, "I have one."

Everyone became suddenly silent, surrendering the floor to Myrna.

"Go ahead." Korn coaxed.

"Sure Myrna, let 'er fly." We all wheedled in compliance.

She murmured softly, "You've heard of the song, haven't you? 'Nothin; could be finer than to be in Carolina,♪ in the mor-or-or-nin'?♪ Right?"

"Oh sure." We chimed in unison.

"It's the only parody I know." She began crooning in a soft pleasant soprano voice. ♪ "Nothin' could be finer than your tongue in my vagina in the mor-or-or-nin'.♪ Nothin' could be sweeter than my lips around your peter in the mor-or-or-nin."♪

A burst of laughter, applause and in total surprise someone spurted, "Omigod! Wow!"

Unsuspecting Delores and I were smack, dab, shot out of the saddle! Quiet, wholesome, shy Myrna had just upstaged both of us. There's no limit to the ad lib ludicrous surprises at a Gopher shindig. Oh yes,

Myrna had certainly passed initiation admittance, with flying colors, into our **Party Animal** coterie.

The afternoon was rapidly slipping away, as it does when friends are having fun. The merrymaking diversions of dancing, singing, eating, drinking, plus the nonsensical chit-chat of swapping blarney lies and telling jokes constituted to hastily disappearing hours.

Geno and I, somehow or other became fixed on a variety train of topics as though we were crusading a battle or contest of intellect, resulting in stimulating conversation that never ended in uncomfortable silence. Discussions moved, as we settled in a bar room booth, in so many diverse directions and theories I was intrigued. I hadn't compatibly experienced an exchange of ideas; profound, indepth thoughts in nearly 20 years, since Roger, my first husband and I had exchanged soul mate, wrenching, sharing times in the early years of our marriage before alcohol had sadly taken control of our lives. All the men in my life, ever since had been somewhat shallow and superficial with little intellect acuity. Chatter had mostly hovered around nonsensical subjects or humorous jargon, pale in comparison.

I was charmed by Geno's indepth, philosophical thoughts ideas and ethics. Topic after topic discursively arose and it seemed we were exploring or perhaps challenging each others minds. Whatever it was, I was captivated by the intensity in his beliefs. Whether the topic was family, religion, careers politics, etc, I was even more amazed that his views were concertedly almost always parallel with mine. It was substantially as though we were clones in thought. "No wonder," I mused, "I previously had never been drawn to him." We were too much alike! Only **opposites** attract."

As we continued our innocuous, impassioned exchange of views, we unintentionally became oblivious to the blaring jukebox and the noisy, lively party around us. Then friends interrupted and lectured us on our discourteous indifference and pointed out our inconsiderate behavior by not mixing with our Bash Buddies. All in kindly, affection of course.

"Say, you guys, get with the program!" Vivian scolded, as she began pulling Geno from the booth. "Dance with me, you Terd." She shifted her attention in my direction. "Don't hog him all to yourself, Dottie." she chided amicably. "He's the best Jitter-bugger partner here on the floor when—I mean **IF** you can **GET** him on the floor?!"

"Yeah!" Delores piped in, "You have to dance with me too, Gene. You're too good a dancer to just waste all that talent plopped in a booth on your fanny all day!"

"Oooh, ooh, oooh, I'm soooo-sorry." I swooned. "I wasn't hoggin' the Jitter-bug King. We were only yackety—yackin', swappin' lies." I lamely apologized, grinning. I thoughtfully pondered, how it reminded me of my brother Gerry, who was a skilled dancer, as well, and one of the few men who had accomplished the jitter-bug steps. He too, was always hounded by the gals to dance, dance, dance until he was exhausted. His sisters were among the most powerful of the badgers!

Vickie came a trippin' down the stairs with Little Joe's sister, Rivea, trupsin' behind. I knew Little Joe would be only minutes behind them. That would certainly make Jan's day! Unless of course Ben showed up as well! Ahem.

"Hey, You're late! Where you guys been?" I teased as they sashayed over to our little group. Vickie was toting a screwdriver in hand with some other bar's advertising on the glass.

"In church!" Vickie joshed. "Right, Rivea?"

"Yah! Right! We even brought along our **Church Key** to prove it." Rivea dangled her auto key chain in front of our faces, from which also dangled a beer bottle opener. A little laughter emerged from the Gopher coterie.

Vickie, glancing around, remarked. "I see the party's a swingin'"

"Yes, but you've missed a lot of nonsense already. Shame on you!" I charged. "Just look at that pregnant Party Animal!"

"We never miss anything wherever we go, you Schmuck. Wherever we go we create a ton of our own nonsense!"

"I have to agree there!"

Everyone watched Dick open his numerous gifts, some serious, some gags and then we all proceeded to fill our faces with pot luck to uncomfortable, over indulged capacity.

"But, Geno," I interrupted as we perched in the booth, having pushed aside our soiled plastic dinnerware and paper plates, piled with crumpled discarded napkins, "I have always felt that Public Schools were more suitable for my children. Special schools, like the parochial, for instance, give kids a wrong message, the assumption that they are perhaps better than other kids. This can create a very diverse, selfrighteous interpretation to young vulnerable, impressionable minds. In other words, giving rise to prejudicial bias attitudes."

"You may have a point there, Dottie." Geno concertedly admitted. "And they're not the greatest of schools, either." he added. "Third grade, Sister Larenzo would wrap her knuckles on, my head and say, "Not much in there!" I said "Nothing wants admittance to nothing." But I don't think she ever understood my sarcasm. I'd go away by myself and really cry, cuz I was so **Dumb!** Miss Gurjette found me once in the coal room. She was a seventh or eighth grade substitute teacher. She hugged me and not saying a word, repaired my injured self-esteem. She was my very first true friend in that Catholic School. She wasn't a nun either!"

"Tsck—tsck." I made the tongue sound. "In second grade I was Teachers Pet! The teacher, Mary Murphy, gave me a doll at Christmas for doing errands for her. I was helping because she had broken her leg during summer vacation and came back to teach on crutches. . See, that's the difference from Public to Catholic schooling!" I giggled.

"That wasn't the school, Screwball! That was **You**.!" he tittered. "You have a way you know. I s'pose even as a child. But back to the nuns. They are mean just like the rumors. They clonk you hard over the head or across your fingers with their rulers or pencils for the least little thing, like chewing gum in class or talking."

"Yes, I've heard the stories," I admitted, "About their cranky dispositions, but I've never really believed it. Kids will be kids and sometimes gentle discipline just doesn't work. Or sometimes kids over dramatize, just for parent benefit or attention, the actual severity, staging what was a soft disciplinary tap to a harsh vicious slap!"

"Anyway, my mother was or rather is a devout Catholic. She believed Catholic Schooling was the way to go. The only way!."

"Is your mother living in Burtrum too?" I asked

"She's in a nursing home, not too far from Burtrum. Close to Alexandria. She lives in a wheel chair most of the time and has many, many health problems that stem from her size. She's really huge. I guess you'd say she's very obese. She's had knee and hip replacements and still can hardly walk."

"Wow! For sad. How about you're dad. Can't he take care of her?"

"Dad's gone. He was a saint. Soft spoken. Never raising his voice in anger. A very humble man."

"You loved him a lot, obviously."

"His name was Albert and he did everything for mother. He loved her so much, so unconditionally. He'd bend over backwards to please her and I don't think she ever really appreciated him. She was always complaining, complaining, complaining. He'd buy her everything she'd ask for. He bought her a new stove and she'd whine. It was too big, it was too small, she didn't like the color, whatever. Nothing was ever right."

"That's sure a complete turn around with my folks." I replied. "My mother was very passive, taking everything dad would dish out and there wasn't much good in that dish! Believe me, nothing worthy of praise."

"Are your folks passed on, then?"

"Oh no. I guess I shouldn't be using the past tense. That's only because I don't live there anymore, of course, but they're both well and alive. I don't have much respect for my dad. And Mother—well, I always felt sorry for her. Still do. She's had such a hard life."

"Is she Catholic?" he asked.

"Her parents were devout Catholics, very christian people, but after she married Dad, she just rolled with the flow. Too scared, too introverted, too passive to make waves. She did, however, sneak us kids off to Catechism behind Dad's back."

"Sometimes I think organized religion is only one step behind organized government." Geno declared. "There's no freedom in government policy. Oh they promise and plug freedom, tell us we have choices but we don't. They don't follow through with campaign promises. You know my definition of freedom is **SELF CONTROL!** What is the hardest, the toughest and sometimes the most impossible thing to control?" He asked, raising his eyebrows equivocally.

"I don't know? What is it?"

"Our selves!"

"I don't understand where you're coming from." I said.

"Well, say we have a vice; like vanity, pride, smoking, drinking, sex, or anger. When we don't exercise restraint to these vices, we don't have control of that segment of our being. We don't have freedom of control."

"Did you learn that in catechism?"

"No. It's just my ultimate conclusion or opinion."

"I'm afraid I'm not capable of the perfect control you describe. I'm only human." I turned both palms upward and remarked facetiously, "I'm not perfect. Look at my hands. **No holes."**

"You're missing the point, Dottie. The serious point."

"I don't want to be that serious." I flipped.

He went on, disregarding my frivolous attempt to turn to jest.

"Do you realize the government doesn't **take away** our freedoms. We willingly **give away** our freedom! Man is so stupid!! Man just gives it all away! Labor gave away it's right to work by creating Unions. Management gave away it's right to free enterprise by Greedy Incorporation! And O.S.H.A. is an organization designed to control management and unions!! Well, okay, that's another story."

"Geno," I interrupted, "I know **very little**, no, let me put that another way—I know **absolutely nothing** about politics, government, or law. It's way over my head and I'd like to keep it there." was my apathetic reply.

"I have a book I'd like you to read, Dottie." he insistently suggested. "It's called 'None Dare Call It Conspiracy' by Gary Allen and endorsed by Senator McCarthy. It's all about our dirty corrupt government and it's under the table "Shenanigans". The corrupt truths they hide from a naive public. The crooked banking business of our country, so forth and so on. I'll bring it with me next time I come to Duluth."

He was so intense I wanted to steer him to another subject although I did, concertedly agree to his opinions on crooked, corrupt government. "It may be true, Geno, but what's the use sweating over what we can't change? The rich get richer, the poor get poorer, the crooked tax collectors are full of greed and that's been going on since Biblical times!"

I felt slightly intimidated by his knowledge on so many topics and yet simultaneously intrigued by it, as well. Our visit wasn't the usual "Duh" chit-chats I encountered in the dim lights of my Night Life

199

world! It was definitely different, definitely a stimulating breath of fresh air.

"Geno, you can't change the world, just don't let the world change you, is a fairly, meaningful cliche, Don't you think?"

He smiled a dimpled smile. "We should never talk religion or politics." he compensated, "Especially not at a party, anyway.

"Well you do have some interesting points." I agreed, trying to remain stoic. "Like control of our vices. I do have a vice completely out of control, so I have no freedom of control over it. And that's my tongue! It's obsessed with verbal diarrhea."

"You're a screwball!" he laughed.

"In all seriousness, I do have an uncontrollable vice, maybe more correctly diagnosed as an ailment."

"And what might that be?" he asked, with faint curiosity.

"Food! I have no control over food. I've struggled with my weight all my life. I don't eat to live, I live to eat!"

"Nonsense!" with a simpered smile I knew he wasn't taking me seriously.

"Not nonsense. I have a very real eating disorder. It stems, I think, from my traumatic childhood with a disfunctional father." **I mused,** "Why am I effusively spilling my personal history and inadequacies to this almost stranger acquaintance. How absurd!"

He skewed his eyebrows in confusion and silently paused, waiting for me to continue.

"No, I'm really serious." I spurted, then midstream in my mind I decided to back up "Woah" and make light of the subject. "So serious, in fact, I even wrote a poem about it."

"A poem? Really."

"You know that version of a children's poem; Jack Sprat could eat no fat! His wife could eat no lean. And so between the two of them, they licked the platter clean!"

"I knew you were joshing me. What could Jack Sprat have in common with Dottie Lou?" he smirked, snickering inherently.

"Well, food, especially FAT can make you fat and even sick! So I wrote a second verse for myself about the evils of all that fat! It goes like this: Trouble is fat plugged her veins, And woe to Fat, 'tis said. Jack got a dog to eat the fat, Because his wife **Dropped Dead!!**—And that's the Rest of the Story!" I chanted.

"Funny Face, You're the craziest girl in The Whole U.S.A.!" he purred, provocatively. "And—you write poetry! Well I'll be----"

"Sure. I've been writing poetry and short stories, too since I was eight. My first poem, in third grade, was published in our huge Bruno School Paper! Of course this gigantic exposure in the monthly paper of that huge school of 100 students in twelve grades torpedoed the production to such excess because of the relentless demand by an audience of parents, aunts and grandma's." I giggled

"Wow! Unreal! What a coincidence." Geno remarked, a surprised glow on his face. "So do I!"

"So do you waht?"

"Write poetry. I've been creating lines of rhyme for years."

"You're puttin' me on!" I denounced disparagingly.

"I'm not putting you on, Dottie Lou. **No Way!** In fact, I'll prove it to you. Next time I come to Duluth I'll compile you a poem. Just for you."

"Yeah, yeah, yeah. You just do that Chocolate Brown Eyes-**full of shit!** Come on let's dance." I coaxed. "The B.S. is getting mighty deep here. Cowboy boot depth!"

"Okay, we'll dance, but make no mistake, I will write you a poem. I'll be back in two or three weeks. I'll surprise you with lines of rhyme that will prove it was just written for you. Not plagiarized."

"Yeah, yeah, yeah. And the farmer hauled another load away." I chanted in casual song. "And Geno, yes, you bet it wasn't hay!!"

"You'll see!" he insisted in earnest. "We sure do get into some complicated discussions. Don't we? And that's no bull either!"

"We certainly do. I love visiting with you, Geno. We're certainly never lost for words. Usually I have to talk to myself to get an interesting conversation initiated."

He laughed. "Do you ever get into heated disagreements?"

"Not generally, and I always do get the right answers to my questions."

♫♫♪

CHAPTER FIFTEEN

After Larry and the boys returned from Canada, I saw even less of Larry as I had previously. Any extra time he had was devoured by the Skiroule Shop, preparing for the approaching winter sports season. He solicited several guest spots on the Bob Junkert radio program, "Speaking on Sports", promoting the new Coleman line of Skiroule sleds. He spoke, enlightening snowmobile enthusiasts, over the air, on the fundamentals of snowmobiling, the mechanics of it, the need of warmth in clothing to withstand the elements and the racing aspects of becoming a first place winner. Frosting on the cake, was the opportunity to promote the new business on radio time.

Dale, having rode and raced Larry's 292 TNT of the previous winter, had proved it to be the fastest sled in the Heights, winning many races plus vaunted, teen-age prestige among his buddies. So needless to say, Dale's face drooped dejectedly and his disposition attested **glum**, when Larry insisted the TNT be traded in on a new Skiroule.

Dale named it the "Green Bean" and put his artistic skill to opus again, painting the name, splashed across the hood. Dale professed, emphatically, it didn't have the power of the TNT of the Ski Doo line. **"Not Even Close!"** However, Larry stubbornly asserted with clout, it to be the **Top of the Line** in performance, ambiguously entertaining the necessary sales pitch to encourage interest and sales for the new line.

Big plans developed and projects took shape in preparation for the Winter Sports Show, which was being assembled at the Duluth Arena-Auditorium on Halloween week-end, Friday, Saturday and Sunday, inclusive.

Kenny and Larry reserved a space for a Coleman display booth and area to exhibit the new sleds, plus a line of Skiroule, accentuated, snowmobile wear, as well as the usual line of Coleman camping equipment and excessories.

In one of now rare instances Larry shared the evening meal with us. We casually chatted over dinner discussing the many business prep, plans, obstacles, just catching up on the recent developments of the Skiroule Shop and its progress.

"You know, Hon, Coleman has really designed quite an excellent line of clothing; suits, sweaters, etc. Quite exquisite in style and fashion, too. Numerous ensembles in green and white, the Skiroule colors." Larry devulged as he earnestly munched on his salad.

"Similar to the yellow of Ski doo?" I asked. "That was certainly a gorgeous two-piece sweater set you surprised me with when we were going together."

"Yes, much like that, only nicer." he smirked.

"I suppose, much nicer, since you get a smidgen of the profits!" I snickered.

"That doesn't hurt." he chuckled. "We're setting up a whole line of the clothing to exhibit at our booth. A big variety, Something to interest the taste of everyone, from the course, rowdy pragmatic dresser to the finesse of the elite."

"I'll have to get an outfit, I s'pose now to match the "Green Bean", huh? I still like riding my trusty ' ole Ski Doo. You know I love that old sled."

"I have to find a model with pizzazz to wear some of the outfits for exhibit. Maybe sit upon a Skiroule looking chic and trendy." Larry remarked.

"I noticed they're advertising, in the paper." I added. "A Winter Sports Style Show at the Arena too, where the models parade, wearing the latest attire in "Outdoor Sports Fun" That's how they printed it."

"Yes, that too. This is really a splendid opportunity for Kenny and I to get some real promotion and exposure to start this new business; get it off the ground and booming!!" he bellowed with the usual idiomatic vonGillern confidence.

"I'm free during the day. I could certainly handle that." I excitedly remarked. "In fact, I'd love doing something like that. Right up my alley! It's my kind of expertise. Well, I'm no expert, of course. That's for sure, but I know fashion and I certainly exhibit it every night on stage." I tittered, rattling on garrulously, non-stop, with elated exuberance. "I know the gestures, like in vocalizing. That's a natural, common sense thing anyway." I casually turned my head, side to side, flinging my hair in an impetuous, prestigious motion for effect as I giggled, struggling with a mouthful of mashed potatoes. "It will be such fun and exciting to model the new Skiroule line of garments." I ejaculated. I was inundated with exhilarated thoughts and immediate roused planning.

Larry's mouth collapsed at the corners and a somber, unsettling frown skulked his face. In a derisive stammer he muttered. "Well uh—ummm—Well I--," then drew a deep breath and blurted, in a stringent voice, "Dottie, surely you must know you don't have the figure for something like that! A model? Really! How absurd! I've asked Eileen, Ray Parkers wife to model the line for us."

"Oh---." The sound barely escaped from my throat, trailing hardly audible. Everyone continued eating in silence. Just the tinkle of silverware against plate filled the awkward tension of the room. One of the kids cleared a throat, uncomfortably. All faces demurely remained turned downward to their dinner plates. No one spoke.

Tears began to burn in the corners of my eyes. I bit fiercely on my lower lip to refrain from acknowledging my maimed self-esteem. Blinking furtively, I tried to suffocate tears about to spill. I thought, "Never show him it hurts! Show him you don't give a **rats ass** about his booth, his exhibits, his business. Right!" Then angrily with pained indignation I mused. "What normal, sensitive husband wouldn't want to swagger, proudly, his singer, recording artist wife, and I might add **cute,** at his exhibition booth. Vaunt her in the Winter Sports Style Show parade of elegance and class! Proudly and boldly introduce her to everyone.

Apparently not **MY** husband! Evidently, either he was inadvertently insensitive to my feelings, blind to my appealing appearance, or perhaps he'd rather not let it be known he even had a wife. My ballot went to number three.

Dinner remained silent to finish. I swallowed my wounded pride and didn't mention it again. It was no wonder my heart was never bonded or attached to Larry's projects. My heart was with my kids and the Gopher was my second home, where I never failed to be **Somebody!** My friends weren't critical. Admiration and prestigious success was my every day reward. I was loved. My many friends were not **fair weather.**

Saturday afternoon I decided to make an appearance at the Winter Sports Show, as Larry had numerously suggested.

"Come and visit our booth. Take a look at our unique creativity." he urged. "We've put a lot of hard work, time and effort into making this a success, Kenny, Sylvia and I. We have quite an exquisite line of Coleman products to offer the public. Dottie, maybe you'll see an ensemble you like. One you just can't live without." A chuckle. "If you do, I'll get it for you." Was this perhaps, an attempt at redemption, I pondered? He smiled ruefully.

When I arrived Eileen was gracefully perched upon a Skiroule sled in a modish one-piece, green and white, elaborate outfit; very chic, very jet-set, well not jet. I guess you'd correctly term it snow set. She was silhouetted against a gigantic winter scene background, splashed on a huge banner for extra drama.

The top portion of the garment was long sleeved, in white knit, joined at the lower hip to a slack bottom in soft white vinyl fabric; hip-hugger style. Where the knit top joined the vinyl bottom the seam was concealed by a wide Skiroule green patent leather belt, fastened by a huge buckle. The belt was threaded through white vinyl loops. The garment was snug and fitted to the contour of the body from the top to the bell bottom legs. A long zipper stretched down the back, full length, from the pert, miniscule, stand-up collar to the tail bone for entry.

The garment was, indeed, elegant, fashionable, provocative and Eileen wore it well! Beads of heated envy cascaded down the nape of the neck and to my cheeks. Frustated anger smoldered within and I wondered if she was another one of Larry's trophys. Her husband, Ray, was one of Larry's friends and also his pit man. I was well aware of, from past experiences, the loyalty Larry coddles on his friends. Ahem.

The cat-woman in me cringed and invisible, ferocious feline claws emerged, inwardly, as I malevolently noted Eileens ruddy, wind damaged, face, 15 years older than her svelte body, skin stretched across bony cheeks.

"So, she has a petite, tiny, hour-glass figure!! **So what!!**" I soliloquized, comforting and solacing my injured pride from Larry's rejection. "People look at your face before your waist!!" I smiled to myself. "Yes, I had just created a new poetic cliche.

Poor, urbane, debonair Eileen! She was, Thank God, oblivious to my shallow, unsanctimonious, cruel, catty thoughts. Lord knows, they were certainly undeserved. She had innocently been caught in a crossfire between Larry and I.

"Did you see anything you really like, Dottie?" Larry queried.

"I like that outfit Eileen is wearing." I replied. "It's got style, reeks of class."

"I'll get it for you."

"Thanks. I see Jodi Miller is the headliner on the Grandstand. I really like her. I'd love to catch her show. I sing a couple of her hits, Queen of the House and He's So Fine. When is she on?"

"She did one show already today and she'll do another tonight."

"So I've missed her, then, cuz I gotta work tonight."

"I took her to lunch today." Larry boasted.

"Yeah, I'll bet." I laughed dubiously. "She's all hung up on the charisma of Larry vonGillern." I sighed, "Like so many. Huh?"

"I think she's got the Hots for me." he grinned, swaggering.

"She has big wheel, big name artists in her life; musician side men; a whole crew on her bus, and she's stuck on a Skiroule dealer from the hicks? Oh boy, isn't that something?" I whined, irony dripping off my tongue.

"Well, I did take her to lunch. I'd never push it, Hon, cuz, of course, I'm married to you, but she did come on to me pretty strong."

Funny, I thought how men take every little gesture of friendship from the opposite sex as being an invite. Larry regularly boasted, feigning his charisma with women, so it wasn't serious, fresh news to me. Sometimes it may have been true, but in this instance, I would have bet big bucks, Jodi Miller hadn't even given him the time of day. It was just a spurious stretch of his imagination. And maybe he was **merely part of a group** that went to lunch, not a tété-a-tété arrangement as he had implied. Perhaps with Larry's usual stretching of facts, he had actually, in all probability, accompanied a **bunch** of folks, standing in line, waiting for a hamburger at the Hot Dog stand in the Arena!! I chuckled out loud, enjoying my facetious thoughts.

"What's so funny?" he asked.

"Oh, nothing." I shrugged my shoulders, grinning profusely. "Let's go take a look at that Skiroule Fashion garment rack. See if they have anything in my size."

* * * * * * *

"Hey, Dottie, telephone!" Dick, the bartender shouted above the noise of the crowded bar.

"For me?" I mouthed, finger poking, repeatedly to my chest. He nodded yes. "Must be Larry," I assumed. I hurried off stage to the waitress station and quickly nabbed the phone.

"Hello."

"Hi. Geno here."

"Geno? Where are you?"

"In Pine Bluff, Arkansas,"

"You're kidding? Arkansas? That's a helluva long way from Duluth!"

"Yes, I know, but I just got lonesome for the Gopher bunch."

"You like us crazy, bizarre Gopher Dugans, Huh? Well what's on your mind?"

"You didn't wish me a Happy Birthday! You didn't even have a birthday drink with me."

I laughed a nervous titter. "It's your birthday?"

"A couple weeks ago." he casually bantered. "I spent it all alone, feeling sorry for myself, in a Holiday Inn in upstate New York."

"That's not my fault then." I snickered. "You should have joined us here. Well anyway, Happy Birthday, Geno, belated."

"Thank you. I was just sitting here in the Lounge of a Holiday Inn, sipping scotch and water and feeling dreadfully sorry for myself. Kinda lonely. I just wanted to hear a familiar voice from the Gopher, preferably yours. I guess it's my home away from home."

"Hey, I always call the Gopher my second home too."

"Well, I'll let you go. Sorry to pull you away, off the stage, from your gig, but I thought it was your break time. Our clocks must not be synchronized."

"They took the break, anyway, when I was called to the phone."

"I wanted to hear your voice."

"Hey, you're makin' me nervous."

"I hope not. I'll be in Duluth, the other office, next week. See you guys then. Say Hi to the Gopher---whatta you call 'em—Bunch, Gang—no, Oh I remember—Dugans. Sing me a song too."

I snickered. "Okay. Will do. It'll probably be "Crazy", just like you." I joshed. Bye now. See you, whenever."

"Bye."

Click. I smiled, puzzled, thinking. "That's quite strange. I wonder what possessed him to do that? hmmm—Pine Bluff, Arkansas. What a screwball."

* * * * * * *

"Who or what are you gonna dress up as?" Delores asked.

"I always enjoy dressing as Grandma from the Hillbillys sitcom. Nobody ever guesses who it is. That's easy cuz I still have all the stuff from before. The jug for my rheumatism tonic, my farmers red bandanna, my corn cob pipe and a little cloth sack of extra-stale bouldourm tobacco. How about you?" I asked, as we planned Sunday's Halloween Masquerade on the town.

"Jan is going as a big fat, black Mama, and I'm her little white bastard baby. Not very little, though, I'm afraid!"

"Wow! Sounds Hilarious! We know how to have a good time!"

"Yeah. I'll be in a baby bunting, diapered, with a bottle to suck on and Jan is gonna pull me around in a big red wagon she has borrowed from someone. Pulling **ME** around won't be easy!"

"Where should we meet and what time?" I asked. "The Gopher will be closed."

"How about the Zoo Cabaret?" Delores suggested. "At about seven."

"Sounds good. We'll hit all the night spots in Superior first and then come over the bridge to charm everyone in Duluth."

Delores giggled. "I have a couple houses I wanna pop in on, in West Duluth too." Delores retorted. "If that's okay with you guys."

"Sure, and let's end up at Larry and Kenny's Skiroule Shop afterwards. Larry and Kenny are putting on an Appreciation Party at their shop for all of the gratuitous help, volunteered by friends to remodel, decorate and set up the shop for business, plus in appreciation of those who also assisted in organizing the exhibition booth at the Arena."

"Isn't the Winter Sports Show still going on tomorrow" Delores inquired.

"Yes, but it ends at 6:00 P.M. on Sunday, so they'll all be heading to the Skiroule Shop afterwards to celebrate!"

"Does Larry know we're going to crash his party?"

"No. He knows I'm going masquerading for Halloween with my friends, but I didn't tell him we'd stop in cuz I didn't know we would. That just now, sprung off the top of my head. I love surprising him anyway. Course he'll know it's me cuz I've dressed as Hillbilly Granny many times before."

"Tumbleweeds" Korn's baritone voice came booming across the PA speakers, signaling Toby and I to hop to it and get our fannys on stage.

"Oh-oh. Gotta go. It's time to crominize some more."

* * * * * *

When I entered the Zoo Cabaret, and after adapting my vision to the dark night club atmosphere, I spotted Jan and Delores at a nearby table, but I deluded them momentarily, disregarding their presense.

I ordered a mixed drink from Sue, the cocktail waitress on duty. I knew her quite well. She occasionally hung around with some of the Gopher gals and sometimes accompanied us when we'd burn up the road on my record promotion excursions.

I pulled out my red bandanna from my apron pocket, in which I had tied up an abundant supply of pennies. I untied it at the bar and told the waitress in a cracked Granny voice, It's my life's savings and would you please count out the amount for my drink 'cuz I dun no tended no school for countin' and learnin' stuff?" Mixed drinks were 60¢ in the 70's.

The waitress was very irate and very agitated, nesciently revealing she didn't have a clue it was Dottie Lou! She summoned the policeman at the door and persuaded him to check my Tonic JUg, to find out if I had brought liquor into the establishment not purchased there, which of course was illegal! She was diligently attempting to get me booted from the bar.

When I put my lips to the officers ear and whispered, he just smiled a simpered smile and said, "She's okay, Sue." We all, later, sniggered, hysterically, over the scene, when we disclosed to Sue who we three were. She was awkwardly flustered and apologized repeatedly only adding to our laughter.

As I've never smoked, I had confronted egregious difficulty lighting up the tobacco in my corn cob pipe and when finally finding success, I couldn't continue to keep it burning so I gave up, put it back in my apron and joined diapered Delores, clad in her big pink baby bonnet and booties to match. She was perched beside her big corpulent black Mama. Every once in awhile Delores would suckle on her bottle, coo and smile up at her Mama, flashing her eyelashes, as contented babies do.

"What do you have in your bottle, Delores?" I asked. "I've got orange juice in my rheumatism tonic jug."

"Mine's just water. I wished I'd have put some brandy in it too. Give me more **GUTS!**" Delores declared.

Jan giggled, inertly, caught up in the moment. "As if you need more **GUTS!**" her white teeth gleaming bright against her ebony painted face as she laughed.

We three Halloween Tricksters made all the rounds of every place we had played or worked. As bars were nearing the closing time, we scuttled our fannys in the direction of the Skiroule Shop. We were moderately assured they were offering cocktails there and the clocks didn't register any closing time. Also if you were in cahoots with the proprietors, the price would be gratuitous.

Being very coy, we **quietly** slipped through the door, as **quietly** as is possible after tipping hi-balls all over town. We were well aware, Larry would know it was us, as he'd seen my Granny masquerade in the past, so it would be impossible to dupe him. However, we assumed, others would not have a miniscule inkling of who was crashing their party!

There were approximately twenty people, presently partying and about as sober as our trio. I recognized Stock Car people and snowmobiling friends, but they didn't recognize me. Larry's Hardway Snowmobile Team was rollin' with the flow. No one was in costume so all heads turned towards us as we entered, except for Larry, who was so proccupied and so involved at the far end of the room he was oblivious to the volcanic eruption we were creating.

He was face to face, almost nose to nose, huddled lovey-dovey with the Arrow Chevrolet **"Big Head"** secretary! Both with elbows on the counter in each others face, at the farthest corner, away from the gala of the party.

"What's that Arrow Chevrolet Secretary doing at a Skiroule Appreciation Party?" I mused, fuming with mixed emotions. "What is **SHE** being **Appreciated** for?" Then suddenly she saw us, Larry mouth to her ear must have given us away, because in a flash she slithered from his corner to the other end of the shop, diffidently mingling with the croud. Larry momentarily dawdled behind the counter as if busy with something, then slowly sashayed over to us with an innocent, "Hi. You guys been havin' a good time?"

"Sure. We still are?"

We were offered cheese and crackers and free drinks or beer and we untimely hung around enjoying the awkward, uncomfortable agitation our surprised entrance had created.

I extinguished any thoughts of divulging my irritation or suspicious intuition as I watched subtle emotions displayed between the two of them. I just casually toiled at lighting my corn cob pipe and swiggin' on my rheumatism tonic jug. I couldn't help but discern Larry and "Big Heads" unmasked eyes and smiles connecting every now and then, across the room, entertaining and embracing little tender body messages they assumed were discreet and undetected.

Did it hurt? I swallowed an unwontedly lump lodged in the depths of my throat. Of course it hurt, but I didn't let my emotions betray me. I feigned stoicism, vicariously acting jovial, tough and slap-happy like Granny from the Hillybilly's is supposed to act. Happy, tough, and **Dumb!!**

♪♪♪

CHAPTER SIXTEEN

"You know, you sing Patsy Cline better than Patsy Cline!" Geno asserted, as we perched in a booth on my break.

"Don't be silly! No one sings better than Patsy." I replied.

Geno was in town and with Halloween just having waved goodbye to Goblins, "The Devil Made Me Do It" and scarecrows, my mind was still visualizing Autumn beauty, although snow was inevitable and just around the corner.

"You've been gone three weeks and you missed the entire beautiful picturesque colors of autumn, here." I had deliberately changed the subject. "No where, in the states, are they as vivid and vibrant as here in the North!"

"I was on the East Coast, New England, and the autumn hues were breathtaking there too." he replied.

My thoughts flitted to Scarlet Summac waving in the cool breeze and a sky, a robins egg blue, with little, scattered pillowy puffs of clouds tippy-toeing across a quiet sky. "How nice it would be," I mused, "to hike through the woods on an autumn afternoon, picking colored leaves to press in a book, with someone as perceptive and sensitive and profoundly indepth as Geno. Picking agates along a Lake Superior shoreline, embraced with awesome colored forest borders, dipping toes in water too cool to swim but exhilarating nevertheless. "NO, NO, Dottie." My mind whispered to unwise foolish thoughts. "Don't even **think** of going there, Dottie!"

"A penny for your thoughts?" Geno uttered, jolting me to the present. "You sure left me there, for awhile, Dottie." he perceptively reproached. "Where did you go, so deep in thought?" he enigmatically queried.

I smiled placidly, not offering an explanation, creating an aurora of mystery, I supposed. "Mystery is always fascinating and intriguing." I laughed, flirting, impishly. "Right?"

"Anyway, about Patsy Cline," he went on. "Will you learn all the good songs that Patsy Cline sang?"

"I think I already know and sing most of hers." I replied.

"At **my expense**, Dottie, I want you to record them. You have her superb type of a ballad voice." he stated in an authoritative voice, making me uncomfortably flushed and awkwardly flustered. "That's not just my opinion, either." he added with ebullience.

"But Geno, You know it doesn't really sell to sound like someone else. You need to sound like no one else! I need to be different and sound just like me."

"I think a tribute to Patsy Cline by Dottie Lou would sell **very well!**" he logicised, determined.

"I have been jostling around in my mind, a plan to maybe, record an 8 track, in Minneapolis, but I haven't made any definite decisions yet on what material I would use. However the project won't materialize 'til sometime next year. I think toward spring or summer. It's not feasible to release, with success, anything new during the holidays. It's bad timing, because everyone is getting into Christmas Spirit and Holiday music."

"Anyway, it's something to think about, Dottie. Maybe an 8 track tape of "Dottie Lou sings Patsy," he quibbled, refusing to surrender his idea.

I seized my purse and wrap from the dressing room to exit as the evening came to a close. Geno approached, following in step beside me.

"I'll walk you to your car." he said "I have something for you. I think it will surprise you."

"Okay. Whatever. Surprise me!" I giggled.

Outside he suggested I accompany him to his automobile. "Come, sit inside with me for a minute." he urged. He gathered up a briefcase from the back seat and opened it upon his lap as he pushed the seat back with a lever. He retrieved a sheet of paper from the depth of the contents of the briefcase. It appeared, in the dim parking lot street light, to be a sheet of a Holiday Inn stationery. He audaciously asked,

"Remember how you laughed at me a couple weeks ago when I told you I also wrote poetry?"

"Yeah." I mumbled, wondering where this was going.

"And remember how you teased me, saying, I had brown eyes, indicating I was full of shit?"

"Yeah, I think that's pretty accurate." I laughed.

"And remember how I said, I'd write a poem for you? Well, I did just that. On the road I wrote a poem to prove I'm not full of shit!! I do write Poetry." And he handed me the paper with a typewritten poem compiled on the page.

There'll Be No Doubt

Out of your bed O sleepy one
This new day has just begun
In lieu of All your spiritual thirst
Open your heart to Him first
While all this time the special one
Invades the mind in shower song
Who happened on with standards high
Returning belief in Him and why
Remember your sit ups, push ups too
And skip a rope, it's good for you

217

A hearty breakfeast, a little more thought
Attracts realization to what you got
Thoughts collected ready for work
Starting this day ahead of the quirks
All zest in you seen by some
Infectious, liken unto the sun
Dreamer you say, pointedly in rhyme
Arising one morning try this sometime
Arms outstretched give a mighty shout
"GOOD MORNING WORLD"
There'll be no doubt....

By Eugene O'Demarra

He turned the dashboard overhead light on, enabling me to grasp the printed page. I read the poem as he waited in silence, Waiting, I assumed, for my comments of criticism or approval.

"Geno, that's really, really nice. I'm impressed! Is this copy for me?"

"Of course, Silly. I wrote it for you."

"It's so deep, so profound. Certainly expresses your intense Love for God." I scanned the verse again. Putting my finger on the line I read, "While all the time the special one, invades the mind in shower song. You should capitalize "Special One", so everyone would know it's the Almighty you're talking about. Not everyone is as intelligent as we are!" I teased.

"No Dottie. It's not capitalized because the special one is not the Almighty. The special one is you, 'Who happened on with standards high, returning belief in Him and why'."

"I don't know what to say." I murmured. A long silent pause, then "It's a beautiful, indepth poem, Geno. I'm very flattered. I'll put it in amongst my own collection. I have a collection of all my writings, beginning with third grade. I should bring them to you to read, when you're on the road. It might help you to pass the empty evenings away. Yes, I think I will."

"You'd trust me with that?"

"Oh sure. And you're one of very few who would or could understand or appreciate poetry. I haven't shared them with anyone except my daughter, Charmaine."

"I'd like that."

"Yes, I think I will." my voice trailing off, contemplating out loud. "And thanks, again for the lovely poem, Geno. I gotta go now. Are you still in town tomorrow?"

"Yes, one more day here."

"Maybe I'll see you tomorrow then." I said as I scrambled from the passenger seat.

"I'll be here." he responded. "This is the only place I go when I'm in Duluth."

"Okay then. Goodnight."

* * * * * * *

I whirled my Chevy into my Walnut Street driveway, skidding on the wild turn, throwing gravel about. "I'm getting to drive just as nuts as Larry!" I laughed, talking out loud to myself. I flipped the car radio off and finished the Merle Haggard tune that was blasting the air waves, full volume, as I scrambled from the seat, heading for the house. "Mama tried to raise ♪ me better, but her pleadings I denied, ♪ It was only me to blame cuz Mama tried." ♪

Just as I reached the porch steps in whirled Larry's Pontiac likened to a tornado gone beserk. "No I guess I don't drive anywhere as crazy as he does!" I chuckled.

"You home already?!" he shouted, across the driveway.

"It's 2:00 A.M." I retorted. "That's not early. Are you hungry?" I asked as we entered the kitchen.

"As a horse." he quipped.

"I'll make some sandwiches." I said.

"Make me two. I'm starved. I gotta see a man about a horse—No about a snow machine, 16 Horse!" Larry laughed as he uncomfortably sprinted to the bathroom.

I prepared sandwiches from cold left-over meatloaf. Two for Larry, one for me and a King Size glass of ice cold milk, which was an infallible routine for Larry. He sure savored his Moo Juice.

"How are things at the Green Bean Business?" I inquired.

"Boy, has Coleman got a promotion package and a half, to get the new line of Skiroule off on a stampede of business. We get X amount of points for every Skiroule we sell. The points add up to earning tickets to a vacation overseas for all of Coleman's participants, Everywhere they are being sold. The States and Canada too."

"Sounds pretty impressive."

"What a clever incentive someone mustered up!"

"When will that vacation be? If it will be."

"It will be. No doubt of that. It's only a question of how many will be able to go. The trip will be at the end of the winter season. Kenny is working his fanny off tryin' to sell, but he's no salesman. I sell three to his one most of the time, but he's a damn hard worker, real excellence in servicing the machines. **Everybody's good at something.** How would you like a vacation overseas? Next spring?"

"I'd love it! Absolutely fabulous! Incredible!" I chortled.

"We're tryin' like Hell to earn enough points for four tickets; for Kenny and Sylvia and you and I. We don't have enough points for even one ticket yet," he smirked, "But the season is barely starting. So that's good."

"Knowing your high pressure expertise at selling, it should be no problem. I know you guys will do it, come hell or high water."

"If we could just get some snow, things would start booming. The sales would flourish right away." he clamored.

"Well, Larry, its only the beginning of November. When it does arrive in full fury, piled up to your dupa and past, you'll wish you hadn't wished!!" I bantered.

"Never! Never!" he blurted, scarffing down the second sandwich with a huge refill on the moo juice. "Never too much of the white stuff for me."

* * * * * * *

I was leaning on the service bar chatting with Delores when the phone let out a shrill explosion next to my ear, so loud I flinched.

"It's for you, Larry." Dick, the bartender shouted to Larry loitering in the barroom with friends.

"I'll take it upstairs, on the extention, Dick." Larry shouted back, "Where it isn't so noisy."

Dick laid the phone gently on the counter and Larry scrambled up the back stairs.

I don't know what possessed me, but I carefully picked up the phone. Quietly, with a very minute twinge of guilt, I listened to the voices cit chat on the line. It's not like me to invade someone's privacy, but I seemed obsessed with listening in. Maybe subconsciously, I became suspicious when Larry decided to bolt upstairs to talk. Was his decision based on the fact his wife was perched, on her break, next to the telephone?

Delores, standing beside me, waiting for a cocktail order, mouthed, hardly audible. "Shame! Shame! Shame!" She placed one index finger across the other and sliding it back and forth, she gestured a "Shame on you!"

I flashed a simpered smile, with a hint of indiscretion written on my face.

"Hello." Larry boomed.

"Hi. It's me." came the reply.

"Oh Hi." Larry said, not requesting an introduction.

"It sure is noisy, hard to hear you." A female voice replied.

"Oh that's because they forgot to hang up the phone downstairs." Larry explained. "It would be a helluva lot noisier if I'd tried talking to you from down there. It's wild tonight."

"Hmm. IT's pretty hmm wild down here too, Larry." she sighed breathlessly. "I need you."

Larry chuckled, obviously pleased. "Where's the Hubby?"

"He's in Georgia, that two week stint in the Guards. I'm all alone—oooh—oooh, so ve---ry lonely." she cooed. I could almost vision her moistening her tongue and sensually sliding it back and forth across her lips. "Can you get away?"

"For you?"—pause, a soft chuckle—"Always!"

"Will you be able to slip away from Dottie?"

"No sweat. She sits here and drinks with the other employee's after hours. Never gets home 'til three or four."

"I'll put on that slinky green satin robe you like so much and I'll light some candles. And a hi-ball will be ice-tinkling with your name on it."

"It'll be a little while, Jodi, I just got here from the Skiroule Shop. I just got my first drink."

"Well hurry! Christ, I'm really horney!"

"You'll have to let me shower there. I'm all engine **grease.** I just finished working on the neighbors crippled Polaris."

"I'll suds it ivory clean for you." she giggled.

They both tittered.

"We'll never make it out of the shower!" Larry added, flirting audaciously. "I'll be there as soon as I can."

"Fine. I'm waiting."

Click.

I carefully laid the telephone on the counter without hanging it up, scurried to another inconspicuous section of the barroom and quickly struck up a conversation with a gal I knew, so Larry wouldn't suspiciously harbor an indication I had been eavesdropping.

He scuttled over and stood facing us, sipping his hi-ball, imperviously listening to the small talk between her and I. I could tell he was spuriously attentive, as his eyes were narrowed to slits, focusing right over our shoulders as he chewed on a straw. I'd observed this transparent demeanor of Larry's so many times, when he'd be concentrating on something other than the chit-chat at hand, his mind overtly elsewhere.

"I won't be going right home, Hon." he interjected our chatter. "Wilhelm has some parts for my 63½ Ford that I have been looking for for some time now. He wants me to come and take a look and the price sure is right! **Free,** to take off of his hands. He's offered to help me in my garage. The guys are all nuts over my new garage and my comfortable set up for grease monkeys."

I remained silent, seething, just letting him sputter his bogus alibis. "Where does he ever come up with all these invented **Brain Farts!**" I mused.

"How stupid does he think I am? Wilhelm?! Yeah! Huh!" I ruminated. I'd have recognized the voice even if Larry hadn't used her name. They were Jodi and Jeff, a part of his racing scene coterie. We'd been to their house a couple times. Snowmobiling also.

"And there's definitely improvement in the "Thunder under the Hood", as well, and that's encouraging." he continued.

"Racing season is over until spring." I quipped.

"Building and repairing is never over." he quibbled. "You have to prepare for the next season. And then it's back to sleds. Repair and service my sleds and other people's sleds, as well, back in Kenny's and my shop." He downed his drink in one quick gulp and sashayed toward the stairway.

"Oh so it goes." I glumly conceded and headed toward the Lounge to collect my purse and wrap. "See you later, at home." I mumbled, but he had already disappeared.

I tried to quell the gut feeling of nausea. However I should have been hardened to Larry's promiscuous liasons by now. It wasn't **new** news! But suspecting him and actually hearing it factually over a telephone, was an entirely different aspect, of the gut feelings that churned atrociously in the pit of my stomach.

I finished my cocktail and insidiously began scheming, devising a plan to burst his bubble, once and for all! "I'll just pop in unexpectedly and crush their little love nest!" I fumed inwardly. "And Oh yes, I'll steal that **Thunder** of his or theirs, (Orgasm) That he brags about incessantly,. This blast of **Thunder** will be louder than any he's ever heard coming from under his hood!" My angry thoughts continued blasting bombarding, scheming! "In fact," I mused, "I'll blow his engine! His mind! She can blow his connecting rod!! **Who Cares?** I'll smash his head lights! (with verbs). I'll lower his ratio, with insults). I'll—I'll—hmm—I'll punch a hole in their oil pans, while they **change their oil!** I'll—I'll—hmmm—Yes I'll—**Damn I'm Good!!**" I had to laugh at my creative witticisms, in spite of myself. In spite of the situation!

I peeled my Chevy out of the Gopher alley parking lot and charged down the asphalt toward the Denfeld Area of West Duluth. I cruised around their home a couple times searching for Larry's vehicle. I couldn't spot it. In the murky darkness it would not likely be plausible, anyway. However I had never been very adept at recognizing one auto from another. On numerous occasions I had attempted entering automobiles belonging to someone else, merely because they were the same color as mine!

Evading the possibility of being spotted, I decided to park a block and a half away from the house. I ambled to the front porch steps and rang the door bell.

Jodi opened the door, all decked out in a long green lounging robe, slits at the sides almost to her waist. I could see candles softly flickering in the background and up front an expression on her alabaster face worth a million bucks! **But NO LARRY!** And then I realized in my inane, anxious impatience, fury and haste, I had beat him there! How asinine! I was stunned!

"Well! Dottie! How nice." she finally stammered. "What brings you here?"

"I was to meet Larry here." I stammered.

"He's not here."

In my nervous anxiety over bungled plans, I garrulously rattled on, non-stop, making, I'm sure, a complete idiot of myself. Struggling for an inert excuse for being there, uninvited. Then **to revert the subject, I asked,** "Where's Jeff?"

"Oh he went for beer. S'pose, maybe, cuz Larry was coming?" **It was cleverly stated as a** question. "He should be back anytime soon. But as long as you're here Dottie, you may as well come in for a night cap cocktail." She then beckoned gracious, composed charm, which was Jodi, propitiously delivering an affable, cordial invitation. She always portrayed, as I knew her, an air of class, dignity and finesse. A demeanor of prestige, diplomatically adroit, assuming the role of polite, courteous hostess!

I sat nervously sipping a high-ball, while awkward gaps of silence hovered between us. She didn't appear nervous or moved by my unplanned presence. Then Larry suddenly appeared in the doorway. He hadn't knocked, just nonchalantly moseyed in.

Larry was always adept at covering his tracks in any situation. He was spontaneous in assertive reply. Always had a quick dexterous answer to justify any circumstance. I, on the other hand, was always nervously, speechless and stumped if an unexpected, abrupt situation arose. I was that bovine, bonehead, who always mused minutes later, "I wish I had thought of that! or I wish I had said that!" I lacked spontaneous quips at rebuttal. Debating was not one of my natural talents.

"I didn't know you wanted to come along, Dottie." Larry quipped. "I know how you hate stock car lingo. Talk of pistons and oil research and formulas and engines etcetera so I didn't even think to ask. And you usually sip at the Gopher with your friends 'til wee hours of morning.

I didn't reply.

"Where's Jeff? Larry sagaciously queried.

"He went for beer. He'll soon be back. What can I get you Larry? I have brandy or whiskey."

"Brandy will be fine, with seven-up."

"Did you bring Jeff that part for his sled he ordered?"

"Oh sure. I put it on your porch bench outside. Lucky to have one in stock so he doesn't have to wait." Larry glanced my direction to see if I was buying them covering their tracks, I assumed.

"He'll be glad of that."

"If he needs help have him call me." Larry added.

226

Well, of course, Jeff didn't return and Larry feigned dire exhaustion. He claimed, as a result of a hard tedious day at the Skiroule Shop. He was anxious to embrace his pillow and a bundle of zzzz's, real soon, so we finished our high-balls rather quickly, excused ourselves and left for the Heights. I wanted to clobber myself for such inane stupidity. For not taking time to mull over an astute workable plan. For impatiently acting in such haste to get there.

When I ironically asked Larry what took him so long to get there he cooly disclosed, he had bounced upstairs for a drink and ran into Redenbaugh and got carried away, hashing over Snowmobile small talk. The "Hardway Team's" possibilities of up and coming races and "Time just flew by." he spuriously apologized.

I smiled to myself, relishing in my own knowledge of having "Rained on their Parade!" Yes, **Jodi**, with her unresolved sexual tensions and Larry with his abundance of pathological lies, I had indeed **silenced their THUNDER!**

My attempt to catch them in the act had failed however, due to my own blundering. "But what does it matter, anyway?" I mused, "Being caught does not make a man more faithful! It merely makes him more careful! More cautious!

* * * * * * *

"Well, Hi Geno. Wow! Has two weeks gone by already?" I jovially reflected, as he leaned against the service bar, waiting on a scotch and water. He looked in vogue, smartly tailored and impressive in a dark green sharkskin suit. The material had a shimmer that glowed beneath the Lounge neon lights. He appeared as though he had just stepped out from the pages of a men's fashion magazine.

"Actually, it's three weeks." he burbled. "You sure missed my being here! Huh? Didn't know I was gone!" He chortled, a forced snicker, emerging.

"I knew you were gone! No requests for "Funny Face" or "Teddy Bear"! I casually bantered. "But the time just flies by when you're having fun. Sometimes I just lose track!" I careened forward in a conspiratorial whisper. "I did think of you several times, Geno. Whenever I did "Crazy". I tittered amicably.

"Thanks!" he scoffed, pretending provocation.

"You're welcome." I teased.

"How do you suppose Christmas season got here so quickly?" he asked. "It was just Thanksgiving last week, wasn't it? What do **you** do for Christmas?"

"My siblings and I take turns hosting a Christmas Celebration on Christmas Day. It's my sister Pauline's turn this year. Christmas eve I spend with my kids. We sing carols around the Christmas tree, open gifts and so forth. How about you?"

"I will, of course, attend Midnight Mass on Christmas Eve."

"We go to church Christmas morning." I interrupted, abashed. "The kids get too tired to attend church at midnight."

"I love the Midnight Mass." he continued. "It's so profound. So renewing to me. Christmas Day I will go to see my children in Burtrum. With gifts for them, of course."

"And your wife." I added with a mite of irony.

"My ex-wife." he quibbled, lightly.

"She's your wife if you're only separated!" I argued diplomatically.

"You're wrong, Dottie!" he tenaciously retorted.

"Tumbleweeds" Korn boomed over the P.A.

I politely excused myself and flitted to the stage, slithering sensuously, attempting to invoke an aurora of eminence and finesse for Geno's eyes, as I could feel his gaze following me and burning into my posterior sway of hips. Despite my sophisticated savoir-faire approach to the stage, I accidentally tripped on the first step, (the only step) almost losing my balance. I grasped the railing to steady my equilibrium just in the nick of time. So much for a suave, elegant entrance or exit, depending on, from which direction I was being observed. **Story of my life!** I've always exhibited expertise at being the family **KLUTZ!** Genes originating from my dad. I should have been named "Grace"! Perhaps I should have resorted to Comedy Routines, like Ted Windus, a drummer friend of ours, who plays "the pots and pans" (a Toby idiom). He intentionally trips, half falls into the stage and consistently bags a barrel of laughs!

At the close of the gig, I invited Geno to accompany me to my vehicle. "I have something for you." I explained. "It's in my Chevy. I've been toting it around for two weeks now—I mean three." A wink following my simpered smile.

"I bet it's a poem." he chuckled. "Just gotta show me up! Huh? Gotta out do me. Right?"

"Tsck. tsck" I snickered as I slithered into the front seat and he scrambled into the passenger side.

I retrieved a zippered, plaid note book from under the seat, on the passenger side, beneath his feet.

"Remember last time we talked, I told you I had a collection, quite extensive, of poetry and prose I've compiled over the years."

"I thought you were kidding."

"I wouldn't joke about something like that."

"You are full of jokes, most of the time. I like that about you. And that's your collection?" he nodded toward the case I held in my lap.

"Yes, this is it. Since you are into writing and reading poetry, I thought you'd probably enjoy this mediocre collection of nonsense." I punned in friendly banter.

"Wow! But I won't be able to get it back to you before I leave for Alabama."

"I know. I intended for you to take it with you. Read it on the road. Whenever you're bored with nothing to do. Evenings, maybe."

"Do you have another copy?" he asked.

"Oh no. This is it."

"But what if I got killed in a car accident or my plane went down and I didn't get back here with it?"

"Don't be silly! Don't even **think** such dark, gruesome, morbid things!"

"But things do happen." he scrinched up his eyebrows in skepticism.

"Where's all that **Faith** you talk about? God takes care of everything you say. Doesn't He? Isn't everything just a part of His Plan?" I smirked.

"You're right again." he smiled, surrendering an abashed dimple.

"Don't be too critical in your scrutiny and anatomy of this peon author." I laughed. "The first poem I ever wrote was when I was eight. So don't expect any kind of Shakespeare or Poe."

"I'll take excellent care of your repertoire." he promised.

"I know you will. It's precious, but only to me."

"You're really a trusting person to trust someone with your whole life's creativity. I'm really flattered."

"I wouldn't share this with just anyone. I think I know you fairly well. I see your sincerity with people, not only me. And how you love God has a bearing on how I have based my opinion on your integrity. But then, of course, I've been known to be quite naive. Easily fooled. Easily conned. Duh!" I chided, with impish about-face humor.

"Sure, build me up, then tear me down!" he teased. "Like every woman I know!"

"And you know a lot of women?"

"Oh sure."

"How **many** do you know?!!"

"Oh—Oh—Oh----Many, many!: he giggled, convulsively.

"A regular casanova! Huh? Well, I hate to spoil a good conversation, but I really have to get along." I said as I started my Chevy and revved up the engine.

"Sure, sure, Okay, okay! Kick me out on my butt!" he chuckled, but then on a serious note, "I will take very good care of your collection, Dottie. Not to worry."

"Who's worried? Just enjoy."

"Okay, I will."

"Bye now."

I entertained mixed emotions as I torpedoed the Chevy homeward, asking myself, Did I inadvertently just do something very foolhardy; Sharing my innermost written thoughts with Geno?

Our friendship was new and juvenile and my collection was surely a very private glimpse into my soul, sheltering likeness, sacredness and secrecy of a personal diary!

Well, too late for reflection, now.

♪♪♪

CHAPTER SEVENTEEN

The Holidays departed as quickly as they had arrived. Tinsel and wrapping paper disappeared and Collette's seven day visit with us was just a memory and like the Christmas decor stashed away, amongst other favorite memorabilia.

Larry had attended an Arrow Chevrolet Christmas Office party, which I reneged on joining, perhaps because **he hadn't invited me!**

We showered Collette with a child's kitchen furniture ensemble, which she took preoccupied pleasure in, for countless hours each day. It was such a joy to entertain such a "Little People". Scotty visited with us and became her companion, as well.

My children spoiled her, even more profusely than Larry and I. Our home was becoming a graduation to the "Big People", Dale having turned seventeen, Char fourteen and Rogie eleven, all during the Autumn months. What oh what, ever happened to three, six, and nine. A blast from the past, I reminisced. Time evaporates before your very eyes.

Larry and his friends organized a Sunday Snowmobile excursion, in which I was invited. It was my first real ride, of any length, in the new winter season. With me clad in my yellow attire to match my Ski Doo and Larry on the "Green Bean", we took the grand tour. I'm not aware of just where we traveled except it was in Wisconsin and we clocked 85 miles, round trip on Larry's speedometer. I so embraced every intriging, invigorating mile of it. Needless to say, on Monday I could hardly lower my posterior buttocks to the commode for the excruciating pain of my sprained muscles in my thighs, back, shoulders and arms. The joy of straddling my sled up and over hills and around curves, through snow draped evergreens of majestic forests on my unimpressive little twelve horse, "Thelma Thudpucker's Thunderbird," somehow seemed worth all the pain!

Larry spent his hours, incessantly preparing for the Eagle River World Championship Snowmobile Races, which was his "Thunder!" He was supportively, also entering his "Hardway Team" in team competition. A number of his fans were also geared up for the three or four day event. Dale and some of his school buddies were tagging along as well, exhibiting the vonGillern Caravan in ample numbers.

I packed my 8mm movie camera into their paraphernalia pack, grinning profusely and emitted, "Pictures are as close as I'll ever come to attending those races and that's sure okay with me!" I didn't cherish standing around, stamping my feet to create circulating heat to frozen toes, attending to watering eyes and running nose and shaking hands vigorously to warm hypothermia pinching fingers. All this, just to observe sleds scoot around and around and around. This phenomenon I'd experienced in the few local races I had attended.

Larry had, from day one, blustered about his prowess and superior ability, describing how in '68 he had effortlessly run away with **First Place** in the World Championship Snowmobile Races in Eagle River. My embarking into his life must have created a foreboding prognostic little black cloud, because in '69 his machine broke down and he didn't finish the race. In '70 he came in second, beat out by a Polaris. He didn't strut any information on the '71 results and now in '72 he was going to compete on a Skiroule. **(not my fault)**. Skiroule just didn't have the omnipotent supremacy of the Bombardier series.

However, Larry was always optimistic, never letting negative thoughts cloud his enthusiasm. He vaunted the endurance and speed of the Coleman product and likewise boasted the expertise skill of his Hardway Team, bragging, "They are more than competitive among other teams, even after facing the handicap of doing without financial assistance from sponsors!" he belted, adding, "Eagle River is the essence, the hi-lite of winter sled racing and it's a damn prestigious "Feather in your helmet" just to be a part of it! If you happen to **win**—something—well, that's just **frosting** on the cake!!"

* * * * * * *

Geno popped in, right before we were about to begin our evening gig. As I gazed up I caught his entrance. I found myself, brazenly looking forward to his visits, his rapport. With Larry burning up the road to Eagle River, I didn't feel compelled to hurry home, but then, I hardly ever hurried home after work anyway.

"Well, Hi Geno." I warmly greeted him. "Long time no see. In fact, I haven't seen you since last year!" I giggled. "How were **your** holidays?"

"I saw my kids for a little while, but mostly I worked."

"Oh, oh. All work and no play makes for a dull, dull Geno." I chortled, dogmatically.

"And yours?" he asked.

"Very very nice. We had Larry's little girl, Collette for a week and she's such a delight. Hated to let her go home. She is definitely a **keeper.**"

"How old is she?"

"She's four. She'll be five in April."

"That's an adorable age. That's just the same age as my little Jeanette. Sure wish you could meet her. You'd just love her to death."

"Daddy's probably biased." I teased. "My kids are so much older. For them it was like playing house with a real live doll."

"I have your book of prose and poetry safe and sound in my briefcase. Read it all, from cover to cover." he glibly remarked.

"Lots of boredom stuff there." I spoofed flippantly.

"Definitely not dull or boring." he replied. "I almost felt reluctant to read it. It was like peeking through the keyhole, like a Peeping Tom, into the intimate heart and soul of an individual, an invasion of privacy. It was a rare experience, looking into the mirror of another one's life."

"I can see where a person might feel that way." I admitted. "but I do hope you're discreet and trusty enough to maintain it a confidential tété-é-tété."

"Oh absolutely," he murmured. "Trust me, I'm a trusty confidant. I have to admit I was overwhelmed by the insight and heart of my favorite singer." An enigmatic smile crossed over his face. "I feel like I really got to know you, more than ever. More profoundly than in any conversations we've shared."

"I gotta go. It's music time." I said as I observed Toby and Korn starting toward the stage, out of the corner of my eye.

"Sing one for me, Dottie." he sniggered.

Trying to smother the chagrin of flattery from our conversation, I quipped, impersonally, "Sure will. How about, "Hello Trouble!" I tittered.

"That's me!" he chuckled.

* * * * * *

"What's wrong?" Geno asked, as I joined him, having observed my difficulty alighting from the stage. "Did you have an accident in my absence?"

"You wouldn't believe me if I told you." I grimaced, wincing.

"Try me."

"Snowmobiling, would you believe?!" I explained. "I guess you're not suppose to ride 85 miles your first time out for the new season. You're suppose to gradually attune your body to the forgotten, stagnant muscles you haven't used all year!" I laughed. "I found muscles where I didn't even know I had muscles."

"You must be a glutton for punishment!"

"I did it last year too, so it's not as though I don't know any better."

"Well live and learn and play and pay! ha!" he teased, with no apparent smidgen of sympathy, despite my whinning.

"You don't feel any compassion for my pain?"

"Absolutely not. If you're crazy enough to do that, you deserve the pain."

"It was such fun and the pain, of course, is short lived." I retorted, complacently. "It's like labor pain, soon forgotten. I think I just may do it all over again." I burst out giggling.

Pollacks never learn. They're a stubborn lot." he bantered.

* * * * * * *

"You know, Dottie, I've been thinkin'." Geno began, as we talked at his table. "I'm on the road all the time, covering a six—no more like a ten state area for Mack Manufacturing Company, so why am I not helping you to saturate those states with your records?"

"I don't know. Why aren't you?" I joshed him with a simpered smile.

"If you'd give me a couple boxes of your 45's I could probably get them placed on jukeboxes all over the southern and eastern seaboard, places I travel, wherever I stop, wherever I stay. Maybe swing into a radio station here and there too. Mack Grapple doesn't need to know everywhere I go. What he doesn't know won't hurt him."

"That would certainly be a nuisance for you, on the job, interfering with your work, I'd guess." I replied, diplomatically. However his electryfing suggestion was rustling my interest, kindling my enthusiasm.

"No. Not at all. I wouldn't mind. I have evenings to myself, after I do my reports, anyway. I know a lot of my regular contacts fairly well, now, most on first name basis."

"That would assuredly render me a lot of extra exposure." I replied. "You're really tryin' to make a National Star out of this **Country Bumpkin**, huh?"

"I stay, almost consistently in Holiday Inns." he continued. "Dottie Lou could be warbling in every Holiday Inn on the East Coast and all through the South!" he opined in friendly laughter.

"I very well know, every little bit counts." I agreed.

"Do you have some extra boxes of records I could take with me?" he asked.

"Not many." I replied in bogus seriousness. "Just a garage stacked to the beams, an attic and my Chevy trunk about to burst, I can barely close. It's such a lucrative business! They're selling like **Hot Cakes!** Too bad they don't sell like Hit Records!"

"Be serious, Dottie." he scolded. "I mean it! Do you have some with you, here, at the Gopher to give to me?"

"Sure, I have some in my car." I responded, finally serious. "I'll get a couple boxes for you, after we're finished."

"How many are in a box?"

"Twenty-five. I'll give you a box of "One More Memory", my signature release and also a box of "Now I lay Me Down to Cry."

"That would be great."

"It certainly is admirable of you to do this." I remarked.

"I don't know why I didn't think of this sooner."

As we shut down the power for the evening and covered our equipment with the usual sheets, Geno was loitering at the service bar with a cocktail in each hand.

"Wow! You're really thirsty!" I chuckled. "A drink for each hand."

"Hey, Funny Face, you know perfectly well, one is for you."

"I was surely hoping one was mine. Not the Cutty SArk, however. I just could never acquire a taste for scotch. I get an odor, attacking my nostrils, resembling turpentine fumes, whenever I come even close."

"Boy, you have quite the imagination." he smirked.

We exchanged silly and serious chit chat in a barroom booth while other employees laughed and danced and visited all around us. We didn't dance. Inundated conversation seemed to take precedence over shuffling around the dance floor. We never seemed to extinguish our abundance of topics.

"When I went to Mass last Sunday at St. Patrick's in Jacksonville, I noticed they were adding a huge steeple, or constructing another huge church right beside the one they are now using. I couldn't believe my eyes."

"Churches have all the money. Organized Religion. That's what big money is all about!" I commented, smiling wryly.

"Well, I looked up and asked Him, why do these dumb human being strive to build expensive, artistic, materialistic **things** for God. It's almost sacrilegious! Nature is free and it's more beautiful than anything man could ever construe. Why can't we just be humble, indulge in simplicity, compassionately see and feel the adversity of others plights and use these assets to help others, rather than pouring all that money into concrete!!" Geno was intense.

"Oh, but that wouldn't do for the rich. They think God is divinely impressed with their money power, poured into cement."

"I guess so. God needs these powerful bucks poured for His Honor and Glory. Right?" he fervently remarked with discerning irony.

"I'm sure God doesn't give a hoot about materialistic power." I added.

"That's assured."

"It's similar to what I read in the Catholic Herald. The Roman Catholic Church is spending millions to build some huge grandeur, magnificent Cathedral somewhere in Rome, while homeless people in New York City, Duluth too, are sleeping on the streets in cardboard boxes and eating out of garbage cans. I just don't understand where their interpretation of charity is coming from!"

"That's how we take care of the poor." Geno smiled, faintly.

"We build elaborate majestic Chapels so the wealthy can have a warm, comfortable place to **kneel and pray** about the needs of the poor and the depressed!" I added. "Instead of doing something about it."

"That's full-fledged **Hypocrisy!!**" he grimaced.

"But, like I mentioned before, Geno, We can't change the world, as the saying goes. But let's not let the world change us!"

"I suppose that's the only way to keep from losing our cool and our minds, as well." he sputtered in agreement.

He talked, with intensity of politics. An excitement about a political campaign trail in progress. Potential candidates, diligently seeking nomination for the Democratic Party. Hopefuls, challenging each other over fervent platforms, on issues; trustworthiness, morality etc. "Nixon is the popular choice for reelection to a second term." he stated, matter-of-factly.

He cited names of numerous hopefuls campaigning for the presidential position in the Democratic Party; specifying a Muskie from Maine, Humphrey from Minnesota, George Wallace, George McGovern etc. "Hubert Humphry is by far the best man in the presidential race for nomination, Don't you think?"

Listening, I smiled and nodded and sipped my drink. He could have been **speaking in tongues** for what little I was able to grasp.

"Well July will tell the tale. In Florida they're all concerned over busing and America's Indochina involvement. The U.S. was just after the tin and tungsten there, among other resources. We had no business being there, just like we have no business in Viet Nam. It's all about greed! I'd sure like to see the Viet Nam war stopped! Wouldn't you?"

I smiled, I nodded and I sipped my cocktail, but finally, I decisively interrupted Geno's intense assessments of the Campaign Trail, emphasizing obstinately, "Geno, I know absolutely nothing about Politics! When I say nothing, I **really** mean nothing. I don't even know anything about these people you're talking about. I don't even know which party each of thes guys represent. I don't know where they're from or what offices they hold."

"You're kidding?!"

"No." I chuckled, trying to hide my embarrassment. "I'm not kidding! Really. Not kidding at all!"

"Everyone should know who they're voting for!"

"That's why I don't vote."

"You don't vote?! Well shame on you!" he dictated, disconcertedly. "I know for sure, now, you have to read the book I mentioned a while back. I have it in my brief case. "None Dare Call It conspiracy. I'll give it to you to read. You read that and maybe you'll learn what this corrupt country is really up to. How they finance wars and afterwards finance the rebuilding of all the destruction they were responsible for in the first place. It's really shocking."

"But if I read it, will I actually understand it?" I blurted, then diverting the subject, I sputtered, "We've given Organized Religion

Hell! Given our two cents—or rather your two cents on the Campaign Trail in progress, offered our stimulating assessments on helping the homeless and disabled, made remarkable progress on how to further my lucrative record business and well—we've covered just about everything that needs modification. Hey, we've put in a diligent, resourceful night of strenuous, intense labor here to execute all these successful achievements in changing the disfunctional world around us. And we did it all just sitting, perched on our sorry dupas, in a booth at the Gopher sippin' cocktails!" I giggled. "And besides that, it's 2:30 A.M. . Where did the time go?"

"It just fly's by when you're havin' fun." he joshed.

"It's been fun, but me thinks I'd better get my frivolous, frolicking fanny, flyin' forward for home."

Geno snickered, "Bet you can't repeat that. And try it without taking a breath."

"Once is enough." I smirked. "Anyway, my thongue is too tick! I think it's Srandy baturated!"

"Say, Screwball, I'll walk you out." he said. "I've got your book of prose and poetry in my car. You better take it before I lose it. I've had it in my briefcase over a month now."

"And that book of Political Emancipation, that will set me free!" I teased, refreshing his suggestion I read it.

"Oh yes, that too, but Dottie, you have to promise to **really read and study it.**"

Geno opened his briefcase on the hood of his car and searched it's contents, retrieving my poetry and also "None Dare Call it Conspiracy".

"Oh, I almost forgot!" I exclaimed, "The 45's! Let's sit in my Chevy. We'll go through the records and insert a 5x7 promotion picture of myself in each jacket. I have a bunch of them in my music case. Radio

Managers seem more interested, somehow in spinning my records when I include pictures."

"I can't imagine why!" he buzzed, as he dramatically ran his eyes up and down my frame, over enacting a thorough inspection.

I just grinned and added, "Sometime Program Directors don't even open the envelope and **caboom,** into the garbage it's automatically tossed."

With dedicated exuberance, together we stuffed each record jacket with a 5x7 photo, including promotion info. at the base of each picture, my manager, Korn's phone number and we included a title strip for jukeboxes.

"Why don't you move to Nashville and pursue your music there, where it's at?" Geno asked. "You're as talented as any I hear on record. It's a shame, no it's a **sin** not to use the gifts God has given you, to their fullest. And you're not only beautiful on the outside, but people don't begin to know the real you, inside. The real beauty that's you."

"Geno, I think you have me on a pedestal. I'm not all that perfect. I did once have thoughts of pursuing a star-studded dream with a Nashville scenario, national TV and touring concerts. Korn is my manager and we talked about attempting to push and further my career. He believed in me. But then there were three little branches from the old tree, the obvious need of three vulnerable hearts necessitating guidance, who had only one parent for support.

I couldn't subject them to life on a Tour Bus or Nanny's without me. And although they're almost grown-up, teenagers, they need direction and discipline even more than babies do Little kids, little trouble. Big kids, **Big Trouble**, if left too much alone to fend for themselves."

"Those are tough choices, I guess." he agreed. "But anyway, I'll push these records in all the states I travel, all the places I stay, wherever I can. It might help. Anyway it can't hurt."

"You're still hell-bent on making a Country-Western Star out of me!" I laughed.

"If it happens, it happens." he returned. "Whatever the outcome, it will be God's will anyway. Right?"

"Yes, that's the truth. Our fates are planned by a Bigger Power anyway. Every turn in the road I've made, I'm sure, was divinely guided."

"That's called Destiny, I believe. How I wanted to be a Priest! I was positive it was my calling. I tried to pursue the plan religiously, but now, four beautiful children later, I realize it was not **His Plan** for me."

"Will you be back in two weeks?" I queried, diverting the subject, then adding, "To have a couple celebration drinks with me on my birthday?"

"I'll be back tomorrow." he sputtered. "I have a couple days here, left in the office. Hmmm—Oh! So you're having a birthday in two weeks! I'll bet you won't tell me your age?"

"Why not? I'll be forty February 6th. That horrific number that panics everyone. Not me. It's just a number! So many, especially gals, are so paranoid about that number forty!"

"Wow! We're the same age." he ejaculated. "I was forty in October."

"Then we're not the same age. You're way older than me! Heh, heh, an old fogie. ♪ Neh, neh, neh, ♪ neh, neh, neh!" I teased, in sing song witticism. "Hey, we'd better get going before the sun begins to appear in the horizon."

"You're right. It's really getting late! I gotta lotta book work tomorrow. See you tomorrow—no, tonight, Funny Face. It is Saturday, now."

"Thanks, Geno, for taking records on the road. Helping me further my career."

"Oh that's nothin', Dottie. Glad to help."

"Bye now." As he made an exit from my Chevy.

* * * * * * *

The following night, after the Tumbleweeds had completed their Saturday night gig, Geno and I shared a couple hi-balls in the barroom. These Gopher cocktail rendezvous, concurring into harmless chit-chat were unconsciously developing into an inherent uninhibited routine that I found gratifying and looking forward to. Our intellects seemed so compatible, so connected. I relished his reflective, philosophical viewpoint on things, his depth and profound insight, his spirituality and his benevolent propensities. He excerised an intellectual vocabulary, obviously well read, giving me mentally challenged visits. Our talks were never reduced to the usual barroom witless four-letter expressions. I'd never heard profanity emerge. Though I was naive, he made me feel smart. He laughed at my weird sense of humor, usually adding his own deft wit. What a turn around from first impressions, when I had cruelly, uninformed, labeled him conceited, tactless and narcissistic.

It was becoming an intrinsic practice for Geno to accompany me to my vehicle on my usual departures.

Saturday night when we exited the Gopher on approaching our automobiles, he urged I join him in his auto, momentarily stating, "I have something for you, Dottie."

"Oh, oh. Another poem, I suppose."

"That too." he replied, "but something else much more important. Last night I found out your birthday is just around the proverbial corner. Right? I got that information from a very reliable source, so I assume it's accurate." he chuckled.

"Yes, but it's a ways off, a couple weeks." I cnfessed.

"But I might not be in town then."

"That's okay. It's no big deal."

Ignoring my indifference, he continued, "I went shopping today, after I was able to lift my face from the mountain of book work on my desk. And I purchased this gift f---"

I cut him short, interrupting with, "I don't accept gifts from strangers!" I opined, teasing.

"I may well be **strange,** but I'm not a stranger." as he reached across my lap, unlatched the glove compartment and drew out a very delicate, petite gold cross on a gold chain so fine it appeared to be the mere thickness of fine thread.

"I want you to wear this." he stated matter-of-factly,

"No offense, Geno, but I can't except jewelry from you. That's way too personal." I quibbled, attempting to dissuade him.

"This **is not from me!** This is **from God.**" he thundered. "I had it blessed this afternoon, after 4 o'clock Mass at St. James in West Duluth. I've noticed, for some time now, you don't wear a cross. You should always be wearing a cross in Honor and Praise of Jesus Christ, who **died for us!"** he scolded, auspiciously.

I was stunned! I was well aware of his intense Love for God. It was beyond my understanding. It had emerged numerable times in our conversations.

"I don't know what to say." I stammered, uncomfortably.

"Don't say anything." he replied. "Just turn your head sideways and let me put it on your pretty little neck." he insisted as he fumbled with difficulty to open the miniscule fastener. He reached around my shoulders with the chain encircling my throat and closed the clasp. As I turned back he gently pulled the cross, sliding it forward on the chain to the front of my throat and pressed it to the center of my bosom, briefly straightening the position of the cross.

An unsettling, unexpected surge of tingling, warm sensations traveled up my throat to my cheeks, feeling flushed, as his gentle hands had touched my pulsating skin and I realized, in all our chit-chats of tété-é-tété visits we had never actually touched, except, perhaps in a lively impersonal polka or jitterbug. This seemed too personal! Too intensely fervid. Were we trespassing on territory not bordering on mere friendship.

"Well, I don't know." I stammered. "I don't think I should keep this. It's not righ---" He laid his index finger, snugly across my lips, hushing, thwarting my less than firm opposition.

"And on yes." he stated, dismissing my reluctance and objections. "I did write a poem. It's for you and I assure you **it is from me!** I will understand your reluctance, if you choose not to accept that. But refusing a cross, praising **our Lord?** Not acceptable! Never! Really, Dottie." he exclaimed, defeating my persistence to object.

He located the poem and handed it to me as he switched the overhead light on.

"What's this one about?" I inquired.

"It's called, Know Your Way. You may not understand it, Dottie. It's more or less about me, but could easily apply to anyone who deeply, truthfully searches the depths of their own consciences. I typed it because my handwriting is not very legible."

I read as meditative silence prevailed.

Know Your Way

Into your bed O lonely men
For you have seen as no one can
The life you led is it the best
And did you know that you'll rest
Knowing the things that you have touched

Excusing yourself for it's a crutch
For any hearts you have broken
Required some day will be a token
When He and you decide at last
Taking review of all of your past
There'll be not one that'll say go here
It's yours to know the entire sphere
Although your stay has not been long
Have you joined chorus within His song
Have you been unselfish and kind to see
Yielding forgiving, in time of need?
Humble and pardoning are the words
Or has this been one that hasn't heard
He, Informs us time and time again
Be kind, Be kind, to your fellow man
For What You Have Done Unto The Least, He'll say
You Have Done Unto Me you'll know the way
You'll Know Your Way

By Eugene O'Demarra

I felt sometimes his poetry messages were totally between the lines and meanings difficult to interpret.

"I have a little difficulty in the interpretation." I said. "But, Geno, you're awfully hard on yourself, don't you think, if I get the meaning?"

"I guess I am harder on myself than anyone else."

"God is so, so kind and merciful you've told me. Even a song in church relates that. Right? We error often. We're not meant to be symbols of perfection."

"No, we're human, but we're suppose to aim at perfection."

"We all are our own worst critics, I guess. I notice on the top of your poems you always put J.M.J. What does that mean?"

"You don't know?" he retorted, indignantly. "I'm appalled!" he flipped, scolding, but equivocally grinning at the same time. "What kind of a Catholic are you?" he joshed.

I replied in a more serious vein. "I'm not a **very good** Catholic, but I like to think I'm a pretty good Christian! Anyway I don't have a clue about J.M.J. What does it stand for?"

Dottie, Dottie, Dottie. J.M.J. stands for Jesus, Mary and Joseph, the perfect family! I thought you knew that. I put that on all my letterhead correspondences too."

"Wow. I feel so stupid."

"You're not stupid. Don't ever belittle yourself." he rebuked.

"It's late. I have to get going, home to my kids." I said, fumbling for the latch on the door.

"And Larry's waiting too by now." he inadvertently added.

"Well, no. He's still racing at Eagle River. He'll probably be back late tomorrow. There are races still going on, on Sunday afternoon, but Dale, my son, has to be back for school Monday."

"Where is Eagle River?"

"It's straight east of here, almost all the way across the state of Wisconsin. Right on 70."

"I've never heard of it."

"That's because it's a small town. Just a little over a thousand people. Seems strange for Eagle River to be selected as a place to hold World Championship Snowmobile Races."

"That's probably why it was chosen." he chuckled. "You can't very well race snowmobiles in a big city, with four lane highway traffic. There's more than likely a lot of open spaces in Eagle River."

"I s'pose, but we could talk all night, Geno. I really gotta go. Thanks for the lovely cross and chain."

"Don't thank me. It belongs to Jesus." he again rebuffed. "Thank God. Love Jesus."

"Well then, thanks for the poem."

"Right. You're welcome. I'll see you next time I'm in town."

"Okay. Toodle-ooo."

♫♫

CHAPTER EIGHTEEN

Eagle River snow dust had barely fluttered from the hood of the "Green Bean" and Larry was off again, attending the Hibbing Snowmobile Races with his Hardway Team and other companions and friends We'd hardly kissed hello and it was "Goodbye, Hon" with brief, indifferent cheek pecks. Racing was his indulged diversion and I undoubtedly savored my freedom. It was almost a guise of being single.

During the week prior to the Hibbing Races, Larry's energy was consumed and exhausted on the Skiroule Shop with brief interludes of salesmanship at Arrow Chevrolet.

"It's fanatical how far snowmobiles have come from the 1927 Model T version." Larry speculated as he handed me an insert from the Duluth News Tribune.

SNOWMOBILES

HAVE COME A LONG WAY SINCE 1927

In 1927, finding a snowmobile like this Model T version wasn't easy—not many were around. Today, things have changed. Snowmobiling has become a favorite winter sport, and the number of snowmobiles to choose from has skyrocketed. Check these snowmobiles! Of course, we can't promise you'll find a 1927 model.

"1927! Yee Gads! I wasn't even born yet!" I ejaculated. "I never realized they've been around that long. Where did you find this?"

"It's from a full page ad that was in the News Tribune, endorsed by the already successful, established snowmobile names. I assume the Big name brands united together to place the gigantic advertisement, because only big names were included in it; Ski Doo, Polaris, Articat, Moto-Ski etcetera. All the Cadillacs of sleds. Of course Kenny and I can't afford that top-notch advertising. We're just starting out small, money is scarce. If I'd known about this I would have hit up Coleman for a piece of the action."

"They would, probably, have been willing to invest some bucks in that!"

"Kenny and I have to depend on **word of mouth.**"

"You should do terrific with that!" I cajoled, laughing. "You're very adept at verbal diarrhea."

Larry beamed. Nothing ever seemed to stifle his undaunted enthusiasm. "Just think, what massive, immense competition Skiroule has to contend with! What a challenge! There are so many sleds on the market, with many more new ones being introduced every year."

"That's certainly true, but you guys are doing okay? Aren't you?" I asked, with dubious thoughts.

"We're holding our own." Larry scrutinized, confidently. "We don't have money for extensive advertising like the "Big Dogs", but we're selling machines every day, even with "Po Boy" handicaps."

* * * * * * *

"Boy, have I been offered a fabulous deal. It's an absolute Steal! A real Giveaway Bargain!" Larry exclaimed with mendacious contention. "There's no way in hell I can pass this one up!"

"You're always, forever getting or giving one kind of a negotiable **DEAL** or another, Larry." I chuckled, innocuously. "It's old hat. What is your expertise, excellent, astronomical, astounding, overwhelming, staggering, stupendous, (enough adjectives?) Deal, that's pending now?" I asked in ridicule.

"It's a deal on a motorcycle!"

"A motorcycle!" I shrieked. "What for? Now race motorcycles too?" I thundered. "Just what you need to kill yourself on, A HOG! What asinine stupidity will you come up with next?" Adamant anger welled relentlessly, as a wave of heated agitation rocketed from within, sprinting up the nape of my neck.

"And where is all the money suppose to come from for all these childish, big kid toys!" I queried angrily. "You spend six or seven grand a year on building your stock car, which incidentally, you don't have six or seven grand to spend. Now, add the expense of a motorcycle?! Larry, when are you ever going to grow up?"

"I have sponsors that pay a bunch of my expenses!" he quibbled dogmatically, unyielding.

"Sponsors? Huh! How absurd! A few pennies here. A few pennie there. Peanuts! Nothing that amounts to 1/100th of the actual cost of building and maintaining your stock street car. Why, Dandrea gets the whole half of your car for 250 bucks. I haven't forgotten, you know, how you conned Ernie Brottom out of money you owed him for several years, until he finally got so fed up, he sigged the sheriff to serve papers on you at our doorstep. How embarrassing was that?"

"That was just an innocent misunderstanding. He did a boo boo. His records were all screwed up. I paid some money he hadn't marked down in his books!"

I forced fictitious, ironical laughter. "Yeah, that's a usual, frequent vonGillern expertise talent. You always manage to prevaricate some kind of a bogus alibi to justify your actions and escape responsibility."

"Well, what about all the money I win at races? I'm very competitive! There's a bundle of prize money for all the First Places I run away with, throughout the entire season!"

"Oh yes!" I agreed derisively. "A six thousand dollar car and First Place winners purse ranges all the way from 25 dollars to 50 bucks, depending on the track. I don't know where you went to school, Larry, but I was pretty proficient in mathematics and no matter how I examine these figures, It just doesn't compute! Racing is nothing more than a power ego trip." I quipped. "A frivolous expensive hobby!"

"You have your ego builder, too. Your music is all of that and I don't stifle **your** hobby!"

"My music supports my three kids and I. It's not a hobby. It's a Job! **I get paid** explicitly a certain concrete amount every night and it doesn't cost me thousands of dollars before I can pick up that bass and plug in that mike. Gas to get there and a few stage clothes, that's about the extent of my expenses!"

"You forgot to include your biggest expense." he scoffed. "The cost of keeping you supplied in Brandy!!"

"I hardly ever buy a drink! It's all gratuitous, from fans and customers. That's my **smallest** expense!"

"Well, **okay, okay!**" he blurted angrily. "I won't get the damn motorcycle."

"Larry, use your head!" I reproved cogently, but in a calm, amiable, bargaining voice. "You don't have time for another hobby with the demands of Arrow Chevrolet, the Skiroule Shop, Stock Car Racing. Think about that. You can handle one or the other, but not both. A motorcycle?? Then give up the stock car or visa versa." I depicted, diplomatically. "You don't have money **or** time for both."

Larry condescendingly agreed to drop the idea of purchasing a motorcycle. The subject was dropped and I assumed Larry was finally acting like an adult. It was a credulous assumption! Because a few weeks later, I discovered, through careless, innocent conversation with a coterie of his companions who nesciently informed me his motorcycle was stored in their garage. Larry's friend, undoubtedly was unaware that I knew nothing of the arrangement and innocuously let the cat out of the bag. Larry had purchased it the following day and stored it there, merely waiting for the dust to settle from the verbal storm with his unsuspecting wife.

There never was a feasible solution to keeping Larry from financial ruin and bankrupcy. Chapter 11 had been his escape more than once, before he even turned thirty. His concept of values and integrity was that of a mirage, charging and spending more than he made, not taking seriously, promisory notes or the loyal responsibility of reimbursing friends who assisted financially. Larry's insatiable obsession to have whatever he wanted, whenever he wanted, feasible or not, affordable or not always took precedence.

* * * * * * *

It was Good Friday and the very last day of March. People were in a hustle bustle mien planning their Easter Celebrations. Traffic, therefore, was akin to a Chicago freeway. I had attended church services with Charmaine and Rogie in the afternoon, observing the Solemn Service commemorating Jesus death on the cross at St. Joseph's Parish in the Heights.

Now, in the midst of noisy Gopher frolic and a festive atmosphere, it was quite an abstract deviation from what I had celebrated prior, in the afternoon. I found it difficult, at first, to make the transition, with my own conscience fostering guilt over being in a bar singing on Good Friday, but I objectively justified my presence to the dire need and required necessity of providing food for the table and fuel in the furnace for my offspring, so I was soon ambushed into the laughter and the music and the gaiety of any ordinary Friday Night.

Geno made an appearance at the bar and briefed me on his Easter Plans. He was enroute to Burtrum; to spend the Holiday with his children, but decided to stop at the Gopher to wish us all a wonderful Easter Holiday. After all, he quoted, "The Gopher is my second home and you're all my second family." He had made friends with our entire coterie and everyone accepted him as part of our clique.

"Going to see your kids, huh? That's great. Are you heading that direction tonight?"

"No. I'm at the Holiday Inn on London Road for the night. I'll head out tomorrow morning at check out time for Burtrum."

"A little Hanky Panky too, I suspect, with; the little wife. Huh?" I smiled mischievously. "Easter Keister Rendezvous!"

"We don't spend time together—and she's my **Exwife!**" he adamantly maintained, as usual.

"Well, it wouldn't be a sin, you know, Geno!" I tittered, teasing. "We all have needs!"

♪ "No ♪ it's over, Really over.♪" he crooned a line, in jest, from a Jim Reeves ballad, smiling, nurturing my bantering mood.

"A separation is not any different than being married. You're married just like I am. Like it or not." I joshed.

"I have legal papers in my possession, drawn up by a competent lawyer for a four year separation, at which time I can make the decision, whether I want a continuation or a reconcilliation. It was the only approved sanction in the Catholic Church. They tolerate and only ambivalently, the policy of separation, when two people are incompatible. Their biggest concern, I believe, is with the welfare of the children."

"But you will never be able to enjoy a serious relationship, Geno. You will never be able to remarry." I said. "You just have to live a life of celibacy. **Ahem!** Unattached, uninvolved, hanging in limbo. Not touching ground. Can you do that? If you can you're a lot stronger than me!" I giggled. "Why not endeavor with a little Hanky-Panky with your wife—hmmm—I mean exwife. After all, it's not as though you haven't been there before. At least four times!" I chuckled, unable to embrace serious discussion. He ignored my attempt at humor and tenaciously replied.

"After you're finished tonight, I want you to come with me to my automobile and I'll get my legal papers out of my briefcase and I'll prove to you, that exactly what I say is true. I'll show you exactly what it states in black and white and exactly very very legal."

"Don't be so serious, Geno, or testy. It's really none of my business. I'm just making small talk or humor or whatever. You don't need to show **me** anything!"

"I know that. But I also want to give you the addresses of a couple people I've talked with in Springhill, Louisianna, last week. They both want you to send them pictures and records of One More Memory, a couple copies to each and also Lay Me Down To Cry. One is Ron Ridey of KBFF radio station and he insists he can maneuver and stimulate a bunch of air play. He also owns a music center in Springhill."

"That's wonderful Geno. You amaze me. I'm impressed. Maybe I'll have to get you a position on my management team and a % of my gigantic proceeds! No, I'm not making light of your effort. It's really nice of you to bother with my stuff."

"So when you're finished, tonight, I'll get that information. It's in my brief case, as well."

"As long as he owns a music store, maybe I should send him a couple boxes of records to sell."

"That might not be a bad idea."

"I sure do appreciate your promoting this Country Bumpkin in your part of the world. A part I'll probably never see or visit."

"I did give away a lot of what you gave me across the few states I traveled."

"Are you out?"

"No. I have about one-third of a box of each left."

"I can always scare up some more very quickly." I giggled. "As long as you're willing to be bothered with them."

"No bother." he insisted.

I sashayed my way back to the stage.

When the evening had come to a close I exited with Geno to his auto to pick up the names, addresses and miscellaneous info he had gathered for me. While I scribbled short memos to myself in the dim light, he briskly scuttled up an official looking document from among his briefcase paraphernalia and unfolded it upon his lap for reading and viewing.

It obviously resembled my divorce decree, dissolving my marriage from Roger, in legal size sheets covered by a blue, heavier dense sheet. He dwelled on the propriety of a separated relationship and high-lighted with his finger, statements discerning a four-year commitment, the pro's and con's in the formalities of the arrangement and I felt uncomfortably ill at ease and embarrassed. I was fallaciously peeking into his privacy. I pretended to scan the high-lights he was pointing out to me, but not really reading or grasping anything he was explaining.

"I don't belong here." I mused, ambivalently. "This is insane! This is monomania!"

"That's okay, Geno." I interrupted. "I believe you. Does it really matter that much? What does it matter what I think anyway?" I asked. "It's really none of my business! You should be shouting 'Butt off, Dottie'."

"I want you to know I'm not a manipulating, dishonest person I'm not full of B.S."

"Why? Who am I to judge or criticize your decisions. I think you're a nice buy and I like you. Let's leave it at that. Furthermore, most of the time I'm only teasing, trying to get a rise out of you!" I tittered.

"I s'pose I'm just too serious." he said. "That is my nature." he confessed as he slipped the document carefully back into his briefcase.

"Say, I meant to mention earlier, I like seeing that cross and chain hugging your throat. It really looks as though it belongs there."

"I like it too. It feels so light and petite I forget it's even there."

"It's so delicate, so feminine, when I first saw it, I knew, through and through, it whispered dicreetly, "Dottie Lou".

I laughed. "You're more of a poet, And don't even know it!"

* * * * * * *

One Saturday afternoon, a couple weeks after Easter, Larry jubilantly burst into our Walnut Street home with ebullient, volcanic excitement.

"Sold three more sleds today!" he exclaimed. "That gives us enough points for five tickets to Paris!"

"Really! Oh my god! Paris? Paris, Texas? Or Paris France?!"

"Whatta you think? Paris, France, of course! We're flyin' T.W.A. to Paris! What do you think of that?!" he smirked, arrogantly.

"I think it's incredibly awesome!" I screamed with delight. "Wow! Awesome! Fabulous! And then some! Who's all going?" I asked.

"You and I, Kenny and Sylvia and we have enough points for one more ticket. We haven't found anyone to fill that seat, yet, but someone will definitely want to scarf that up. There's no doubt of that!" he beamed optimistically, then added. "It will be a little harder to find someone to go alone. It would be easier if we'd had points enough for two."

"I'll have to find someone to fill in for me at the Gopher!" I ejaculated, as wheels began turning and spinning in my mind. Necessary plans errupting and boarding the rails of the proverbial **train** of thoughts. "When do we leave?"

"Real soon! We leave May 4th from Minneapolis. We have to get passports, maybe shots too. I don't know all the particulars, but it's nine days including travel time from here to Minneapolis. They won't pick us up here in Duluth. Boarding is arranged to be at the Minneapolis International Airport."

The Coleman Company's gigantic promotion scheme to introduce and sell their new snowmobile **"Skiroule"** line had certainly been met with success. New on the market and previously unheard of, the aim to splash it over all the snow states, including Canada had reaped an unexpected avalanche of diverse marketing success.

Working for points collected for the sale of each sled was met with dynamic incentive and motivation. Convinced salesmen, among their many franchises were responding with tenacious, infectious dedication.

Larry and Kenny, in spite of their novice franchise, were proficiently in the top groups in sales performance. The Coleman marketing management let it beknown they were impressed.

Larry entertained an innovative ambition for adventure, always embracing life with uninhibited trial and risk. Certainly these three and one-half years we had shared had not been dull. Scary? Yes. Insecure, unpredictable, but never **Boredom!** Larry had an expertise skill in conniving anyone and everyone, convincingly that what he had to offer was always of utmost excellence, the best in taste, in durability and performance! Who was more well aware of this fabrication than I?! Look what he had persuaded me into in three short years!! Ahem! I mean this with humor.

"I'll have to find someone to stay here at the house while we're gone." I sagaciously relegated. "I certainly can't leave these teen-agers alone for nine days! In two days, without supervision, they'd be tearing the house apart. No one would go to school and they'd be drinkin', sleepin' all day and partying all night the whole time."

"Well, they've had a **damn good teacher!**" Larry arrogantly flipped sarcasm. "Their mother is no **slouch** when it comes to drinking and partying!!"

"Seems like I remember a **passed out Larry** last year, very early, at his garage Birthday Bash!" I quipped. "And so early, in fact, we had hardly begun to party yet. I've got that on my home movie collection." I scowled at him with a disdainful grin. "Seems like I have pictures of Barb Jurek putting a lighted Birthday candle in your inebriated belly button!"

He set his lower jaw in a defiant thrust and squinted at me with eyes half closed. This was a subtle, vonGillern expression Larry harbored whenever he was annoyed or beaten or didn't get his way.

He quickly changed the subject. "I'll talk around, among friends, and see who I can come up with for baby sitters."

"Good idea. They can't be left to fend for themselves." I scrutinized. "The bigger the kids, the bigger the mischief and the bigger the trouble!"

"Yeah, I'm well aware of that!" he agreed, as he flashed a deliberate wink at Dale. "Leave you and your buddies in complete control here! While we're gone? Hah! Never!"

"We can stay here by ourselves." Dale rationalized. "We don't need a baby-sitter!" insisting innocuously, **"We are not Babies!"**

"Yes, Mom." Charmaine piped in. "I've been making meals, all the time on Saturdays, when you work at Freddie's, don't I? We can really take care of ourselves. The house too."

"Not a chance!" I chuckled in reply.

"That's for sure!" Larry buzzed. "Soon as we'd make the first turn off of Walnut Street, Dale, you and Willis would be hot wiring my stock car, just like before!"

"Hot wire your stock car? What's that about?" I queried, intuitively.

"Oh, last summer, they took old number 61 out for a spin!" Larry incisively devulged. "Without my knowledge, of course. And when I wasn't around."

"Why didn't I hear about that?" I rebuked.

"No use to get Mother's panties in a bundle, I thought." Larry explained. "So I didn't tell you."

"So you can tell me now." I scoffed.

"Dale and Willis, hot wired my stock car and took it down the road. That's it. I guess you were at work."

"You did that, Dale?" I asked.

Lowering his eyes he sheepishly replied. "Yes, but—Larry, you bragged and bragged and bragged about how you could burn rubber in third gear, so Dave and I took it for a spin on Morgan to see if it was really true!"

We all burst into laughter.

"That was the truth. I could burn rubber in third gear. That engine was Hot!" Larry chuckled. "It did burn rubber in third gear. Right?"

"I don't know." Dale smirked with a simpered smile. "You caught us before we really got a chance to give 'er guts!"

* * * * * * *

When Larry and I applied for our passports I was a bit apprehensive, as I had lied my age to Larry when our courtship was in it's infantile January stage. I also falsified it on our marriage license application, as well. I don't know if the discovery was a jolt to him or not, when facts, like birth certificates, revealed I was ten years his junior. He never mentioned or questioned any part of the procedure in attaining our passports. I couldn't fathom his disinterest or unconcern. Perhaps our anxiety over the question of shots, put everything else into oblivion. We were ecstatic over learning shots were not a requirement.

We purchased a small "short duration" insurance policy to cover the financial trust and care of our children in the event we should be killed or injured on the trip.

Larry had arranged for his best man, Bill Redenbaugh and his new bride, Bunny, to stay at our house with the kids while we were away. We filled the frig and cubboards with abundant supplies and Bill and Bunny moved in for the nine day stay.

Bill Weisenberg from Larry's snowmobile, "Hardway Racing Team" picked up the fifth ticket to Paris.

♪♪♪

CHAPTER NINETEEN

I called Billy Griffith of "The Country Gentlemen" to inquire if he was available to fill in for me on Bass in my absence. He accepted responsibility for all the gigs except for the Saturday night when, he disclosed, he was booked with his own band. Trying to touch base with Korn, I explained the situation to him, with apprehensive concern.

"Not to worry!" he chortled. "Don't sweat the small stuff, Dottie P. Lou. Don't worry about this **peon** place, when you have the chance to spend your time in Paris, France!"

"But, what about Saturday Night?" I precariously inquired.

"I'll play the bass and I'll get Dick Porter to do the rhythm guitar and he wails a helluva good country song to boot!"

"Uh oh, I may lose my job over this trip." I tittered. "But, Saturday Night is okay. That's settled then."

As I worked the week-end gig, Bill dazzled us with an unexpected appearance at the Club to confirm he'd substitute for me. He sat in with the band and treated us to his renditions of "High on a Mountain" and "Crazy Arms."

All musicians love to Jam and Bill was no exception.

"You cravin' the strings?" Toby asked.

"Yeah, and I just happen to have my trusty 'ole bass in the car." Bill laughed.

So Bill bombastically agreed to filling in a set of music to "get the hang of the Tumbleweed Bag."

As I stepped from the stage to relinquish the spotlight to Bill, I was hand motioned to a table where Geno was perched, sipping a scotch and water.

"I didn't see you come in." I remarked. "It's pretty dark in here. The spotlights were glaring in my ey---."

"No. The fact of the matter is, I'm pretty sneaky." he interrupted, twitting. I could see he was in one of his sporting whimsy moods.

"And Hi there, Marketing President of Dottie Lou Enterprises." I asserted.

"What's that all about?" he laughed.

"An A1 Performance in Promotion." I buzzed. "You're certainly doing a lot of homework. I'm getting responses from a lot of areas along the Eastern Seaboard about that Dottie Lou recording artist. Places I've, myself never touched on before."

"Well, well, well, it must be payin off, then".

"I'd say so. I'm impressed. For instance, there's a Jerry Adams WSEN, Baldwinsville, N.Y. wants five DeeJay intro's to play for five different DeeJays there. Wow!"

"I'm glad I'm doing okay with the Dottie Lou Promotions." he beamed.

"More than okay. I've heard from a Rueben Jackson, WRFS, Alexander City, Alabama; Charles Dillard,WPFA, Pensacola; A Colman O'Neil, Hamel, Noth Carolina, I forget the station letters, and Hamlet, North Carolina, WKDX. Oh yes, South Carolina too, in Baltimore. A John B. Walton at KDJW in Amarillo. Texas also wants me to send intro tapes for several stations."

"You remember all those by heart?"

"Well, all in all, that's only what I can remember off the top of my head. There are several more. I've already recorded and sent out intro tapes to some of them. I'm working on correspondence replys too."

"Evidently a squeaky wheel does get the grease." he chuckled, obviously pleased.

"I can't thank you enough, Geno for all your efforts. That's really wonderful of you to take the time."

"Gotta promote my favorite singer." he chortled.

Oblivious to the performance of the band, I excitedly related the latest developments of my anticipated vacation plans to Paris.

"That's a great opportunity!" he remarked. "Will you get a chance to sing there?"

"Hardly! I'm afraid, I'm having a difficult time getting invited to sing in the states, let alone over seas!" I laughed heartily.

"It's food for thought." he retorted in all seriousness. "You're certainly talented enough."

"It's not that kind of a vacation. It's more or less just a private group of Coleman Companys representatives. Franchise holders, managers, salesmen, secretaries, employees, people involved in their snowmobile business. And of course wives and friends get to tag along."

"When are you leaving?"

"On May 4th, from Minnesota. I'll be gone a total of nine days."

I explained how Larry and Kenny had earned the tickets and what a trip overseas involved in prep. Like passports and baby sitters and insurance and fill-ins for my gigs etc.

"It won't be the same without your voice in the Tumblweed sound." he frowned.

"But the dancing will be the same. There's Vivian and Delores to dance with and oh, of course, **Big-Boobed Jan.**" I giggled. "I'll send you a card from Paris for a souvenir."

"That would be nice. Oh, by the way, I'm out of Dottie Lou records, too. Do you have some here?"

"Sure. Bunches and bunches in my little 'ole Chevy."

* * * * * * *

Geno and I searched my trunk for a couple boxes of my 45's and I extracted from my messy, cluttered trunk interior a large business envelope containing 5x7 pictures and title strips.

265

We sat in my vehicle putting the 45 promo jacket packs together, as we had on prior occasions. By the dingy light I autographed each individual photo.

"This goes pretty fast now, after we got the hang of it." he casually remarked.

"Yes, we're getting really skilled at this." I agreed. "By the way, Geno, I wrote a poem for you." I said, as we completed the record promo packs. "I can do that too, you know." I glibly purred.

I fetched my purse, lying on the seat between us and retrieved the type written poem I had penned, then tossed my handbag onto the back seat. I turned on the dome light for Geno to read by. Handing him my poem, I remarked. "I wrote this poem a couple weeks ago after we had talked in your car, discussing our spiritual and intellectual compatibilities. Our mutual interpretations of so many things. It's entitled "Insight? The Birth of Life.""

Silence embraced the air as he read, ingesting the indepth meaning of my thoughts on when the actual instant of birth occurs.

Insight? The Birth of Life?

I remember times, far passed away.
Superficial living from day to day.
I'd flaunt my youth and laugh aloud
At wrinkled brows that seemed so proud.
For blind was I to that within,
Real beauty, beneath a fading skin.
When minds think no deeper than the tongue.
So Sad! The **ignorance** of young!!
Does life begin with birth of sperm?
Or at first cry from mother's womb?

With pubic hair, do we surmise?

Or with greying temples and tired eyes?

No it matters not what the age may be!

Life really begins when we can see!

"Wow, Dottie." he deemed reflectively. "Incredible. It's very well written. Makes me feel like an amateur. I'm amazed at your perceptive viewpoint describing insight. It comes across very clear, very honest."

"All that flattery. You're making me embarrassed."

"Don't be. Be proud, not embarrassed. You know I read a poem just yesterday by Helen Steiner Rice. Are you familiar with her literary works? Especially her poetry?"

"I'm shocked! I don't believe it!" I ejaculated. "She's my very favorite poet! I have two books of her poetry. It's unreal, of all poets you would pick her!"

"At my cabin, when I'm alone and after I've built a fire in the fireplace and have taken off the chill, I sit and read her stuff. Love her style."

I was mesmerized. I couldn't believe what I was hearing. I was often aware of how compatible and connected we seemed to be on topic after topic. And I was often impressed with his indepth, his perception and grasp of intellectual and spiritual vision. However, poetry is a real profound and personal insight into the very soul of a human being. Not that his visions were so significant, but that they were mine, as well. My thoughts, my values, my perceptions.

"I love the way she meters her poetry, besides her sensitive grasp of words." I conceded.

"What do you mean, meter?" he asked.

"It's like the beat—in time—like in music."

"Oh, I've never really thought about **why** I like her. I just do. Maybe that's part of it."

"I love her poetry so much, I memorized one from her book that I use as a prayer. Along with my Our Father's and my Hail Mary's, of course." I tittered awkwardly, in an attempt to lighten the tense conversation.

"Recite it." he suggested.

"Really?" I could feel my facial warmth and I knew my face was flushed. I was thankful the street lights of the parking lot were too dim and dingy to betray my embarrassment. I surrendered to his request.

> Bless us, heavenly Father,
> Forgive our erring ways,
> Grant us strength to serve Thee,
> Put purpose in our days...
> Give us understanding
> Enough to make us kind
> So we may judge all people
> With our heart and not our mind...
> And teach us to be patient
> In everything we do,
> Content to trust **Your** wisdom
> And to follow after You...
> And help us when we falter
> And hear us when we pray
> And receive us in **Thy Kingdom**
> To dwell with Thee some day.

"That's a real nice prayer. I'm pretty sure I don't have that one. I'll have to look again in the book I have of her poetry. What's the title of the prayer?"

"It just says it's the personal prayer of the author. Another one of her's that I really like is "The Peace of Meditation".

"I have that one. It's very profound. Is that in the same book as the prayer?"

"I'm not sure." I replied.

"I'll have to check that out."

He was still grasping my poem. "Oh here. Your poem." he reached out his hand timidly to return the written page to me.

"It's for you." I said as I returned the sheet to his fingers. "I wrote it for you."

Our hands touched and as he pulled away his fingers brushed across my arm and he momentarily squeezed my arm with a casual gesture of friendship. An unsettling stream of sparks fluttered wildly up my arms and through the veins of my neck. His fingers were trembling as they rested briefly on my arm. His equivocal gaze caught mine in a humble, contrite moment. Dropping my eyes, I looked away. He broke our connecting eye contact, as well. We both, intuitively deemed a compelling fragility of emotions racing through our minds. Perhaps a too-late warning of the danger of our pristine, private visits, unchaperoned by the adamant security of hum drum public places.

Fostering a fleeting impulse, he gently touched my cheek. I couldn't halt the mounting, intoxicating flood of emotions that ambushed my senses. Furthermore, I didn't seem to want to! instead I reached for his face, tenderly fondling his cheeks where usually little obeisant dimples snuggled, whenever his humor was aroused.

With sudden elated emotion, he cupped my face in his hands and his fingers were tremulously caressing my cheeks. He traced my lips with soft gentle fingers. I avidly returned his caresses, unrestrained, exploring his face as well. Suddenly, while combing my fingers through the tufts of his ebony, black hair, his mouth seized mine. Pressing, crushing fiercely with intense, uninhibited passion. His soft moist tongue was taste testing my lips, back and forth, when we rashly, hungrily devoured each others mouths in sensual frenzy.

Instinctively, my arms encircled his neck, shamelessly welcoming his subtle invitation, surrendering totally to the hunger of our euphoria. Kissing, kissing, here, there, planting kisses everywhere. Faces, cheeks, lips, mouths, to the soft closed eyelids and to the tip of the nose. But then, impulsively rushing into a current, out of control, to bared throats and throbbing secrets in a torrent of heightened passion.

I was unaware my bra had been unfastened until I felt his fingers gently massage my breasts and I gasped a gulp of air in ecstatic surprise at the unexpected touch. He attempted, unsuccessfully, to kiss my, out of reach, bosom. An impossible feat in lieu of the erratic position we had snuggled into.

Erratically agressive, we began tearing at each others garments. I fiercely unbuttoned his shirt and began, zealously running the palms of my hands over his warm hairy chest. His hands were sliding up and down the curve of my buttocks and caressing my outer thighs, suddenly diverting to my inner thighs, up—up—up, under my skirt, fondling my genital secrets through the layers of lingerie. When reaching the waistline of my undergarments, he pulled my pantys and panty hose to my knees. I gulped a huge drag of air, catching my breath, like hitting an air pocket in flight, when his supple hands smoothly slipped up my inner thighs to my now bared genitalia. "My Broken Lady".

I fumbled anxiously, all thumbs, at the waistline of his slacks, tearing nervously into closures, wildly unhooking, unzipping, then clumsily yanking his slacks down to below his knees, impatient and sensuously frenzied with desire. As the restriction of his shorts was surrendered his protuding passion was thrust, unconfined, meeting my naked stomach. Geno pulled me fiercely, hungrily over on top of his errection, in this inert, compromising sitting position.

It didn't matter. Nothing mattered. Without apprehension or guilt or embarrassment, without thoughts of right or wrong or good or bad, he probed his love machine into the very heart of the pulsating broken lady. With persistant, intense, escalating thrusts, in this crazy, unplanned, unrehearsed inert niche, Heaven belonged to us, ours! Totally, ecstatically Ours! All ours! Nothing else existed! Nothing else mattered! Nothing and No One! Only our complete oneness, our togetherness, our own **Special Private Utopia!** The ultimate taste of Heaven!

Breathlessly, **simultaneously** we found a profound tenderness together, in those first time precious moments of our love-making the entwining of two inseparable souls and like our clothing, still tangled.

"Oh, how I've wanted to do that for oh—so—so long." he murmured, unabashed, against my ear, his breath rustling my hair.

"Gosh—omigod—I—well, oh, oh. So wonderful." I sighed, softly, my voice trailing off, still quivering.

We both, perceptively found each others lips again. Our kisses, momentarily silencing all needless conversation of a nondescript emotion. Gently, tenderly calming, caressing, fondling each others faces, throats, while we finger-combed each others hair. We had profoundly discovered a part of each other never imagined in our wildest thoughts, in an impulsive, bizarre, unplanned intimacy. We had always suspected a platonic, soul-mate bonding for sometime, that we so often shared. But never anything this impetuous.

The wild pounding of our hearts against each others chests gently calmed to a peaceful patter and still we held each other in quiet subdued tenderness, still ultimately tangled, tangled in our clothes, still planted together as one. Not wanting to separate, to break the intimacy, to spoil the moment with words or dampen it by annihilating a bonding of souls. We just quietly embraced the togetherness, with profound silence of our Spirits, our minds, clutched in each others arms.

Moments later, still peacefully tangled together, coddled in each others embrace, face to face, tears began slowly slipping down my cheeks in silence. And in silence, with the insight and sensitivity that was Geno, he wordlessly began gently wiping them away with his fingers, putting them to his lips, tasting my obvious ambivalent emotions. Not till then a word was uttered, when he softly, wistfully inquired.

"Do the tears mean you're **Sorry**?" he asked.

"No. Not sorry, Geno. Only sad. Sad for the **hopelessness** of these wonderful, wonderful, ecstatic, elated, crazy emotions I'm feeling, right now."

"I know. I know. Me too."

♪♪♪

CHAPTER TWENTY

"What will we do for spending money?" I asked. "I'll be missing a whole week of wages from the Gopher."

"No problem there." Larry asserted. "Kenny and I called an emergency meeting to discuss the appropriation of **"Funds for Fun."** he smirked. "A proposal was made by Kenny and seconded by Larry, followed by a unanimous vote to allocate a grand from the business for each of us for essential traveling necessities." He laughed heartily, enjoying his own witticism.

"Wow! We can have a lot of fun on a thousand dollars." I quipped.

"You bet."

A portion of a participating group, joined us as we boarded a privately chartered 747 at the Minneapolis International Airport.

BOARDING TWA FOR PARIS

We flew, nonstop to Montreal, where another larger group of Canadians joined us raising the total number of passengers to approximately 180 people. And from Montreal, a straight shot to Paris.

The initial excitement was overwhelming and cameras were flashing spasmodically, from every direction and every occupied seat. We were, of course, among the mesmerized tourist clowns, exuberantly snapping shots of each other.

To the rear of the TWA an all night beverage bar had been arranged, set up for party accommodations, so needless to say hardly anyone slept. I dozed a smidgen here and there, but Larry, so intensely hyper, was continually whizzing back and forth and up and down isles, introducing himself and getting acquainted with others. I assumed, candid, gregarious Larry would know everyone on the plane by the time we landed in Paris. I don't believe he laid his body down for a fleeting moment.

After the 747 TWA had touched down in Paris, a shuttle bus, or perhaps several, transported all of us to the **Inter.Continental**, our hotel. We would be staying there for seven nights. Accommodations for showers and shut-eye mostly. However, there wouldn't be much ample time to spend collecting zzz's.

The group was tense, excited and awed when we received our itinerary, at a short, spontaneous briefing in the lobby before locating our individual rooms. The program listed exciting tours, places and events to enhance our stay. Engaging in the numerous activities was voluntary and we could choose to take part or go our own ways, whatever was our whim.

What remained of the first day, after settling in was left to getting acquainted. Acquainted with the city, our accommodations and with each other. Kenny and Larry hailed a cab, late afternoon to take us to an eating place recommended by the receptionist at the desk.

"They serve the greatest, most delectable entree of octopus in all of Paris. Nothing, no one, not another single establishment can compare to that exquisite cusine!" she assured us. "Em—em—good!"

All four of us raised our eyebrows and exchanged dubious eye contact.

"Whatta you think?" Kenny smurfed grinning.

"Nothin' like a little new adventure." Larry chuckled. "Let's try that octupus!"

The cab driver drove on and on and on, with a greedy meter burning up the bucks, finally dropping us at the designated restaurant. The next day we learned the eating place we had visited was a mere three blocks from our hotel! Ahem!! Lesson #1. Legs are very adaptable and adept, are never exorbitant and costly and walking is excellent exercise. We opted to transport our bodies, physically, here and there without insatiable bogus meters running chaos, debilitating our wallets.

As we entered the elegant cafe, an odor meant to be a tantalizing aroma of the delicacy of simmering octopus attacked our nostrils. It was quite similar to the odor of urine! Ugh! We wrinkled our noses and frowned.

"I don't know if I care to try that octopus!" Sylvia retorted, reluctantly. "They must have something more american on the menu, like a good old fashioned cheeseburger and french fries!"

"Ah, come on Sylvia." Larry quipped. "Where's your adventure? How bad can it be? And **we're in Paree!**"

"But the smell!" she scowled, mulling it over. She wrinkled her nose, scrutinizing the offending odor. "Unless we hold our noses when we eat!"

"I'm gonna try it." I piped in. "Why not? Something to talk about when we get home!"

"Yeah, we'll sure never be in Paris again. It's once in a lifetime." Kenny added. "Why not be a little daring?"

If you could ignore the aroma, it was in fact quite delectable. It was cut in thin slices and basted in a delicious brown sauce. To me it seemed quite parallel to the taste of beef heart or chicken gizzard, which I had often savored on the farm.

The following morning, whoever bore an interest in sightseeing, gathered at the main entrance of our hotel and boarded a tour bus which took us on an exciting informative venture, visiting the many prestigious historical sights of Paris. We made non-stop, congruous persistent exploit of our cameras.

Larry doggedly insisted he be photographed with our Tour Guide. We all were well aware of Larry's obsessive, audacious display of importance, as we modestly chuckled. I couldn't help but ponder if his eagerness would have been synonymous had the Tour Guide been of male gender.

The tour bus paused at each sight, enabling everyone to explore and snap photos. Our Tour Guide very proficiently explicated and categorized each point of interest.

Arc de Triomphe
(The Arch of Triumph)

"Arc de Triomphe or The Arch of Triumph", she rattled on in fluent English, with a pronunciation here and there in French, equally fluent, "is here looming glorious and statuesque before you at the base of this beautiful avenue called Champs-Elysées and symbolizes National Honor and Patriotism. The Avenue Champ-Elysées is in itself, a fashionable sight, the most famous of twelve symmetrical avenues."

I absorbed and digested her comments as she rambled majestic descriptions in English, sometimes with a heavy French accent. French was a language I had always embraced and adored. I thought it imbued and gushed of Romance! Retrospectively, in my eleventh grade of High School, when students were asked to participate in a Declamatory Contest, with category choices being; Humorous, Political, Historic or Dramatic, there was no hesitation on my part. I immediately chose, my only option, a French Drama, entitled "Camille". I tried, studiously to master the beautiful French Brogue, embellishing the sound.

"Here in 1806 Napoleon began building his Arc de Triomphe and it was not completed until 1836 by Louis Philippe." the Guide continued. "The tomb of France's Unknown Soldier of World War I lies beneath this Arch. A flame burns continually, as you can see, to honor him. The Arc de Triomphe is 160 feet high and 146 feet wide. Inner walls bear names of Napoleons Generals and his triumphs."

Standing at the front exit, as the bus was in motion she explained how the River Seine ran east and west, quietly flowing through the center of the city. "Several gardens, huge lawns and parks lie on the left bank of the Seine. It's entire course is edged by stone embankments. Streets that line the embankments are called **quays** and as you can see are bordered with many trees to enhance the beauty of Paris. There are many Book Stalls standing along the guays for brousing."

She continued her historicity as we rumbled along Parisian Roadways and Streets, some many lanes, other exceedingly narrow, curving in and out of turbulent traffic I found unsettling.

"There are over thirty bridges that cross over the Seine. Little steamboats called **Bateaux Mouches** carry passengers on the River Seine. There are 130 public town squares, called **agoras** in Paris. Many of them are World Famous, and here is our next stop." she continued as we approached the famous Eiffel Tower.

"The Champ de Mars, (Field of Mars) was formerly a Military Training Field and is now the site of the Eiffel Tower." she continued, as we disembarked and gathered around the base of the Tower. She went on, "It's a wrought-iron skeleton designed by Alexandre Gustave Eiffel in 1889. The Tower is 984 feet high and 330 feet square. Elevators and stairways lead to the platform on top. We will allow approximately thirty minutes for anyone desireing to board elevators and view beautiful Paris from the top. The Tower, now houses several restaurants, a weather station and miscellaneous experiment spaces. The price of its construction was one million dollars. For many years it was the highest structure in the world. But now, presently, the Empire State Building and The Chrysler Buildings in New York have surpassed its height. It was a Military Observation Station during World War I. Since 1953 it has been used to transmit TV Programs. There are no skyscrappers or Church Spires here. Most buildings in Paris are no higher than six to eight storys and seventy to ninety feet tall. You may now take time for picture taking and for viewing, or elevator trips to the top, or for the brave, the stairways." she giggled, knowingly and then began to sashay back to the tour bus.

We snapped numerous pictures of each other at the base of the Eiffel Tower and exchanged favors with others to get pictures of complete groups together.

Kenny-Sylvia-Dottie-Larry
EIFEL TOWER

"Let's get on that elevator!" Larry ejaculated, with hyped enthusiasm, We discovered the elevator, though sizeable, accommodated merely fifteen to twenty people at a time, so we were forced to wait and take turns for elevator admittance.

Lollygaging at the summit, the cameras were flashing everywhere as we viewed Paris in awe from the top. We took turns using and sharing huge telescopes supported on hinges to embellish the magnificent view. It was exciting. It was stimulating,. So much to try to absorb and digest, overly saturating my brain. It just seemed so overwhelming!

As we again snuggled into our seats, the Tour Guide rattled further descriptive historicity of Paris. The tour bus hammered tantivy down the roadways and the Guide specifically pointed to various sights. "Look to the North Bank. There, in part you may view Louvre Palace and the largest, most prestigious Art Museum in the world. It covers 49 acres. There are 140 exhibit rooms and eight miles of galleries. Approximately 5,000 paintings are displayed in the 900 foot Grand Gallery, including Leonardo de Vincis 'Mona Lisa'. There you could also view, if time permitted, the intriguing painting of Faust playing Chess with Satan, bartering for the German Magician's Soul!" she glibly chuckled. We all laughed, politely adjoining her amusement. "The architecture is Gothic as are so many, many structures here in Paris." she added.

"We will now cross the bridge to the Island and visit the world famous Cathedral, the Elise Notre Dame de Lorette. It was built in 1836 to "The Glory of the Virgin Mary." It is filled with statues of Saints and frescoes of scenes from the life of the Virgin Mary. This island is the **Heart of Paris, the very center of the city**. There is a circular sundial, kilométre zéro, in front of Notre Dame. All distance points in France are measured from this **kilométre zéro** sundial."

CATHEDRAL Elise Notre dame
DE LORETTE

As the bus came to a parking halt she announced ostensibly, "We have 30 minutes here."

Larry and I visited the Cathedrals interior and marveled at its elegance, the gigantic bellows, in size and number, the display of reverent majestic statues.

"Gosh, it sure would be awesome to attend Mass here on Sunday!" I emitted, intrigued. My enthusiasm was soon dampened when there was no audible response.

"Wouldn't that be something?" I adamantly continued. "Mass in Paris at the famous Notre Dame? Gosh, what a reverent honor!"

Still no response. Disappointed, I abandoned the thought. I deduced it must be of no significant interest to a non-practicing Baptist, then musing, with regret, "How intoxicated and mesmerized Geno would have been at the prospect of Mass at Notre Dame. How he would have absorbed all the ambient history of Paris, I was so fortunately seeing and digesting."

Larry exuberantly took to feeding the flocks of pidgeons on the sidewalks outside of the Cathedral, as I watched, indifferently. Some were even taking the popcorn from his hands. One alighted on his arm.

"Quick, take some pictures!" he ejaculated.

"Okay." I agreed. I rolled some on my movie camera for him to enjoy when we returned home. It was obvious the pidgeons were accustomed to tourist hand outs.

The Tour Bus transported us to numerous Parisian sights, as the guide dramatically gave descriptive briefing on Parisian and French history. I fantasized myself being entertained on Pig Alley, dancing the can-can at Moulon Rouge and sitting elegantly garbed, in a private balcony square, watching a play at the famous Opera House. I retrospectively examined my inner thoughts on Victor Hugo's "Hunchback of Notre Dame."

We visited a Parisian Cemetery, observed French Fuzz directing traffic on Paris congested streets, strolled along outside markets with fresh fruits and selections of meats and bakery goods, all unwrapped with no sanitation and frequently attacked by hordes of flies.

We visited Parks and Gardens and numerous Palaces and Museums, such as the "Musee de Petit Palais". All structures, monuments, museums, street signs etc. were, of course, in french.

The bus rumbled along North Side of the Seine and as the vehicle slowed to a crawl, the guide casually announced. "We will now visit Montmartre, the highest hill in Paris. You may have lunch in the

Montmartre district. It's noted for its cafes and Nightclubs. It's also a gathering area for artists and writers. Montmartre is in the Bohemian District of Paris and is inhabited by many painters. You will be able to watch them in action, as they sit and paint in numerous places here on Montmartre Hill."

On foot we followed the guide up the street to a quaint, Sidewalk Cafe. Glancing up, I noted it was called "Restaurent á la Mére Catherine", "Mére" meaning Mother, in french.

"Must be a Ma's and Pa's restaurant." I sputtered. "Has to be excellent food with both "Mére" and "Catherine" on the Marquee. Catherine is my grandmothers name so it can't be all bad!"

"We have allotted free time, here, for everyone to spend however you choose." the guide declared. "We will resume to the Tour Bus in exactly one hour." And she disappeared to her own whims.

The four of us ordered sandwiches and beverages. Kenny and Sylvia ordered sodas and of course Larry, his usual gigantic glass of Moo Juice, **(lait).** My beverage preference was the usual coffee **crutch.** It was the third time I had ordered coffee **I was unable to drink.** I finally realized it was not because of any particular restaurant menu. It was because I was in France! Their interpretation of a palatable, choice formula for coffee was **thick** and **black** and so strong it was nearly the consistancy of syrup! It turned out to be my final attempt to drink coffee in Paris. I was briefly devastated, being coffee was my daily crutch. How I regretted not having initially packed a small coffee pot and a bag of Folgers in my luggage. We carried our lunch to the Sidewalk tables, where we indulged in idle conversation, watching people as we ate.

After lunch we strolled the area amongst numerous painters, stopping now and then to admire their efforts. Larry was mesmerized over a painting of a Parisian Cathedral.

"I'd sure like to take that one home to Minnesota." he said. "Is it for sale?"

"Qui."

"When will it be finished?" Larry asked the preoccupied artist.

"Deux." he held up two fingers of his left hand as he continued painting with the right hand, without looking up.

"Two days?" Larry asked.

"Oui, two day." he replied, indifferently.

Larry began negotiating on a price. "How much for the painting when it's done?"

"Hundrad dolla." the artist inadvertently replied, murdering the English language with a heavy French brogue.

"Way too much!" I heard Larry reply.

"Ayety dolla, no las." the painter quibbled.

"I'll give you fourty dollars." then enunciating very slowly **"For— tee—do—lla! No more!"** Larry cavilled emphatically, gesturing with his hand at **"No More!"**

"Auarante? For-tee dolla? Steal!!" the artist yelled. "Hundred dolla. Cent. Wort mo." he argued.

"No want!" Larry smirked, shook his head no, turned to leave, slowly making a bogus motion of departing. I chuckled, inwardly, thinking how Larrry was attempting to communicate in broken French-English, as well, but without much success.

"Wait!" The painter thundered. "Quarante dolla, I take. For-tee."

The smug, confident, gregarious salesman grinned from ear to ear, winked at us and started making arrangements with the bearded artist. Larry slipped him $20 deposit, negotiating on him paying a balance of $20 when we'd return in two days for the painting.

I laughed as we began strolling back toward the area where our tour bus was parked. "You may as well kiss 'dat twenty dolla au revoir, auf wiedersehen, adieu, adios, goodbye!!" I giggled, teasing. "You'll never find that same artist here at montmartre, **I'll bet**, two days from now!"

"Oh yeah. He'll be here." Larry confidently replied. "No sweat!"

"I don't know." Kenny blurted. "I think my vote's with Dottie."

"Well, what's twenty bucks anyway, halfway across the globe?" Larry joshed, grinning.

Back at the hotel, in our room, Larry, addressing Kenny, Sylvia and I, exclaimed in heightened enthusiasm,

"Where should we go now? What should we do? The day is still fairly young. Hell, there's so much to see!! Should we hit the Night Clubs? We don't wanna miss a thing!! No, not a thing. We'll never, ever be in Paris again!!" All this as he languidly stretched out across the bed. Kenny, inadvertently flopped into a padded chair, unmoved by all this exhilarated eagerness.

Less than five minutes later Sylvia tapped me on the shoulder and without conversation, pointed to our gregarious over-achievers!

"Let's go to the Lafayette Shopping Square and look around." I whispered.

"That's an excellent idea." Sylvia agreed.

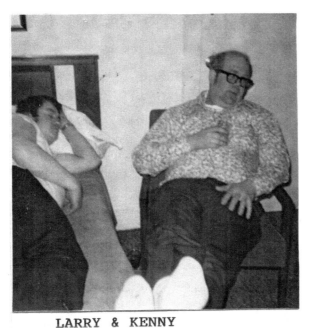

LARRY & KENNY

"UNDAUNTED ENTHUSIASM"

We gathered our shoulder bags and softly tippy-toeing from the rumble of zzz's, we exited the room and sashayed down the stairs of the Inter.Continental, but not before surreptitiously snapping a couple blackmail pictures of our two exhuberant companions!!

♫♫♫

CHAPTER TWENTY ONE

The majestic Lafayette Cathedral was constructed in the 14th century and was later converted into a Department Store, presently the largest in all of Paris. Over 200 Boutiques and many adjacent stores lined the shopping square.

Sylvia and I browsed around from boutique to boutique, store to store.

"Sylvia! Look at these gorgeous dresses! Over here!" I exclaimed.

She sauntered over. "But where in the world would you ever wear one of them?" she lamely affirmed, as she finger examined the feel of the material. Sylvia was a consistent, hard core, jeans and sweat-shirt gal.

"On the stage!" I declared.

"Feasible for you, maybe." she conceded. "Sure not for me!"

"Just think!" I gushed. "To sing on stage, clad in a Paris Original! How elegant. How impressive! They're probably not originals, but who would ever be the wiser in Duluth!" I giggled.

I diligently examined the clothes racks, the innumerable choices of sophisticated garments and soon found one appealing to my taste. Sylvia, curiously located a partly concealed price tag.

"Jesus Christ!" she boomed. "Look at these prices!"

"Wow! $250!" I ejaculated, as I peeked over her extended arm. The price was listed in American dollars as well as French currency. I began investigating. "Here's one for $450." I blantantly screeched and then quickly glanced around to see if our tacky, tourist conduct was being observed by other customers. "I'm gonna try one on." I said.

"Are you crazy? What for?"

"Well just for fun. I'm sure the clerk won't recognize that we're poor as church mice." I whispered.

I located a fitting room after selecting an exquisite blue lace. The tag read $325. Emerging from the fitting room I slowly sashayed, swaying my hips voluptuously and tilting my head in a come hither gesture, I sighed in a low, sensuous, breathless Marilyn Monroe imitation. "I'm Mademoiselle Dot—tee from Gay Pair—ee!"

"Oh take it off!" Sylvia quipped, chuckling. "Let's mosey down the shopping streets and find some Pair—ee Sweat—ee Shirt—ee!" she chanted, mimicking and mocking me.

"Well, no harm in dreamin' a little. I think I'll just weasel some bucks from that big Skiroule wad Larry's carrying around for Paris Original Gown!!"

"Fat Chance!" she laughed. "Lotsa Luck!"

We strolled past a Beauty Shop on an adjacent Avenue.

"Hey. Wait a minute, Sylvia. Let's top in here. I'll see if I can get an appointment to have my hair done. That would be fun. An elegant, sophisticated hairdo for that Dinner-Dance tomorrow night."

"Oh you and your **elegant** this and **elegant** that. You're completely wearin' the guts outa that word." Sylvia teased. "Better find out how to say it in French for variety."

With a little subtle persuasion, the hair dresser agreed to allow me an appointment for the following forenoon, squeezing me in a slot where there actually was none.

* * * * * * *

The four of us took to hoofin' the streets the next morning searching for a reasonably priced breakfast cafe when a French Photographer, with a camera slung over his shoulder, approached Larry.

"Monsieur, I take photo of you and Mademoiselle. Souvenir of Paris." he coaxed, emphatically.

"That would be nice. **Elegant**." I purred, grinning, as I winked at Sylvia.

"How much?" Larry asked.

"Two dolla." was his reply.

"Okay. Oui." Larry conceded, apathetically.

It was a Polaroid camera. The Frenchman hurriedly snapped an unrehearsed, informal shot as we casually stood by. He released the flipped out photo and retrieved a small cardboard frame from his paraphernalia in which he quickly inserted the, still not yet completely developed picture. Handing it to me, he asked, "You like?'

"Well, it's us I guess." I wrinkled my nose, unimpressed. "Us on a Paris Street."

Larry reached for his wallet. "Two dollars. I guess it's worth that."

"Dit-on!"

"Quoi? Deux? Non!!" shaking his head. "Oh la la! Sixty dolla!"

"You said two dollars." Larry angrily retorted. I mused, "Humm, Larry just met someone expert at his own game."

"Non, Par-don. I say sixty dolla!"

"Dit-on!!" Larry laughed, ironically. We had learned how to say **"Rip-off"** in French. The term was quite often as necessary as "Bonjour" in Paris.

"Sixty Dollars?" Larry tittered. "You can keep the picture, Monsieur! A souvenir **for you** of Paris—from me! And Mademoiselle!" he chuckled again, relishing the game.

"Oui. Two dolla." The swindling photographer conceded.

We shook our head sin disbelief, however we were innovatively coming to realize the spurious expertise talent of the scheming Frenchman versus the gullible, naive American Tourist!

After breakfast, **le petit dejeuner** I left our foursome and sauntered to the Beauty Shop to honor my appointment for a Parisian Coiffure. Sylvia and Kenny and Larry plodded their own directions to pass the time. We agreed to all meet at our rooms in the afternoon around 4:00 P.M., give or take a little.

At a novelty boutique I purchased a few postcards. I addressed a humorous one to the Gopher Gang and a casual to Geno. I located postage stamps at a vending machine in a nearby drugstore and later I dropped the cards off at the desk to be mailed. It was one of their included courtesies.

I wasn't very pleased with my three-hour hairdo. It was lopsided, loose and floppy! To salvage it for the evening I had to pin it down with numerous bobby pins. I had to almost, completely reconstruct the style in my hotel room. Judy King was my personal hairdresser in Duluth and her handiwork was expertise by comparison. Her styling usually lasted, with minor touch-up for four or five nights on stage. Perhaps the Parisian fickle elements were responsible, in part, as the weather was continually humid and misty most of the time. I guess that's Springtime in Paris that the world sings about.

We busied ourselves with prep for the evening Dinner-Dance on the itinerary, planned and hosted by Coleman, to be held in a huge ballroom on one of the floors of the Eiffel Tower. Showers, **une douche,** were in order, as was special sophisticated attire to hug our perfumed, powdered, fresh fragrant bodies.

We stood in line at the Tower elevators in our fine garb and Sylvia, yes Sylvia was in a dress! Clad in elegant attire and high heels and with the men in suit and tie, we were an incredible, exquisite striking foursome.

We entered the ballroom and immediately observed that the setting, the decor was just as exquisite and elaborate as our dress. We found seating next to the Canadians we had become somewhat acquainted with over the past three days, sharing tours and festivities. It seemed natural and intrinsic to hang with the same people on a respite holiday as such. One begins to feel bonding and comfort in associating with the same people, sharing tours and dinners.

The tables for the féte were richly set in white linen with matching cloth napkins. Candles and many lavish bouquets of flowers adorned each table. Placed beside the top rim of each plate were three stemmed wine glasses of variable height and size.

"Boy, they must think we're mighty thirsty!" Kenny tittered.

"We are!" Sylvia giggled.

"This is France. When in France do as the French do!" I giggled. "Get sloshed on wine, wine, wine!"

Larry's gesture summoned a maitre d, one of many scurrying around in haste to prepare for our group. Larry relished having any old excuse to visit with the staff, especially if they were female. It's the distinctive behavioral trait of a salesman!

"Why do we all have three glasses?" he inquired.

"Monsieur," she laughed. "Every elegant dinner is served with before, during and after dinner wines. And it's proper etiquette to provide a different glass for each wine."

"I knew that." he buzzed, sheepishly.

Soon after receiving our before dinner Chardonnay, salad was served on our plates. As soon as we finished the salad, the plate was so quickly removed it almost eluded our awareness, and replaced with a clean dinner plate.

A vegetable-potatoe entree, **aperitif,** was served on the clean plate and likewise removed as soon as we had finished, to be replaced by another clean dinner plate, as well. The main-course, **plat,** was then served upon the clean plate and in the same manner removed, with a clean desert plate in its stead.

"Wow! I have to tell Rogie about this!" I remarked. "He hates to do his turn for dishes so badly, that he hides the dirty dishes in the, under the sink, cubboard, pretending he did them."

"Hey," Larry piped in, "When we get home we'll tell him, 'We're dining Parisian Style' whenever it's his turn for dishes!"

"That would probably cure him of hiding the dirty dishes!" I ejaculated, laughing.

After casual conversation and sip-sip-sipping, still another serving of after dinner Rosé wine, the maitre de appeared, toting a gigantic silver tray, all of two feet or more in diameter, completely covered with a scrumptious assortment of desserts. We were invited to make a dessert choice and indulge. The delicacies were displayed so artistically, arranged with hardly a repeat, making choices unusually difficult to make.

I opted for a huge slice of a magnificent pie, perhaps banana or coconut creme, being pale maize in color and topped with crushed nuts and coconut. I felt the saliva flow immediately as I was always intrigued with sweets. The love of sugar has always been my hangup.

We paused and waited for our complete table to make their selections so we could all etiquettely begin savoring our desserts together. I cut a small, I assumed dainty, portion from my pie. My fork seemed to struggle with a dessert not nearly as soft and creamy as I had anticipated. Rolling it around the tastebuds of my tongue, I stopped short, mid bite, wrinkled my nose and impudently announced. "This isn't dessert!!" It's **Cheese!!"**

Everyone laughed convulsively.

"Didn't you know the French serve various cheeses as dessert?" Someone at our table asked.

"No. I'm afraid not!" I said flustered and embarrassed. "I expected something sweet! I'm a sweet freak! I like cheese okay, but, I'd have chosen a much smaller slice if I had known."

During the later half of our meal a five piece orchestra entertained us with soft, ambient background dinner music. The group, all men, were clad in dark suits, white shirts and matching ties. I was fascinated by their performances, as they played American music. Music I was familiar with, Stardust, Smoke Gets In Your Eyes, Tenderly, etc. but sang lyrics in French! "How cool!" I mused.

A spokesman from the Coleman Company Management took over the stage P.A. for a half hour, talking and giving recognition to a number of people, one by one, who were responsible for all the programming and arrangements of the Coleman Paris Trip. He also presented awards to Best Salesmen Achievement of various franchises and areas. He devoted some aggressive time to future plans for the expansion for the anticipated growth and success of Skiroule. Increase in advertising was discussed and promised. "We're looking forward to another gigantic, even bigger year in **Sales and Snowmobiling!"**

Finalizing his speech and following an exuberant display of applause, he announced that the band would be performing for our dancing pleasure throughout the remainder of the evening.

I didn't see much of Larry at our table, as he continually gregariously bounced around, flitting from table to table, group to group, here and there. I assumed he was attempting to capture recognition and make some browny points, diligently rubbing noses with the management and the **"BIG CHEESE,** whomever he assessed as **Important People.**

With full stomachs we were engrossed in casual chit-chat. The Canadian couples visited with us, comparing kids, jobs, family, our life differences. Now and then a couple from our table would rise and embrace the dance floor. Larry twirled me a couple two-steps in between his meandering from table to table.

Sylvia and I were engaged in small talk, in Larry's absence. We conversed in raised voices, as we were overridden by frolicing noise of chatter and laughter of 180 people.

The melodious strains of music had paused briefly and someone at our table sputtered, "Shhh! Listen!"

From the stage Bandstand a voice thundered, somewhat distorted by the noise of the party. (féte)

"Paging Dough-Tea-Loo! Paging Dough-Tea-LOO!"

"They're paging you." Kenny said.

"Paging me!?!" a chortle, mixed with a ludicrous "Humph" spilled from under my breath. "Are you crazy?" Another absurdity chuckle and, "No one's paging me!—Not in Paris!" I babbled.

"Sure sounds like it to me." Sylvia remarked.

"Nah!" I scoffed, giggling. "Not remotely possible!"

"Paging Dough-Tea-Loo, paging Dough-Tea-Loo!" again came buzzing loudly, over the P.A.

"You better go see." Kenny urged. "Just go up there and ask."

"Ask what? That would be so embarrassing. I wouldn't know what to say. Besides, I can't speak French!" I quibbled.

"Just pretend you're requesting a song." someone suggested.

More persuasion erupted from several directions. Reluctantly I rose, disconcertedly, and shuffled to the stage. As I approached the foot of the stage near a series of foot lights, the front man of the band leaned over to talk to me and asked, "Mademoiselle Dough Tea Loo? Oui?"

"Oui." I stammered.

It was then I realized they were, indeed paging **Me!** Larry and the others in our group had been in **cahoots** all along. Had requested the band to petition me to sing. Larry had coaxed the band to vaunt the talent of his wife, knowing how much I would delight in such an opportunity. To sing, here in Romantic Paris, with an elegant French Orchestra! Tears were suddenly filling my eyes. How Awesome! How incredible! How wonderful!!

Somehow, between us, with his command of French and my blubbering English, we by some means, managed to interpret enough information to agree on a couple selections for me to sing, somewhat familiar and compatible to myself and the band as well.

High-spirited and pretentious I stood, ostentatiously in the midst of a prestigious French Band, in a fabulous ballroom on a floor of the majestic Eiffel Tower of Paris on May 6th, 1972 and made my euphoric debut, singing "Harbor Lights" and "Fascination" as my unbridled heart pulsated so furiously it felt as if it was about to take flight from my chest. It was overwhelming! It was incredible!

I believe—No! I **know** it was the absolute high-light in my entire trip to Paris and only after the evening came to a conclusion and we were all back at our hotel, did any of us realize that no one, not even myself, had perceived to snap a picture of me as I stood singing, mesmerized and totally embracing the moment. Every table was cluttered with innumerable cameras.

It was to be, my one and only excursion overseas in my entire present lifetime of 72 years!

♪♪♪

CHAPTER TWENTY TWO

The following day, after a late breakfast, we hopped a bus to Montmartre to explore the progress on Larry's lay-away purchase of an original Paris painting.

Kenny, Sylvia and I ribbed him disparagingly, mercilessly, all the way to Montmartre, attempting to cushion him for an inevitable disillusionment. Another probable **"Dit-on!"**

As it was our second time at Montmartre, we were able to locate the same area we had visited, prior, without difficulty. We began mulling about, among the ambience of numerous artists, searching for the bearded French painter Larry had negotiated with.

"He's over there!" Larry gestured and pointed across a bustling path, swarming with activity. The painter was perched upon a stool, studiously engrossed with a paint brush in hand and a canvas in it's early stage of creativity. As we approached he raised his eyes over glasses without raising his head and in a cool pleasant voice purred a **"Bonjour."**

"Hello." Larry greeted him in return. "My painting? Is it finished?"

"Oui, a droite." He pointed to the right of where we stood. There propped up against a make-shift stand was Larry's finished exquisite painting of a French Cathedral.

And "I told you so" complacent smirk stretched amiably across his face. He grinned, ostensibly, from ear to ear as he fumbled for his wallet.

"What did I tell you?" he quipped.

Kenny, Sylvia and Yours Truly were condescendingly forced to **eat crow!**

* * * * * * *

After a brief siesta to refuel our staminas in preparation for a full, capacious evening, on the itinerary for our group, we showered and dressed in our most ostentatious garb to accent a sophisticated dinner aboard a **"bateaux mouches"** on the River, **(fleuve)** Seine by moonlight. The enchanting, intriguing Romance of Paris!

We gathered together as instructed, in the lobby, to board buses to transport us to the boarding site on the **fleuve** bank.

We again arranged to be seated in the company of our Canadian Companions, as we were becoming fondly acquainted, familiar and at ease with our little coterie.

It was night time, so there wasn't much possibility of viewing scenery, sights, or monument landmarks. It was not intended to be a sight-seeing tour. It was definitely a planned evening with the beguiling, romantic, ultimate Passion of Paris!

An accordian player, musician, charmed the romantic atmosphere with French love songs and soft intriguing dinner music, serenading us with beautiful, mysterious french lyrics we didn't understand, but somehow portraying the intended mood of Love and Intimacy.

A photographer sashayed about the tables, snapping pictures of couples, by request, as we relished a scrumptious cusine, with an abundance of choice wines, indulging whatever our esthetic preference or taste may be, and never leaving for a minute, a glass half-empty!

Larry, with a gesture of obeisance, asked the photographer to snap a picture of us with our new Canadian friends. We autographed each others photo folders and emphatically promised to keep in touch. We conscientiously vowed to write or phone each other when we returned to our own environments.

Maybe it was the wine or the music or just the atmosphere or the concept of cruising down the River Seine in Paris, escaping all reality of responsibility, that overwhelmed us with so many capricious, fickle promises! "The road is paved with good intentions!" Everyone was mesmerized! Everyone was enchanted. Everyone was ecstatic! Everyone was in love! **Perhaps everyone was Drunk!!**

We never heard again from any of the Canadian Crew. We never wrote or called anyone, keeping in touch as we had so impetuously promised.

Yes, Paris is the city of Romance, French love songs, Can-Can Dancers, the lure of Gothic Architecture and Artists on Montmartre Hill **(colline),** exquisite féte in the Eiffel Tower, luxurious Designer Clothes, and a moonlight excursion on the River Seine for Lovers. Even the language gushed of Romance. Yes, Paris, was indeed, the **City of Romance!**

Larry had clout. Larry was adventurous. Larry loved risk taking. Larry was unpredictable and gregarious. But **Romantic?!!!** I think not. Perhaps the void in my heart was not his fault. Perhaps my reflections on the sensitivity, the warmth, the profound, philosophical rapport of the Soulmate I had only recently encountered had dampened the sentiments I should have been embracing.

Being giggly, lightheaded and a bit sloshed, we shambled, noisily, up the stairs to our own individual rooms. Our stomachs were full as was my camera, chock-full of memories for our scrap book.

As we, a little drunkenly disrobed and scrambled into our night clothes, we reminisced and chattered about the evening's frolic.

"Sure are a nice bunch, those Canadians." Larry remarked.

"This fe—te," I feigned a dramatic bogus pronunciation of fete, **feh-tay** as I giggled, tipsy. "Sure has been fun!"

"And we're not even finished yet."

"We're seeing so much in such a short time," I speculated, "and it will all too son be forgotten, I'm afraid, when we get back to routines and busy lives."

"You did take a lot of pictures, though. Didn't you?" he asked.

"Sure did."

"We have another Tour in the morning." Larry asserted. "So we better get some ZZZ's."

"Larry, I'd like to get a Paris dress." I said, ignoring his suggestion to hit the pillows. "A dress to wear on some of my more classy, sophisticated shows. Something different. Something really reeking Paris! Whatta you think?"

"Sounds Great! **Go for it!**" he boomed.

"However, to **go for it,** Larry, I'll need some cash. At the Lafayette, I saw a real nice lace in turquoise for only $200."

"Two hundred bucks! Are you nuts?!"

"Couldn't you give me two hundred dollars for a nice dress? You said you and Kenny, each, had a grand to spend."

"Well, yes" he mumbled, "But—"

"You sure haven't had to spend much of that grand, have you? Meals, that painting, a few souvenirs. Almost everything is prepaid by Coleman. Rooms, tours, special dinners. Right?"

"Well, yes—but—" in an obviously disconcerted grumble.

Again I interposed, "So why couldn't I have a dress out of that money to remember Paris by?"

"You must have your own money!" he curtly retorted.

"Well, some. I spent my own money on the Beauty Shop. Cards, stamps and a few souvenirs. I didn't bring much with me. With your thousand to spend, I didn't think I needed much."

"Get the dress out of your own money!" he scoffed.

"I don't have enough left for that dress."

"Get a cheaper dress. I can't give you two hundred bucks, so just forget it."

"But Larry, this is only once in a lifetime!"

"A dress is a dress is a dress is a dress. What's the **Big Deal**, anyway? I don't have the extra bucks for that kind of extravagance!"

"Where did all the money go?"

"It didn't go. I'm saving it for my Stock Car for when I get back to Duluth!"

"Oh I see." I mumbled, ruefully. "Once in a lifetime in Paris is not a **Big Deal**. The big Deal is **Your Stock Car!** I should have guessed. Racing always comes first! Always has. Yes I see."

"Don't be such a Big Baby!" he scoffed.

I didn't reply, only turned my face to the wall. "I still have eighty bucks." I mused. "I should have known better than to go without my own money. I can still buy myself something. Something nice. Something useful. Maybe a parisian handbag."

* * * * * * *

Nine A.M., sharp, we boarded a sight-seeing Tour Bus for our guided tour **(visite guidée)**, which took us to many castles, embraced by gardens and gardens and many museums and palaces **(musee** palais). We visited the Place de la Concorde, Place of Peace, in the heart of Paris and viewed the guillotine on which Marie Antoinette was beheaded in 1793. In some Palace or museum we were invited to view the bed Napoleon slept in. After awhile my head was spinning, as the Palaces seemed pretty much the same.

In one museum Larry, as usual, detoured from the customary designated route of the **visite guidée, mumbling** to me. "We'll catch up later." Larry's usual reckless, impetuous curiosity, unconsciously led him to a display of automobiles. I sware, he could actually smell gas, oil and metal when in the wherabouts of a collection of vehicles a mile away!

"Look!" he ejaculated, as he pointed. "A collection of cars. An MEP Citroen Toe-Tall." (Total)

"What's that?" I asked.

"I'll be dammed if I know!" he laughed. "We sure are picking up a lot of words and slang in French, but nowhere to use them after this trip! Hey, let's get some pictures of these automobiles! Get your **brush** on the seat of that shiny red "Brush" and I'll take your picture."

Due to my proficient expertise knowledge, **ahem!** and education and experience in auto mechanics **ahem!** and the racing circuit, **ahem!** I am unable to volunteer any discriptive enlightenment on the pictures we snapped!

Fontainebleau was next on the agenda, a town 35 miles southeast of Paris, famous for the magnificent Chateau de Fontainebleau, situated on the outskirts of the town. The Palace was a summer residence for many French Kings, where they hunted the grounds since the 12th century. It was one of Napoleon's favorite spots to visit and the Courtyard was the scene of his surrendering of the throne in 1814.

The Tour Bus rambled along countryside. Destination, Versailles. I attempted to capture French terrain with my 8mm movie camera through the window glass. However, the speed of the bus was too rapid to seize much of the farm **(ferme)** fields, where tractors plugged along in cultivation. Likewise, we so swiftly whisked through a little French Village that the town and the scenic countryside I had attempted to capture only resulted in a fuzzy blurr on my movie screen in later viewing.

Versailles was nestled twelve miles southwest of Paris and hosted the site of the historic Palace of Versailles. The huge Palace was ½ mile long and is known for its vast glittering **Galerie des Glaces,** "Hall of Mirrors." It is 243 feet long and is illuminated by 17 windows. At night in Louis XIV time, the murals, mirrors blazed with light from three thousand candles. The Treaty of Versailles, ending World War I, was signed in this Hall of Mirrors.

The Palace Park had a formal pattern of walks and gardens and lawns and majestic fountains. In its center a broad walk of law, called green carpet, **(topis verte)** in French, stretched along a mile long Grand Canal. One branch of the canal ran toward two smaller Palaces. The Petit Trianon and the Grand Trianon. The Grand Trianon had been Eisenhowers Headquarters during the war.

After wearisome hours of walking and walking and viewing, we were accorded a brief interlude to indulge in a late luncheon at the **"Palais Trianon."**

Around 3:00 P.M. we returned to the Inter.Continental, everyone complaining a bit of sore dogs and exhaustion, not to admit getting minutely bored with Tours, Museums and Palaces. The itinerary revealed the evening left was entirely of our own choosing.

Kenny and Sylvia excused themselves to their own room pleading fatigue, as did Larry, to catch a rejuvenating snooze before we'd be getting together for dinner.

Although, I too, was spent, obstinately I clutched my handbag after relating to Larry, I was still determined, still consummed with the notion to purchase something **special** for myself from Paris, I trudged, alone to the Lafayette Shopping Square.

I meandered from boutique to boutique, inspecting dress rack after dress rack, scanning for a garment with a more frugal price tag. Nothing stirred my emotions, arousing an **"I can't live without that!"** aspiration. My heart was fixed on a dress for stage wear, one perhaps a little notorious, but with a flare of elegance as well.

Everything I, condescendingly viewed in the conservative price category seemed frumpy, not exciting, glamorous or meretricious in any aspect and pale by comparison to the turquoise lace I had fancied and admired.

"Maybe a pants suit!" I ambivalently pondered. "A one piece like my green chiffon. If I can find one just a smidgen sensual. Eighty bucks sure doesn't buy much in Paris!"

"Hey Dottie!" the seamstress in me suddenly thundered! "Why not material? Some elegant fabric? Make my own ensemble!! A dress, exquisite and **one of a kind!"** I had designed and tailored most of my own stage clothes, even my wedding dress, so where is the problem? Yes! Yes! Yes!"

I soon found a well stocked fabric shop. I sashayed about, scrutinizing and probing into bolt after bolt of material and finally detected a suitable, luxurious red lace that I could visualize draped across my shoulders and embracing my curves.

It didn't take me long to figure out that the exquisite red lace fabric, for perhaps a tea length garment would still cost a hundred dollars or better.

As I wistfully fondled the delicate lace, with adamant vibes I mused, "There's gotta be a way, somehow to solve this dilemma." Suddenly my torpid, **out to lunch** brain came to life!

"Why not a **"Hot Pants"** outfit. It was presently the audacious rage in the Twin Ports. It would certainly take a lot less material; Short Shorts with a striking top.

Giggling to myself inconspicuously, restraining my excitement, I settled on sufficient yardage from the red lace bolt of fabric. The total came to $73.38. I would still be able to vaunt, impressively the possession of an Elegant Paris Ensemble! So what if I designed and tailored it myself! I might even enhance the story a bit. Manufacture some bogus details. "A rendition equal to the expertise duping talent of my mendacious husband!" I soliloquized, tittering, as I slithered up the steps of the Inter.Continental to our room. I entered tippy-toeing to an unbroken symphony of Larry's ZZ's. Tiredly, I claimed the remaining half of the bed to embrace a few ZZ's of my own.

* * * * * * *

"Yes. this is what I'm wearing!" was my adamant reply. "We'll be airborne by this time tomorrow, heading home. We may as well make this last evening one to remember and I want to dress with finesse."

"I better change to a suit and tie, then." Larry muttered placidly. "I was planning to dress casual. I thought this was merely a wine tasting insignificant affair. Just visiting a few wine cellars."

"Didn't you hear the Coleman Spokesman announce in the lobby briefing that it was a semiformal wine tasting féte?" I giggled with ebullience.

"A wine tasting féte. Ridiculous. So what's that?"

Well you already know féte means party, celebration in French. The **nuit**, night finale of this ree-sep-she-awn" I drawled **is** the wine cellar tour. It's an elaborate, sophisticated dinneur, Monsieur." I tittered in a simpered deliberate attempt at a French accent.

"Boy, you sure get a kick out of murdering the French Brogue!" he retorted, shaking his head.

"I love that **Romantic** language. It sounds so—so—**Swan—Yay!**

"Swan-yay? What's that in French?"

I giggled, mischievously. "That's not French, Larry. Roger, my first husband used it all the time to describe class and exquisite elegance. I think he made it up!" I laughed again.

Larry sighed and muttered with apathetic doldrums, "We may as well mosey our butts downstairs to the lobby and Join the others." He yawned and rubbed his eyes.

"Are you actually, finally getting burned out?" I teased. "Isn't there enough excitement to hold your interest anymore? You sound tired or bored or both!"

"It's the tail end of this fête," he smiled. "And I'm getting a little anxious to rev up that 63½ Red Ford."

"So your mind isn't on French Chateau's and Chardonnay anymore? Huh?"

"We'll be getting home on the 11th. First Stock Car Races start on Mother's Day Weekend and Mother's Day is the 14th. So that doesn't give me a helluva lotta time to get Trusty 'ole # 61 a Purrin'."

"I guess that's understandable." I remarked. "My thoughts are leaning in the direction of Duluth and home too. I wonder how Bunny and Bill are faring with a bunch of teenagers. Quite a handful I bet!"

After jovial Bonjouir's everyone languidly strolled behind the formally clad Tour Guide. We passed through corridor after corridor of concrete. Every now and then he'd halt the group and volunteer some historicity on the Museum and the expertise of wine making.

"We are now in Musee Du Vin, a museum dedicated to wine. This is a renovated 15th Century Cellar." he said. "If you will look around, you'll notice this **cave,** cellar is peopled with strange wax models. All the figures are engaged in numerous poses in the art of making wine."

He explained the differences between Alsatian Wine and Burgandy. We were indulged with diminutive shot glasses and wine was passed around for us to test taste and savor, to attempt distinguishing differences between red, rose, or white wines.

```
Larry & I with our Guide
  in Wine tasting Cellar
```

We again followed the guide through numerous corridors, winding through cellars until we finally entered a large room, prepared in advance for our party. It was set up with white linened tables, with all the excessories to wine and dine us in class and style.

The service was buffet style, however. The buffet table was all of thirty feet long with every delectable choice of cuisine imaginable to satisfy the most particular of pallets. A mere teaspoon size taste of each entree would have more than filled the plate and mesmerized the tongue, as well.

We found a seating spot to our liking, collected a plate and joined a long line of half-tipsy wine-tasters. After filling our plates we returned to the seats we had selected. And again wine was served by matre de's during our meal and likewise, sip, sip, sip, after.

"I wonder how do the French function in daily responsibility with all this **sip, sip, sippin'?"** I remarked.

"They must be some goddamm happy people! **All the time."** Sylvia said, "I could handle that!"

We laughed.

"And just think. Tomorrow we take flight and leave it all behind us." Larry added.

"It sure went fast. Didn't it?" Kenny muttered. "Back to the Skiroule Shop to sweat."

* * * * * * *

Needless to say, there was a lot more sleeping and a lot less conversation over the Atlantic Waters on the return trip. The cocktail Service Bar on the 747 TWA was engulfed in the **sound of silence** and the bartender had disappeared without ceremony. Even gregarious Larry had abandoned all his exploitations and was plopped, lethargically in his seat!

♪♪♪

CHAPTER TWENTY THREE

It was over a week since we had returned from Paris and I was glued to my portable Kenmore sewing machine of eighteen years of service. Many a stage costume had been designed, created and sewed at this little dependable machine; and many matching vests for Korn and Toby as well.

I had, prior, arranged my portable Kenmore in my bedroom upon an old vanity cabinet I had scarfed up from a neighborhood rummage sale. There it remained continually set up for any spur-of-the-moment need. The kitchen table was strewn with pattern pieces of red lace fabric and makeshift patterns I had assembled and cut from brown paper grocery bags.

I had designed a two-piece **"Hot Pants"** ensemble, ad-libing from segments of other previous garment projects, filed away in my sewing cabinet repertoire.

Larry burst into the room from the garage, hands and coveralls full of grease and inundated with the fragrance of **ahem**, of motor oil and gasoline.

He exclaimed in an ebullient voice. "Hey Dottie, some of our friends suggested I ask you to accompany us to a nice dinner tomorrow evening. **Their treat!** They're taking me out for my birthday."

"On a Monday?"

"They picked Monday so you could go with us."

"I'm up to my eyeballs in this outfit I'm sewing. I only have Mondays off now that the Gopher has picked up Tuesdays too."

"It's my birthday this week, you know." he uttered pensively.

"I know. What do you need or I should say, want for your birthday:?" I asked, indifferently.

"I could use a new Truck!" he clowned, tittering.

"I suppose you could! Well I'm too broke for a gift right now, but I'll get you a nice card."

"Nah, just come with us." he urged.

"Well, if my adoring, thoughtful, sensitive, liberal, compassionate husband would have bought me a dress in Paris, I wouldn't be having to spend this time at my sewing machine. **Now would I?**" I quipped, with sarcasm. I was still angry and seething inside over what I had determined was self-absorbed parsimonious narcissistic selfishness!

"I guess that means **"no"** to the dinner invite, huh?"

"I guess so. I'd like to finish this outfit tomorrow."

"Okay." he replied, ostensibly and left without ceremony.

With shrewd prepensity, just that morning, I had purchased a birthday card for Larry from Target before returning home from Mass with the kids. I had very painstakingly selected a doting, sentimental card with a warm impassioned message in verse. I schemed to unscrupulously plop it in tomorrows mailbox.

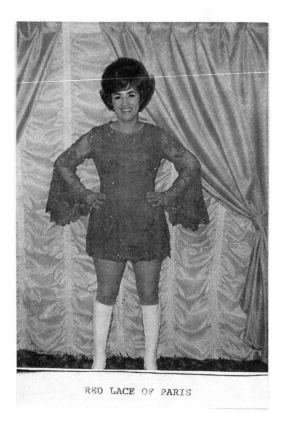

RED LACE OF PARIS

My irritation over his inconsiderate King Midas hording of the money intended for Paris spending, for his own selfish interests was still consuming my mind, fuming angrily inside.

I ambiguously addressed and endorsed the card as follows. It read:

My Dearest Larry,
It's always you I set apart
As someone closest to my heart.
I have learned the full extent
Of what your thoughtful ways have meant.
And even as the years have flown
The warmth I feel for you has grown.

You've always been, you'll always be
Someone who means the world to me.
    Happy Birthday,
With my deepest, devoted Admiration.

        Love,
            Larry

                * * * * * * *

The party was in full swing downstairs of the Gopher Lounge, as The Tumbleweeds entertained a crowd even more copious than usual. The basis being, it was a special celebration. A going away, adios, au revoir party for Cal the bartender, who was leaving the employment of John Dandrea and his many friends and associates at the Club, as well.

With abundant avidity, we enhanced the festivities with our spirited Country Music and enthusiastically joined in the tipping, toasting to Cal's new Lot.

Geno was once again in town and he was intuitively included in our clique, as he had become an accepted fixture at the Gopher. When my intermission arrived, he was playing pool in the adjacent barroom and as I approached, he was stretched across the pool table, eyeing up a potential shot. However, his eyes were not on the pool balls. They were flirting shamelessly with me, gazing over the table, locked secretively with mine. He smiled and winked. I melted. Little dimples were etched upon his cheeks and his eyes imbued an awareness of our secret intense hunger for each other.

It was Saturday night and hardly tiddly minutes later, Larry came noisily scuttling down the Gopher stairway. It was an unexpected sojourn and very unorthodox for Larry to return on a Saturday night and with his whole Pit Crew. An effusive explanation warranted that they had been rained out in Ashland and the Stock Car races had been cancelled.

With Larry and Geno, both present, I felt awkwardly agitated, uptight and shaken. I was grateful and relieved to be zealously occupied with my music. With only three, 15 minute breaks to mingle, I aimlessly moved around among friends, addressing various fans and tactfully avoiding confrontations with either.

Fostering guilt, with no justification for my prior, impetuous, impulsive surrender, I mused, "That tryst should **never** have happened. That was a terrible mistake! It must **never** happen again!" I believed it was a godsend, Larry had rained out and showed up at the Gopher.

At closing I slipped away abstrusely, without having spent time with either. I skulked, apprehensive, shaken but grateful, having secretly exited, unnoticed.

But, as my Chevy revved and sputtered out of the back parking lot, honeward bound, my heart sunk and ached for not having spent a single moment with Geno. I was wretchedly missing our tété-á-tété companionship; Our sharing of so many connected ideas; Our casual, candid bantering. How had it all become so complicated? My body ached with the memory of the tender warmth with which he had held me. Touching, kissing, fondling. Hands roaming the secrecy of my trembling thighs. "No, Dottie! You must not go there! **Not now! Not Ever!**"

* * * * * * *

"I think I've finally got it all together. The synthetic oil formula is finally up to snuff." Larry blurted after the races. "My #61 is really percolating now!" he thundered.

"Did you win?"

"Well no. I blew a tire. Put me back some."

"Last week?"

"No, I had trouble with—uh."

I laughed, badgering lightly. "Yep, it's just like the old adage! I finally fixed my nose, so now my mouth don't work!"

Hobby stock car racing seemed like **little grown-up boys** playing around with expensive **grown-up little boy** toys!

However, synthetic oil was really making progress and Larry was very happy with it's performance in his #61. Major Petroleum Mamufactures had scoffed at the idea of marketing synthetic motor oil. But after intense periods of research and development, in 1973 the first synthetic motor oil to exceed API Automobile Service Requirements had reached the shelves for street vehicle customers.

Larry had hoped to be, somehow, included in the ground floor of this gigantic endeavor. He was proud and puffed up over having been involved in the experimentation ground work. He vaunted his participation with the product on the Race Track. But for Larry it never materialized to anything, financially or otherwise.

* * * * * * *

Korn, with his fizzing, effervescent glass of Alka-Seltzer in his hand and me with my fresh, hot brimming cup of coffee, brushed elbows on stage as we busied ourselves turning on PA and other musical equipment for the beginning of another evening of music.

"Well, hello there, Dottie P. Lou." he sniggered.

"Hi Korn. Medicinal Cocktail for the tummy?"

"As usual."

"I'm glad I don't have your stomach." I added. "You feel okay?"

"Hell yes! I feel more like I do now than I did a little while ago!" He joshed, always brushing off a serious subject with the little whimsical nonsense he often used. "Anything new a happening?"

"I learned a new song. I'm gonna lay it on you tonight."

"Uh—oh! A tough—ee?"

"Nah. Just standard commercial four chord country. **'Happiest Girl in the Whole U.S.A.'**"

"Oh. Donna Fargo. That's ¾ waltz time, I do believe. Not many chords."

"No, it's an easy one. Say Korn, I've been thinkin'"

"Uh-oh! That's dangerous territory for a Pollack!" he laughed. I mused, "Maybe that's where he came up with the P in Dottie P. Lou. P for Pollack." He had never ever explained why he always addressed me as Dottie P.

I snickered and continued, "I'd like to get another recording session in Minneapolis for a 8-track tape. It's what's popular right now. The goin' thing. Whatta **you** think? Any suggestions?"

"Piece 'o cake." he glibly replied.

"You'd set it up for me?" I asked, wistfully.

"Sure thing. Hmmm-" he muttered, deemed to be in thought. "**I bet we** could use Sherwin Linton's **Black Gold** label. Maybe his band too. How soon do you wanna do it?"

"This month, if that's remotely possible." I said.

"I'll get on the phone Monday. See what I can come up with." he promised. "I'll talk to Sherwin. Nothin's too tough to do, for Dottie P. Lou" he laughed. "Hey, I'm a poet and didn't even know it. Shucks I did it again!"

We both giggled.

"You're a doll—Well not a doll." I winced. "whatever a guy is that's—ah—oh, I know. You're a Prince. **A Helluva Prince**, Korn."

"Prince or Whatever. It's mostly Pauper, and we'd better cut this chit-chat and get our fannies a movin' and our tootsies a pickin' and a grinnin'. It's that time again."

In the middle of the first set, I glanced across the dancing crowd and spotted Geno perched at his usual table, Sitting across the room. Even with his face partially shadowed in the soft dim night club neon's, I could see the want in his eyes. My knees turned to jelly and tremulous spasms of weakness made me feel giddy and unsteady. Drawing a deep breath, on second thought, I pondered. "Perhaps the want is merely cascading through my veins instead."

I tried to concentrate and lose myself in the music, forcing my mind to ignore his presence. However, out of the corner of my eyes, I couldn't help but notice him motioning Delores to his table for service. He meticulously folded a cocktail napkin and pointedly handed it to her.

A request, I assumed, as she nonchalantly sashayed to the stage railing and handed the folded napkin note to me.

"Omigod!" I muttered barely audible, as I read the note. A surge of warmth sizzled up the veins of my throat and to my cheeks and I was positive my face had turned a torrid crimson, as my emotions bludgeoned my composure.

The note read, "Dottie, I'm **so-so aching to be inside of you.**" It was followed by a gigantic question mark.

"A request, Dottie?" Korn asked, jolting me back to the ambience of our public.

"Oh—oh—yes." I stammered, sprinting my mind back to reality. "Yes, uh—a request for Geno. He wants "Let's Go All The way" Nursing clandestine embarrassment, I quickly added, "Norma Jean's #1 Signature Hit!"

"Gene wants Let's Go All The Way?! Well **who doesn't?"** Korn tittered, flashing a usual flirtatious, ambiguous reply. "We can do that Gene." he added.

* * * * * * *

"Can I see you tonight?" Geno asked, on intermission, as I slipped into a seat beside him. "We didn't get a chance to even talk last time."

"Larry showed up unexpectedly by surprise. What could I do?"

"I know. I sure was disappointed."

"Not anymore than I."

"Will you spend some time with me, after you're finished with the gig? I could use some more records. We could chit-chat in my car?" He asked, wistfully.

"We made some grave, intimate mistakes last time." I said. "Maybe we had better stick to the barroom booths for our chit-chats."

"It would be merely to visit." he implored.

"Our visits **have to be** just that. **Visits!"** I assured him half-heartedly, as I reminisced our last trip turned to tryst, with tender passionate memory.

"Can you really promise that?" he asked with a dubious simpered smile.

"Our careless, impulsive craziness just clouded the beautiful **Platonic** relationship we've shared the last couple years, Geno. I've so enjoyed our talks. We can't let that recklessness happen again."

"No, I s'pose you're right. I will try to control and restrain my feelings, my urges to hold you in my arms." he muttered with a hint of irony.

My heart throbbed at the mental image of him holding me in his arms. I squeezed my pubic muscles and my inner thighs tingled with spastic memory. My vow, **not to go there,** was little by-little, slowly dissipating, my willpower steadily weakening, my calculated determination crumbling. My sensuous reverie was simply fogging and dimming my reasoning, that **"it had been a terrible mistake!"**

"I don't sincerely think I can seriously keep that promise, Geno, without your help!" I quipped. "My strength turns to mayhem when you suggest those little intimate details." I smiled. "But I will try."

He tittered, softly, without reply.

"We'll talk after I'm through singing." I said as I rose to return to the bandstand.

He smiled with a docile tenderness that left me unhinged and confused. "Sing something special for me." he coaxed.

"Sure. How about, "I Never Once Stopped Loving You?"

"Yes, and I never once stop—uh-umm—I mean, yes, that would be nice. Thanks Dottie."

We were barely into the second song of the final set, when on the overhead stairway, above the stage, came the thundering, scrambling of abundant footsteps and through the doorway emerged Larry, **Parker's,** Kenny and Sylvia and a clutch of their friends and fans.

My heart sunk. I mused, disconcertedly, "I wonder why Larry is so often, so diligently bolstering the economy of the Gopher Lounge latterly!" He very infrequently made appearances in places I performed. Was he aware, perhaps, of Geno's and my attraction to each other? Questioning my assumptions, I was nebulously absorbed in skepticism. Could it be merely coincidence? Or was it merely because John Dandrea's Gopher was one of Larry's most generous Sponsor's for his Stock Car? Or was I just being riddled with self reproach of my own creation.

Larry vonGillern in his 63½ Ford #61

As my eyes wandered across the room to Geno's table I could see the frustated disappointment in his face.

He signaled my attention with an obvious nod of his head sideways, gesturing toward the barroom, indicating that I indeed, had **"company a comin'"** I nodded, placidly, a **"Yes I know."** in mental language.

It was impossible for anyone to miss a Larry vonGillern entrance. It was always noisy, flamboyant and accompanied by a conglomeration of people.

After the Tumblweeds had concluded our performance and covered our equipment, I ambled across the room to stop briefly at Geno's table, before joining Larry's coterie of friends. I perched, very impersonally, across the table from him.

"Well, so it goes." he stated, flatly, dispassionately. "I guess I'll see you next time I'm in town, in two or three weeks." He began to rise from his seat.

"No. Wait." I implored, feeling defeated.

"Don't look so sad, Dottie." His eyes were cloudy and rueful. "He has rights!" Geno flipped, diplomatically trying to camouflage his feelings, but disappointment was etched in his face.

"Wait! Wait! Don't just jump up and leave!" I pleaded. "I just couldn't stand that."

"What else is there to do?" he replied as he sunk back into his chair. "I leave in the morning for Mobile."

"I just can't handle this charade, Geno. Pretending I hardly know you. Inventing impersonal conversation when anyone may be listening. Not touching. It's been so l—ong—uh-well—I—this makes it six— uh weeks since—since—well," my words trailed off, disoriented and inaudible.

Instinctively he reached for my hand. However, impulsively, I jerked away from his clasp, assuming our little tété-á-tété may be a clandestine observance from an informant eye. How did our friendship become so complicated? So clumsy and uncomfortable So caustic?

I noticed miniscule tears creeping from the corners of his chocolate eyes, when I impulsively had drawn away from the touch of his hand. I knew I had ultimately, inadvertently wounded his feelings by my rejection of his familiar hand clasp.

I drew in a disconcerted gulp of air, then released it to an ambivalent sigh. "What's the use?" I thought. "This fighting, this ignoring, denying the ultimate abstruse intensity between us, the insatiable hunger defeating our sense of morality. I stared wistfully into his somber, lanquid eyes and audiciously murmured, "Geno, I'm going to socialize in the barroom, briefly, with Larry and his friends. When I leave, in a few minutes, from the rear of the Gopher in my Chevy, **Please follow me** in your car. I'll drive a few blocks over toward Shopper's City, down Ramsey Street. I'll park my car at a legitimate legal spot. Then I'll transfer to your vehicle, very quickly and very discreetly. We'll go for a drive somewhere." I paused, boldly penetrating his stunned gaze. "Okay?"

My cogent, dedicated vow, **not to go there,** had dissipated like the morning fog into oblivion.

"Yes! Yes!" he finally gasped. "Dottie, Dottie, my little **Funny Face!** You really know how to completely shock me! And yes, I'm parked in the back too, as always. I'll be there."

Discreetly, after a smidgen of idle chit-chat in the barroom I excused myself and inconspicuously slipped through the now empty dance area, up the back stairway and through a sparsely occupied cocktail lounge with merely a handful of die-hard drinkers still loitering over last minute ordered beers. I sashayed across the dark, now closed, restaurant area and out the back door to my auto.

With tremulous fingers I fumbled for my keys and clumsily, but hurriedly, inserted the key to the ignition, started the engine and spun out of the parking lot through the alley and up Ramsey Street. I anxiously checked the rear view mirror and immediately observed the head lights of a vehicle trailing behind. A few safe blocks out of the Gopher area I swung left and down Wadena, near Shopper's City Store. Swiftly locating a parking spot, I killed the motor and dashed eagerly from my vehicle to the one that had swung around beside mine. I scrambled hurriedly into Geno's and there, double parked, very indiscreetly in the middle of the street, with escalated emotions exploding we impetuously, sensuously flung into each others embrace, furiously kissing. We were lost in the unbridled overwhelming hunger between us, passion kindled by weeks of starved celibacy. We avidly lapsed into intense passionate kissing; everywhere, gobbling lips, tasting cheeks, eyelids, throats, hungrily devouring each other in unrestrained passion.

Lost to the emotions flowing through my veins, my groins, I finally caught my breath and whispered, giggling. "Geno, we can't just stay **HERE,** locked in each other's arms in the **middle of Wadena Street,** in front of God and everybody!"

"I guess not, but I could just eat you up!" he laughed. I loved the way he laughed. "I just can't stop kissing my Dottie Lou. I'm so hungry for you, to touch you, to hold you. I want to taste every iota bit of you—all over. It seems like forever since I held you in my arms, Dottie! Since I made love to you!"

He then bolted his vehicle into motion, leaving the city lights of West Duluth. Winding down Ramsey and Central Avenue, we disappeared into the night, along with our tossed aside virtues, vows and caution, leaving behind the extinguished neons of a frolicking city, replaced by dim street lights flickering in a city soon to sleep.

We whizzed through Morgan Park and selected a side street out of Gary, New Duluth that angled toward Midway Road and Highway #61, searching for secluded country privacy. We soon spotted a quiet side circular entrance to a cement plant, where Geno swiftly veered in.

He switched off the headlights and before the engine completely ceased turning, we were already audaciously disrobing each other, tearing at clothes that went flying, airborne, to the back seat.

Geno smoothly slid downward into the seat on his back and sensually, persuasively pulled me down, over on top of his, now, nakedness, as I fondly clasped his firm, aching manhood in tender caresses. He indulged me in control position. How could he possibly know this was my inexpressible fetishism, a deviation from the norm. It **certainly** had never been up for **discussion!** I was consumed by his profound sensitivity and indepth insight to my needs. He never ceased to amaze me. He seemed to know, without tutoring, my very thoughts, my wants, pampering my every whim, exploring all my secret vulnerable points of sensual seduction.

We exhausted two plus hours in our little private love tryst, whispering, fondling, embracing, exploring, and then just holding each other in our semi-nakedness, as we talked and talked and talked.

It was there in his arms, I discovered the euphoria and elation and surprise of multiple orgasms. I was never aware these sensual wonderful heights in succession, could be an authentic reality. I had always assumed they were merely fictitious fantasy of the romance novels I had read!

It was there, in the wee hours, as the sky was captured in transition between darkness and dawn, he cupped my face gently in his hands and gazing tenderly into my eyes, murmured softly, "Dottie Lou, I sure do love you!" And even that was poetry. "I have for quite some time." he added. "Longer than you know."

"And I love you." I assured him.

We talked and rambled on and on, enhancing clandestine closet discussions on all our dreams, the beauty of our love making, the bonding of our souls. At times it was tearful for the sadness. The sadness of hiding, sneaking, lying, when we wanted so much to shout to the whole world, "Can't you see how much Dottie Lou and Geno are in love!? How perfect, how beautiful are their souls in togetherness! Heaven sent and arranged, the celestial bonding of two beautiful souls in love!"

At home I found Larry asleep. I quietly, prudently slipped in between the sheets, with Geno's fingerprints all over my skin, his lip impressions and tongue tracks, warmly, discreetly etched over almost every inch of my body.

I was feeling no guilt or remorse. Perhaps I should have been ashamed, but I was only feeling such a great sense of fulfillment, tranquil peace and tender memory.

I reminisced, retrospectively, the memory of these past several weeks, of the fork in the road that had taken me in a direction I would never had ever imagined, without caution or remorse. Geno had taken me, at 40, to places I had never been, had never imagined in my wildest dreams. I just couldn't let go. I was so deeply connected to the soulmate love of this man I could see **no turning back.** He had so completely, recklessly captured my heart. He was sensitive to my every vision. Our every hope in life's journey was always on the same page.

"How could something so perfect, not be your will, Lord?" I asked, trying to negotiate with God, trying to justify every precious moment. Something so perceptive, so profound? Tears trickled down my face silently, into my ears as I laid on my back pondering, mentally weighing a feasible consequence of such a complicated situation. **I'm Married!** Will the pain of severing our relationship be my ultimate future? Melancholy gripped my heart. "I'll not dwell on it tonight." I mused and like Scarlet O'Hara ruminated, "I'll think on it **tomorrow!"**

Larry didn't stir and the following morning he didn't even inquire where I'd been or what time I had come home. Perhaps he hadn't hurried home, as well, but my guess was he was self-absorbed and just hadn't noticed. Our life style had never been, from day one, a blueprint plan of permissions or explanations. We were both so career involved and absorbed in our own visions, it never occurred to question each other.

♫♫♫

CHAPTER TWENTY FOUR

With the prospect of a future release of an 8track tape, I 'surmised a trip to a professional photographer was in order and way over due, since my last effort at promotion pictures had been way back in '68.

My newly designed Red Lace Hot Pants ensemble was complete, ready to wear and I concluded it would make an excellent razzle-dazzle for the face of my 8track cartridge. I contemplated to set for a bust pose, as well, to be used for 8x10's and 5x7's to include in the jackets of a couple proposed, consectutive releases from the same session for air play, juke boxes and personal stage sales.

I thumbed the yellow pages for a reputable photo studio and made an appointment for an immediate setting. It was imperative that I "jump the gun" to be prepared, in advance, so no lapse of time would be lost in marketing when the recordings arrived.

When the professional, final bust proof was ready, with the usual retouching, the master photo was sent to A.B.C. Pictures of Springfield, Missouri, where orders for lithographed reprints were available in large amounts at reasonable prices. They would print my submitted, detailed promotion information on the margins below the pictures. The pose in my Red Hot Pants outfit, I would present to Sound 80 for the face of the 8track cartridges.

* * * * * * *

"Where's your bass?" Korn asked as we began shuffling my paraphernalia from my vehicle to his.

"I didn't bring my bass. I thought Dickie Mobakken was going to play bass for me so I could concentrate solely on singing."

"Oh, that's right." he muttered. "I forgot."

We were leaving early A.M. from Korn's residence in West Duluth for my recording session at Sound 80 in Minneapolis.

"You've got all the songs you're plannin' to do?"

"Sure. Extra copies for everyone too. And the keys I sing them in."

I had contrived an assemblage of songs I already knew and had been singing on gigs, determined not to waste precious, expensive studio time in learning new material. Almost every selection screamed, gushed and imbued of Geno. Discreetly, in my own heart, unbeknown to anYone else, I was inwardly, spiritually dedicating the entire 8track project to the love of my life.

Songs like: "You're My Shoulder To Lean On", "Rainbow Guy", "He's So Fine", If You Think I Love You Now," (I've Just Started), screamed of my obsessive infatuation with him.

As we entered Sound 80 and met with Korn's line-up of Studio Musicians and Staff, lovable Dickie Moebakken, with his winning, dimpled, flirtatious grin was the only face familiar to me. He had, over the years, been tagged with the pet name, "Teddy Bear" among fans and friends and I was greeted with his usual lovable Teddy Bear hug.

Dick had filled in for me with vocals and Bass on numerous occasions in Duluth, before he had changed residence to Minneapolis, joining the Sherwin Linton Show. There, showering his many talents as vocalist, comedian and bass, on the ambience of Minneapolis fans.

Dick was a dear friend and well received by everyone. He tickled us with his friendly comedy and so many times we had chuckled over his quaint Walter Brennan impersonations.

Just a little history of Dickie from Mary Ann Ludolph:

By Mary Ann Ludolph

ST. PAUL MN – Our centerfold this month would be a mountaineer about to burst into song for a fill of the jug but it's none other than Dick Moebakken, virtuoso of the bass guitar, outstanding vocalist, first rate comedian and member of the Upper Midwest's No. 1 traveling country show, Sherwin Linton and the Cotton Kings.

The irresistable Dick, often referred to as the lovable teddy bear, has a very special way with people, giving the impression of being a somewhat saintly (?) imp or perhaps a slightly tainted bearded angel. Whatever – he quickly establishes a rapport with his audiences any entertainer would envy.

Dick is a native of Duluth. He was musically influences by his dad and uncle Al, from whom he learned the basic guitar chords when he was a youngster. During the 50's. Dick played with rock and roll bands, although he always had a love for country music. One of his first country gigs was in 1962 at Freddy's Bar in Duluth with Gene and Toby, now known as the Tumbleweeds. "Great people," Dick says. "After that I played with many groups and even did some commercial jazz. I went where the money was. Sherwin Linton was the biggest influence in my life for the better. I am now playing the music I like best, with job security and I still have time for my family. What more could I ask for?" Dick's family consists of his wife Mary, two sons Rick and John and daughter Vicki.

When the band is in the Minneapolis area, Dick spends a lot of time at home in the kitchen. "I love to cook," he says. "My grandfather's recipe for wine making always impresses my friends when they drop in."

Dick has been with Sherwin Linton the last 7 years. .He & the group's tremendous frontman, Red Freeman, have worked up some great comedy bits and Dick's Walter Brennan impersonation always brings a rousing response from the audience.

Almost all of the studio musicians Korn had contacted and convinced to enhance my session were, complimentary, from Sherwin Linton's Band. With his arm around my shoulder, Korn glibly asserted, "Meet Dottie Lou." and enthusiastically went over a friendly line-up of introducing all the guys who would be working for me on the session.

"Dave Knight will be doin' the honors on steel and Jerry Hermis," I shook their hands. "Plays a mean, mean lead guitar. He's just as sharp on the guitar as that goat-ee he sports."

My attention slipped to the thin dark mustache sporting his upper lip, with the ends hardly the thickness of a farmers match, curled up, very stiff and uniform, perhaps waxed.

"And Dottie," Korn continued, "meet Tom Jung, our engineer. One of the very best. He and I will work together on sound and levels. Our youngster, here, still discovering Babes is Mike Grunke. What he doesn't yet know about chicks he makes up for that with his talent on the "pots and pans". He's our Drummer. I'll play rythmn, of course, and obviously, our Party Straffer pal, Dick will—"

"Oh Yeah." I interrupted and winked with inside percipience. "Yes', I **know** our Dickie Poo Bass pickin' Buddy."

He grinned mischievously, returning my wink. We all snickered.

We harnessed a gruelling eight hour session, recording nine songs, until most of the musicians had to hurry away for an evening gig with The Sherwin Linton Show at the Flame, downtown Minneapolis. Some were a little extra happy from frequent visits to an **Uhmm**--! refreshing, stimulating cooler I had deliberately improvised for medicinal **HELP** to sustain our Stamina! Ahem!

Dick generously promised to return and meet us the following week to assist us in the finishing touches as time had run out for the present. We were to over dub our back up voices on several selections. A few hours of engineering, re-mixing and attaining balance remained to be perfected with next weeks assistance from Tom Jung.

Korn and I stopped off at the Flame to catch the first set of Sherwins Show, before heading back to Duluth, and to thank him for loaning us his talented musicians, their having rendered my Sound 80 session a success.

I named the 8track "Just Plain Country". It consisted of the nine selections created at the Studio and three from a prior Nashville Project.

* * * * * * *

It was Saturday night at the Gopher, following the Thursday we had concluded the final mixing of the Sound 80 session. Korn and Dick and I had dubbed in back-up voices and I had opted some harmony to my own voice.

I hurriedly scuttled around the corner, grasping my usual first cup of coffee from the restaurant upstairs and almost crashed, head-on into Geno around the corner of the waitress service station. Hot coffee slushed about as we collided. My knees suddenly buckled, and my hands began to tremble, when surprised by his presence. "Surely my shaking knees must be obvious to the eye!" I soliloquized.

"Oh my gosh!" I stammered. "You almost got a shower of hot coffee. I'm sorry."

"No problem. None on me!" his spirited laughter was infectious. "Just a little puddle on the floor. Shame on you, Dottie!"

"Nice to see you're back in town again." Smiling demurely, I attempted casual conversation. "How long will you be around Duluth **this** time?"

"Just tonight and tomorrow. Do you play somewhere tomorrow night?"

"Sure. At the Kro Bar in Superior."

"I think I should be able to make that." he glibly remarked. He seemed to be so in capricious control of his emotions. I aspired to share in his inherent talent for composure, not nearly as well, however. "I don't leave 'til Monday morning. Lets sit at a table." he suggested. "You have time?"

"Yes." I glanced at my wrist watch. "About ten minutes."

We sat at the table he usually occupied, still vacant as the evening was yet in its early stages.

"I thought of you today when I did my laundry." He laughed. He had the warmest laughter when he was proudly seized with something clever. "A little ripple up my arm as I whipped in my underwear, thinkin' of my Dottie."

"Sure great!" I teased in return. "You think of me when you toss your dirty shorts! Huh? How flattering!"

He laughed mischievously. "Memories make me horney!"

It was an inside joke we, lovingly shared. The analogy was innocently based on the times we'd arrange to meet at the Piedmont Heights Laundromat just to discreetly be together. What could be more innocent than a rendezvous to do our laundry. We'd legitimately wash our clothes and chatter, sit in the car, like a couple of teenagers waiting on the dryers. It was not so much a carnal tryst, but merely an inconspicuous theft of moments together in embrace and sharing.

"Just like **An Old Hunk Of Coal,** A Basket of Dirty Laundry, Hmmm—uh—there's just got to be material there for a good 'ole

Country Ballad!" I giggled, again, but he didn't laugh and a seriousness flickered in his eyes. Silence. Had I gone too far? I nonchalantly flipped to another topic.

"I have some new promo pictures to show you. 8x10's and also 5x7's for the 45 disc jackets."

"I know. A bust pose in a blouse with a gigantic round collar."

"How do you know?"

"I saw one posted upstairs."

"Did you see anything else significant about the pose?"

For Bookings & Records
GENE NORELL (Mng.)
(218) 727-1418 or 724-8193
1505 Walnut St.
Duluth, Minn. 55811

DOTTIE LOU

Black Gold
Records
Mpls., Minn.

"No. Should have I?" He feigned indifference, smiling faintly.

"Nothing important at all? Or maybe different?"

"No. Nothing." he replied cunningly stoical.

"You saw nothing unusual? Like somethin' around the throat of the subject?"

"No." then he chuckled hilariously and added. "Yes, I saw her little gold cross, ever so petite and dainty, just like the subject posing." He reached across the table and squeezed my hand, dispersing his turgid teasing.

"My aren't we just full of little pranks and jokes tonight! You're sure in a high-flyin' mood!"

"That I am! Maybe cuz it pleases me to see you wearing the cross."

"And if ever, someday, you see me without that little gold cross, you'll know I don't love you anymore."

Then a serious, demure expression spread across his face, enduing me unable to discern the reason for his change of emotion. It was time to begin our gig, so I began to rise from my perch. He quickly grasped my hand in a gentle squeeze and murmured, "Remember, Dottie, that cross, Sweetheart, is for the **Love of Jesus,** not for **me** and don't you ever, ever take it off!"

Ione popped in and waved to me as she sashayed across the dance floor and ebulliently joined Geno at his table. A tinge of jealousy skirted my thoughts, momentarily, as I observed their heads together in chit-chat and laughter and even more disconcertedly as they danced and danced and danced.

Geno smiled and winked at me as they gracefully waltzed across the foot of the stage. Delores did manage to squeeze in a twirl or two, jovially breaking up the twosome, giggling as she cut in, in her usual mischievous flirty style.

It almost seemed like it was a prepense planned date. Ione and Geno would undoubtedly appear as an **item** to anyone observing from the sidelines.

I mused, halfheartedly, "They sure do make a striking couple, dramatically complimenting each others semblance, Ione with her gorgeous, blond coiffure and an hour-glass figure, in contrast to Geno's slick, dark, ebony hair and a meticulous, fastidious taste for style in a dark sharkskin suit and a matching tie."

Ione was **single,** a definite advantage in a relationship. My thoughts were sabotaging any rational kind of deduction.

"Don't be stupid, Dottie!" I mused, Ione was my dear friend and confidant and I was certain her loyalty to me would surely outweigh any thoughts **beyond friendship** with Geno. Many a straffer we'd shared. Many inner private secrets had passed between us. Many tears on shared shoulders we'd divvied. Innumerable trips we had partaken, on serious business, in indulgent pleasure.

I sighed and soliloquized. "Yes I **am** relieved that **she** is the one keeping Geno company instead of some, come hither, glamorous, "Hit On" pursuing stranger!" A miniscule inkling of possessiveness fluttered through my heart, and nevertheless, a smidgen of envy imbued my mind as well.

♪ "A gambler and a Rambler, I stay out every night. I tell you folks, I'm ragged but I'm ri----ght"♪ was melodious refrain, indicating another night of music had faded into memory. Geno, with a cocktail in each hand invited me to share a barroom booth to visit.

"One for me and one for my Special Platonic Soulmate." he opined as he slithered into the booth, not spilling a drop. He seemed to be in an exceptionally auspicious, cheerful frame of mind.'

"You sure seem to be in a happy-go-lucky mood tonight." I declared.

"That I am!"

"Oh, and thanks for the beverage, Geno."

Ione sauntered over to our booth. "Well bye, you two Love-Birds!" she buzzed.

"Shush! Not so loud." I exclaimed with a warning forefinger pressed against my lips. She tittered.

"I'm headin' over the bridge to catch a drink or two before they close." she volunteered. "See you two love---guys next time I see you. Toodle oooh."

"Okay, Ione." We both ejaculated at the same time, and she was gone.

"You're suppose to make a wish when you say something at the same time." Geno teased.

"How do you know I didn't?" I giggled and winked, raising my glass to my lips, as the ice tinkled harmoniously to the hum of barroom chatter.

"I guess I don't."

"How did you fend the evening with my gal friend, Ione?"

"She's a lot of fun, a good dancer and quite a conversationalist."

"You two were quite the **chummy** pair, I'd say."

"Little jealous?"

"Me? Never! Why, **should I be?**"

"We spent the evening, mostly, talking about you. But she **is** a sophisticated lady and elegant as a Lippizaner Stallion thoroughbred!"

"A horse?! Really! Not too complimentary I'm afraid!"

"On the contrary. We're not talking about a horse is a horse is a horse. We're talking about the beautiful White Lippizaner Stallions! You've heard of the Arabian Lippizaner Stallions of the Spanish Riding School in Vienna, haven't you?"

"No, I'm afraid not."

"You're kidding?"

"Hardly. Not in the least."

"Dottie, Dottie!" he sighed. "Everyone's heard of the Arabian Show Horses. A famous breed of perfectly trained horses of which the Lippizaners are the most beautiful and impressive horses in the world."

"I know a little about everything and not much about anything." I laughed, trying to make light of my obvious embarrassment of being so uninformed.

"Ione holds her head high and struts with finesse. She just, somehow, reminds me of the magnificent ceremonial maneuvers of those perfectly trained, impressive stallions. And that is a compliment.."

"Well, it appears you've certainly done your homework. And yes, that does describe Ione's demeanor. But to me she's a darn good friend."

"Say, what's your opinion on that Watergate Explosion!?" He excitedly changed the subject. He was indeed in a rare mood.

"An **explosion** of a water gate? What kinda' gate is that?" I asked, feigning animated surprise, while trying to stifle a giggle.

"Oh I know. Politics is not in your bag of interests."

I chuckled. "Yes, I heard about Watergate. How could I not? It has monopolized the news channels incessantly for days. It's just not an important issue for me to follow or get in a dither about. Politicians are a never ending fiasco of corruption anyway. Nothing changes! And it bores me!"

"Well, humor me with a little boredom." he quipped. "I think their so-called fiasco will surely blow Nixon's possibility of a second term. He may as well kiss the Presidency Goodbye!"

"I can see I'm in for a briefing of political issues, like it or not." I smiled wryly, as he continued and went on about, how McGovern was building his campaign platform entirely on attacking Nixon's credibility instead of sticking to the major issues.

"I think Muskie has a better chance as a candidate for the Democratic Party at the National Convention. Don't you?"

"You're asking me?" I tittered.

"Sure. You vote don't you?"

"Sometimes."

He glanced at my languid facial expression, masked with a responsive smile and said. "I know these are not interesting subjects to intrigue and captivate my precious Dottie Lou, but it's the only way I'm able to obliterate the real issue between us, which I've been camouflaging with small talk."

"And that is?"

"The issue of **us.**" he equivocally retorted, surrendering obvious unstable emotions.

"You are certainly in a strange diverse mood tonight." I said.

"That's because I've been cowardly trying to shun and evade the truth."

"And that is what?"

"The truth is, those "cloud-nine" guiltless, intense, intimate moments we share are **all wrong!** Very, very wrong! I know that and you do too. We're not a couple of reckless teenagers. We are two sensible, mature Catholic adults. We **Know** right from wrong."

I tittered in an attempt to lighten Geno's intense seriousness. "I'd rather be sorry for something I did, than to regret something I didn't do." I said. "Anyway, that's my **philosophy.** I'm really sorry you're **so sorry** about us." I quipped with a hint of sarcasm.

"Well, not really sorry—hmmm—maybe—uh—well." he stuttered, awkwardly, seemingly lost for words.

His serious mood had momentarily rubbed off on me as I somberly submitted my own theory. "I know, of course, Geno, we're not a couple of reckless teenagers! But, **We Are Catholic!** And that's the problem. Catholic teachings inhibit we mortals to a perpetual **guilt trip!** That's Catholic doctrine. All this sanctity, however doesn't make us more saintly, more virtuous, more endowed with inundant Herculean strength to avoid sin. It merely keeps us from enjoying it! The tiny, many times insignificant, no-no's of Catholic belief keeps us tormented over the most diminutive of rules. It's the Catholic way. Even eating meat on Friday or missing one single Sunday Mass will send us to eternal damnation! Right?!"

"God will get you for that!" He finally let out a chuckle, and shaking his head added, "You're one of a kind, Dottie. My Dottie Lou."

I precariously scanned the barroom to detect if anyone may be picking up on our private conversation. Patrons had diminished to only a handful of people, mostly employees. Not much noise was left to camouflage our voices.

Detecting my uneasy caution, Geno lowered his voice and continued. "I'm stealing moments that rightfully, morally belong to Larry. You are, after all, **married** to him. You **sleep together.**"

"You are still married, Geno."

"I'm separated and I'm **not sleeping** with my Ex. That is an entirely different situation."

"Hmmm—" I soliloquized. "Who's jealous now?" He didn't realize how little Larry and I saw of each other, in bed or otherwise.

"So then you plan to avoid seeing me? To stop moseying around the Gopher? Maybe entirely avoiding Duluth?"

"No, I'll still visit, listen to **The Tumbleweeds,** dance and mingle with everyone. We will always be Soul Mates and Platonic Friends,

Dottie. How can we not? In fact we are just that right now. The only difference will be the celibacy."

"You don't love me anymore?" I whispered.

"No. I didn't say that! You're over reacting, Dottie. What's more comforting and profound and rewarding, **without guilt,** than the sincere, spiritual and intellectual **friendship** of two, you and me, very warm-hearted, compatible people?"

"Love is friendship on Fire!" I said. "I didn't make that up. I heard it in a movie once." I smiled ruefully and softly inconspicuously murmured. "I just don't understand this at all. Your reasoning, I mean. I love you, Geno. We enhance each other. It feels so good to be with you. You make me feel so special! But, if it's abstinence you want, who am I to disagree. I'm certainly not one to dispute your wishes."

"I love you so much." he patronized, as he glanced around insuring his privacy. "And it's been so hard to convince myself to even bring up the subject to you. I feel I'm letting you down in some ways, but, Dottie, it's really the only way. Morally, the right way. I've been going out of my mind with guilt."

It was the first time an awkward ambiance of **silence** hovered between us, continuing for what seemed like an eternity. We finished our cocktails, jingling loose, half melted ice cubes against the interior of our low ball glasses, to fill the void of silence. I slipped a small fragment of ice to my lips and gently crushed it between my teeth in silent rueful thought and swallowed the cool comforting pieces, liken to comfort food.

"Can I walk you to your Chevy?" Geno asked, finally breaking the thick poignant silence.

"Sure." I paused briefly, then kiddingly smirked, "I promise I won't ravish you in the parking lot!" Then with forced half-hearted laughter I added, "Hmmm—Maybe on second thought, you might not be safe.

I haven't touched you in a couple weeks, My body is starved. It's very dark back there. What if I lose control?" I meekly, flirtatiously bantered. "I may seduce you."

"I'll take my chances." he returned, with a tiny passive grin pursed across his face.

He walked me to my car. We hugged our Platonic goodbyes. He promised to come and see the Tumbleweeds at the Kro Bar in Superior the following night.

I cried to the hum of tire against asphalt all the way to "Lonely Street" of Duluth Heights.

* * * * * * *

The Kro Bar was a dive. A saloon location, skirting the border of the bowery district of Superior. Clientele were of a vast, diverse variety. The bar was rowdy, rough and consisted of the Tumbleweeds middle class following, but frequented by the wild, the homeless, the unemployed, the derelict, as well.

So therefore, it was of no surprise when we were bombarded by the arrival of several of the notorious "**B.P.M's. The B.P.M**'s were a well known Motorcycle Gang, noted for terrorizing the area, putting Bar Owners and patrons ill at ease in their presence. In minutes they could create havoc and chaos and completely vacate an establishment with raucous behavior, barroom brawls, uncouth, repugnant conduct and four-letter profanity. Toting arrogance and short fuses, at the pugnacious hint of rebuttal from anyone, their subtle mood could escalate to violence and leave a Pub in shambles. They boasted their outlaw conduct and proudly flaunted their obnoxious title, vaunting bogus prestige, indicating and bragging that B.P.M., deciphered meant Balls, "Pussy and Motorcycles!"

Arrogant Bill Craven was a member of this gang and I thoroughly detested the aberration. Thwarting an over zealous ego that was definitely masked by ignorance, he flaunted what he assessed was **"clout"** in wild animal acts.

As I intentionally ignored his presence, slapping my bass fiddle with over-emphasis and gusto, he waltzed, solo, among the dancing couples with a glass of tap beer in his hand. He'd slurp and burp and slurp and burp some more, purposely ostentatiously pounding his chest and burping liken to a demented African Ape.

He shoved and pushed his way to the foot of the stage for an upstaged performance. I observed his conduct out of the corner of my eye, excluding him the satisfaction of any recognition or attention to his exhibition. He faced the stage with a couple feet of space between him and the band. I could see his eyes on us, thirsting for the band's attention and admiration in lieu of his melodramatic production. There he guzzled the glass of beer down, without taking a breath, then stuck his fingers down his throat and barfed the entire beer up, all over the dance floor, laughing convulsively over what he assumed was a **Spot Light** performance, as he exited the dance floor. My stomach turned, lurched in disgust and I was afraid of losing **my** dinner, as well, and, not for show!! "Oh my yes," I mused, ironically, "I am so impressed!"

The **B.P.M's** were, in my opinion, a bunch of foul, putrid, uncouth animals, lacking intelligence or class! Perhaps, Bill Craven was not an accurate, authentic paragon of the group as a whole, but his behavior certainly gave them a distorted, irreparable reputation.

A number of my friends owned and drove motorcycles and some were also a part of the "Thunderbirds", a Motorcycle Club, which seemed more down to earth, friendly and with some noteable human finesse. Toby and Korn owned Harley Davidson's and frequented time with a number of the "Thunderbirds". Some even joined my house party's and were gentlemen and ladies by character, so it was probably, the Beast and not the **"B.P.M.'s** gang as a whole.

During my first break I observed Craven sashaying along the lines of barstools around the Kro Bar's Horseshoe Bar. He was biting female customers on their rear ends as they perched sipping their beers. Every now and then a scream arose when Craven had made contact.

I chatted, briefly with Eddy Shaw, our employer and proprietor of the Bar. He spouted, rather indignantly, that the **"B.P.M.'s** had stormed his Pub the day before on Saturday afternoon. They had become unruly and when he had politely asked them to leave they had vandalized his place, throwing barstools into the center shelves of stacks of liquor bottles, breaking decor, mirrors, stools and various contents of his establishment. People usually avoided the **"B.P.M.'s.** Bar owners pussy-footed around them, trying not to make waves lest a small storm might quickly transcend into a hurricane if they became riled. So everyone patronized them and precariously tolerated their atrocious conduct.

Geno and Ione had auspiciously missed the entire exhibition, as they arrived, **together,** just prior to our second intermission. The **"B.P.M.'s** had already abruptly disappeared, moving on to their next halla-ba-loo of chaos. At least that was my assumption.

I was flabbergasted to see Ione and Geno arrive together. They selected a vacant table straight across from the band and Geno immediately sent a complimentary round of drinks, up, for the Tumbleweeds.

As I joined them on break I feigned mild irritation and scoffed, "Hey. What's this? My best girlfriend and my secret love out for Hanky Panky? I would have never guessed!" I stifled a giggle.

"You know better than that, Dottie!" Ione impishly purred.

"We thought it safer if the public thinks Ione and I are an item." Geno explained, "merely for discretion."

"To curb those wagging, suspicious, gossiping tongues." Ione added.

"Well, more power to you. If it works." I flashed a saccharine smile.

"How about if we all, the three of us head out to the Silver Star when you finish the gig?" Ione suggested.

In Superior on Sunday nights all bars closed at midnight. However, the County was opened until 2:00 AM. The **Silver Star** was located in the County on the outskirts of Superior.

"Sounds great to me! I ejaculated.

"And then I'll get to dance with my "Funny Face!" Geno smiled, dimples emerging from tanned cheeks.

The **Silver Star** was packed. The midnight dashes on Sunday nights to the County was always fun, as it was a conglomeration of umpty musicians roaming in from many different bands playing the Superior Clubs and some loitered in from Duluth bars, as well.

We knew almost everyone there. Our fans that followed us from the **Kro Bar** and also some bar owners would arrive, relishing a relaxing un-winding after closing, liken to Eddie Shaw and his wife, Myrna, our employers; Leo Grenier, Dennis Cummings etc.

Korn and Toby were "belly up to the bar" ordering drinks as Geno, likewise, was getting cocktails for Himself, Ione and I. We snatched the last empty table in the lounge having arrived slightly ahead of the midnight rush.

Freddie Osberg & **The Chaparels** was the band on stage. Ted Windus sprinted hurriedly to the stage to chat or just hello his musician friends intentionally tripping over the edge of the stage and half fell into the bandstand. He picked himself up, hand brushed himself off and grinned from ear to ear.

Ione and I laughed heartily. We were well aware of Ted's stunt man buffoonery. Even after having seen it so many times it was still hilarious to us. He was quite adept at stunt entertaining and very entertaining.

"Is he hurt?" Geno gasped in serious concern. Geno, not being from our area, was not at all familiar with Ted's comic displays.

Vic Martinson and Bunny Waterhouse from the **Green Apple Quickstep** waved a 'Hello'. Band members poured in in abundance from Beiner's, Johnny's, The Zoo, The Cove, Frankie's, etc. Some were muddling about, looking for close friends, as the dance floor filled, breast to breast and butt to butt.

"Everyone knows by now that I'm Ione's beau, but could I anyway, twinkle toes with the Kro Bar's singer?" Geno winked and grabbed my arm feigning permission from Ione.

And dance we did. Almost every song they played we construed as "Our Song". It felt so great to be mingling, independently as a patron and I discovered Geno and I danced very well together especially the jitterbug, as if we had been doing it for decades.

"What cologne do you wear?" I asked as we plunked, breathless after a grueling fast jitterbug. "It sure is nice. I meant to mention that before."

"It's called **Brute.** I wear nothing else. Like the brute I am!" he chuckled. "You like?"

"The cologne or the brute you are?"

"I hoped both." More giggles.

Ione was Geno's date in spectator eyes we hoped and the necessity for caution and wariness had all but dissipated.

"We have to do this more often." Geno suggested.

"Hey, I'm not always available as a chaperone!" Ione teased. "Sometimes I may just want a lover of my own!"

"Oh shucks." I twitted. "But I'll drink to that."

344

"We drink to everything, don't we?" she added. "How about you give Geno a ride back to his motel in Duluth?" Ione asked. "You have to go to Duluth to go home."

"You go to Duluth too. So?" I pretended indifference. "But I guess I could give him a lift, if he promises to behave!"

"Hey, you guys talk like I'm not even here. Don't I have anything to say about this arrangement?" Geno quipped.

"You know, Dottie, I live in Gary, New Duluth and Geno for the moment, lives at the Holiday Inn on London Road." Ione briefed me. "That's an extra five plus miles east and then five miles or more back west for me. It's way more **on your way,** Dottie."

"Okay, okay. I guess I can give him a ride." I sighed and smirked, feigning reluctance.

"Oh you two conniving females." Geno ejaculated. "Maybe I'll just ask the first good looking gal I spot here, to give me a lift! Ha!"

"And you're confident that that wouldn't be very difficult. Right?" I cajoled. "You conceited, scheming, good-lookin', devious Irishman!"

I dropped Geno at the Holiday Inn. Even before the car came to a complete stop he opened the passenger door to exit and I muttered, "Don't I even get a hug for my efforts?"

"Of course."

I scrambled out of the drivers side of the Chevy and standing in the parking lot, under the street lights, we held each other in an embrace that didn't seem to harbor closure, long and snug, without words. I could feel the hungry beat of his heart against my tingling breasts.

"Goodnight, Love." He finally whispered. He brushed a swift, sisterly kiss against my thirsting lips, as he murmured, almost in a tease, ♪ "There Must Be a Way" my "Funny Face," ♪ using song titles for dialogue, a little game we often played with each other.

"Just One ♪ More Memory?" I asked.

"We have to be strong, Dottie. Love will make us strong."

"Strong? Like I said, Geno, 'Love is friendship on **Fire!**"

"A fire can surely be cooled as well as kindled."

"Well, "God help us!" I said. "You're really serious about this celibacy thing. Aren't you?"

"I have to have peace of mind, somehow! I don't want to be responsible for hurting anyone. We all, eventually, have to pay dearly, for hurting the **least of His.** I don't want to lose my soul. What you do to the least of my Brethren, you--, well, you know the passage, Dottie."

"All I can say, Geno, is, as Patsy Cline says, 'Darlin' ♪ You're Stronger Than Me'."

And I softly crooned a couple lines of Patsy Cline's song as he slowly walked away. He never looked back. Not once.

♫♫

CHAPTER TWENTY FIVE

"Omigod! I don't believe it! How disgusting!" I shrieked, a grimace stretched across my disdainful face. I was catching up on news from the Duluth Sunday paper, as I paged, over Monday morning coffee, through the many sections.

"What? What?" Larry ejaculated, as he scurried around the house preparing to leave for the day.

"Can you believe the Editor of the Duluth News Tribune devoted the entire Cosmopolitan section to the **'B P M's'!!** How disgusting!!"

"What's so disgusting about that?"

"Apparently you don't know or haven't been in the company of any of them."

"I know some of them."

"Oh, I suppose in the racing circuit. There you would come across that kind of low-life riff-raff." I snapped. "That dirty obnoxious, repugnant bunch of animals don't even deserve a write-up on a roll of toilet paper in a First Street Bowery john, let alone the Cosmopolitan section of the major paper of the Twin Ports!"

"Uh-oh! For instance, they're not the high class and finesse of your musician clientele, I gather. Like the excellence of the elite of **Freddie's Town Pump** on the Duluth Bowery or the elegance of the **Kro Bar** customers on the Superior Bowery!" Larry rebuked, smiling, but with cogent irony.

"I have my reasons." I scoffed, defending my biased opinion. I related to him, the incident of the **B P M's** odious behavior the prior night at the Kro Bar and Saturday afternoon's pillaging of Eddy Shaw's Pub.

"However, they really do a lot of good, too; volunteer and charity stuff." Larry cavilled. "I imagine their recognition stems from that, mostly."

"And that gives them a sanctimonious license to act like animals, destroying property?!" I scowled. "Listen to this," And I read from the paper. "They are so misunderstood, resulting in cruel, unjust publicity; the spokesman of the article states."

"Boy, you sure are prejudiced. Opinionated too!" Larry rebuked. And the passage; 'What you do to the least of my brethren' echoed in my head, still fresh from last nights conversations with Geno. An embarrassed flush spread to my cheeks and I opted dropping the subject.

"You're heading out to the shop? Huh? Or going to Arrow Chevrolet?" I asked.

"I think I'll have to hit both today. I have some serious negotiations with Kenny and the Arrow Chev staff too."

"Oh. You do?" with raised eyebrows.

"By the way, while we're both here, at home, at the same time, there's something I want to discuss with you, as well. Coleman Company in Minneapolis has offered me a top notch position in sales with their company and I have to give them my decision by the end of this week."

"Way in Minneapolis? That's 140 miles, more or less. How in the world could you drive that every day. It's all of four hours! Oh, but maybe only two and a half for you." I laughed.

"I wouldn't be driving every day, Bimbo! They said they'd provide full accommodations until I can find a room or an apartment or whatever, down there."

"Are you taking the position?"

"That's what I have to decide. The Coleman Big Cheese are determined I board their team!"

"What about #61? You certainly wouldn't give up your racing hobby! There's no question of what comes first on **your** priority list."

"It's a 9 to 5 job. I'd come back in time on Friday's to race Superior and leave on Sundays after the Proctor races."

"What about if you break down. You know I'm fully aware of how much time you spend in that garage between races, fixing this, repairing that, running here and there for this or that auto part." I grinned perceptively.

"I'm sure Redenbaugh could be talked into supervising that, with my pit crew. Just like when we went to Paris. I'm sure the guys would all pitch in to help. Have #61, spittin' fire, all ready to race when I'd get home."

"Sounds like a heavy, grueling, exhausting schedule to me. It wouldn't take long before you'd be totally burned out!"

"That schedule would only be for a couple months, anyway. Racing ends in September."

"It's your decision, Larry. I can't help you there. It's your life. Whatever brought this negotiating all about anyway?" I asked. "The contacts, I mean? Clear from Minneapolis?"

"Because they were so impressed with my salesmanship, here in Duluth in their first season of the Skiroule Sleds that they are adamant I become a part of their management team."

"Did you talk money?" I asked. "After all, if you are so so importantly needed, the green bucks should be discussed right up front! **Top priority!** Flattery doesn't buy groceries."

"We haven't as yet, but it will be discussed before I agree to anything. IN all seriousness, I'm sure their offer will be well worth my efforts."

"Well do whatever suits you, Larry. Salesmanship is definitely your calling. There's no doubt about that! You excel in persuasion and pressure, very convincingly. Look what you talked me into!!" I smirked with a coy simpered smile.

"And you loved every minute of it!" he laughed, with his usual bolt of confidence.

Larry joined the Coleman staff the following Monday morning. He left for Minneapolis directly after the Proctor races with a quick change of attire and a little case of essentials in clothing and toiletries.

Our third anniversary arrived without ceremony, as it was in the middle of the week and Larry was gone. On the weekend after the races, he stopped in at the Gopher to share a belated cocktail in acknowledgement. I had Delores snap a photo of us, me in my gold, bronze stage dress I had created at my Kenmore sewing machine. Larry was in white jeans, smudged with race track mud and sporting an arm in a sling from the recent motorcycle accident that only reminded me of his hiding the purchase in the neighbors garage. The purchase was a thorn, my having frowned and disputed his erratic decision due to financial difficulties.

As diverse as Larry and I appear, in attire, in this photo is analogous to how we differed in ideas, and values and sophistication.

Our unceremonious 3rd Anniversary
Me stage attire-Larry racing garb

The Tumbleweeds were booked to front a gigantic three-day Country Western Extravaganza on the Iron Range. We frequently booked many such shows, the demand arising from our popularity with the success of **One More Memory** beginnings. I always had a fresh disc on the charts, thanks to deejay, Tim Michaels. This activity also kept us from getting stagnant at our home club, The Gopher. This perpetual two state exposure encouraged record sales as well. **Just Tell Him I Said Hello** on Sherwin Lintons Black Gold label was presently climbing the charts. No, no dust was allowed to gather on Tumbleweed toes!

We engaged Twin Ports Jimmy Armstrong's band, with Don Herold as front man, singer, to fill our Gopher gigs in our absences'. Don and I had worked together in earlier days before Tumbleweed time. Indeed, life was one long, never ending, exorbitant exciting journey.

The Iron Range show was embellished by notable Country Western headliner artists, such as George Kent, Charlie Walker, Red Simpson etc. We were the front band for all artisrs appearing as singles on the festival.

GEORGE KENT-GENE NORELL-DOTTIE LOU-CHARLIE WALKER

I took my youngest son, Roger with me to introduce him gradually to the music entertainment scene. He was a born **ham and a half** by instinct or perhaps mother's genes and was quite proficient on the rhythm guitar. For someone who had had a difficult time conquering the task of merely tying his shoe laces in Kindergarten, he certainly was quite adept at mastering Uncle Harry's lessons in guitar finger pickin'.

Roger, my Protégé Son

I had guest shot him on several occasions as early as age 9. I located a shirt jacket for him to wear in the same hues as the Tumbleweeds blue vests, vests I had designed and sewed for them, so he'd be in sync with my group.

He belted with confident compression and stage presence, not a smidgen withdrawn or introverted, a Glen Campbell tune **"Sweet**

Dream Baby" that was presently mesmerizing his 11 year old music repertoire.

The weekend on the Iron Range was soon followed by Dave Dudley's Annual Country Concert at his resort in Staples, near Danbury, WI. Dave always presented a line up of music from 1:00 Pm until dark when a jam session would continue the festivities. The Tumbleweeds always fronted the event.

THE TUMBLEWEEDS

Dandrea dropped Tuesday nights from the agenda as the added night was not yielding crowds to any significance. He changed our schedule back to the original Wednesday through Saturday we had started with. I was pleased with the cancellation because it rendered extra time off in a schedule way too busy to accommodate music, three kids and **Mischief too!!**

Fun was what it was all about. With Tuesday's open I initiated some pure pleasure, also filling the vacancy with promo activity to market my 45's, encouraging sales of my new release with juke box operators and stores, including visits to the air waves to further stimulation on the KAOH charts.

However, music was always a saccharine excuse to camouflage our overindulgent party mischief. And I had so many willing friends to assist in get-away extravagant soiree's! Two of these, more than willing, **partners in crime,** were noneother than Ione and Delores!

After we had finished some of the local business we opted to find some innocuous cocktail tipping, dancing and bar hopping. Live music on a Tuesday night in the Twin Ports was not too selective, but we knew of a few. Charlie's in West Duluth entertained hard rock six nights a week, which was not our cup-ó-tea. We headed for Superior and the ZOO. Out on the town were a lot of my fans and I soon spotted Betty Coyle and Barb Olson among the patrons. Betty was all dolled up, sporting an exquisite hair do, in excellent taste.

"Who does your hair, Betty?" I asked. "It's so neat. Elegant in fact."

"I do it myself."

"You're kidding."

"No, I do hair styling for a few of my friends too."

"How come you never did mine?" Barb joshed. "I thought I was your friend." she giggled. Everyone tittered.

"Where did you learn to do that so well?" I queried in amiable curiosity. "I can't count the number of times I've tried to style my hair and it comes out shi---nglenails!"

"I went to Beauty School for a time, but I quit half way through. Never finished my schooling so I never went into a shop and all that stuff, not anything like that."

"Would you do mine sometime?" I asked.

"Sure. I style hair in my own apartment. I live in Park Place so just stop in anytime. If I'm there, I'll do it."

Delores and Ione and I bounced from place to place, bar to bar. We stopped in to give the **Green Apple Quik Step** a listen. As we came through the entrance the band abruptly stopped, right in the middle of their song to the surprise of a dance floor occupied in earnest. Vic Martinson, the guitarist of the group, immediately rendered a series of solo licks on his electric guitar, which began at the top of the guitar neck, low notes, and traveled from the lowest position to the very highest. He improvised the very exact progression that was the intro of a release I had on LP entitled **You Know Where You Can Go.**

Vic would always perform this little feat whenever I appeared revealing to me he knew I was there. Then he'd announce, over the mike, "Dottie Lou has just entered the building!" and heads would turn searching my whereabouts.

I giggled and waved a hello to Vic and his group. They in turn, laughed and returned to the theme, continuing their rendition of whatever tune they had been playing when we had first arrived. (I so cherish all the beautiful bonding relationships created among musicians. These are some of my favorite memories.)

Finalizing the evening at some local Night Spot in Superior, we opted for coffee and tummy suppresants before heading home. We leisurely strolled into the usual favorite Superior hang out, Kitches Cafe, close to the waterfront. It was crowded as usual with many fans and friends about.

I spotted Hank and Randy, police officers, at a table as we sashayed across the room in search of a parking spot for our fannies. With my senses in a mischievous, half-tanked mood, I stopped momentarily at their table and planted a big smooch on each of their faces and then casually, amiably sashayed away to an empty table. Carl Farrel, a musician friend, soon joined us at the table.

"You know the cops pretty well, huh?" Ione tittered.

"They're a couple that hang out with us a lot at the Gopher, **after hours.**" I explained

"They have an excellent sense of humor, too." Delores added volunteering a bit of Gopher history. "Real nice guys."

"Not many cops I know would allow what you just did." Carl remarked.

"Oh I think most cops are friendly and most do have a sense of humor too." the waitress, overhearing our chatter, added, as from a tray she placed cups of steaming coffee in front of each of us. "They all come in here to eat. Are you guys ready to order?"

"Hmmm--." Delores sighed as she picked up a menu.

"Oh, that's okay." the waitress responded. "I'll come back in a few minutes."

"Good idea." I said as I made a feeble attempt to scan the menu. "A few minutes would be fine."

George Gwinn, Carl's side kick, moseyed over and joined our table. "As long as you're plantin' them all over the place, plant one here." He said, as he placed a finger to his lips. "I saw you smoochin' the cops. Makin' browney points, huh?" He chuckled. "Hey, see that other cop over there, by himself, eating. Fourth table down on the right?"

"Sure." I said. "I don't know him though."

"You may be lucky you don't. No brownie points there." George retorted. "He's an older cop and ornerier and crabbier than hell! Not any sense of humor in that terd!"

"George has had a little confrontation with him in the past." Carl explained.

"Oh I bet he has a sense of humor too." Ione smirked.

"A few drinks and we all have a sense of humor!" I laughed.

"Not him! sober or otherwise." George replied. "I really doubt if he'd ever actually take a drink. I dare you to go over to **HIS** table and give **HIM** a smacker like you plopped on those other two cops!"

I giggled, musing, then softly muttered, "Yeah, maybe not."

"In fact, Dottie, I'll bet you five bucks you can't do it. You don't dare to it." George added.

"Five bucks, Hmmm—I can't really believe he'd get mad just over a little smooch." I glanced toward the police officer, as he diligently guzzled eggs and hashbrowns, oblivious to our intent evaluation of his detached, conservative mannerism.

"You'd probably end up in his squad car, Dottie, caged and peekin' through those little squares of steel!" Carl chuckled.

"Five bucks?! Do it Dottie." Delores coaxed.

"One thing Dottie and I never fear," Ione added boldly, "Is the confrontation of **ANY** man. Right, Dottie? Any age, any size, in worn out jeans or in sophisticated uniform. No matter."

Several hi-balls had challenged me with enough spurious courage to surrender to my usual wild, unorthodox prank exhibitions. Encouragement from my girl friends certainly fanned the flames.

"Okay." I agreed. "But only if—well, how about five bucks from **each** of you guys. It seems hardly worth the effort to even bother kissing an old duffer for a mere five bucks!"

"Okay. Bets on." in unison they smirked.

I rose from my chair and casually sauntered to the officers table. Leaning over I planted my cheeks into the palms of my hands as I rested my elbows on his table. As I stood, bent over in this position, I gazed directly into his eyes, now having his undivided attention from his eggs and murmured softly,

"Don't look now, but, I'm sitting with two guys and two gals across the room from here. They've tried to convince me that you are such a crabby, ornery old duffer that you would get very, very angry if I were to give you a kiss. I disagreed, of course. I told them to me you appeared to be a gentle, gracious, modest gentleman and certainly would never be angered by a simple friendly kiss."

He smiled faintly, glanced in the direction of our table, then burst into a wide grin. He tapped his finger gently on his cheek indicating it would be okay to plant a little kiss there" Oh no," I whispered. "On the lips. Nothing personal, if that's okay with you. You know they're watching us."

"Sure." he grinned.

I gave him a paltry, impersonal kiss on the lips, thanked him and moseyed back to my table, approaching with outstretched palms to indicate a collection of a five spot from Carl and George.

"Well I guess I can order now." I giggled as I slid into my chair. "In fact I can eat well tonight. Maybe steak!"

As Ione and Delores and I left Kitche's, I noticed a squad car still present in the parking area.

"Hey guys, we started this day with **heavy promotion.** I smirked, "May as well end our day just like it began, with **Heavy Promotion!"**

"Now what's on your devious little mind, Dottie?" Ione asked.

"You know those stickers, the adhesive music notes I have in my purse, advertising my new 45 release we've been promoting all day?"

"Just Tell Him I Said Hello." Ione remarked

"And a nifty way to say **'Hello'**, don't you think?" I asked.

"Whatever are you think—ing--, Naughty, naughty Dottie?" Delores blurted, a question that wasn't an inquiry. "They are next to impossible to remove!!" she continued. "Wait 'til all those people you gave them to today try to take them off, wherever they stuck them. They'll soon change their **admiration** for Dottie Lou."

"You s'pose?" We all giggled.

I fumbled through my purse to retrieve one of the stickers. I bounded to the squad car with Ione close behind me as **Look out. After peeling away the adhesive,** I quickly plopped it over the rear bumper, smoothing out any wrinkles, hastily, but carefully, for a successful firm adherence.

"And now we better get-a-rollin' outta here—**And Fast!**" I sputtered, as we scurried back to my auto. Set into motion, I immediately revved out of the parking area.

"You'll get us all in the slammer, yet!" Delores shouted, scolding.

"Nah." Ione tittered. "Not to worry. Apiece of cake."

I just laughed and listened. "Hey, let's stop at KDAL and harass **Little Joe.**" I suggested. "Bet he'll give me a little interview on his all night show. Probably spin my new 45 release."

"Sure. Sounds great." Ione agreed. "I'm sure not ready to sleep yet, after that squad car decoration!"

"That sure woke me up too!" Delores retorted. "Dottie! You are crazy!"

"You think?"

I never, ever heard a word about the **Squad Car Caper!** I had to assume it had to have been Hank and Randy's vehicle. They were our fun duo cops who often spent leisure after hour bonding with the **Gopher Coterie.**

* * * * * * *

Larry's expertise salesmanship and in lieu of his many contacts at the Airbase had launched a one nighter for the **Tumbleweeds** to entertain for a special Appreciation Party at the N C O Club.

Looking over the couple wigs I wore, I discovered it was definitely discarding time! They were frizzled and overdue for the trash bin. And my dismal, limp tresses had lost the luster of the last set, so I called Judy Hill, my regular hair dresser for a spur-o-the-moment appointment only to discover she was out of town and unavailable. Then I remembered Betty Coyle having said she would love to do my hair and at **Anytime!**

"You said **Anytime,** Betty!" I snickered when she answered her Park Place doorbell. "So, here I am!" I giggled at the astonished look on her face. "It is **Anytime!**"

Shyly clinging to Betty's leg at the door was a little girl with auburn bouncing curls, hiding her face against her mom's leg. A ter Betty invited me inside and promised to fix my dull frumpy mane, the little girl, not so shy now, followed her mother around the room.

"Who's this pretty little princess?" I asked. "And what is her name?"

"Tell her your name." Betty whispered.

A soft, almost inaudible, "Lonna" escaped from her timid demeanor, as she quickly, again buried her face to her mother's hip.

"She's usually more brave than this." Betty emitted. "Dottie would you like some coffee before we get started?"

"That would be great." I replied. "Coffee is definitely my morning drug, you know!" I tittered.

"Well Lonna, What do you think of Dottie Lou, my friend? She's a singer." her mom asked.

Lonna turned her head to her mother and whispered. "She's got curls. She looks like me."

We laughed.

"Dottie, I don't drink coffee, so I'm not too good at making it." Betty benevolently apopogized, as she bustled about in prep of the brew. "Not much experience here, I guess." she added. "I'm a pretty good hair dresser, but not much of a cook."

Betty was 10 or more years my junior, so I did not initiate any advise or instruction in coffee brewing in risk of intimidating her earnest efforts.

Wow, I struggled to force down, with a lump in my throat, a cup of her coffee that was so strong it almost needed a spoon to pry it from the cup!

"How's that?" she asked in her amiable effort to please.

"Really, really great!" I lied, not wanting to sabotage her attempt at coffee!

However, as coffee brewing was not one of her talents, hair styling certainly was and I left with a proud, elegant coiffure.

♫♫

CHAPTER TWENTY SIX

I snatched the phone from its wall cradle to be suddenly warmed by the soft, mellow, evocative voice of Geno.

"Isn't your hamper full by now of dirty laundry?" he joshed. "'bout time to attack the laundromat criteria, don't you think?" he purred, sensually.

"Oh yeah." I laughed. "It's stacked sky high!"

"Can you talk?" he asked.

"Oh sure. Larry is in Minneapolis. He landed a sales position with the Coleman Company and he only comes to the Twin Ports on weekends to race."

"You won't be able to get away on weekends then, huh?"

"Oh yes. I can then too, 'cuz he's always gone then too, somewhere, here and there, working on his stock car. Rebuilding the last races break downs. Anyway, I don't have to have an excuse to do laundry." I chuckled.

"Well, if you can get away, I have a request."

"You want me to come and wash my clothes?" I interposed.

"Well, that was second choice. First choice is better. How about meeting me for lunch at **The Bellows** on London Road.?"

"How long have you been in town?"

"I just got in a couple hours ago. Then I started missing you. Aren't you hungry?"

"For you?! Oh boy! Am I ever!!"

"No, no, no, Naughty Dottie! Just lunch and **platonic** conversation."

"Okay, okay." I sighed. "It was just wishful thinkin', out loud, I guess."

"Will you come?"

"Would absolutely **love, love** to—ahem—yum-yum, ah-ah—ooh—ooh—ooh." I sighed. "Oh you mean to The Bellows? Darn."

"Yes, to The Bellows!" And his infectious laughter ran little heat waves up the back of my neck and down my arms.

"Okay then, Geno. I'll meet you in an hour at the Bellows." I surrendered, my insides aching for his touch.

Click.

Entering from extreme bright sunshine blinded my vision momentarily and I stopped and stood still to adjust to the dim atmosphere lighting of **The Bellows.**

I soon located Geno at a quiet corner table inconspiciously off to the side, hidden from the busy bustle and chatter of other patrons. He arose as I approached. We hugged briefly and my senses embraced the fragrance that was Geno's own usual signature scent, not a cologne I recognized by name. We settled into soft padded swivel chairs. He had already summoned a waitress to take our cocktail orders.

"It sure is great to see you again, Dottie. It's a very lonely life on the road. I missed you so much."

"Not anymore than I missed you."

"No comparison." he cavilled. "You have family, friends and fans surrounding you at all times."

"I can't argue with that. I'm certainly hardly ever alone, even to think." I agreed. "I have something for you to listen to on the road. I made a cassette of my 8track new stereo cartridge, so you can play it on your boombox or in your auto cassette player as you travel. No one knows, except yours truly, that almost every song on it I selected especially for my Geno, about my Geno. I think You'll love it."

"Really! I'm dumb founded, wellmostly dumb, not founded. Haven't found myself yet." He chuckled, trying to make light of my tribute to him, personally. I deemed it was an attempt to camouflage embarrassment over the special attention.

He whispered, "I have something for you too, Dottie Lou. Another poem. A story poem and this one is true. It really happened on the road, somewhere in North Carolina. I was going to give it to you tonight at the Gopher, but as long as we're here together, I may as well give it to you now."

"Someday I'll write a book." I stated meditatively. "About the night life I've lived and witnessed. A musicians struggle for recognition, fame and money, the lost relationships and values sacrificed. It could be a best seller!" I joshed. "The things I've seen and heard and **done.** I'd have to change names, of course. That's for sure, or I'd be bridled with many lawsuits. I added giggling. "Not to protect the innocent, but to silence the guilty. Are you going to come to the Gopher tonight?"

"Sure. You must know by now, I just can't stay away, Dottie. It's my undying love for the Tumbleweeds. Well okay, I guess I have to confess, it's love for **A Tumbleweed,** not plural. It's not Toby or Gene I'm mesmerized with. Nice guys, but just not my type." He chuckled as dimples emerged as usual.

"Don't knock it if you haven't tried it!" I tittered.

Geno handed me his poem, on Holiday Inn Stationery. I squinted under the lighted atmosphere candle at our table to read it with difficulty.

Tale of Two White Tails

Two white tails in the night
Two white tails, rigid with fright.
Eight brown eyes in reflection
Eight brown eyes knew not direction.

The night found one driving his best.

Two lights came speeding out of the west.

Hi-lights catching a rear view mirror

Causing one to squint and to peer

A reflection in the opposite direction

Eight brown eyes was the detection.

Four little beauties from the forest came.

Two in the ditch and two in the lane.

Breaking momentum to a crawl,

As precaution and protection for us all.

Caution lights blinking in agitation.

The motorist passed in aggrivation

The collision being a spectacular crash

Dead one ended upon his dash.

Stopping the vehicle behind the mess.

Assistance offered in his distress.

His cussing could be heard a far,

Doing a one eighty returned to the car.

Not without a little chatter,

But then, dear God, It didn't matter.

Perturbed, disgusted, engaged the car,

Taking off like a shooting star.

Stopped in the first town, reported the pest.

Who slaughtered two of the forest's best.

Venison's God's gift to us all

"As food, give grace, He'll tend to the fall.

Two white tails, rigid with fear.

Two white tails, absent next year.

Two white tails next spring will not fold.

Robbing **child's sight** of this precious gold.

"New surprises from you every day, Geno. It's very well written. At least I think so. This happened when you were traveling, on the road?"

"Yes, at night, after work, heading for a late dinner and motel shut eye. The idiot barreled out around me to pass when there should have been no passing. It was around a sharp curve. He was in a stupid, belligerent hurry and there around the curve sprinted the innocent unsuspecting deer in the road."

"And you put the story to poetry. How nice. Is it mine to keep?"

"Sure."

"Thanks. I'll add it to our little collection that's repeatedly growing."

"I should write about the politics that's going on right now." Geno remarked. "That will be a much, much bigger disaster happening. I guess McGovern cinched it at the Miami Beach National Democratic Convention. He's no competition for Nixon. Even with Nixon's battling with the Watergate Cover UP and even with that sabotaging his reputation, McGovern is no competition for him. He is a **bad, bad** choice for the Democrats.

"Is there anything better out there anyway?" I asked. "It's **ALL** corruption in my estimation. Only difference is some get caught and some don't!"

We had ordered food and it was just setting in front of us, untouched and getting cold as we chatted, holding each others hands at times, knees knowingly touching under the table. We were both disregarding the intimate pulses passing between us, ignoring it all with incessant chatter. But always prominently present were the vivid memories of past passions, stimulating those foreboding sensual desires that throbbed between us.

"I think Edmund Muskie would have been a far better choice." Geno continued. "More people trust Nixon than McGovern. McGovern is a History Professor, but people are dubious about his credibility. Even more so than Nixon."

"He would have been your choice? Muskie, I mean?" I asked, smiling; unknowledgeable and feigning an interest in the political aspect that Geno was so passionate about. It was a sensitive issue in his life, perhaps stemming, I assumed, from his stint in the service as a SFC in a war. Perhaps the Korean War. I didn't know. I didn't ask.

"Sure, Muskie is a far better choice." He went on, "Nixon is duping the public about ending the war in Viet Nam. And the naive, trusting, ignorant public **Believes Him!!** If he gets reelected, **no doubt, feel certain,** there will be another four years of war!"

"We'd better start enjoying this food, Geno, before it turns completely cold. Don't you think?"

He laughed and squeezed my hand, without comment. We both dug into our selected entree's, my sea food platter and his New York strip.

"What do your days consist of when you're gone?" I asked to change the subject theme.

I call on corporations and big businesses to try to sell them on our large array of **superior** quality machinery and equipment. I try to convince them our stock will procure a profitable asset to their businesses. The meat of my job is as a sales representative for **Mack Zapple Inc.,** meant to persuade our contacted clients to eagerly place a hardy order with me. I do this from state to state through the south, the southeast and as far north as New York State."

"Wow! that's a lot of travel. Way more than my music ever entails." I ejaculated.

"Then, I locate a motel wherever I end up at the end of the day and have a late dinner there. Mostly Holiday Inns. Evenings, or whatever is left of them, I type my reports, in my room, of my orders, my expenses and my progress, successful or not, for Bud, my Boss. And that's about it."

"That's during the week. What about your weekends?'

"Sundays I go to Mass in some local church and lay around my motel reminiscing about my Dottie Lou and the Gopher Gang."

"You can always find a Catholic Church among all those **Southern Baptists?**" I asked, with a little chuckle.

"Oh sure. You know, Dottie, there's a Catholic Church in Savanah, Georgia that I attend whenever I'm in that area. It's the most beautiful, exquisite, elegant, magnificent church I have ever seen. I'd sure like to take you there someday. What an awesome experience it would be to go to Mass there together!"

"What is so special about it? The services or is it the decor?"

"Dottie, it is so beautiful it would take your breath away. It reminds me of the Notre Dame Cathedral in Paris, France, but even more ostenatious. It has steeples towering almost reaching the clouds; in Gothic architecture, I think. Just magnificent! It's all painted in **white** with vast opulent gold trim."

"White and gold? That would be awesome." I replied affirmatively. "Rich, luxurious, I once had a gown like that in white with gold trim."

"Every window, vestibule entry and steeple is in gold trim. You'd have to see it to actually grasp the beauty of it. And when the sun shines on it, well, you just can't imagine! Someday, make no mistake, I will take you there!"

"Sure." I laughed. "How about next Sunday?"

"Okay." he glibly chirped, responding to my light innocuous humor. "Bring your Bible or your Catholic Missal."

"I don't have a Bible."

"You don't have a Bible!" he ejaculated. "**Shame!** Shame on Dottie Lou!"

"You know, Geno, I just read last week that there's a new modern version of the Living Bible, called The Way, copyright in 1971, all written in modern every-day language."

"I've never heard of it."

"And the article said it was the top Best Seller of literature in 1972; even ahead of sex and cooking recipe books that came in second and third."

"Really! Well, where Have I been?"

"It comes in both Catholic and Protestant versions." I added. "You know for a number of years Catholic Doctrine didn't allow us to even have a bible."

"Really. I wasn't aware of that. Why? I wonder."

"I think they didn't want us coming to our own conclusions, our own interpretations."

Bible Rated As More Popular Than Sex Or Diets

The best-selling book of the year 1973 was not a sex book. It was not a diet book. It was a Bible: The Living Bible to be exact. Although sales records indicate the book buying public bought millions of diet and sex books, the Living Bible was again the No. 1 hardback best seller. Dr. Atkins' diet book and The Joys of Sex ran a poor second and third place.

This is the second year running that The Living Bible has soared into the rarified number one best seller slot.

"One million copies were sold in October, another million went out in November, and half a million by the end of December", according to Dr. Kenneth Taylor, president of Tyndale House,

publisher of The Living Bible. Seven million copies were sold during 1973.

The total Living Bible sales adds up to a staggering 13½ million volumes since it was first published in late 1971. said Dr. Taylor.

The book's popularity stems, in part, from the fact that it is written in easily understandable contemporary language.

"The average person's need to understand the Bible has contributed to the phenomenal sale of The Living Bible," observed Dr. Taylor. "The fact that it's published at this time answers that need and insures continued public acceptance by all faiths."

Besides, more than 13 million people must be right.

"Well Bible passages can be interpreted in many different ways by many different people. So which interpretation would actually be the right one?"

"Perhaps, but we were forced to accept and live by Catholic Rules, designed by men, enforced by men. Kind of a dictatorship wouldn't you say?" I laughed, with a touch of irony.

"Not anymore." Geno replied, defending Catholic Doctrine. "Things change. Nothing remains the same."

"Anyway, I've never been able to grasp the intended messages of Biblical passages most of the time, probably why I've never owned one."

"No excuse, Dottie." he scolded, shaking his head. "I'll see if I can find you a copy." He said. "It's called **The Way?**"

372

"Yes." I muttered and in alternative thought, uttered, "Thank you, Geno for the nice dinner. It was a nice unexpected reprieve from household responsibilities. But I guess I'd better now get this Pollack Dupa home, fix something for the kids and get ready for my gig."

"Don't forget, I want a box of your new release to distribute to contacts on my route. Loretta, in Mobile, will immediately put it on her jukebox for sure. She likes me. Well I'm a big spender. She put **One More Memory** on it for me so I can listen to Dottie Lou whenever I'm in town at home base."

"Loretta?"

"She owns the little Pub I spend time in when I'm in Mobile. You'd like her. **One More Memory** is also on the jukebox at the Holiday Inn in Mobile too. Plus a DeeJay friend spins it in the area also."

"I'll get you a box of them from my trunk when we get outside." I said.

We finished our six or seven, plus, cups of after dinner coffee and re-entered the bright blinding sunlight of daytime, squinting and hand shielding our vision, until our eyes had adjusted to the dramatic change in light.

Fumbling through my messed up, cluttered trunk I located a box of 45's for Geno.

"Well, up the hill for me. I s'pose you're at the Holiday Inn, just blocks from here?"

"No. I'm at a different motel this time. Actually, in your direction, up the hill on sixty avenue east."

"Really."

"I have a room with a huge picture of the impressive Royal Lipizzaner Stallions of Vienna, right above the headboard of my bed. Remember, we talked about them a couple weeks ago. They are, in my opinion, absolutely so perfect, so striking. It's quite a coincidence that I'd get a motel room and there, gracing the wall, this splendid picture! How unusual is that?!"

"Wow! That's weird! A strange phenomenon? That gives me goose bumps. That's not a customary, typical painting for a motel, where people steal! I'd never even heard of the Stallions before you. Motel pictures are usually scenes of landscape, rivers, trees, mountains, flowers etc."

"Is it a sign, you think?"

"Maybe. For us?! About us?"

"Why don't you stop for a minute and I'll show you the painting. It must **be a copy of** a painting. It's on you way, anyway."

"Where did you say you were hangin' your hat, **today**?"

"Just follow me." he suggested.

"Why did you decide to stay here instead of your usual Holiday Inn?" I asked as we entered his room.

"Oh, just some stupid brainstorm about avoiding you. You'd expect to find me in a Holiday Inn where I usually stay. I deemed if you don't know where I'm at, we can't get in trouble. Kinda dumb. Right?"

"I'd say. And now you show me where you're at anyway. I'm not some kind of a sex stalking monster, you know. I try to understand and honor your compelling wrestle with celibacy. However, even if you may be instilled with a rigid battle of prior Catholic teachings as an alter boy, I do not harbor the integrity and discipline of a nun. I may not agree with your reasoning but I certainly honor your decision."

"Look here. That's the picture of the Lipizzaner Horses! Isn't that magnificent!" he blurted, changing the delicate subject.

Above his bed on the wall, hung a huge, gigantic picture of the Stallions, three horses, prancing in a procession, as in a ceremonial parade or ritual.

"They were beautifully painted." I agreed. "A very talented artist must have loved them as passionately as you to capture the essence of their elegance."

"As I told you before, their name comes from Lippiza, a small village on the Adriatic coast. They are born black, turn grey and finally white as they mature."

"Wow, you sure have all the details of their actual history and existence."

"Well, a person usually study's whatever really interests a person."

"Yes, I truly believe that. I have a head just saturated with music stuff, chords, words keys, arrangements, with probably 3,000 or more songs in my head."

"Well you see that's what I mean."

"Gosh your room sure smells good. It's that cologne you wear all the time. I've noticed that before. Sometimes I can smell you before I can see you. How about that?"

"Anyone overhearing that might take it the wrong way, Dottie. Thinkin' I'm stinkin'!" we both laughed.

"It definitely is your signature." I remarked. "Makin' a statement, huh? I haven't noticed the fragrance on anyone else. Whatever is it called?"

"It's called Brute. That's all I ever wear."

"It's really nice. I will always be able to locate your whereabouts by merely following my nose!"

"Funny, funny, Dottie. You're such a screwball." he smirked,

"Well," I sighed, "I better run along. Things to do and places to go." I languidly announced, sporting a simpered smile as I sashayed toward his wide-open entry door.

With the entry facing the south west, an iridescence of elongated shafts of afternoon sunlight cascaded across the floor leaving a shadow of the open door. Little lines of shadow, also emanated along the floor from open venetian blinds.

"Will I see you later at the Gopher?" I asked as I lingered at the doorway.

"Oh sure. Gotta see the gang and dance a little if I can snuggle an available, willing partner." He moseyed over to me at the doorway.

"Okay, see you later Alligator." I chortled the overused usual jargon of aphorism. As my hand gripped the open door handle Geno initiated a small gentle hug in a non-sexist goodbye with "After while a Crocodile" response.

His innocuous hug was lingering beyond formality and I snickered and retorted, "That is, if you'll let me go!"

He softly brushed my lips with a **Sisterly** kiss and whispered benevolently, "Bye, my Funny Face." With half-closed eyes I found myself peeking into the chocolate-brown eyes I knew so well, detecting the essence of that familiar notorious hunger I also knew so well. Sporting a hunger that was definitely not roots of a **Sisterly** affection!

His arms suddenly slithered from the cuddle of my shoulders, unlocking the spurious attempt to goodbye and nimble traveling hands roamed, ravishing, squeezing the curves of my buttocks, then graduating lightly to the curves of my outer thighs.

I gulped in hypnotized surprise when his hands, no stranger to the secrets of my chassis, nor my significant points of stimulation, guided his fingers, sliding them abruptly up my throbbing inner thighs. With a surrendering sigh, my arms found home in the nape of his neck in a yielding embrace. Intoxicated and obsessed, as we were, lusting mouths devouring each others lips in mania, unashamed, uninhibited, lured into the essence of a way-too-long self denial, thus tossing every hint of a vow of abstinence to the wind.

His hands tremulously fumbled around my waist band searching for the enclosure of my slacks. My hands, as well, were quivering as I clumsily unfastened the buttons from the front of his shirt. Greedily I ran my fingers through the opening, caressing his nipples, his warm hairy chest, anticipating with inundant eagerness, the wonderful intense entrance of him into the warm wet longing of me.

He reached for the edge of the door and with his foot in one hasty exuberant thrust, slammed it shut, hiding our love away from the outside uncharitable world.

As we lay in utterly spent exhaustion with renewed attachment, closer than ever, bringing us deeper and deeper into the point of no return. The ultimate bonding of our souls.

"No way to turn back." I mused. As if I'd ever wanted to.

We lay clinging to each other in nakedness, transfixed in a disarray of white tangled sheets, oblivious to the time and dissociated from the world around us. Nothing existed in that moment except our obsessive love for each other, our sensual unchartered passion, fanning the flames of surrender as the Lipizzaner Stallions just paraded rhythmically, ceremoniously to the magnificent splendor that was us—as one!

As I dressed Geno slipped on a robe and sat beside me on the bed's edge. With a rueful smile he murmured. "I promised myself I would never do that again."

"Why?" I frowned.

"Where's that **freedom of control** I boast about?" he remarked almost apologetically. "I'm inexcusably weak!"

"I'm inexcusably happy!!" I sighed.

"This is just not right." he mumbled. "It's not fair to you. It's not fair to Larry and it's not fair to me."

"Love is never fair, Geno. In fact, at times it's damned sight painful. And selfish. Yes, sometimes very selfish. Self absorbed."

"Do you have any idea what it does to me. Us just sneaking around like this? Knowing you will never ever belong to me? That I can never have you for my own?"

"Well, you're certainly not talking marriage?"

"Isn't that where love usually goes?"

"Sometimes. But how? You can't get married anyway!" I quibbled. "You're only separated. So why torture yourself over things not even remotely possible, anyway?"

"My four year separation will be up about this time next year. It will then be finalized. At that time I have to make a definite decision as to a continuation or a divorce."

"One year from now—hmmm." I mumbled aloud and ruminated in private thought, trying to digest the meaning of his sudden announcement. Is he trying to plant a seed directly at me, hinting cleverly, inwardly that I should examine my own situation as well?

He went on, "You have no idea, Dottie, what it's like on that lonely road. You're in my every thought. I turn the car radio on full blast to change my train of thought, but then the songs are songs you sing. Do you have any idea how that tears me up?"

He arose and forlornly sashayed to the window. With his back to me, staring outside, in a choked voice he muttered so softly, almost inaudible, "I think you enjoy seeing me miserable."

I realized then, he was in an emotional distraught mood. "Is this the dark side of him he has spoken of, warned me about?" I pondered. "Why is he so depressed?" I cogitated in serious thought. "So negative, while my cloud is gliding, prodigiously in a heaven bound unabashed euphoria?"

He jolted my private musings with, "I'm not ever going to make love to you again, Dottie."

"You can't possibly mean that." I protested despairingly.

I love you so much! But I'm afraid at times I love you more than my God and that is **very very wrong!** I should love God first, most, above all else. Please don't hate me for my crazy convictions."

"Hey, He's my God too and I interpret His messages, His guidance very, very differently than you do." I cavilled. "He knows how much I love you. He doesn't condemn me for that! I'm sure it was His plan that brought us together in the first place. It wasn't coincidence! It was a won—der—ful mir—icle--." My voice trailed off, softer and softer to a silence and a gnawing doubt he was planting. I couldn't go on explaining how I so trustingly believed in God's plan for us. I began to cry. All my words and thoughts refused to emerge and my heart was heavy as he was sadistically emasculating our exquisite, precious sunshine afternoon into a grey, dismal, negative overcast.

The rushing of tears couldn't release the let-down I was feeling from my intoxicating euphoria. Without restraint I welcomed the waterfall explosion of my emotions. He took me in his arms and we held each other, both wept in each others embrace for a period of wordless humbling, each of us, in our own way, analyzing the futility of our love.

"I know I can't stay away, Dottie. I'll come to hear you sing every chance I get. I want to keep our special soulmate friendship always in my heart."

"That's it?!"

"The Bible states without negotiation, what will occur, happen to our souls when we disobey His—well, wait a minute." He unlocked our tender embrace and strode to the bedside night stand and fumbled in the drawer for the usual motel Bible.

Shuffling through the pages, he muttered, "Well, here it is; Matthew 16:26. 'What profit a man if he gains the whole world but loses his soul'. That's what will happen when we are disobedient to God."

"I guess you should have been a priest after-all, if you feel so passionate about God's rules and regulations."

"But I got married, instead, had four kids, so I guess, maybe I missed my calling." he stated, flatly with compunction.

I knew although our tears were over, momentarily, that he meant in all earnestness to end our intimate, heart wrenching, soul connected relationship. It was over. His God-fearing sense of foreboding fire and brimstone; the result of sin and loss of soul had long ago been embedded in his mind, ambushed by the brain-washing Stockholm Syndrome of Catholic Doctrine.

His intense love for God, the fear of the consequence of sin had harbored an adamant guilt struggle with his conscience. It would never permit him to continue in the most gratifying, passionate, soul-bonding relationship, the magic that was us, I had ever known. He had taken me to depths, awakened in me, something I had never experienced with anyone else. My sensuality had been in hibernation, dormant for most of my adult years. He had so moved me sensually, emotionally and intellectually to places I had never been. The loss would be devastating.

* * * * * * *

I routinely traipsed up the stairs and poured my usual creamed cup of java. I then ambled to the upstairs lounge area to chat briefly with Vivian as she dexterously cleared a table near the bar entrance. Addressing her with my usual "Hi," adding a few nonsensical remarks, I moseyed toward the barroom stairway that led to the dance area down stairs in lieu of my usual restaurant back stair exit. Entertaining a startled halt, I spotted him perched in the wall booth adjacent to the stairway, engrossed in conversation with perhaps a colleague or coworker. Not expecting to see Geno after our afternoon tearful goodbye, seeing him again so soon was an awkward start.

A hesitant "Hi" rattled my broken composure. Not receiving a welcome invite I chose to slip in beside him, nevertheless, as he reluctantly slid over to make room for me.

After a brief introduction, his colleague, seemingly uncomfortable, perhaps embarrassed, arose and excused himself with a simple, "See you tomorrow, at the office."

I voluntarily switched to the opposite side of the booth as the fellow disappeared through the barroom exit. Geno gawked at me across the booth, completely silent, obviously uncomfortable. For a moment I too was lost for words. "How should I begin to break this God-forsaken awkward silence?" I ruminated. "Perhaps I should have pretended having not noticed him in the first place and just disappeared down the stairway." Tears were stinging in frustration at the back of my eyelids. How I ached to hold him, hug him in tender solace just for a few fleeting moments. How I needed him, his magic to assure me all was normal and okay between us. I licked the salty dryness from my lips.

"I know you misunderstood what I was trying to explain to you this afternoon." he finally spoke.

I felt wounded in my heart with the afternoons poignant hurt still fresh in my mind. "Understand?" I thought.." I only understand how incredibly entranced and hypnotized I was with our magical love-making." I longed to touch his face, brush the full softness of his lips against mine, feel the sensual warmth of his throbbing, pulsating heart against my chest, the rigid fire and uncontrolled passionate excitement of him against my groin, seeking entry. It was overpowering, the memory of our ecstatic afternoon tryst!

"I knew what you were saying." I said. "I understand perfectly your meaning, but that doesn't mean I agree with you. Your reasoning seems radical and absurd to me. Too much conservative Catholic idealistic education has been pounded into your head, by enthusiastic priests, in your beginnings."

"Dottie, this is not about us. It's about God and the outcome of our Souls. I'll still be around, as a friend, a Soulmate. You know that. What's more beautiful and profound than the Platonic loving togetherness we share? And that's accepted and in fact, welcomed in God's eyes."

"How can you expect me to stand on stage across the room from your table, sing your requests, knowing I can never, ever hold you. I can't agree to your emasculating our precious love-making." I quibbled, ruefully. "If you don't ever intend to make love to me again, Geno, I'd rather you didn't come around at all! **Platonic?** It's not my cup of tea! I'm sorry."

"There, the ultimatum is out on the table." I mused. I rose to leave. He was silent. I plodded down the stairway to my stage. To my gig. To my life.

He never came downstairs that night and I was devastated! Tears welled in the corners of my eyes in brilliant penetrating flood lights. Perhaps, I had spoken too hastily, too harshly, too soon! Not seeing him at all was even worse than I had anticipated. More painful than any kind of abstinence.

My interpretation of our love affair was certainly from a very different scenario than Geno's. I rationalized in thought. "How could anything so beautiful, so complete, so compatible, so connected, **be so wrong?** Not feasible! And why would God suddenly, out of the blue, give me so much extra freedom, in Larry's absence to the Cities, if not to pursue this new opportuned godsend relationship?" I ruminated.

Hurt and confused, I kept candidly trying to negotiate with God!

Downstairs my exciting night life now seemed dull and without purpose. My vocal delivery of an emotional love ballad seemed hollow and didn't have any spark of significance anymore.

"Every ♪ fool has a rainbow, ♪ but she never seems to find." ♪ I belted to my fans through the ambiance of a smokey haze. "The ♪ reward that should be waiting ♪ at the end of the line."♪ Yes, a bed of roses, in exchange for a hammock filled with thorns, the song emanated, interpreting; Loves results, the consequences, the pain, "And ♪ go chasing after rainbows, ♪ everytime a dream ♪♪ is born."

CHAPTER TWENTY SEVEN

I heard the raucous roar of Larry's auto engine rev into the driveway just as I was about to leave for my Friday night gig at the Gopher.

"Hi. Goodbye!" he sputtered as he tore through the house gathering his racing garments. "I'm already late for the Superior Races!" He boomed flustered. "Gotta go."

"I'm running late too. How is the new job working out?"

"Can't talk now. I'll tell you all about it after the races. At the Gopher or home, whatever."

A swift peck on the cheek and out the door he bolted. Redenbaugh had been at the house earlier to load Larry's #61 on the trailer and I assumed had taken it to the race tracks.

I saw very little of Larry as he somehow managed to maneuver the three night schedule of racing, Superior, Ashland and Proctor, plus the usual stock car repairs, in his garage, on the numerous unanticipated break-downs in between races. I could discern his usual gregarious attitude and easy going disposition was steadily becoming burned out, irritable with a short fuse of endurance.

Without strategy or contemplation it seemed our rapport had drifted into a brotherly, sisterly arrangement, which on my part I deemed acceptable and adaptable, and Larry was too busy to really care about my whereabouts, my comings and goings. That was okay with me.

Barb and Gerry were visiting the area from Aitkin and popped in unexpectedly for a Saturday morning visit. Barb had always embraced a special bonding with Char since she had lived with them, having attended almost a complete term of school in Aitkin where Gerry taught. Char had baby-sat numerably for the kids, Scott and Debbie, and had even accompanied Barb to the East Coast as a baby-sitter when she flew to meet Gerry there, in lieu of a return vacation from his two week Army Guard Camp stint. So they were always more than anxious to visit the kids, especially Charmaine.

Scott and Rogie were so absorbed in their shared afternoon biking, soft ball, marbles and whatever young boys, hanging out, do, that Scott asked his mother persuasively, if he could stay and visit with Rogie for the weekend when his family went to Askov to spend the time with Barb's family and our parents, as well.

On their return from Askov late Sunday afternoon to collect Scott, enroute to Aitkin, Larry suggested taking the boys with him to his Minneapolis apartment for the week. "Company for him" he said.

So with Dale working at the Bjorklunds Transmission Shop in West Duluth and self sufficient Charmaine, soon to approach her fifteenth birthday, with little demands on me, I was favored with profuse freedom to pursue self indulged days with my own personal prized hobbies and recreational relaxations. To sleep in, uninterrupted, read leisurely, sew, play my guitar and learn the new Country hits that were up on the charts. I was squandering my days in sheer self-absorbed delight.

Busily, I kept myself never idle, trying to smother and repress any thoughts of Geno from my mind. But then a visit to the mailbox sabotaged all my good intentions. There snuggled amongst the stack of marketing jargon, magazines and utility statements was a letter from Geno. The postmark was Prichard, Alabama.

My hands shook tremulously as I brusquely ripped open the envelope. Enclosed was a little bundle of Praying Hands stickers.

"I have to see you, Dottie." a hand written text message read. "I'm going completely out of my mind. I'm so sorry if my stupid craziness has hurt you. I guess this Irishman is really mixed up in interpretations of Right from Wrong, Good from Bad and Love versus Loneliness. I just can't stand the missing you! "Why am I torturing myself?' I ask. After typing my reports in my room a couple nights ago and with so much time on my hands to think and think, I was so damn lonely I was inspired to write this poem to you."

Beneath his message was a type written poem with a praying hands sticker adhering near the title.

At Times Our Love is Quaking

When simple men of simple means
Gather together to compare dreams,
And ask what fate determines these,
And what men know of what all this means?
Who tells these men there is no way?
For any gain we dearly pay!
But listen closely, one will say,
I'll reach that Mountain Top **"ONE DAY!"**

It seems at times our love is quaking,
Please, Dear Lord, no heart breaking.
Our love needs not rings or paper,
Just be blessed by our Maker.
Is too much asked, Oh Lord, we pray,
Requesting Eternity and **ONE DAY?**
Just Eternity and "One Day!

My heart was pounding, vehemently against my sweater. Surprise?! Dubious, ambivalent emotions clutched at my heart with an analytical gut feeling, asking myself, "Is this for real? Or will he just change directions again in a week or two?!"

I instantly penned a return poem answer as poetry was our usual idiosyncratic technique of intellect reply and posted a praying hands sticker in the right hand corner, top of the page.

I never deemed our love was quaking!
Was not prepared for a heart breaking!
If only You'd asked **HIM,** sincerely and clear
To guide our Love in the time we spend **here.**
Then **TRUST Him, BELIEVE Him** in all that He'd

say.

If only you'd asked **HIM,** He'd have shown you
The Way!

It was my day off so I decided to do the laundry in Piedmont Heights. Then I swung over to Shopper's City for miscellaneous supplies, including the week's grocery list.

As I sashayed through the department store's furniture and hardware accessory departments I stopped abruptly, dead in my tracks, stunned by a display of a section of framed pictures. There propped on a shelf, a painting or a copy of a painting, I assumed, was exhibited a huge, magnificent picture of the Lipizzaner Stallions, and only one, identical to the one that had been hanging on the wall in Geno's motel.

I stared in awe at the whimsical coincidence. Is it a portent omen?" I sighed in reflection. "A sign? A message?"

On impulse I seized the picture from the shelf, plopped it into my cart and headed for check-out. At home I excitedly propped the painting against a blank wall and impetuously snapped a number of photos of the impressive Stallions. Then a couple extra shots to be assured of successfully arriving at a clear, sharp image.

After developing, mischievously smiling, I inserted the photo into an envelope and addressed it to Geno, now having received his Alabama address. On a more serious note, I attached one of his Praying Hands stickers to the photo and added a three line positive prayer I had copied from the Sunday Newsletter at St. Joseph's Sunday Mass.

The Royal Lipizzan Stallions of Vienna

It read:

I Believe I am always divinely guided.
I believe I will always take the right turn of
the road.
I believe God will always make a way where there
is no way!

I wanted to accentuate a little propitious positive thinking to sabotage any further off-the-wall renewal of his platonic, celibatic nonsense.

Geno arrived in town the following week, unannounced, and snuck in and perched his special table. With cocktail in hand, he emphatically requested Korn to sing, especially for him, a Carl Smith tune, "I Just Loved her *AGAIN For The LAST* time."

I could hardly contain my excitement as I impatiently struggled with the time dragging, in waiting, to finally hear Korn warble, "I'm ragged but I'm right," the signature closing song of another night at the Gopher finalized.

Geno and I gulped our unfinished cocktails in the corner booth, intoxicated, not from liquor, but with each others presence and the inner knowing of what was yet to come. We climbed the stairway to the back exit and in separate vehicles peeled out of the parking lot, off to our clandestine Holiday Inn tryst.

Geno hadn't mentioned the photo, perhaps hadn't yet received it. I didn't ask. I didn't want to dampen in anyway, our ecstatic obsession with each other.

We spent Tuesday, Wednesday and Thursday nights locked in each others arms, my leaving his motel room only just before dawn to arrive home before my children would awaken.

We talked and talked pensively about a future, sometime, somewhere, somehow, **"One Day,"** expressed in anticipation and promise, from the contents of his new poem he had compiled and sent to me. It was our ultimate vow of a **"One Day"** Together! He had taken his beautiful poem, had it perfected on 8x10 parchment paper in opulent black and gold Old English lettering. It was exquisite and ostentatious. It was for me to frame for my wall, he said. But, of course, I just snuggled it, hidden amongst my music paraphernalia. I was married!

We were in an amazing state of prodigious euphoria. Platonic and abstinence and celibacy were nouns totally annihilated from our vocabulary or our entity.

All too soon it was Thursday night or almost dawn on Friday and he talked of his having to leave for Alabama in the morning. As I dressed to leave he presented me with an old Irish poem he had recently come across.

"This is to us." he murmured. "It's not mine. I wish it were. The author is unknown."

It had an incredible passionate message, a positive outlook on the acceptance of whatever life's future might hold.

> The clock of life is wound but once
> And no one has the power
> To tell just when that clock will stop
> At late or early hour.
> **NOW** *is* the only time we have
> **Give Love,** Toil with a will
> Place no faith in tomorrow
> Tomorrow those hands may be still!

* * * * * * *

A mere three or four hours had lapsed since we'd hugged and kissed in a lingering goodbye. I was still maudlin from his tender, memorable touch and had not yet sudsed his fingerprints from my skin when the phone screamed a shrill wake-up call from my night dreams.

"Hello."

"It's me, Sweetheart."

"Omigosh! Hon. Where are you? I thought you'd be on your way to Montgomery by now!"

"I am, but I only got as far as the Quik-trip Convenience store at the Barnum exit when I realized I just had to hear your voice. Just one more time."

"Wonderful, my Love." I sighed.

"Would you mind," he proposed, "Scooting over here to Barnum I just need to hold you in my arms, just once more, before I leave the area."

"You're kidding." I laughed, the same old weakness pulsating rising and flowing, warming my veins as it moved to my throat, my arms, my groins. I squeezed my thighs tightly together, sensually remembering the passions of last nights love-making.

"No Sweetheart, I'm not kidding. I'm just aching to hold you again. If you need a more feasible excuse to scoot over here to Barnum, well, bring me another box or two of your 45's of **Just Tell Him I Said Hello,** with the pictures inserted inside. I'm completely out and need some more to distribute on my route."

"I really don't need any other reason, Darling, to fly away to your arms. And yes, I'll be there as soon as is possible, as fast as this crazy Pollack can whizz out of here, with a legitimate excuse. Ahem! Records, yeah! Love you, my crazy Guy."

"I'll be right here in the parking lot, waiting." he sighed.

"Yes, yes, Hon. See you soon."

Click.

I scrambled madly around the house, tossing garb together, fervently splashing water on my face, then grabbing my purse and a couple of boxes or 45's, with keys dangling from my trembling fingers, I dashed crazily out the door. Gunning the engine, I hurriedly peeled out of the driveway, screeching the wheels of my 'ole Chevy out onto the road, with only one destination obsessing my mind.

Maple Grove and Midway Road extending and crossing over Highway 2 to Highway 61 would be the shortest, quickest route to Barnum.

Upon nearing the one set of railroad tracks on the entire route near Highway 2, there in view emerged a long lazily approaching freight train, only three or four hundred feet from the crossing, clanging along, loudly and profusely blowing horns, nonstop, cautiously warning me to **HALT** my approach to the tracks!

"I can't wait for 125 cars!" I told myself. "They're moving so-so slow and what if they stop entirely? A ten minute wait for sure!! No way!" Pedal to the Metal! I bombarded the gas pedal, screamed across the tracks, with the scent of burning rubber, as the engineer incessantly laid on his horn expressing his obvious anger. I glanced back as I cleared the tracks, with him in view, shaking a vehement raised fist in my direction!

Flying down the highway with the feeling of Eagle Wings, my heart was pounding, as it always did with the very thought of him, still here in Minnesota and only a few breath minutes away from our embrace.

Upon entering the Convenience Store parking lot, prodigiously searching, I immediately detected Geno's auto and I pulled in along beside him, jolted out of my vehicle and seconds later I was clinging to the warmth and fury of his arms, the fragrance of **Brute** tickling my nostrils, with his embrace holding me so desperately compelling I thought he'd crush my bones.

"Darling, Sweetheart, Darling!" he murmured. "Oh how I needed just to hold you. To hold onto the precious few moments left before leaving. I just couldn't get you out of my mind this morning."

"I know." I whispered. "I know. Me too. How well I know. But why should we? I love you being in my mind."

We hugged and kissed and talked and laughed and talked some more, in between cupping and touching each others faces, holding hands, with the sun fondly and warmly caressing our faces, streaming through the windshield embracing our infatuated obsessive stolen hour this magnificent August morning.

"We just can't let the sadness of parting overwhelm us like this," he wistfully intimated. At the mention of goodbye tears slowly dribbled from the corners of my eyes. He reached up a finger, tenderly wiping away as he softly crooned, almost in a whisper, "She ♪ needs someone to hold her when ♪ she cries."

All too soon he was departing, his auto wending away toward the entrance of the 4-lane divided highway, south bound, back to his Alabama job. Dismally poignant, I waved and the emptiness gripped my persona as I sat parked and watched his car slowly disappear out of my sight and down the busy freeway, vanishing somewhere among a caravan of moving vehicles.

He wouldn't be returning for a couple weeks and it would be lonely, but he called every week night to talk and phone visit when he knew I would be alone.

Languidly I engaged my Chevy, heading back toward Duluth Heights and home. Through a few tears, yet smiling to myself, I whispered out loud, "Yes, we must be **totally crazy!** Me, even risking my life **racing a train!!** Just for a few precious lingering, loving Goodbyes!" As the music has said time and time again, as Dave Dudley sang in one of his hits, ♪ **There'll Always Be That** ♪ **One."**

We were definitely infatuated, mesmerized; definitely obsessed, but we were also, definitely **Magic!** We had brought to our relationship something in understanding and insight to each other that embraced a very special bonding. A blessing to cherish that not everyone is given. Some people don't even think it exists! This once in a lifetime **bonding of souls.**

"Yes, I'd rather be sorry for something I've done, than for something that I didn't do!"

♪♪♪

CHAPTER TWENTY EIGHT

I nonchalantly sauntered into the house, a melody still on my lips, humming softly the last refrains of a song I had been listening to on a local radio station on my way home after my gig. I was earlier home than usual. School had resumed and there were school lunches to improvise, clothes to be ironed, etc. I seemed to manage successfully my best efforts at night when I was hyper and unwinding from the excitement of the night life crowd.

I gently tippy-toed into the bedroom where Larry was already vocalizing a nonharmonic strain of ZZ's as he mumbled incoherent gibberish.

I attempted to noiselessly remove my pickin' clothes and quickly, unceremoniously slip into my nightie.

It was Tuesday night, just a day past the Labor Day Weekend Racing Extravaganza so I knew he was exhausted. He had even chosen to disregard his scheduled day of employment in Minneapolis.

His racing trophies were all packed in three gigantic cardboard boxes, one on the kitchen table and the other two on the counter top. This prudently informed me he had recently been down to the Skiroule Shop where his partnership had hence been slowly, slyly terminated to enable him the necessary freedom for his new Coleman position in the Twin Cities.

He had nummerably grumbled to me in no uncertain terms, that he had been forced to withdraw his partnership without any kind of reimbursement from his partner. It had been a verbal partnership without written agreements or contracts. "No papers." he had sputtered. Nothing except a joint tax statement, had given any evidence a partnership had ever existed. I wasn't aware of any of the particulars. Never pressed my curiosity into Larry's many incredible grey arrangements, or questioned the authenticity of his ventures. His comings or goings I never disputed. I wasn't even aware of why he was home in lieu of a working day for him on his new Coleman employment.

"Gosh, I think I'll prepare the stew for tomorrow's supper, after school." I ruminated. I usually found it easier to prepare family entree's ahead for a quick bake or warm-up when kids would barge in, off the bus, ravenously hungry.

Being it takes an hour or two to floor, pound and brown the beef, peel and cut up vegetables and potatoes etc, I decided to quietly smuggle the clock radio from the bedroom for some musical companionship as I coasted the kitchen drudgery.

The electrical cord of the clock radio was pinched tight and emerging from somewhere behind the headboard of the bed. Carefully and quietly I attempted to release the cord by raising the corner of the mattress just a mere smidgen, but with little success. It was stuck tight!

Suddenly to my stunned surprise, Larry sprang from the bed in a fit of infuriated anger. He was battling the impossible schedule between the Coleman Minneapolis job and the Twin Ports three nights of Racing. It certainly didn't make for a virtue of patience and the result was a very frazzled short fuse. He was definitely getting burned out!

Retrospectively, I had once seen him, during an angry fit, leave a fist hole in the dry wall of the hallway over some trivial incident I couldn't recall, but he had never hit me and he was usually quite patient and compatible when things went haywire, as they often did in racing.

"God damn you!" he thundered in a stringent voice. "You don't give a damn for anybody's sleep but your own! Do you?"

"I'm sorry!" I responded ironically, rolling my eyes to what seemed immature childlike nonsense to me.

He seized the clock radio cord and yanked it fiercely from behind the headboard and hurled the radio across the room **where** it crashed against the chest of drawers and lay shattered in numerous pieces upon the carpet.

"You son-of-a-bitch." I muttered, softly under my breath, as I slowly picked up the pieces of glass and metal and plastic from the floor. He followed me with his eyes as he scrambled back under the covers to resume his interrupted zz's.

I carried the debris away and dumped it into the kitchen garbage can all the while crying softly. Crying for what seemed an equivocal mayhem, but mostly because it had been my birthday gift of a few months prior.

I was so devoid of emotion and apathetic with Larry's and my stoical relationship. Everyday I longed so to be somewhere else. With the double life I was living a lot of the trauma was of my own doing, my own fault. More and more I pondered making changes. "I've had it." I mused. "Coming home to this really fans the flame of indifference. Life is way too short for this."

Thoughts of closure stumbled through my mind as I began clearing space for preparing my beef stew. "Better take his stuff to his garage." I ruminated. His private domain. A place I felt was not a part of me.

As I carried the boxes in my arms to the garage, **Would you Believe** one trophy just happened to **SLIP** from my grasp and shattered into pieces on the garage cement floor.

"**OOPS!**" I grinned. "Strange, and a First Place trophy at that!"

"**OOPS!** And there goes another one too?!" I couldn't stifle the devious, derisive giggle that followed.

I smiled an appeased simpered smile as I browned floured beef chunks in a pan of burbling safflower oil. "Hmm—God works in mysterious ways." I ejaculated. "Well, perhaps, not God!"

* * * * * * *

It was middle September and Larry had just returned with the boys from the Canadian Invitationals. The kids were off to school Monday morning and Larry and I were at the kitchen table. Me with my usual cup of java and Larry downing some milk with toast, sausage and eggs.

Our times home together were very infrequent, so this was an exception to the rule. Usually he'd be back working at Colemans on Monday.

"I s'pose I'd better get packed for Minneapolis." he mumbled. "Can't miss Tuesday too."

"I don't know how you're able to keep employment with all those race track absences." I said.

"You know why? Cuz, **Damn I'm good!** That's how!" he chuckled.

"Yes, I know you're indispensable, Larry." I smirked, ironically.

With each of us in our own selfish self-absorbed lives, I deemed there wasn't much reason to cling to what little we had. I was just waiting for the right opportune time to spring the bombshell on him.

"What better time ever, than **now?**" I mused. I took a big gulp of courage diaphragm air and diffidently tossed the impetuous question onto Larry's lap, taking him by complete precipitated surprise.

"Are you actually happy in this marriage?" I asked. "Truly satisfied with the way things are?"

Our marital commitment had stretched into three plus years. There were not many angry outbursts, no major disagreements, however no significant bonding or incredible chemistry either. Just a blah indifference most of the time.

"Are **You?**" he flippantly chortled.

"I asked you first." I replied with a nervous giggle.

"What do you have in mind?" he quipped.

"That's not an answer, Larry. That's a question." I protested.

He laughed.

I went on, "Well, we really do go our own ways most of the time, anyway. We pass in the hallways when you're enroute to your stock car racing or I'm on my way out to my gig. How much do we really **need** from each other?"

"Not much quality time eh?" he smiled. "But what about the fantastic sex?"

I rolled my eyes, but ignored his frivolous witticism. "This house is just a place to flop when we're tired." I stated flatly.

"And this is upsetting you?"

"Not tremendously." I replied, trying to be tactful, yet indifferent.

"Do *YOU* like being married?" he asked, obviously trying to analyze where I was coming from.

"Is that a trick question?" I asked.

"No, but that's not an answer, Dottie. That's a question." he returned, grinning impertinently.

"Okay, okay, you got me." I continued, "It is a bit confining, all this commitment. We both have our own finances, which we don't share. We both have and own our own houses, our own transportations, our own careers. It just **doesn't** make much sense. What's the point of being married?" I cavilled.

"But, we're not actually very demanding on each other." he added. "Half the time we aren't even aware of where the other half is, much less care. Right?"

"That's what I mean. We don't really **need** each other. **What's the point?"**

He chucked, then turned his attention to downing a second glass of milk while he munched a buttered toast, gone cold. "But, isn't that a good thing?" he added complacently.

"Not really. Do you like being married?" I candidly repeated the ignored question. I tried to be casual, grinning and emphasizing the YOU.

"Hmmm—I guess I can take it or leave it." he replied. "For one thing, I really would like to date other chicks." As if he hadn't started dating a mere six weeks after we had said "I do!"

"I guess maybe, I would like that too." I agreed, trying not to sound too anxious.

"As long as we both mutually agree." Larry remarked. "Why don't we get a divorce? I don't have a problem with that, unless it is a problem with you."

"No problem." I replied.

"We have to have two witnesses. That I know. I'm not a rookey at this, you know." he laughed. "It's old hat with me. You're my fourth marriage! Why don't you get one of your Gopher friends and I'll get one of my racing pit buddies to volunteer to make me a free man."

"Sounds good to me." I replied. "I'm sure Delores would help me out. She's done this before too."

"Would or could we still be lovers? On occasion?" Larry sheepishly asked.

Off guard, his carnal request had taken me for a jolt!

"Your kidding?!" I said. However, looking at his facial expression I realized **he wasn't!** I hadn't anticipated anything in this vein of closure.

"Will he renege if I say no?" I mused, uneasily. I decided to feign a positive interest. "May—be—" I stammered. "Oh I s'pose—what the hell." I lied, knowing my real intentions were anything but a continuation. I was definitely permanently **Moving On!"**

With raised eyebrows in bogus sexual interest I blothered, "There'll be times, I suppose, when I'll be squirming in dire need of sexual release.

When that happens, I'll look you up!" I giggled, trying to make light of his subtle suggestion.

"We are **dynamite** together! Don't you think!" he bombarded, trying to pry a trophy boast of his performance from me. When I didn't reply he added, "Yeah, you're good. Good for at least a couple times a month!!" He laughed heartily. "The last of the worlds oversexed nymphomaniac females. I can handle that!"

My face turned hot in silent anger. "Forget the insult!" I mused. "Walk softly. Don't arouse any animosity. Rebuttal is not worth losing ground. Not now, with freedom so close."

"One more thing." he proposed. "I would want it to be **me divorcing you,** not you divorcing me, because I already have had three. It wouldn't look very good for me to have another marriage 'hit the dust'. I have to think of my reputation!" he guffawed in amusement.

"That's okay by me." I agreed. "I don't reall---,"

"Another thing," he interrupted, "I wouldn't want it to take place in Duluth and have it smeared all over the Duluth News Tribune! How about having it arranged in Carlton?"

"That's fine." I agreed. "But if **you** divorce me, however **You'll** have to pay lawyer and court costs." I chuckled.

"Oh ho-ho-ho No. No way!" he sniggered. "It's all 50-50. Under the table, we compromise. I pay half!"

"Oh I guess." I conceded. "No sweat." I would have agreed to just about anything to snatch my freedom and the opportunity to freely move on with my life.

"Only one lawyer, though." I dictated. "No sense for us to pay two layers as long as we're in agreeable, friendly arrangement. Right?"

Larry contacted attorney Adrian Blake McDonald of McDonald, Munger, Fillenworth & Bang to arrange a court date of December sixth to wholly dissolve our bonds of matrimony.

* * * * * * *

* * * * * * *

"Yes, I'd like that a lot." I responded.

Geno was proposing an afternoon picnic in Jay Cook Park for the next day.

"Where should I meet you?" I asked. Now that Larry and I were in agreement over going our own separate ways I felt a weight had been lifted, deeming clandestine trysts unnecessary.

"How about here, at the Gopher?" he suggested.

"Sure. I can leave my car parked in back for the afternoon. Dandrea won't care I'm sure."

We motored out through West Duluth and into Fond-du-lac. We casually cruised miles of picturesque scenic wilderness in Geno's rented auto, stopping now and then, just to take in the beauty of early autumn. Everything is so much more awesome and breathtaking when you're in love. Colors are more vibrant. Greens are greener. Wild redbeckia, with little piercing black centers winked at us in the breeze, their golden faces basking in the sun while crimson sumac gently swayed with the wind as we drove along through winding terrain.

Geno slowed to a crawl, then stopped, as we entertained watching a doe and an almost full grown fawn twitching their pointed ears raised in curiosity at our approach. They stood in the middle of the road and after a lengthy pause suddenly darted across the road with their fluffy white tails bobbing up and down in departure.

We sashayed through meadow and park-like forest, picking flowers and rocks on natures pathway along the falls, searching agates, entertaining an occasional embrace, totally relishing the languid, lazy afternoon, lost in each other or perhaps found. It was awesome. It was profound.

The area was mostly deserted. Flow of traffic or pedestrian was minimal. We had inherited the tranquil domain almost all to ourselves, as we pilfered beautiful hours of escape from the eyes of the world. being thus consumed and absorbed in each other manifested absolute oblivion to any activity around anyway.

We talked and talked, laughed and laughed, never runing out of topic, hesitating now and then to brush lips or gently hug and squeeze waistlines or hands as we gazed, hypnotized by the white frothy foam forming on the rushing waters of the falls. Utter relaxation from a fast lane world!

Loving and laughing at each others inane attempts at nonsensical lines of poetry was our usual thing whenever we were in each others company. Sometimes our jargon witticism tidbits were a bit suggestive and naughty, sometimes profound and philosophical.

"Hey, look at that bluejay up in the tree." Geno intimated glibly.

"Loving the **Splendor** that is you and me." I replied.

"And she knows our secrets, true, but alas,

Will probably tattle on our **Splendor** in the

grass!"

We both laughed cordially, as we squeezed each others hand. Since we always tried to out create each other, Geno was compiling again as he shook a scolding finger at me and chided.

"He knows my Dottie is urging a **RISE!**

If I can catch her, she's in for surprise!"

I giggled.

"It's no surprise. Even bluejays can see

This **Special Love** God's given you and me."

"Wouldn't you just love to camp here, Dottie?" he said dreamily in far away seemingly meditative thought. "Dive for lily roots, snare game, make a reed shelter, watch animals play, lie around and gaze at a star studded sky and make love and make love and make love to a serenade of crickets and frogs."

"What a dreamer you are." I tittered. "A regular Don Quixote. And yes, that would be awesome, only what would we do as mosquitos munched our tender tootsies?" I giggled. trying to add a realistic vein to the fantasy.

"Hey, don't be such a realist!" he scolded. "It's my dream, my choice and there are **no mosquitos** in my fantasy!" he declared emphatically.

"But also," I teased, "I can't dive for lily root. I don't even know how to dive. As a kid I was barely able to master dog-paddling."

"I'd teach you." he said, dimples dancing as he grinned with eyebrows raised in suggestive flirtation. "I'd teach you lots. Yes, lots of stuff! Then turning to poetry he recited softly:

"Out in the night on a dark hill

Stood pines around me, spicy and still,

With a heaven of stars over my head,

White, topaz and misty red."

"That's beautiful, Geno." I said in humble surprised seriousness.

He chuckled and winked mischievously. "It's not mine, Dottie I wish it were. That's Joyce Kilmer. But I know the Poem is right as rain and rain is lovely drops of love from God and **that is mine!**"

"I saw a ghost one night last week." I interposed.

All long and lean and lanky.

As I walked outside of the house

In the darkness black and inky.

He waved his arms and legs at me

And the moon began to shine.

Ah Shucks! Just Daddy's underware
Left flappin' on the line!"

"You screwball." he smirked.

"And that's not mine either." I giggled. "Seventh grade, author unknown."

"How did that come about?"

"It was an English assignment, a lesson in public speaking to recite in front of the class. I don't remember where I found the poem."

"It could have been yours. You're always coming up with uncanny, amusing tidbits."

"You know I tried to write a poem for Delores, at her request, the other night. I had my, one for the road, glass of brandy water squeezed between my thighs while I was driving the car. It was late and I was on my way to an after hour party at Marcie's and Phil's place, when a couple of good cool lines popped into my head. Well, you know you have to write them down right away when they come to you or you lose them."

"You need to carry a tape recorder."

"Yes, I know. I've thought of that too. Well anyway, I tried to stop my chevy at a certain spot under a street light so I could see to write. Well what happened then made me forget completely, the poem lines for Delores and brand new rhyme popped into my head. Just like that. It went like this:

I'm holding my drink right between my knees
Cuz I'm late for a party at Phil and Marcie's.
A poem for Delores I'm trying to write
By dim street light in the wee of the night.
Well, I put on the brake instead of the clutch
And now I got **Brandy** right up my crotch!!"

"You're crazy." he chuckled. "Did you show Delores?"

"Oh sure. But the fact of the matter of importance is that incident wasn't a bit funny, Sweetie! It was icy cold and it was wet! Very, very wet! and that's the truth!" I finalized the explanation with a Lily Tomlin signature idiom from the popular **Laugh In** TV sitcom, when she rolls a tongue "air poop" from her lips.

"What did Delores say?"

"You know Delores. Always comical. She said, 'I bet, at least that was one time you had a tight one!'"

"Huh? She what? A tight what?"

"You know. My crotch got tight."

"Oh. How would she know?"

"I guess, maybe she could assume." I said.

We both giggled heartily.

"Good thing I wasn't there when it happened." he purred impishly. "I'd have gotten smashed between your thighs. On brandy and I only drink Scotch!"

"Naughty! Naughty, Geno! Shame, Shame!" I ejaculated in a high pitch and we both chuckled.

He squeezed me in a gentle hug and murmured softly, "I sure do love you. And I sure love to hear you laugh." he said. "Laughing comes so easy with you."

"It's easy because I'm so happy." I responded. "That's how it is when two soulmates are so in love."

"Yes, we sure are." he said. "But anyone can be lovers. It takes so much more to be a soulmate and a true friend. I think I've discovered all that in my Dottie Lou."

"Don't put me so **High** on that pedestal, Geno. I'm afraid of heights and I'm bound to fall. No one can stay up there, that high, for long." Unbeknown to his usual perceptiveness I was serious.

He spread a blanket on the grass and we sat with our legs in Indian fashion and munched the sandwiches I had prepared, sipping soda between bites.

After satisfying our tummies I tickled his ribs and mussed his hair as he lay sprawled, full length on his stomach on the blanket. I gently rubbed his back and indolently pinched little zits, urbanely smoothing the pink pinches away.

"You know, I want to learn to play the guitar." he rambled on as I languidly continued scratching and rubbing his back. "Hey, I'll give you only two hours to stop that!" A little chuckle followed.

"Do you have a guitar?" I asked.

"I'm going to buy one."

"It takes many, many hours, Geno, of committed, dedicated practice; endless repetition, over and over. It's not an overnight accomplishment."

"I know."

"It doesn't come easy. I can't begin to stress enough the amount of discipline it will take. Improvement happens very, very slowly, so slow, in fact, it's difficult to actually see the progress."

"I know. But music is so much a part of your world. I love music and I wanna be a part of that world too. You look like you're in some special kind of **seventh heaven** when you're singing."

"That's fairly true." I agreed. "I think every performer does actually become somewhat oblivious to who or what's around them when they're doing their thing. We become sorta entranced with the emotional impact of melody and delivery of lyrics."

"Well, I'm determined. I'm going to give the guitar a whirl. What's there to lose?"

"I could show you some guitar chords for a start." I said. "I play a little guitar too. I know a few chords."

"That would be great. I have a lot of free time in the evenings and week ends to practice. It would keep me out of the bars. Better for my health." he winked.

"I only know chords to accompany singing. Not actually playing a melody. Do you sing?"

"In the shower and only country music. You could teach me **there,** how to sing and I could teach you----" he chuckled, intimating. "Well never mind. We can negotiate those details later, **there,** under the soft spray of the water."

"Oh sure." I smiled. "Well Honey, I have to work tonight. We'd better head back to Duluth. Gosh this time sure went fast."

"I know, but what a wonderful way to spend an afternoon. It doesn't get any better than this."

And our lazy afternoon had so quickly disappeared. A leisurely kiss on the lips, one more hasty embrace, pack up our paraphernalia, dispose of the garbage and we were back on the road, about to join the inevitable chaos of the worldly rat race.

And I knew I was hooked on this guy! There was no turning back. I had never felt more connected to anyone in my entire memory. This was love based on so many innumerable profound interests. Our passions for music, poetry, religion; Our love of nature and God. Our perceptions and intellect were so very on the same page, same directions, like clones. Uninhibited communications in every category: Yes a unique bonding of soul, not mere body. This was not merely a romantic sex tryst, a tété é tété of lust. This was **Special,** indeed.

However, I did have to admit. He had taken me to places I had never been before and I don't mean vacation spots!

♫♫♫

CHAPTER TWENTY NINE

So many autumn birthdays and so close together. All three of my kids were autumn babies. I arranged little traditional parties for Rogie and Charmaine at the house with a few of their close playmate friends.

Geno popped in and it was noted that it was his birthday also, a week before Rogie's, so a celebration was in order there, as well.

We slipped away with Ione and her boyfriend, Medford, to what we deemed, discreet, on a quiet Monday later afternoon and evening to honor the birthday boy.

We chose to bar-hop and just hang-out in Gary New Duluth. It was Ione's stomping ground and hang-out area. Many people knew here there, so we soon decided to find a more prudent area. We motored to Cloquet and the Cloquet Labor Temple to dance to the jukebox.

The Lounge was almost deserted with merely a bored bartender and a couple guys playing pool. Not much intriguing action on a Monday night, but we welcomed the unoccupied privacy. After all, as an intimate foursome, we weren't searching people. We were making our own excitement, our own action! The place was cozy, private and comfortable and that just suited us perfectly.

But the party of all parties of that autumn was the one Larry and I threw for Dale. His initiation to 18 year old **Stud, Macho, Manhood!** Dale had been one of Larry's pit men and go-fer's for three years so Larry harbored a lot of surrogate fatherly effort and enthusiasm to make Dale's birthday shindig a party of all parties. We used his house in West Duluth for the celebration. We invited a coterie of Dales and Charmaine's friends to hobnob with a mix of Larry's and My adult friends, as well.

In my book research, through the viewing of my old home movies, displays much evidence of a mixed attendance and there sure didn't seem to be a generation gap at all! Not that the kids were so precociously adult and mature, but rather that the adults were a bunch of zany, wild, undisciplined kids!!

Vickie, Korn's wife, unbuttoned Dale's shirt as they danced in the tiny living room. She caressed his hairy chest and masculine nipples as Barb, Dale's girlfriend, looked on from the sidelines with sparks of arbitrary anger.

"Just a joke, Barb. Having some fun with your birthday boy." Vickie giggled in impish, comical gusto.

I had elaborately decorated and frosted a birthday cake, that in reality was a 12pk of Budweiser, a tribute to Dale's initiation to adulthood. However, I also presented him another gift; a brown paper bag filled with gum drops, an all day sucker, crayons, a coloring book, little boy push cars, kids candy etc. to let him know he was still a kid and would be expected to follow rules and accept parental guidance and discipline at home.

* * * * * * *

I didn't see much of Geno in late October or November. He thought it best for him to remain inconspicuous in lieu of perhaps complicating matters with his presence during the strategy of Larry's and my divorce actions. I had to agree.

He called me at home a couple times a week, very earnestly reminding me to **VOTE!**

"The right to vote is a gift, a fought for, hard earned legacy to our freedom." he stressed emphatically. "Don't take that privilege too lightly. You will take time to vote, won't you?"

"Oh sure." I lied. I felt I was not qualified in knowledge or wisdom in political matters to make an intelligent decision. Geno, on the other hand, was well informed and passionately zealous over government and political issues.

"Are you puttin' me on?" he asked.

"Who? Me? Would I ever put the shuck on you!?" I tittered.

"I have a poem I've written about the political issues in this presidential campaign, like watergate, for instance. But I don't suppose you'd understand it."

"Probably not."

"I'll mail it to you anyway. Maybe you will learn something that will help you understand politics plus maybe inspire you to get more involved."

He mailed me his political poem and he was right. I didn't understand it!

Here is a horse the media can ride.
It does sway from side to side.
They have accused and now they wait,
Sitting back, they adjust its gait.
Viewing the spectrum with a fix-on,
They will try to implicate Nixon.
Agnew rides that horse of spirit.
He don't give a damn who hears it.
All involved care not the country's fate,
Expose, Expose, The Watergate!!
The gullibles watch the entire diversion,
Knowing not the true **excursion!**
They champion the minority rights of one,
But trample **All** the rights of some.

Oh people , my people, turn the tide!
Divert the Comm's from our Countrside!

And Nixon was certainly re-elected with or **without** my vote!

* * * * * * *

In late November **The Tumbleweeds** fronted another Country-Western Concert at the Duluth Arena, featuring Donna Fargo (Funny Face) and Freddie Hart (Easy Lovin').

Fredie hart & Dottie Lou

DONNA FARGO CHATS WITH
DOTTIE LOU *Back Stage*

Of course, My being the correspondent for the Minneapolis C W News-Scene Newspaper, Dottie Lou relating Monthly the Duluth-Superior happenings in Night Club, Concert Scene as she had been doing for sometime, sent them a splash for their December issue:

Twin Ports Area Proves Attraction
PAGE 7, NEWS-Scene—December, 1972
For Top C/W Talent

DULUTH, Minn. – Duluth and Superior folks are not lying in the weeds as far as country music is concerned, according to Country & Western NEWS-Scene correspondent Dottie Lou.

"Things are really happening here," she reported. "We have about 10 local C/W combos working five and six nights a week in our Twin

Ports area, not to mention the out-of-town talent that entertains us from time to time."

Twin Ports Area Proves Attraction For Top C/W Talent

PAGE 7, NEWS-Scene — December, 1972

DULUTH, Minn. — Duluth and Superior folks are not lying, in the weeds as far as country music is concerned, according to Country & Western NEWS-Scene correspondent Dottie Lou.

"Things are really happening here," she reported. "We have about 10 local C/W combos working five and six nights a week in our Twin Ports area, not to mention the out-of-town talent that entertains us from time to time."

Among national headliners in the area lately were Dave Dudley, Donna Fargo, and Freddie Hart. Donna and Freddie shared billing on the KAOH country music spectacular at the Duluth

Donna Fargo (left) chats with Dottie Lou.

auditorium. With them, said Dottie, were Billy C. Cole ("we are proud of him, since he is from our town and was a DeeJay here in the past") and Ronnie Lyght, "a promising local boy on his way up."

Also, on October 9, Dottie Lou and her band, "The Tumbleweeds," were suprised with a visit from Tom T. Hall at the Kro Bar in Superior, where they perform.

Dottie added that NEWS-Scene readers might want to look for her new release, "Every Fool Has A Rainbow," b/w "He Don't Wanna," on Sherwin Linton's Black Gold label. The release has been out for about a month, she said, and is being played on WHO Radio, Des Moines, and over stations in Kansas City and Denver as well as many in the midwest.

Among national headliners in the area lately were Dave Dudley, Donna Fargo, and Freddie Hart. Donna and Freddie shared billing on the KOAH country music spectacular at the Duluth auditorium. With them, said Dottie, were Billy C. Cole ("we are proud of him, since he is from our town and was a DeeJay here in the past") and Ronnie Lyght, "a promising local boy on his way up."

414

Also, on October 9, Dottie Lou and her band, "The Tumbleweeds," were suprised with a visit from Tom T. Hall at the Kro Bar in Superior, where they perform.

Dottie added that NEWS-Scene readers might want to look for her new release, "Every Fool Has A Rainbow," b/w "He Don't Wanna," on Sherwin Linton's Black Gold label. The release has been out for about a month, she said, and is being played on WHO Radio, Des Moines, and over stations in Kansas City and Denver as well as many in the midwest.

♪♪♪

CHAPTER THIRTY

In the afternoon of December 6th we met at the Carlton County Courthouse, Delores Havron with me and Howie Hanson, one of Larry's pit men, with him.

"Dottie, I think you should sit and wait out here, on the bench in the hall." Larry suggested, hesitantly. "You don't want to know what we'll be saying about you to get this marriage dissolved."

"We have to convince the Judge that Larry just can't take your physical beatings anymore!" boomed Delores, adding her usual vein of humor to the strained moment. We chuckled.

"I s'pose it **would be** rather embarrassing to listen in." I responded in total agreement. "And I really don't want to know."

To this day, I don't have a clue as to what was said or what I was accused of. It was immaterial to me. I sat idly on a bench in the hallway, patiently awaiting the proceedings to come to closure. In less than a half hour the three emerged from the courtroom smiling.

Larry announced cheerfully, "We are free, Dottie! That calls for some kind of a celebration! Don't you think? Are you buying the drinks or the dinner?" he asked jovially.

"I guess I'd better spring for the steaks!" I replied joining his gregarious, infectious mood. "The way you guys all drink, I'd have to apply for a loan somewhere to pay for all that." I giggled, bombarded by ludicrous laughter from the others. It was of course totally bogus, as Larry was an amateur drinker in comparison to my friends.

I sighed as a feeling, a rush of relief swept over me like a huge weight had been suddenly lifted from my chest and my heart.

We engaged in a frivolous evening, the four of us. Dinner, cocktails, dancing and then Delores and I excused ourselves and separated from the guys. We all departed in our own separate directions in our own separate thoughts, with Larry and I, I assume, reflecting the onset of our separate, single lives.

The Honorable Donald C. Odden, Judge of District Court at Carlton, MN, did on December 7th execute the dissolvement of the bonds of matrimony between Larry and I, opening a new chapter in our separate lives.

Very few divorce journeys are embarked on, on friendlier terms and never, ever as bizarre as the vonGillern matrimonial closure. Unorthodox by any definition!

There were no outburst of anger. There was no haggling over real estate, personal property, possessions, alimony or quarreling over custody of children. We agreed; he could keep his and I could keep mine. Just a little added humor there.

Larry had silently, intuitively discovered I was not, as he had assumed, financially flush and in the money to finance his hobby racing and I discovered he was not the ideal surrogate dad. I believe these had been our initial prospects to tie the knot in the first place, although neither of us would willingly admit it!

We each signed quit claim deeds to our houses, surrendering any claims to property we both had owned prior to our marital commitment. #5 decree stated that each party be awarded their respective and absolute property, all personal property on our respective pieces of real estate. I accepted and totally understood the removal of all tools and mechanical paraphernalia from the garage, but was inwardly a mite irate when he confiscated the color TV from the living room he had given to the children as a Christmas gift!

However, he did leave me the Ampeg Upright Electric Bass he had presented to me the same Christmas for my musical career. It was a real asset to my profession. And of course, who could not appreciate a huge established, newly constructed two-car garage. I was so tickled to be free of this commitment that I reneged making any waves over a mere TV set. Water over the bridge.

Although I had to concede that there were, however, many plusses in my life from Larry's impact in the three plus years we had lived as husband and wife. I had to admit, as the cliche goes, **Out of all bad comes some good.**

Larry had a reckless spirit of adventure, untamed, a very reverse of my conservative nature. Therefore we had shared some wild heights of adventure I would never have explored on my own. Each aspect of life is so diverse and yet every relationship is unique in its own way.

Innumerable **firsts** for me arose, stemming from Larry's uninhibited careless spirit of adventure; He introduced me to the world of snowmobiling, Coaxing my reluctant disposition to battle sub zero weather, nursing stinging cheeks and pinching toes and fingers. Riding double, I was to discover he was way too crazy for me, dodging trees and flying over unexplored hilly terrain, around ninety degree sharp turns without the slightest consideration for safety. Therefore I learned to drive my own sled!

He lured me into joining him in the splendor of tent camping without sleeping cots, bare ground, and in the pouring rain! I chuckle to remember the surprises and bombshell of that adventure.

Another **first,** an exhilarating nine-day trip to Paris, France with 200 other Snowmobiling activists from all over northern USA and southern Canada. I would never have encountered that adventure, except for Larry's proficient skill in Salesmanship.

And my first ever air-travel flight originated on our honeymoon excursion, visiting California sights with a **first** time adventure in a gambling casino in Las Vegas, that was highlighted by an Elvis Concert on the strip! Perhaps all of this was at his sister's expense, but I was to learn, That was Larry!

Another **first** was a flight in a tiny **private plane,** taking his four year old daughter home to Michigan after spending time with us. And I was scared as hell, petrified, by his omniscient insistence that we take off in a threatening, black electric thundering sky and rain starting. There, I stubbornly adamantly refused to board the plane. We were in a small air strip somewhere in northern Wisconsin, with radio waves warning all air travel foolhardy.

Another **first,** his introducing me to the Hobby Stock Car Racing Scene, where I did meet a lot of very nice people. I had relished most of his crazy adventures, but was never able to grasp the thrill of this, seemingly unsophisticated form of entertainment. I just couldn't embrace the thundering, battering of roaring engines on my sensitive eardrums or the grinding and spitting of sand form my teeth!

And that was Larry! All the firsts forced upon my whimpy, cautious nature by this extroverted, rambunctious, over-achiever were so very opposite of me. He had a driving consistent will to never give up on any dream, desire, no matter how foolish, right or wrong, good or bad it may be. These could extend from building a car with no funds to losing 20 determined pounds in two weeks, to snapping his own shoulder joint when it would pop out snowmobiling, then remount his sled as if nothing had occurred, and shoot off into the white terrain, blazing another (off limit) trail in a cloud of billowing flying snow!!

Larry just thrived on having a steady flow of people around him at all times, consistently, while I flourished on **Privacy,** enjoying my own companionship, as a loner a large percent of the time.

In lieu of Larry's imprudent persuasive nature, he had unassumingly influenced my becoming more out-going and extroverted; more willing to tackle risky, precarious endeavors. His influence had, likewise, induced me to realize pride in my house and belongings.

"Your bass is so **ratty!**" he complained. "It looks so tacky on stage."

I had never noticed or dwelled on the appearance of my instrument. Only on its sound, its tone; or on my house either.

"You should have more regard for your stage presense." he nagged. "Dottie Lou should appear elegant and exquisite as any other Country Music star should!"

Thus came the unexpected arrival, at Christmas, of a brand new Ampeg Electric Bass. Needless to say I was a bit excited. a bit overwhelmed. A trophy wife image, I surmised.

"You shouldn't be vocalizing with vacant spots in your mouth." he scolded. "When you open your mouth in song all the dark holes stand out like sore thumbs. A Daisy May image."

Thus he arranged an appointment for me with a dentist he had sold a snow machine to at an obviously reduced **"vonGillern deal"** price. The dentist implanted three bridges in my mouth as a return favor to Larry at a very reasonable price. I had to pay for it of, of course, but the cost of the procedures was exceedingly frugal and feasible for me.

Yes, **Out of all bad comes some good!** Each relationship is so very different and yet **Special** in its own way. We were friends. We've remained friends. I loved Larry. But I guess I was never **in love** with him and Geno had taught me the difference.

♪♪♪

CHAPTER THIRTY ONE

I don't know who started the snowball that sparked the undulating avalanche of changing lives in the Gopher's **Peyton Place.** It was like an out of control snow ball of carnal seduction rolling down the hill, becoming larger and larger and rolling faster and faster as it gathered its wayward momentum, exploiting a consecutive pattern of divorce as predictable as the rising of the sun. My decision to divorce may have added energy to the wayward avalanche in progress.

Men have affairs and one night stands usually without temperamental commitment, but women usually become emotional and decisive in extra marital rapports. With the female species, (my opinion, only) it is imminent their affairs lead to somewhere, something secure, some kind of closure.

Jan divorced Ben to pursue a love tryst with Little Joe. Vivian waved a goodbye to John for the sensual advances of a womanizing cop. Delores divorced Jerry. We still don't have a clue as to **why.** Except, perhaps, assuming, a desire to be in the in crowd, to belong to our coterie and the freedom we embraced and I dissolved my marriage with Larry to pursue a future with Geno.

It's curiously whimsical how one can rationalize **Our own** faults and motives and label **Our own** sexual liaisons as morally right and acceptable. Jan was, of course, **trashing around,** Vivian had a **back street affair,** but Dottie was celestialy blessed and Merely in love! Ahem!

* * * * * * *

The next morning I wired a telegram to Geno at his Pritchard, Alabama office, stating simply; "I'm white. I'm free. I'm available." Signed simply, "Dottie."

Earlier, in letters, Geno had intimated he'd be in Duluth around the middle of December, so I wasn't expecting him for a week or better. Thus my surprise was overwhelming when he flew home just one day after I had reported my new found status to him in the telegram.

Unannounced and unexpected I spotted his silhouette in the night club low light, in the doorway of the Gopher Lounge, next to the waitress station just as I was warbling, Donna Fargo's, **Happiest Girl in the Whole USA.** With my heart pounding with excitement, I was, at least, The Happiest Girl in the whole Gopher Lounge.

I ached to hug him, to touch him. As my knees trembled, I Knowingly realized I had better control my obvious wild emotion until my 45 minute set was complete and an intermission interlude would be announced by Korn. Stumbling through microphone cords and music paraphernalia I scrambled to Geno's side as soon as the last note of the break song had barely faded into the ambience of the smokey Gopher atmosphere. He was leaning against the service bar sipping a cocktail. He winked as I approached the counter.

"Hi Funny Face." he grinned. "Surprised you, didn't I? Huh?"

"You bet."

We embraced and in my arms he sighed and very softly whispered in my ear, "I love you, Dottie Lou."

"Gosh, I just sent you the telegram yesterday and here you are!" I ejaculated.

"I know. I told Bud, I'm leaving right away and no negotiating! I grabbed a flight to Duluth and here I am. I just had to see you. You know we haven't seen each other since the middle of October?!"

"It has seemed longer."

"I couldn't stand another day not being here. I hope Bud doesn't fire me, but if he does, he does."

"Wow! I wouldn't want you to lose your job over this." I said.

"Ah, who cares!" he joshed. "Then I'd have an excuse to stay in Duluth."

And so began my first taste of freedom. No more having to hide, to pretend. It felt great.

"You know, Geno, You're too late for a front table, tonight, don't you?"

"My loss." he remarked. "I guess I won't be able to see my Dottie Lou very well from here when she sings to me. Huh?"

His dark chocolate brown eyes mischievously caressed mine, then wandered about, boldly undressing me. How he could arouse such sensuous excitement in my veins with only a look! That look! My legs were trembling like jello and how I wanted him, right there, that instant, starving for the velvet touch of his body. Too many weeks of absence and abstinence!

"Will we be having coffee later after you're through?" he facetiously tittered in ambiguous metaphor. I assumed it was for the benefit of evesdroppers.

Slyly returning his banter I winked and replied, volunteering my own carnal metaphore. "Is little Mack ready to share coffee with us?" We had named him, or rather Geno had named him after the Big Mack Trucks and machinery he marketed.

"You bet. He's lonesome and feeling very neglected."

"Well be sure and invite him to our **"coffee clutch"** too."

"Wouldn't have it any other way." he laughed recklessly.

We winked at each other, grinning, knowing a planned "coffee clutch" was certainly top priority on the agenda! ahem!

"We could play the guitar and sing." he suggested, whimsically, "to pass the time. I did buy one like I said I would."

"Yes, a fabulous idea. I'll show you a few chords."

"Yeah, bet **you could** show me a few things." he chuckled, returning to ambiguous metaphor.

"We'll see **Teacher! Who teaches who!**" I giggled. "Gotta go. See you after the set."

I sashayed casually back to the stage to begin the final fourth set of music for the noisy, country-music lovin' crowd. At closing I suggested taking my own car to Geno's motel as it was on my way home.

"What about that coffee?" Geno teased as I jingled my ignition car keys nonchalantly in my hand.

"Oh yes, coffee." I replied, jokingly, bemused. "Don't they offer that in every motel room now-a-days?" I giggled. "And don't forget to bring in the **guitar.**"

"oh sure. it's a good thing we have things like coffee and a guitar to pass the time away. Otherwise we'd be so so bored with absolutely nothing to do!" he chuckled, with an obvious mischievous hunger flashing from the sensuous depths of those dark chocolate brown eyes.

* * * * * * *

In Geno's absence I sang, with his and my future escalating through my mind. Sometimes I'd complete an entire ballad with lapse of memory of even having sung it. Where were we headed? I had asked myself. Would he be able to accept and cope with my career? Or would he be paranoid and possessive as Roger had been? Or would he demand changes?

The floor was breast to breast, crammed with couples dancing as Korn crooned, ♪ **I'd rather be sorry** ♪ **for something I've done,** ♫ **then for something** ♪ **that I didn't** ♪ **do.** I embellished the chorus with harmony. "What a true profound philosophy of life!" I mused. Kris Kristofferson surely had a way with words, a talent for such philosophical wisdom in all his brilliant, powerful lyrics. Almost all of his ingenious efforts had become #1 Hits!

Yes, I loved my career! I loved the feeling of accomplishment in the delivery of a song. I loved the attention. I would never be able to abandon this dream for anyone. That was obvious.

I smiled at fans as they glided by, acknowledging their special presence and then I glanced to the floor, in the dim lounge light, at their shuffling feet and perceived what I thought appeared to be a stream of water running across the dance floor!

A broken water pipe? The stage was way across the room from bar or bathroom plumbing. Nothing dripping from the upstairs lounge above our heads, I noted.

My gaze followed the puddled floor away from the dance area toward the smokey area of remaining tabled customers and abruptly I became aware of the obvious source of the waterway. A drunken patron was leaning against one of the center building support pillars at the edge of the dancing area, fly open. penis in hand, eyes closed, relieving himself against the pillar as though it were a sturdy old tree in a secluded forest. He was obviously so inebriated he didn't have a clue to where he even actually was!

Couples danced about, unaware of the toilet performance going on around them. I swallowed a curdled lump and quickly focused on my bass and our country music vibrating off the concrete walls of the Gopher.

Yes, I loved my career, but sometimes the low life was difficult to handle. Passages of scripture would come to mind to haunt. What you do to the least of my Brethren—Love your neighbor as yourself—and

I wondered, momentarily if perhaps, it was time, my time for a change of direction.

* * * * * * *

We entered the Holiday Inn and Geno immediately toted a small portable liquor cabinet from atop the desk. From the contents he lifted a 5th of Cutty Sark Scotch and proceeded to prepare a couple night-cap cocktails for us. I was slowly becoming accustomed to his Cutty Sark, after hours, in absence of brandy.

"You can take this little traveling liquor case home." he suggested. "It's a gift from Bud to me. A Christmas gratuitous of appreciation intent from employer to employee, I guess, for my input in **Big Mack** marketing.

"How nice." I remarked.

It was covered in a grey spotted upholstery material and quite sturdy. It was approximately one foot square in size with a carrier handle like luggage. The interior housed space for two quarts of beverages and inside the top cover were clampted four glasses, a bottle opener, a cork screw and two shot glasses.

"It also has a security combination lock so the kids can't get into it." Geno asserted.

"I will certainly need that at my house." I added. "Teenagers, you know."

"It's just set at zero's now, but you can set whatever combination you want."

He closed the case, set the combination and reopened it in a little instructive demonstration of the operative proceedure.

"I can get it stocked for our own enjoyment needs at your house so whenever I'm there we'll have our own private stock."

Then he reached for me in a seductive change of avenue, touching and embracing. We began, slowly, removing each others garments, bit by bit. I was a little intoxicated and in a clowning prankster mood so, in jest, I feigned fiery passion while giggling and hurriedly unbuckled and unzipped Geno's slacks and quickly whipped them down to his knees. Smoothly I dropped to my knees and on my haunches, still giggling, I hastily yanked down his fruit of the looms, over an unexpected erection. When the waistband had cleared the upright protruding manhood, the quick abrupt release had sprung it up and out in a bouncing momentum and thus it clobbered me, sternly, on my chin with a firm hard thump!

We both burst into laughter, starting from a surprised giggle, rising to an expanding chuckle, then escalating into convulsive, infectious hysterical laughter.

Between bursts of guffaw, I ejaculated in spurts, "Geno, do you have a **legal permit** to carry that **dangerous, concealed weapon!?**"

We both plopped upon the bed in laughter, rolling in embryo positions, our clothes still half on, half off. The laughter became unable to halt, like a cascading avalanche completely out of control.

Trying to repress the noise we were creating, with a finger to my lips, I emitted a weak "Sshh. Shush. It's 3:00 AM and these walls are paper thin."

That only added fuel to the fire and we again roared in hysterical amusement.

Finally partially composing himself, Geno blurted, "No, I do not have a permit."

Laughter bombarded the room again.

"What do you s'pose our connecting room occupants are thinking?" I panted.

"Maybe we should invite them in."

"They wouldn't get it." I giggled.

"You bet they wouldn't get it! It's all mine and I don't share!"

Unrestrained laughter followed again, with the tears rolling down our cheeks. I guess you would have had to have been there to capture the light hearted humor, the jovial, unbridled, uncensored, unrestrained new soaring freedom we were embracing.

The time escaped so rapidly and dawn was all too soon beckoning us to another day.

Geno pleaded, "Please stay 'til morning. I have to check out early to catch a plane back to my desk in Mobile. Just let me hold you a little longer, to wake up to your arms around me and your hair tickling my face."

"Oh I wish. Do I ever wish I could. Can't do that. Kids, you know." I answered softly as I rose to dress.

"I know. It seems like I just got here and it's time to leave. It's only ten days until Christmas, Hon. I have to be with my kids then." he murmured wistfully, as he lay on his back, arms stretched out behind his head, watching me dress. "I want so much to be here with you at Christmas." he continued. "To get something real nice for you to wear for the holidays or on stage. Attend Midnight Mass together. It really hurts not to be able to be a part of your Christmas."

"It's okay, Hon," I stressed, murmuring. "I have commitments too. That's how it is when you have kids."

"I'd sure like to buy you something real, real special."

"Darling, the most real special thing you could ever give me for the holidays," I tenderly explained, as I plopped on the bedside, struggling with my shoes, "is what you give me all the time, just loving me. ♪ **My Darlin', My Darlin' I wanted** ♫ ♪ **to call you My Darlin'**". I entertained a soft quiet melody for him as I fumbled with the closure buttons on my wrap. **"For many ♪ and ♪ many a day. My Darlin, ♪ My Dar-----"'**

"Wait!" he dictated, interrupting my refrains. "I'll get dressed and walk you to your car. It's pretty late to be wandering out there alone."

"Or early?" I tittered. "It's okay. I'm a big girl, you know."

"But, it's also a chance for one more hug, one more kiss." he chuckled softly.

My auto was half-way across the gigantic Holiday Inn parking lot. It was the 14th of December, A warm calm winter night, but winter just the same.

He wouldn't hear of me going out alone when I tried to convince him it was totally unnecessary. It seemed like never in my relationships since Roger Sr. had I ever had someone fuss over me to this extent of thoughtfulness and I was glorying in the attention. It was impressive to find a man not driven by power and materialism who embraced the simple things in life, the soul searching ambience of nature and God and love and bonding.

He kissed me goodbye, reassuring me with, "Only a little while, my Precious."

The surrounding aroma of Brut tickled my nostrils as he sashayed across the lot with me. He was attired merely in slippers and a terry cloth robe between his naked body and my clothed one as we kissed and hugged and squeezed each other amicably in the deserted parking lot.

"Well, well," I teased, as I slightly opened his robe to reveal his hairy nakedness underneath. "I can't imagine me, being so smitten and so in love with the Minnesota Flasher!" We both laughed. I added, "You better get **Little Mack** inside before he catches pneumonia!"

I swung my auto out of the parking lot, down the street toward home and the Heights. Just a short block down the avenue an automobile emerged from the shadows, peeling out, squeeling tires, following me.

It was 4:30 or 5:00 AM. I was startled and disturbed, uneasy by the sudden, unexpected encounter. After following me a mere one block the vehicle pulled alongside of my Chevy and the occupant rolled down his window. I stared in utter disbelief, braked my car and came to a full stop, realizing it was Larry!!

He stopped as well, and there we were, double parked in the middle of vacant First Avenue East.

I rolled my window down. He seemed very hyper and a little disoriented, as he exclaimed in an agitated voice.

"I watched you and O'Demarra come out of that motel. I saw you when you went inside, earlier too. I know what's going on!" he scoffed arrogantly.

I was shocked! He had been stalking me! Watching me, somewhere in the parking lot, all the time I had been there. He disclosed that he had observed Geno, walking me back to my auto, kissing me goodnight.

Astonished and outraged I sputtered, "Larry, maybe you haven't noticed, we **are not** married anymore! My life is my own business!"

"I know." he stammered, retreating apologetically. "But, you promised me, we could still be lovers, even if we aren't married anymore." Then he wistfully, pathetically implored, "How about some sloppy seconds?"

I laughed. "Thanks, Larry, but No Thanks." Adding derisively "I never ever intended to continue our relationship, Larry. **I lied!** How does that now feel? To be on the **receiving** line of **Deception!!**"

I drove away, relishing the satisfying, sweet taste of vengeful, not so nice, justice.

♪♪♪

CHAPTER THIRTY TWO

On Monday, after the weeks music gigs were over, Geno called me from Mobile around 9:00 PM.

"I'm back at it, with a red bruised nose." he stated.

"A bruised nose? Who punched you? Bud? For taking that extra time off?" I jabbered questions, not waiting for reply's.

"No. It's just raw and bruised from the grindstone!" A little coy chuckle followed.

"Funny, funny." I singsonged.

"Your day off?" he queried.

"If you call laundry and grocery shopping a day off."

I related to Geno the incident regarding Larry's seedy shadow surveillance of our after-hour activities during the night and while we said our early morning farewell in the Holiday Inn Parking lot.

"I guess I'd better change motels!" he quipped.

"I think so. No sense in inviting harassment. I Icy, I miss my Fx," I giggled. "But my **Aim is getting better!**"

"Funny. Funny." he replied, mimicking my earlier retort.

"Speaking of humor, I wrote a poem for you about the incident in your motel. My discovery that you carry a very dangerous concealed weapon! It's in the mail."

"You're kidding?!"

"Oh no! A lawless violation like that deserves some poetry recognition! Don't you think?"

"Recite it to me."

"And spoil your enjoying my letter?"

"I'd still enjoy it second time."

"Oh I s'pose. It goes like this.

'You know those were the days, my friend,

When he would wop me on the chin.

He'd bruise my face and then he'd charge

And hide his head in my garage!

But I could read him like a book.

I knew **exactly** where to look.

You just can't dupe a gal like me.

Cuz' plain as hell it was, you see.

For that silly **game** I'd surely fall,

'Cuz, he never meant to hide at all!'

"You're somethin' else."

"So I've been told. Not always complimentary, however." I added.

Then Geno sent me a poem about Larry's little unexpected parking lot sojourn. Our letters were consistently filled with correspondence in rhyme and Geno, true to habit, sent me his analysis of Larry's little parking lot interruption in poetry. I abruptly realized Larry's watchful eye must have frustrated and annoyed him. I deemed it merely humorous. His poem seemed to evoke a mixed up summary way more serious than my interpretation.

NO BRAG! JUST FACT!!

One fourteen, this is right.

One fourteen, our delight.

One fourteen was **his to rile!**

Not for you to reconcile.

In depth the mystery of One-o-nine.

A **MOVE** created in fear of mine.

Discovered in love without legal bind.

There you left it all behind.

Truth in the eyes could be seen.

A desire for you always keen.

Ney, a **Devilwoman** do I behold?

Rather **An Angel,** it can be told.

Caresses of love in my making,

Only for you-yours for taking.

A tear in her eye not expected,

yet knowing her depth and ability to see,

Wasn't really a surprise to me.

Your love is infant, young and supreme

Not etched by "True Love" as I've seen?

When customer kisses I receive,

The demand is there for T.L.C.

* * * * * * *

I had barely dozed off after Friday Night's Gopher gig when I was brusquely awakened by the incessant screaming of the phone on the kitchen wall. Rubbing my sand filled eyes, I scrambled from the covers, stumbled to the kitchen counter, mumbling to myself, "I just gotta get an extension phone by my bed. Hello."

"Hi. It's me." Geno's low seductive voice bombarded my still morning silence.

"My god, It's 3:00 AM!" I ejaculated as I glanced at the kitchen clock. "Where are you!?"

"I've just checked into the Holiday Inn in Superior."

"Just now?"

"Yes. I drove all the way this time. I wanted to have my own car for transportation on this end."

"I thought you said you couldn't make it to the Twin Ports before the Christmas Holiday."

"I know I said that, but I just couldn't stay away that long. Not at Christmas."

"Good."

"I'm gonna catch some shut-eye and then I want you to meet me here tomorrow morning at o nine hundred hours. That's 9:00 AM."

I laughed. "You mean **THIS morning**."

"Yes, **this** morning. In a few swift hours."

"Are you crazy!?" I laughed heartily.

"No doubt of it. I'm taking you for Brunch in Minneapolis."

"Minneapolis! No way! I have to work tomorrow night. I mean tonight. I work at the Gopher on Saturday nights, you know. Or did you forget?"

"Yes, I know you work tonight, but I'll have you back way in time for your Gopher gig."

"Why Minneapolis?"

"I want to take you shopping. Perhaps Daytons. To get you something real special for Christmas. Then we'll have lunch and head right back. Christmas Eve is tomorrow night so then I'll be gone. I have to spend Christmas Eve and Christmas Day with my kids. But now, right before Christmas you can't deny me the pleasure of getting something special for my Angel, "Funny Face.""

"My Crazy, Crazy Rainbow Guy." I sighed. "Okay. 9:00 AM it is."

"See you soon. I love you."

"Me too."

Click.

* * * * * *

Snuggling beside Geno, we chatted, laughed and sang along with the radio all the way to Minneapolis, with only one stop at Tobies in Hinckley for a way over due potty call and a brief pause to collect cups of java to go. We totally ignored the little spasms of tummy growls, seeking our attention, in lieu of not wasting needed travel time.

I was astounded by the effect and impact my freedom by severing marriage ties had made on Geno's attitude. His former precarious outlook had ostensibly taken on an about-face turn. His occasional negative aspect on the moral interpretation of our relationship had all but vanished.

We spied a vacant spot near Dayton's, parked the car and casually sashayed into the gigantic, block square of department store.

"I'll just mosey around here to kill time." he suggested, "while you search for an elegant long dress to wear New Year's Eve 'specially for me. **My choice.**" he added obstinately.

"Oh my! Gosh!" I stammered. "You're kidding?" I studied the adamant compelling expression on his face and surrendered with, "You're not kidding!"

"No. I'm not kidding." he sagaciously emitted.

"Okay. Wow!" I was lost for words.

After a lengthy search I came up with two gorgeous, floor length gowns to choose from. I carried them over to where Geno sat on a customer bench, languidly awaiting out my exuberant shopping spree. I held them up, for him to make the choice.

One dress fashioned a smooth black gabardine, full body, in an A line Princess style, emphasizing a dramatic silk or chiffon narrow, pleated ruffle around the neckline, cascading to the waist and continuing down the front embracing a continuing entire hemline in spectacular ruffle accent. A huge three inch rhinestone pin, round center with star studded points jutting out, accentuated the ruffle at the waist, suggesting a closure that was bogus. A long zipper at the back gave entry to the garment.

The other gown was a scarlet dress in chiffon over soft taffeta in a style almost identical to the black except it was accentuated by a wider four inch chiffon ruffle. The color was brilliant, loud, almost boisterous, while the black gown was subtle and sophisticated. Both garments were sleeveless.

The red dress made a statement that was me. It characterized my daft taste in exorbitant colors. The black was definitely signifying subtle, discreet class, refined urbane sophistication.

"Your choice, Hon. Which one do you like the most?" I asked as I held them up for his inspection and approval.

"The black is so—soo exquisite and sophisticated." he said, then excusatorily paused, looking into my eyes and added. "You're more attuned to the red one, aren't you?"

Attempting to hide my biased opinion, I graciously succumbed to his choice.

"Whatever you like, Geno. Which ever one you'd like to see me in on New Years Eve is fine with me. They're both so elegant."

"Okay, let's take them to the check-out counter." he said as we carried them to the cashier.

"We have to choose one of these." I nodded to the girl at the register.

"Which will it be?" she smiled. "They're both so lovely. Hard to choose. Right?"

"Box them up." Geno beamed. "We'll take them both."

I was stunned! What superfluous extravagance!

"That's not necessary." I feebly protested.

"You'll be beautiful in both dresses, Dottie, but I want you to wear the black for me on New Year's Eve."

Geno spent Christmas with his kids and I wore the red taffeta chiffon to my family Christmas, which I spent with my kids and relatives at Gerry and Barb's home in Aitkin, MN where Gerry was teaching school.

We took family pictures.

Dad—Mom—Me—Pauling—Lorraine—Gerry

I proudly explained to my folks and siblings how my new present Significant Other had purchased the dresses for me and that he couldn't be with me because he was spending Christmas with his own four children in Burtrum, Minnesota.

There were no comments made from my family over my excitement over my new fork in the road of my Life's Journey. A few frowns prevailed and a speedy change of the subject arose. It was rebuttal sufficient to remind me of my status with my family. A portrait of my life, not too pretty in their eyes. A Catholic does not get a divorce! A Catholic lady does not engage in pre-marital sex!

I was, indeed, living up to my "tag" as the **Black Sheep of the Family.**

♫♫♫

CHAPTER THIRTY THREE

Geno sashayed into the Gopher on the Saturday night before the New Years Eve extravaganza was due. Only one more day remaining on the scenario of a splendid eventful and innovative 1972, initiating the ebullient course of my new journey.

"Where are you staying tonight?" I asked as we scrambled into his vehicle after exiting Jerry Lee's Truck Stop at 2:30 AM where we had just polished off early morning omlets.

"I'm at the **Superior** Holiday Inn." he said. "Don't want vonGillern stalking us so I changed **States!**" he laughed.

"I don't think he'll bother us again, anyway." I responded. "He knows it's really over. He was just grasping at straws."

"Can you stay with me tonight?" he asked. "All night?"

"Yes. I've arranged to do just that. With the kids, I mean. Also I have tomorrow nights stage get-up with me for the New Years Eve gig at the Kro bar."

"Wonderful. That's great."

As we approached his motel I noticed Jack Frost had painted the glass on the door entrance, lightly, embellishing his cool artistic strokes, the grand finale of a memorable 1972 December night.

With his fingernails Geno etched into the frost, **Dottie Lou O'Demarra.**

"Whatta you think?" he smiled, squeezed my shoulders and kissed the tip of my nose, then flipped a questioning, "Well?"

"What do I think?" I repeated. "I'm flustered, elated. My heart is about to jump the curb! It's a very genuinely fine sophisticated name, Geno. I'd be right proud to be called Dottie Lou O'Demarro!" I tittered like a star-struck teenager.

"You're really staying the night?" he asked as we approached his room, 109, the number.

"Yes, I sure am. I'm all yours in Room 109." And I softly murmured a parody to Tammy Wynette's **Apartment #9** with, "the ♪ sun will surely shine, ♪ in apartment one-o-nine ♪ And we can spend the day together tomorrow too." I added. "And I can stay right up to the New Years Eve Bash at the Kro Bar!"

"What a great, unique way to close out the old year and bring in the new!" he purred.

Geno and I spent the day leisurely enjoying our newly acquired freedom. I played his guitar and we harmonized country songs together. On Holiday Inn stationary I scribbled the music chord pictures for him to practice in my absence. I was acquainting him with chord progression, teaching him how to accompany his own voice, in sync, with the rhythm guitar.

As he attempted, repeatedly, the stiff finger stretch to the frets on the neck of the guitar he blurted, "Will my fingers ever reach far enough? Will my finger tips ever stop hurting" He sighed, "I'm allergic to pain, you know." Then a brief soft self-conscious chuckle.

"With time." I reassured him. "You'll form calluses on your finger tips that will eventually be hard as rock. You'll see. You'll wonder why it ever seemed so difficult."

"I sure hope so. I wish I had your confidence."

"It takes patience, dedication, incentive and time. A whole lot of time!"

"Well I have plenty of that in the evenings."

He chose several selections of his favorites to practice when alone on quiet evenings in motels and I scribbled the chords above the words for him.

We compiled little nonsensical poetry to each other, giggling like little kids, wiling away the amiable, comfortable hours together.

We ordered room service for our empty growling tummys, spending the entire day never leaving the Motel. Clowning in jest, I compiled silly lines of parody to Apartment #9 and sang it to him as Apartment 109, with him adding his own witticism here and there, exploding eminent, contagious laughter from both of us.

We voraciously embraced nonstop moments in insatiable hunger, **libido magic,** starved for the intimacy put on hold, by necessary absences of employment. As much as we gorged the sensual intimacy, we also embraced the intellectual exchange of views on countless subjects, heart to heart submission of each others innermost private desires and dreams, intellectual as well as the rapacious physical.

After each intimacy we'd suds and sponge each other in the gentle spray of lukewarm showers. However, after oodles of lengthy sensuous sudsing and rinsing this prolonged dutiful episode of overindulged, obsessive cleanliness merely sent us back, surrendering to pillow talk and tumble!

The aroma of soap and Brute and desire imbued the ambiance of our room, enhanced by male and female body heat. We were mesmerized with intimate kissing, tasting, loving and exploring the essence of each other.

"What's your fetish?" he asked. "Breasts, throat, thighs, toes?"

"You're my fetish." I sighed. "Every inch of you."

"You know, it seems almost sinful to be this happy." he said, leaning back on his elbow, enjoying a leisure cigarette, then in thoughtful cogitation, "Just think. Only days ago, Hanoi was being bombed in the horror of war right during our **Saviors beautiful Birthday Celebration!** They couldn't even stop that **slaughter** for Christmas!"

I just couldn't fathom anything so dreadful as war in our enchanted ecstatic moments of euphoria. His dark eyes were far away and serious in memoir.

"Why can't people love each other instead of all the hatred?" he said. So often, in reminiscence, he'd flip to politics and the horrific ravages of war.

I mused, "perhaps it stems from his stint in the Korean War." Aloud, I added, "You can't change the world, Hon. Just don't let the world change you!"

Changing the mood, I hungrily, shamelessly kissed his body from the tip of his nose clear to **kingdom come,** until he rolled me over and, in return, initiated tasting every throbbing inch of my anxious, awaiting body as the fragrance of the perfumes of our love-making was damp and sweet and inviting.

I had been in and out of two marriages unable to dissipate the tenacious hang-ups originating from my disfunctional beginnings; the carnal transgressions of my father. It had influenced, **big time,** my embarrassing difficulty in sensual performances. I was compelled to hide my body from intimacy, in daylight pulling shades, inhibited and unable to experience full abandonment in my own sexuality.

Geno had undoubtedly initiated my recovery from the humiliating hang-ups that had poisoned my mind with shame and low self-esteem of my own flesh. His patient, profound tender lessons in performance and surrender had completely obliterated my imprisoned obsession of sexual inadequacy. He made me feel so beautiful in nakedness, assured me lovingly, of a confidence in my own inner skills and a unique awareness of the beauty of my own body.

I discovered, from our bonded, magnetic relationship, that love surely **begins in the mind!** I had loved **first** his philosophical, profound, indepth grasp of intrinsic basics and principles. We had discovered an amazing togetherness; agreement in almost every aspect of shared values, beliefs and views. Conversations had connected our minds and bared our souls into a magical bond.

In lieu of those profound moments, I deduced that the intellectual connection of minds initiates and instigates the inevitable dawning of love. And **from this love** the intriguing, stimulating drive of sex results, **not the other way around!**

We made love again and again and dawdled the erotic afternoon in sensual intoxication, dozing now and then in each others arms until it was time to prep and dress for the New Year's Eve Bash at the Kro Bar.

As I entered the Kro Br on Geno's arm, I was draped in the elegant long black gown he had requested I wear for him.

"Well there you are!" Eddie Shaw, the boss exclaimed emphatically. **"Where Have You Been!?** I've been trying to locate your whereabouts all afternoon!" he remarked in wistful disappointment.

"Am I late?!" I ejaculated. "I thought we were scheduled to begin at eight! Weren't we?" I asked, dumbfoundedly.

"Oh sure. But it's been so busy here all afternoon I wanted the band to start an hour earlier." he explained. "Korn and Toby have been here for some time now, waiting, hoping to get started. Boy, are you a tough gal to get a hold of!"

I mused, in thought, "I sure am tickled pink you couldn't find me, Boss." with a faint, simpered smile etched across my face. Then I heard my own voice replying in bogus apology, "I guess so. I'm so so sorry, Ed. If only I'd known. I was gone around town. Shopping, Carousing."

I grinned at Geno as he mischievously winked, his miniscule dimples creasing ever so slightly. Ed assumptively stared at Geno as if expecting a response or an explanation. Geno, with lifted eyebrows, merely shrugged his shoulders and glibly replied,

"Gosh, I have no idea where she could have been. I couldn't find her either. She sure is the mysterious one!"

I glowed, sparking a clandestine grin of secret memory, loving and basking, mindfully, in the ultimate splendor of the afternoon----of the day----of the year! Yes, 1972 was so soon to close, gone forever. It had been so unique, so good to me.

The Tumbleweeds would be saying farewell to their seventh year together as a group. We were on stage, again, warbling with the usual country music enthusiasm, playing all the memory-making, impassioned tunes of our generations repertoire, looking forward to whatever might lie ahead in a brand new year.

And I was singing with gusto and emphatic earnestness for my fans, the magical lyrics of "Shine ♪ on me sunshine, Walk with ♪ ♪ me world. It's a ♪ skippity-doo-dah day. ♪ I'm the **Happiest Girl** ♪ **in** ♪ **the whole U.S.A.** Oh, ♪ Shine on me sunshine, Walk with-- ♫ --"

Yes Indeed, I certainly was, the Happiest Girl in the whole U.S.A.!!

♫♪

LaVergne, TN USA
19 July 2010
189917LV00004B/4/P

9 781452 003795